SPATIAL, ENVIRONMENTAL AND RESOURCE POLICY IN THE DEVELOPING COUNTRIES

Spatial, Environmental and Resource Policy in the Developing Countries

Edited by
MANAS CHATTERJI
State University of New York,
U.S.A.

PETER NIJKAMP
Free University,
Amsterdam,
The Netherlands

T. R. LAKSHMANAN
Boston University,
U.S.A.

C. R. PATHAK
Indian Institute of Technology,
Kharagpur,
India

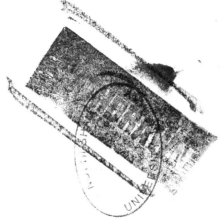

Gower

Published by
Gower Publishing Company Limited,
Gower House, Croft Road, Aldershot, Hampshire GU11 3HR, England

and

Gower Publishing Company,
Old Post Road, Brookfield, Vermont 05036, U.S.A.

Reprinted 1986

British Library Cataloguing in Publication Data

Spatial, environmental and resource policy in the
 developing countries.
  1. Developing countries——Economic policy
  2. Developing countries——Regional planning
  I. Chatterji, Manas
  330.9172'4   HD87.5

Library of Congress Cataloging in Publication Data

Main entry under title:

Spatial, environmental, and resource policy in the
 developing countries.

  1. Developing countries——Economic conditions——Regional
disparities——Addresses, essays, lectures. 2. Developing
countries——Economic policy——Addresses, essays, lectures.
3. Regional planning——Developing countries——Addresses,
essays, lectures. I. Chatterji, Manas, 1937-
HC59.7.S63 1983   338.9'009172'4   83-16448

ISBN 0 566 00650 2

307007

Printed and bound in Great Britain by
Antony Rowe Limited, Chippenham, Wiltshire

Contents

1 Preface

MANAS CHATTERJI, PETER NIJKAMP, T. R. LAKSHMANAN
AND C. R. PATHAK

One of the most important problems facing mankind today is the
immense disparity in the level of income and, consequently, in the
standard of living among people in different parts of the world. What
is more disheartening is that the growth rate of income of the poor
countries is consistently far below the rate of economically advanced
countries. Based on the resulting difference of income, countries are
generally divided into two groups, namely, developed and
underdeveloped. The term "underdeveloped" has been used with different
connotations in the literature on economic development. Sometimes it
means a low ratio of population to area, sometimes a scarcity of capital
as indicated by the prevalence of high interest rates, and sometimes a
low ratio of industrial output to total output. instead of using the
term "underdeveloped country" it may be more appropriate to use the
expression 'developing country'. A reasonably satisfactory definition
of developing country may be: (1) a country which has good potential
prospects for using more capital and labor and/or more available natural
resources to support its present population at a higher level of living;
or (2) a country which can support a larger population on a level at
least equivalent to its current level, if its per capita income is
already fairly high. The reasons for a less high development are many.
Among these are poor natural environments, severe climatic conditions,
niggardly endowment of resources, past social and cultural development,
and restrictive political practices. All these factors confine the
production far within the maximum possible frontier, leading to low
output. Frequently a country is faced with the vicious circle of low
output, high propensity to consume, low savings, and low capital
accumulations.

Another aspect of the problem of economic development concerns the
regional or spatial dimension. Unfortunately, insufficient attention
has been paid to this area until recently. Considerable theoretical and
empirical work has been done on the problem of allocation of resources
over time but not over space. Clearly, the spatial aspect is important.
This is particularly so for a country like India, which is striving for
economic growth despite extreme regional variations within a framework
of a federal democratic system of government. The situation is basically
the same in all the so-called poor countries, especially those countries
which were under foreign rule for a long time. Examples are Indonesia
(Java vs. other islands), Burma and Thailand (capital cities and rice
growing areas vs. up-country), Brazil (Northeast vs. Central-South area),
etc. The formation of Bangladesh from former East Pakistan is a classic

example of regional devisiveness. The general pattern is economic disparity between the capital or port city and the rest of the country. Of course, this pattern is deeply rooted in the economic history of any of these countries. Typically, industrialization has started at a few focal points (mostly port cities). These points were deemed convenient to the rulers and were not necessarily optimum locations. In addition to economic development, these points obtained an earlier start with respect to education, health care facilities, and all other benefits and drawbacks of Western civilization. The cases of Calcutta, Bombay, and Madras in India are good illustrations.

It is well known that the cities and ruban areas in the developing countries are facing serious problems of employment, population growth, housing, transportation, and lack of social amenities. The magnitude of such problems has reached such a point that immediate action by international organizations is needed. First, there is an increasing and concentrated amount of growth and investment in the capital and major cities. As a consequence, the agricultural sector is neglected, and the flow of immigrants from rural to urban areas has increased. Second, due to the rapid industrialization, the urban centers have become hotbeds of political instability, thus leading to riots and politically-motivated urban unrest. These problems, along with the tranditional factors, such as ethnic and racial rivalry and religious and linguistic differences, will endanger the basis of the political system of a nation. The confrontation of urban and rural interest groups has also complicated the situation. Thus, the conflict of interest will be a major concern in urban and regional development. The third factor is the inavailability of resources, such as energy, which will affect the agricultural and rural sectors, and thus, adversely, endanger the urban areas.

With all this in mind, we must look beyond the immediate question of providing social amenities and take a wider perspective. The papers included in this book, written by a wide variety of international experts in this field, address such problems. They have been selected out of a large number of papers presented at the International Conference on Urban and Regional Change in the Developing Countries, held at the Indian Institute of Technology, Kharagpur (Calcutta). We hope this book will help to devise strategies to address the issues which will be the foremost facing mankind in the future.

Manas Chatterjee
Peter Nijkamp
T. R. Lakshmanan
C.R. Pathak

PART I
Planning Issues and Techniques of Analysis

2 Techniques for analysis of urban-regional and resource management in developing countries

MANAS CHATTERJI

One of the most important problems facing mankind today is the immense disparity in the level of income and, consequently, in the standard of living among the people in different parts of the world. What is more disheartening is that the growth rate of income of the poor countries is consistently much below the rate of economically advanced countries. Based on the resulting difference of income, countries are generally divided into two groups, namely, developed and underdeveloped. The term "underdeveloped" has been used with different connotations in the literature of economic development. Sometimes it means a low ratio of population to area; sometimes a scarcity of capital, as indicated by the prevalence of high interest rates; and sometimes a low ratio of industrial output to total output.

The reasons for underdevelopment are many. Among them are poor natural environments, severe climatic conditions, niggardly endowment of resources, past social and cultural development, and restrictive religious practices. All these factors confine the production far within the maximum possible frontier, leading to low output. Frequently the vicious circle of low output, high proprensity to consume, low savings, and capital accumulations results for a country.

Another dimension of the problem of economic development is the regional, or spatial one. Unfortunately, insufficient attention has been paid to this aspect until recently. Considerable theoretical and empirical work has been done on the problem of allocation of resources over time, but not over space. Clearly, the spatial aspect is important, particularly for a country like India, which is striving for economic growth with extreme regional variation in the level of activities within a framework of a federal democratic system of government. The situation is basically the same in all the so-called "poor" countries, especially those countries which were under the rule of foreigners for a long time. Examples are Indonesia (Java vs. other islands), Burma and Thailand (capital cities and rice-growing areas vs. up-country), Brazil (Northeast vs. Central-South area), etc. The general pattern is economic disparity between the capital city (or port city) and the rest of the country. Look at the economic history of these countries. Industrialization typically has started at a few focal points (mostly port cities). These ports were deemed convenient to the rulers and were not necessarily optimal locations. In addition to economic development, these points obtained an earlier start with respect to education, health care facilities, and all other benefits and drawbacks of Western civilization. The case for Calcutta, Bombay, and Madras in India are good illustrations. However, this situation also exists in rich countries, such as the U.S., the U.K., and other countries in Europe, where numerous pockets of poverty remain in the midst of affluence. Thus a regional approach is necessary to deal with the economic, environmental, and resource problems. The theoretical basis of regional planning is furnished by the discipline of regional science, which, like all other social sciences, is concerned with the study of man and his continuous interaction with, and adaptation to, his physical environment. However, regional science limits itself to the study of problems for which a spatial or regional focus is central. It concerns research and studies on the structure, function, and operation of regions from an economic, social and political point of view. In several important ways regional science is related to other social sciences, such as economics, geography, sociology, political science, and anthropology. Each of these disciplines does involve the study of man related to physical environment.

Basic to regional science is the concept of "region." At the present stage of scientific development this concept is rather elusive. Though inescapable as a tool, the region acquires a concrete form and character only with respect to a given problem, whether the problem concerns the testing of pure spatial models at the one end of the continuum or a pressing situation of reality at the other end. In this sense, the set of regions (or hierarchy of sets of regions) associated with each problem at a given time is unique. Yet we may anticipate that as regional science develops and becomes better able to cope with problems of a more general nature, the diverse sets (or hierarchies of sets) of regions will tend to blend into one another to ultimately yield the best set (or hierarchy of sets) constantly changing over time. Some of the most important tools in regional science are the following:

1. Location theory and comparative cost analysis
2. Regional demography
3. Regional and urban history approach
4. Economic base and related urban growth theories
5. Regional and interregional social accounting, intergovernmental transfer
6. Regional and interregional input-output models
7. Interregional programming and other optimization techniques
8. Industrial and urban complex analysis
9. Interregional multiplier and business cycle analysis
11. Central place theories and application of classification techniques, such as factor analysis and discriminant analysis to analyze regional problems
11. Spatial regularity models
12. Regional systems and simulation
13. Regional econometric model building
14. Interregional general equilibrium theory with political, social, economic, and ecological variables
15. Spatial organization theory, graph theory application to regional problems
16. Nearest-neighbor approach. Point distribution, pattern recognition, and application of mathematics of topology to point distribution, remote sensing, and other abstract models

drawbacks of Western civilization. The case for Calcutta, Bombay, and Madras in India are good illustrations. However, this situation also exists in rich countries, such as the U.S., the U.K., and other countries in Europe, where numerous pockets of poverty remain in the midst of affluence. Thus a regional approach is necessary to deal with the economic, environmental, and resource problems. The theoretical basis of regional planning is furnished by the discipline of regional science, which, like all other social sciences, is concerned with the study of man and his continuous interaction with, and adaptation to, his physical environment. However, regional science limits itself to the study of problems for which a spatial or regional focus is central. It concerns research and studies on the structure, function, and operation of regions from an economic, social and political point of view. In several important ways regional science is related to other social sciences, such as economics, geography, sociology, political science, and anthropology. Each of these disciplines does involve the study of man related to physical environment.

Basic to regional science is the concept of "region." At the present stage of scientific development this concept is rather elusive. Though inescapable as a tool, the region acquires a concrete form and character only with respect to a given problem, whether the problem concerns the testing of pure spatial models at the one end of the continuum or a pressing situation of reality at the other end. In this sense, the set of regions (or hierarchy of sets of regions) associated with each problem at a given time is unique. Yet we may anticipate that as regional science develops and becomes better able to cope with problems of a more general nature, the diverse sets (or hierarchies of sets) of regions will tend to blend into one another to ultimately yield the best set (or hierarchy of sets) constantly changing over time. Some of the most important tools in regional science are the following:

1. Location theory and comparative cost analysis
2. Regional demography
3. Regional and urban history approach
4. Economic base and related urban growth theories
5. Regional and interregional social accounting, intergovernmental transfer
6. Regional and interregional input-output models
7. Interregional programming and other optimization techniques
8. Industrial and urban complex analysis
9. Interregional multiplier and business cycle analysis
11. Central place theories and application of classification techniques, such as factor analysis and discriminant analysis to analyze regional problems
11. Spatial regularity models
12. Regional systems and simulation
13. Regional econometric model building
14. Interregional general equilibrium theory with political, social, economic, and ecological variables
15. Spatial organization theory, graph theory application to regional problems
16. Nearest-neighbor approach. Point distribution, pattern recognition, and application of mathematics of topology to point distribution, remote sensing, and other abstract models

17. Regional allocation of resources within a fixed time horizon
18. Survey methods in regional planning, problems of implementation
19. Transportation studies and diffusion models
21. Housing and rent studies
21. General areas of management of public systems, such as hospitals, educational administration, and the like
22. Regional and interregional energy modeling
23. Entropy and its application
24. Fuzzy systems and their application
25. Catastrophe theory and its relevance in regional decline
26. Statistical ecology
27. Application of mathematical biology to regional growth
28. Application of conflict management to regional systems
29. Regional grouping of nations
31. Multinational corporations and regional growth.

Let us discuss the applicability of these techniques for a proto-typical developing country, namely, India, keeping in mind that applications to other countries can be done on a similar basis. Population is the basic variable in economic planning in India. The current population is nearly 651 million, which means that a population over twice as large as that of the United States is living in an area one third of its size. It is generally agreed that the present population of India is quite high in relation to the developed resources and output. There is, of course, some difference in opinion about the degrees of intensity of the problem. It is encouraging that the Planning Commission, the Central Government, and the people of India are quite aware of this problem and are taking necessary measures. Much data has been accumulated on this subject through census operations, government surveys, and scholarly research by Indian and foreign demographers. However, one aspect of the problem has not been given much attention so far. It is the regional pattern of population distribution and growth. The density of population in India varies widely among Indian states. For example, it is high in Kerala and low in Jammu and Kashmir.

If we study the rate of change of population over the past century, on a regional level, interesting features may be revealed. Such factors as birth rates, gross reproduction rates, net reproduction rates, and other demographic indices for these states (or more meaningful area units) will show large amounts of variations over the years. These variations are not random. They can be explained by the physical, economic, social, and polit-ical characteristics of these regions, and their interregional linkages. It is wrong to neglect these differences and treat the population problem on a global or all-India basis.

Again, there is wide variation in the demographic structures of urban and rural India. More than 81 percent of the population of India is rural. The characteristics of the population in urban centers in India vary by region and depend on such factors as rural-urban migration characteristics, the size of the center, history of growth, distance between urban centers of different sizes, and many other spatial variables. In short, the population distribution pattern varies regionally, and it is to be expected that it will change radically in the future when the locational configuration of activities changes due to the successful implementation of five-year plans. So what is needed is not only analysis and projection of Indian population as a whole, but also for each of its meaningful regions. Methods of regional demography and projections can be applied. For the purposes of regional projection, the following traditional methods can be used:

    a. Comparative method
    b. Extrapolation or mathematical function
    c. Regression or correlation method
    d. Regression and covariance analysis
    e. Growth component analysis

Migration was not so important in Indian population history until recently. The nation is committed to a rapid occupational shift out of agriculture, a shift of most of the natural increase in the farm labor force from farm to non-farm work. The question is whether the occupational shift need involve a geographic migration, and, if so, to what extent. This occupational shift may be village centered, metropolitan centered, or town centered. It will be extremely useful if it is possible to project migration under "normal conditions" without government intervention, and then to project the impact of various instrumental policies designed to influence migration. Many methods of regional migration are available. Some of them are theoretical as we see here:

$$M_{ij} = \frac{P_j}{d_{ij}} \, f\,(z_i)$$

where M_{ij} = migration to destination i from source j.
                  $f(z_i$ = function of z_i, where z_i measures the attractive forces of destination i
                  P_j = population of source j, and
                  d_{ij} = distance between source j and destination i.

Many such theoretical models in the field of regional science have been developed and empirically tested. A regional approach to the analysis and projection of population and migration are not only important for economic planning, but also for providing health care benefits. So, one of the starting points for urban planning in India may be the construction of regional or metropolitan life tables.

After the analysis and projection of population and migration in different regions of India are made, the next task is to estimate regional income. Although the state income figures are not readily available, it is possible to indicate the regional variations from data on agriculture. Over the years many methods of regional income accounting have been developed in regional science. Most of these methods were constructed to suit the conditions in the developed countries. However, they can easily be modified and combined with other accounting frameworks specifically designed for developing countries.

One approach is to have a triple-column income-output expenditure table. This table would show in the first column by what groups of individuals or institutions the income is earned; in the second column, in what industries they are earned; and in the third column, how they are consumed or invested . In this table each transaction would appear three times, once as it becomes part of income received, once as it represented the value of a particular kind of good or service produced, and once as it entered into some form of consumption or investment. This system permits the effective utilization of every scrap of economic information by providing a considerable number of cross checks. It thereby reduces the area of unconfirmed estimate to the smallest possible range and presents the sum of available data deductions that can be drawn from the material. Actually, the specific form of the table may vary significantly from study to study, not only because of variations among basic characteristics of regions and available data, but also because of difference in study objectives and meaningful conceptual frameworks.

In a country such as India, a considerable portion of economic activity is concentrated on subsistence agriculture and handicraft, andthere is a significant volume of barter transactions which do not pass through a formal market. Thus the standard Western world functional classification (wages, rent, interest, and profit) should be replaced in many cases by a more meaningful classification related to a subsistence economy or a combination of these classifications with a standard Western world set of categories. Such combinations may be desirable when an underdeveloped region has an important export sector tied to the industrialized sector in the country or abroad. Otherwise, imposing on an underdeveloped region a set of social accounts appropriate for industrialized regions will lead to overstating the importance of money transactions and thus destroy the measure of welfare. So this is an area where the Indian regional scientists can contribute significantly by developing new definitions, ideas, and techniques which will be appropriate not only for income accounting in underdeveloped areas of India, but also in other like countries.

When we come to the question of income accounting for developed open regions in India, the applicability of the tools of regional science become easier. The industrial economy of India is concentrated on a few urban centers, such as Calcutta, Bombay, Ahmedabad, and a number of other centers, such as Durgapur, Bangalore, Bhilai, and Rourkela, which have become important in recent years. In this sense, income accounting in India is not so difficult. If we have a set of regional accounts for these industrial regions, then what remains is to account for the agricultural sector for which we can use the area and output figures for different agricultural crops. The income accounting of urban areas is not only useful for income accounting for India as a whole, but also for urban planning. Consider, for example, the case of the Calcutta Industrial Region, which is facing a serious crisis. One of the prerequisites for planning in Calcutta (now being considered under the auspices of the Calcutta Metropolitan Development Administration) is to prepare a regional social accounting of this region, i.e., the income coming into this region and going out, income and expenditure of different constituent municipalities (which may help us to determine investment outlays in supplying different civic amenities at a future date), and also the import-export relationship of this region with the rest of India and abroad.

Income accounting for Calcutta may reveal many interesting facts which are not presently apparent. For the construction of such accounts it may be necessary to conduct special surveys and refashion some of the existing materials. Again using the data on costs and revenues of different civic amenities by the municipalities, we can construct a regional model for projection of these items at a future date. This model will be extremely useful for deciding the optimum size of each of the municipalities.

Regional income accounting can be supplemented and its value greatly enhanced by the analysis of interregional commodity flow. Such analysis points out the manner and extent to which any region (1) does and can avail itself of the natural advantages of other regions through imports, and (2) does and can compete with other regions in the disposal of its products in the several regional and sub-regional markets. The money flow counterpart of it can provide us with a rupee tag and a common denominator for the exchange of goods and transfer of assets. Thus flow analysis can help formulate monetary and fiscal policies both within a region and in India as a whole. When commodity flow analysis and money flow studies are completed, regional balance of payment studies can be undertaken to assess the current financial position of a region's economy and its general economic health. The interregional commodity flow data for India are reasonably good, but no significant use has yet been made of this material. The flow data can give a clear picture of spatial movement and how it affects regional activity. However, they possess somewhat more than descriptive value. They can very much help future transportation planning. When commodity flows are tied with interregional money flows and, in particular, with (1) the spatial system of individual locations implied by comparative cost and industrial complex analysis, (2) the technical interindustry linkage system of interregional input-output, and (3) the efficiency system of interregional linear programming, then commodity flow studies attain maximum value. The same is true for money flow analysis.

The Indian economy is basically agricultural. It depends on the vagaries of nature in this respect. The level of total economic activity over the years varies greatly, depending upon agricultural production. The fluctuation takes different forms in different regions. Even in the industrial sector, the total industrial activity depends on such big industries as jute, textiles, and tea. The ups and downs of these industries in a few regions influence the national cycles. Industrial location policies should consider the implications of such regional cycles. Other things being equal, it is generally more desirable to develop in a region an industrial mix whose cyclical tendencies tend to balance out or at least do not intensify each other. Thus one valuable avenue of inquiry has been concerned with the industrial composition of regions and the cyclical fluctuations of different types of industries as they may offset each other. We discover that in the short run at least certain industries are basic, particularly those which serve national markets. Their fluctuation leads to changes in local income, which in turn influence retail sales and various service trades. In short, the fluctuations of basic industry have a multiplier effect. In India, there are many regions which depend solely on the export of one commodity. When there is a change in the export of this product, the direct and indirect impact of this change is considerable. Regional and interregional multipliers can be devised for evaluating this impact. For Indian regional scientists there is considerable opportunity to develop the theoretical basis of such regional cycle and multiplier analysis. The problem of regional social accounting, commodity flow, money flow, and regional cycles are intimately related to the policy of industrial location.

All methods discussed so far, namely, regional studies, commodity flow studies, balance of payment studies, economic base studies, multiplier studies, etc., are all partial in nature. What we really need is a general interdependence approach which represents a fruitful avenue for depicting and investigating the underlying processes that bind together the regions of a system and all the separate facets of their economies. The regional and interregional input-output model is one such approach. It presents (1) the production and distribution characteristics of individual industries of different regions and (2) the nature of interrelationships among these industries themselves and with other economic sectors. The basic principle of regional and interregional input-output models is well known. It consists of constructing an input-output table which gives the input purchases and output sales by different sectors for each of a set of regions. Such a table itself presents in an internally consistent fashion a comprehensive set of data on both regional economies and interregional flows. Construction of such a table is extremely important from the standpoint of data collection and statistical discipline. It tends to impose on data collection agencies a common set of definitions, concepts, and terms. This requirement also helps to avoid costly duplication and overlapping of efforts to increase the comparability and usefulness of the resulting statistics. The construction of such a table is costly and time-consuming. Among many problems to be found are the choice of particular types of industries to be defined as sectors, the type of regional and interregional situation to be examined, and the clear identification and statement of the objective of the study.

More importantly, the input-output approach serves as a technique to project into the future the magnitude of important sectors and linkages for the economy. From the flow table, input-output co-efficients are constructed by dividing the elements in each column by the sum of each row. It is generally assumed that this interregional input-output co-efficient matrix remains invariant over time. Regional goals are formulated consistent with national goals and existing situations in each region. Thus the projected output figures for each sector required to achieve these goals are obtained from

$$X = (I-a)^{-1} F$$

where X is the output vector, I is the identity matrix, a is the input-output co-efficient matrix, and F is the vector of final demand (reflecting both national and regional goals).

For a vast country, such as India, instead of having a national input-output table, a set of regional tables can be constructed. The application of this technique for deciding optimum strategy in India has been very limited. However, in many other countries, developed or underdeveloped, input-output analysis has been used extensively for various purposes, in various forms, and under various assumptions. Its applications are not limited to economic planning alone; they extend to major problems in regional, physical, and environmental planning. It is true that this technique has many limitations. It involves sweeping assumptions, and it abstracts from many important realities of folk,

regional, and international life. Yet, after all its limitations are
set down, the fact remains that it provides essential scaffolding for
cementing various partial studies. The input-output model can be
supplemented by industrial complex analysis.

An industrial complex may be defined as a set of activities
occurring at a given location and belonging to a group (sub-system) of
activities which are subject to important production, marketing, or
other interrelations. An example is the production of iron and steel,
starting from coal and ore-mining through pig iron and steel ingot
production to the many final fabricated steel products. Starting from
the mining of the raw materials, ore and coal, each successive stage or
activity constitutes at least part of the market for the immediately
preceding stage; conversely, each stage looks to the preceding stage for
its basic inputs. The location pattern of steel ingot production cannot
be ascertained without knowledge of the location of pig iron production.
However, the local pattern for pig iron production can not be
established unless the location of its market, i.e., the production of
ingot steel is known. Many such complexes exist. The petrochemical
complexes in Bombay, Madras, and Cochin, the jute complex in Calcutta,
the textile complex in Bombay, and the electronics complex in Bangalore
are a few examples. The task is to select meaningful complexes for each
of a set of regions. This can be done by applying the industrial
complex analysis. In this method we examine in order transport cost
differentials, labor cost differentials, scale economies, and
localization and urbanization economics. All this inquiry is conducted
in a restricted, but flexible multi-regional inter-industry framework
which permits changing factor proportions and changing activity mix.

Viewed from several standpoints, the crucial problem facing Indian
planners is how to select a set of policies which will maximize national
or regional income subject to certain social, political, and economic
restrictions. This issue brings us to the method of linear programming.
The problem of income maximization in the face of scarcity of resources
is particularly important for India on the regional level. For example,
there are many areas in India suffering from water shortage. How can we
best employ the available water in terms of a predetermined goal for a
region which may be short on both capital and skilled labor. How can we
exploit this resource most efficiently to attain certain income, employment, and other objectives. Here linear programming on a regional level
can answer such questions.

When there are several regions, each with its particular set of
limited resources, inter-regional linear programming (in which the
objective is to maximize or minimize some linear function, subject to
certain inequalities over a system of regions) can be helpful in
attacking basic problems. Like inter-regional input-output and
industrial complex techniques, inter-regional linear programming
emphasizes general interdependence. Unlike inter-regional input-output
techniques, it is an optimizing technique, and compared to the
industrial complex technique, it can treat a much broader framework in
the analysis of an inter-industrey system.

Given a set of limited resources, a set of constant production
co-efficients, and a set of prices (except on the factors in limited

supply), how can we program diverse production activities in order to maximize profits, social gains, total income, per capita income, employment, goods, social product, or some other magnitude. In particular, say, in the more limited context of transportation planning in Calcutta, the question may be how to schedule the suburban train services so that the transportation cost or bottlenecks are minimum, subject to some restrictions with respect to demand for services and availability of supplies. There are many examples of linear programming models being applied in business, industry, and planning (both regional and national).

The generalized inter-dependence schemes as crystalized in inter-regional input-output and linear programming are powerful analytical tools. However, they are unable to capture fully spatial juxtaposition economies and diseconomies. The structure of a system of regions is more than the sum of the interactions of sets and patterns of units or sectors. The agglomerative forces arising out of concentration of population at different locations is something for which a different approach other than linear programming and input-output is required. This approach must be able to measure the attraction among the areal units and must discern the regularity in such attraction, if any. Gravity, potential, and spatial interaction models are designed for these purposes.

A rather general form of the interaction model is:

$$T_{ij} = \frac{(W_i P_i) \; (W_j P_j)}{d_i b_j}$$

where T_{ij} represents the actual trip volume or interaction between any originating sub-area i and terminating sub-area j; P_i is the population of the area i; P_j is the population of the area j; d_{ij} is the distance between i and j; W_i is the weight factor of the population mass at i; W_j is the weight factor of the population mass at j; and G and b are constants.

A rather general form of the potential model is

$$_iV = G \sum_{j-1}^{m} \frac{W_j P_j}{d_{ij}^b}$$

where $_iV$ represents the potential at a point i from all other points. The other symbols have the same meaning as before. These models, together with others, can be fruitfully applied for analyzing regional problems in India. Problems linked to inter-regional migration; transportation; market area identification; distribution over space of population, business organizations and urban units; and participation of the populace in decision making can be in part attacked by these models. In India, the urban population is low, but the problems in the urban areas have assumed a serious nature, particularly in the field of transportation. Gravity models can be of great help in analyzing and planning intracity transportation.

So far we have discussed the problems related to general economic development. In recent years the problems of resource availability and resource management have posed serious challenges to regional development policy. It is thus important to integrate resource models with developmental models. An example of such an energy econometric model can be found in Chatterji (1981b).

The future of democracy in India hinges on both the ability of the different states to cooperate with each other in nation-building and on international cooperation in the region. Frictions do appear and will appear, particularly from the fact that different parties now administer different states. However, resolution of the problems can be achieved by cooperative efforts through establishment of interregional bodies and under the guidance of the central government. The analysis of these problems and their resolutions can be greatly clarified by careful study of diverse cooperative procedures now available in the fields of conflict management and peace science. We hope more efforts in these directions will come in the future to contribute to the Indian peaceful revolution toward a better way of life.

References

Airov, Joseph, (1959). <u>The Location of the Synthetic Fiber Industry</u>, Cambridge, MA: The M.I.T. Press.

Chatterji, Manas, (1982a). 'An energy-econometric model for the developing countries,' in <u>Energy and Environment in the Developing Countries</u>, (ed.) Manas Chatterji, New York: John Wiley and Sons.

_____, (1982b). 'Energy, environment, and growth in the developing countries: An overall perspective and plans for action,' in <u>Energy and Environment in the Developing Countries</u>, (ed.) Manas Chatterji, New York: John Wiley and Sons.

_____, (1982c). 'Regional and interregional energy-econometric model building,' in <u>Regional Development under Regional Stagnation</u>, (ed.) W. Buhr and P. Friedrich, Baden-Baden, West Germany: Nomos Verlag.

Chatterji, Manas and Umit Akinc, (1981a). 'A critical evaluation of location-allocation modeling,' in <u>Location Developments and Urban Planning</u>, (eds.) W.F.J. Van Lierop and Peter Nijkamp, Alphen aan den Rijn: Sijthoff a Noordhoff.

Chatterji, Manas, (1981b). 'Urbanization, energy, and environment in the developing countries,' in <u>Urban Problems and Economic Development</u>, (eds.) Lata Chatterjee and Peter Nijkamp, Alphen aan den Rijn: Sijthoff a Noordhoff.

_____, (1981). 'Energy modeling with particular reference to spatial systems,' <u>Regional Science and Urban Economics</u>, 11: 325-42.

_____, (1978a). 'Regional planning, national development, and conflict resolution,' in <u>Regional Planning and National Development</u>, (ed.) R. P. Misra et al., New Delhi: Vikas.

_____, (1978b). 'System modeling in space,' in <u>Applied General Systems Research</u>, (ed.) George Klir, New York: Plenum Press.

_____, (1977). 'Spatial modeling,' in Proceedings of the First International Conference on Mathematical Modeling, Vol. II. Rolla, Missouri: University of Missouri Press.

_____, (1976). 'World energy situation,' In Energy, Regional Science, and Public Policy, (ed.) Manas Chatterji and Paul Van Rompuy, Munich: Springer Verlag.

Fisher, Joseph, (1957). 'Potential contributions of regional science to the field of economics,' Papers of the Regional Science Association, 3, 17-23.

Isard, Walter, (1969). General Theory: Social, Political, Economic, and Regional, Cambridge, MA: The M.I.T. Press.

Isard, Walter, (1961). Methods of Regional Analysis, Cambridge, MA: The M.I.T. Press.

_____, (1956). Location and Space Economics, Cambridge, MA: The M.I.T. Press.

Isard, Walter and Panagis Liossatos, (1979). Spatial Dynamics and Optimal Space-Time Development, Cambridge, MA: The M.I T. Press.

Isard, Walter, and Thomas A. Reiner, (1966). 'Regional science: retrospect and prospect,' Papers of the Regional Science Association, 16: 1-16.

Smith, Thomas, (1957). 'Potential contribution of regional science to the field of geography,' Papers of the Regional Science Association, 3: 13-15.

Viner, Jacob, (1963). 'The economics of development,' in The Economics of Underdevelopment, (eds.) A. Agarwala and S. Singh, New York: Oxford University Press.

Wetmore, Louis, (1957). 'Potential contribution of regional science to the field of city planning,' Papers of the Regional Science Association, 3: 16.

Whitney, V. H., (1957). 'Potential contribution of regional science to the field of sociology,' Papers of the Regional Science Association, 3: 24-28.

3 Some notes on the methodology of development planning

T. H. BOTTERWEG, L. H. KLAASSEN AND J. G. VIANEN

1. Introduction

In development programming, the question whether to plan "from the top down" or "from the bottom up" has become traditional. The "top down approach," adopted in many countries and strongly stimulated by the developed world, is bound back in many models operated in developing countries, but often inspired by economists and econometricians who have come from developed countries. The "bottom-up" approach lacks the mathematical elegance and strict logic of the "top-down" approach, andperhaps for that reason has found less favor with economists. Probably for the same reason, we find "bottom-up" planning techniques far less discussed than "top-down" ones. Nevertheless, there is much more planning going on at the base than on the macro level.

This note will briefly discuss the "top-down" approach, the meso approach, and the "bottom-up" approach, pointing out their advantages and disadvantages.

2. The Top-Down Approach

2.1 Macro analysis

The purpose of development programming, by any method, is to realize meaningful projects, i.e., projects of real economic or social importance that contribute to a country's development objectives, such as income, self-sufficiency, balance of payments, national budget, and employument. So, a programming method should be appreciated primarily for its capacity to identify such meaningful projects and judge their contribution to the development of the country. A method that fails in that respect is sterile, for it does not serve social and economic development, the ultimate object of programming.

In macro planning, mathematical models are mostly used; they make it possible to test how much certain essential economic quantities hang together, and thus to determine their development in the near future. However, such an estimated model is not indispensable to plotting macro development; quite a good outline of economic developments to be expected can also be obtained from a macro-economic study in which some essential quantities are examined separately.

In 1975 the World Bank presented in one of its publications an

14

up-to-date survey of (macro) programming models developed in the course
of time and actually applied (Blitzer, Clark, and Taylor, 1975). It
gives a good description of the kind of models that are used in the
top-down approach. We will quote a passage by T. Watanabe referring to
the normal case where the available statistical material for individual
years is limited and the time series too short (Watanabe 1975, p. 119).

> With a relatively short period of time series
> observations in national income accounts and
> relatively poor statistical information, it would be
> useful to construct a simple aggregate economic
> model and to use it for ex post forecasting in order
> to improve data reliability, especially of national
> income accounts. A simple aggregate economic model
> may include a consumption function, an investment
> function, an import function, and related identity
> equations. The consumption function may be
> specified as a function of income variables (e.g.,
> disposable income, national income or GDP) and other
> variables such as the size of the population. If
> the model is viewed as demand oriented, the
> investment function may be described as the function
> of changes in output variables (e.g., GDP or some
> form of capacity utilization), exogenous government
> investment (including foreign investment), and other
> related variables; where estimates of the existing
> capital stock are available, they should also be
> added. The import function should be specified as a
> function of output variables (e.g., GDP or some form
> of capacity) and other related variables such as
> relative prices or changes in foreign trade
> indicators.

However, the author seems to expect difficulties in applying this
kind of model for planning purposes, for he goes on to say:

> Simple aggregate economic model building might not
> be useful for short-term ex ante forecasting, since
> the dualistic nature of developing countries is a
> significant barrier to drawing meaningful forecasts
> from this kind of model. For example, a mixture of
> fundamentally different technologies, traditional
> (labor-using) and modern (labor-saving) may generate
> biased forecasts from levels of output, employment,
> or imports. These considerations would lead to
> another type of analysis such as the Leontief input-
> output model, for forecasting purposes. (Watanabe
> 1975, pp. 119-21)

He continues:

> although both simple macroeconomic models and input-
> output models may be more useful in assessing data
> reliability through ex post forecasting than the
> rough ex ante forecasting, future economic projec-
> tions are an important application of economy-wide

models. As has been pointed out above, predictability itself may sometimes be poorer using these former models than when using more naive types of forecasts such as a simple blow up of GNP components or sectoral output levels. However, one of the more important gains from attempting to use models to make forecasts lies in the ability to draw implications from the model's solution regarding structural interdependence in the economy. Furthermore, the appropriate sensitivity analyses which are required in order to test the feasibility of economic planning can only be made within a modelling framework. (Watanabe 1975, p. 121)

In the top-down approach it is important to know not only how the national economy develops, but also how its development relates to the development objectives. The two elements are integrated in macro analysis, where the model's parameters are the results of the historic development, and the value of variables such as national investments and consumption is calculated from the desired economic development of, say, national income.

Note that the information used in such analysis is not equivalent: Taking the future increase of income as a starting point, one calculates the consequences with the help of parameters (whether average or marginal) corresponding to either the historical or the present situation. That is a remarkable procedure, since the desired growth of national income or employment can be expected only from the realization of concrete projects. For instance, a decision about certain sectoral developments implicitly assumes that, on an aggregate level, a series of projects will be carried out in each sector, and that at a later stage (which indeed is seldom reached) efforts will be made to identify useful projects for each sector.

2.2. Sector analysis

Let us take a first step down towards the project level with the help of the input-output tables already mentioned. As Taylor aptly expresses it,

The models discussed so far have been aggregative, consistent with national accounts data, and designed to make macro-economic projections about the evolution of GNP, total employment, the balance of payments, and so on. However, for many planning purposes -- particularly as a basis for discussion between sector specialists and those concerned with macro-analysis -- more disaggregate growth forecasts are desirable. These are almost always built around an interindustry flow table. This is still an essentially macro-economic construct, since even the most detailed input output tables rarely reach down to the plant (let alone the farm!) in their classification. However, the tables do provide a halfway house between macro and micro and are useful for precisely that reason. (Taylor 1975, p. 42)

In the top-down approach, sectoral and regional planners are supposed to adapt the development strategy drawn up on the macro level to sectors and -- as we shall see in the next section -- regions, allocating in a tentative manner the available means to the sectors and regions distinguished. They will introduce a kind of efficiency criterion in the shape of the contribution individual sectors make todevelopment objectives. In concrete terms, a sector's intake of scarce resources such as foreign currency, financial means, and manpower, is weighted up against its contribution to, say, national income. The use fo input-output tables makes it possible to do what partial sector analysis cannot: take into account how far economic activities are interwoven.

The step we have taken towards the plant or farm we are anxious to reach is a small one, and we come upon a well known, nasty snake in the input-output grass, called fixed input-output coefficients. The various methods designed to overcome the problem (trend-wise extrapolation, use of marginal coefficients, etc.) all share the disadvantage of straying too far from reality. Input-output coefficients differ widely because there are essential structural differences within even the most detailed sectors. For that matter, is it not the very purpose of programming to let new activities spring up in a country, activities other than the traditional onesµ The objective is, indeed, to bring about changes in the sectoral structure, changes that, ex post, will modify the input-output coefficients.

But what we do find, as a second remarkable fact is that fixed input-output coefficients, or coefficients changing according to a fixed time pattern, are used to find a set of activities intended to change sectoral structures and thus input-output coefficients.

2.3. Regional analysis

Obviously, determining the sectors where one may find likely projects is not enough; the best region for the location of such projects is essential too. Therefore, the macro and sector approaches have to be regionalized. As to how that should be done, let us cite Mrinal K. Datta-Chaudhuri:

> Our brief survey of interindustry models for multi-regional economies seems to lead to a few broad summary conclusions regarding their usability:
>
> (i) these models are not yet very useful as practical guides to making rational choice with respect to the regional allocation of resources, at least in the context of today's computational technology. In the judgement of the present author, regional or locational choice is extremely important for geographically large and culturally diverse countries, and the possibilities of savings in resource use by making rational choice in their area are significant. But the construction of meaningful computable models seems to be beyond our scope today.
>
> (ii) For short-run forecasting problems we do have usable models but these models are constructed on

assumptions of the stability of the interregional
trading coefficients and/or attraction coefficients.
This makes them unreliable for use in the long-run
planning context -- particularly in underdeveloped
countries where the marginal changes are likely to be
significant compared with existing averages.

(iii) Interindustry analysis can be used imagina-
tively in a partial context in formulating development
strategy for a particular region or an urban center.
But it is difficult to formulate such partial models
that will have general applicability in many different
situations. However, measurement of interindustry
linkages is essential for formulating reliable regional
development programs. Input-output analysis provides
the obvious framework for posing these policy
problems. (Datta-Chaudhuri 1975, pp. 256-57)

So much for Datta-Chaudhuri. What he suggests is not so much to
regionalize the sector forecasts, which would be in line with the
top-down approach, as to repeat on the regional plane what has been
done earlier on the national plane, that is, couple input-output
analysis for each individual region with regional and macro forecasts.

This brings us to the third remarkable fact to be underlined: at
the very point where it ought to lead us towards projects in certain
sectors and in certain regions, we leave the top-down approach because
it becomes too complicated and make a side-step to the regions, to
recommence the national procedure -- a side step which is alien to the
systematics of the top-down approach, and which would indeed fit the
bottom-up approach better, as we hope to support later on.

2.4. The project level

In the top-down approach there is but a weak link between the
macro, sectoral, and regional levels and the projects that eventually
are to gove substance to development. On high hierarchical levels are
developed the criteria by which projects prepared at the base are to be
evaluated. Theoretically, the criteria should be used to assess not
only the projects' contribution to national development, but also the
differences among the contributions of selected projects, so that a
priority list of projects can be drawn up. In that connection one
could think of accounting prices for the inputs and outputs of the
projects.

Three questions seem to arise:

1.   Can the top-down approach lead to the selection and weighing
     of concrete projects?

2.   If so, will the selected projects be the ones that serve the
     country's balanced economic and social development best?

3.   Is the method consistent?

We can say yes to the last question, but we cannot give a positive answer to the first two from what has been written above.

3. Meso Approaches

   3.1. Introduction

         In the preceding chapter we have seen that at the stage of
macro planning, a nation's overall development in the near future is
laid out. Macro planners work with rather broad social objectives
formulated in consultation with leading politicians and social
organizations that are interested in the development of the nation.
The social objectives are mostly translated into economic targets such
as growth of national income or an equilibrium in the balance of
payment. On the macro level a first assessment is made of the
financial resources available, and the main bottlenecks that hamper a
country's development are identified. To analyze quantitatively
non-economic elements is difficult on the macro level; it is not for
macro planners to study institutional and social bottlenecks.

   On the other hand, broad objectives of social development are not
easily recognized by such economic agents as firms, ministries, other
private or public organizations, and consumers. That is why a
conceptual link should be laid between the rather broad macro
development objectives and the goals of individual sectors and
regions. In other words, the social objectives should be made
operational and reformulated in terms of concrete targets that are easy
to recognize. Reformulation on the meso level the exercise yeilds a
list of development projects. In this section the meso level is under
discussion; we shall give our comments on some aspects of planning on a
level halfway between the "top" and the "bottom." The focus will be on
sectoral planning, but regional planning is in many respects linked
with it. At the end of the section we will give some attention to the
problems involved in selecting and weighing projects.

   In essence, sectoral or regional goals, apart from setting the
scene for sectoral and regional development programs, also make up the
framework for productive development projects on the micro level.

   Macro planning cannot stand on its own; it should be linked to
sectoral, regional, and/or project planning. Planning based solely on
the identification of projects, without a proper built-in allocation
mechanism, might lead to misallocation of national resources.
Moreover, on the project level one could easily neglect to compare the
efficiency of the project in hand with that of others.
Underutilization, for example, is a problem that is beyond the scope of
one firm, and should be studied on the sectoral level.

   Would it be possible for macro planning and project planning to be
directly linkedμ In particular, in large countries or countries with
intricate networks of economic activities, to define a consistent
complete program of development projects to be studied, financed, and
implemented is technically very difficult. Kornai (1967), Goreux and
Manne (1972), and Vours, Condos, and Goreux (1971) may have
demonstrated that in theory economic activities can be planned in an
optimum way with the help of very detailed economic multi-level
models. In practice, such a refined planning process is difficult to
implement within the social organization of developing nations. It

demands a central planning organization with power to develop plans and
a team of highly competent model builders, neither of which tend to be
found in developing nations.

A more efficient procedure would be to make use of the institutional and organizational capabilities available in developing nations.
These can be found, or developed, on the meso level, where all the
parties concerned have common economic interests. They may be of help
in implementing development programs defined on the sectoral or
regional level.

3.2. Sector planning

Sector planning should be based on sectoral analysis, by which we
understand the integrate analysis of a given sector and its relations
to the economic system. Such an analysis can provide the information
required to formulate a program that leads to the identification of
promising projects on the sector level or the micro (firm) level, and
to an investment strategy. Out definition of sectoral analysis leaves
open the question whether sectoral programs will be drawn up with the
help of explicit sector models or based on the partial analysis of
individual sectors.

Partial sector analysis does not explicitly consider the results of
any macro planning done in the country, but uses as input macro-
economic information based on certain assumptions. The plans founded
on such analyses are designed more or less autonomously and not
integrated in a general macro-economic framework. They are operated in
many developing countries, and the results are no more disappointing
than those of planning by means of integrated development models.
Waterston (1977) states:

> Il convient de signaler que les résultats obtenus
> avec les programmes sectoriels établis en dehors des
> cadres macro-économiques n'ont pas été notablement
> inférieurs ... et il est arrivé même qu'ils soient
> supérieurs ... à ceux qu'ont produit généralement
> les programmes sectoriels intégrés aux plans macro-
> économiques.

Partial planning does not necessarily imply that the information that
is analyzed is inconsistent or has been collected ad hoc. For quite a
few sectors highly detailed models have been built to consistently
simulate the relations within the sector, or optimize its production.
Especially in the agricultural sector much experience has been gained
in studying, with the help of sectoral models, the contribution of
agriculture to output, income distribution, employment, and balance of
payments. Policies and programs dealing with taxes, training, credit,
land reform, prices, and marketing can be evaluated. The relations
with the overall economy are mostly weak and hypothetical, however. A
good example is the model developed for Guatemala by the government of
Guatemala and USAID (Fletcher et al, 1971). A large-scale model of
Nigeria's agriculture, also considering different regions, has been
developed by the Michigan State University (Johnson 1971). A sectoral
model built entirely from the bottom up has been used for agricultural
planning in the Punjab. One of its outstanding features is the
preference function of the farmer. This model is a regional rather

than a national sector model (Mudahar 1971).

The framework for analysis should preferably be general enough to do justice to relations among industries and sectors and to link up macro-economic analysis and analysis on the meso level. Few such models have as yet been constructed for, and applied to, developing nations. Most of the existing sectoral models are experimental and as such of limited use for policy purposes.

Things can be said for and against partial as well as multi-sectoral analysis. Using the two approaches complementarily is a challenge to the countries. A multi-sector model helps to detail the results of the macro model and to allocate scarce national resources to the various sectors of the economy. There is, however, a risk of too mechanical an analysis, one which considers only economic variables and pays no attention to the institutional and organizational capacities of a country. Multi-sector planning, being akin to macro-economic planning, should never be applied in isolation. Planners are indeed justified in first making rudimentary analyses of individual sectors. But how should we define or disaggregate the sectorsµ In multi-sector models, aggriculture is often taken as one sector, while the industrial sector, mostly far less important in developing nations, is sub-divided into many sub-sectors. Another question is this: how available and how reliable are sector dataµ It should be kept in mind that the information to be collected has to serve planning, and ultimately, implementation, and should therefore apply to the future rather than to the past. Another thing to remember is that next to economic problems, the patterns on the meso level should be given due attention, and the sectors disaggregated accourdingly. For it is on the meso level that economic agents should join in the discussion on sectoral development plans.

While the economic impact on the national economy of sectoral development programs based on partial sector analysis can be studied thoroughly interindustry relations cannot adequately be accounted for. A multi-sector model constructed with the help of provisional economic data obtained in partial analyses and capable of taking into consideration elementary information on the social organization on the meso level may at least give a rough idea both of how much individual sectors contribute to the national objectives (for this purpose translated into provisional sectoral development goals) and how desirable they thus are for national development (Kuyvenhoven 1978). To give an example, investments in the textile industry may be found to contribute more to the national objectives than investments in the footwear industry. In this way, a key can be developed by which to allocate funds to selected industries and to the economic activities with solid forward and backward links to these industries (clusters or bunches of industries).

After the first run of the multi-sector model, studies delving much deeper are required to work out a development program for the industries provisionally selected. To that end, the industries are subjected to a partial analysis that, while heeding the input and output aspects of a sector, ignores the multiplicative effects of its expansion on the national objectives. A detailed descriptive analysis would shed light on the exact position of the sector in terms of the national balances of raw material and final product, production processes currently used, and possible technological innovations, manpower situation, marketing and financing problems, etc. To verify the results of the first run of the multi-sector analysis, the interindustry relations of the sectors involved should be investigated thoroughly. In the same phase the development projects should be identified and a tentative list composed of projects that satisfy the sectoral goals, derived from the national objectives by means of the multi-sector model. If necessary the multi-sector model should be taken to a second run with revised and completed information, leading perhaps to a new ranking by attractiveness of the provisionally selected industries.

Ultimately, the performance, problems, and chances of the selected industries should be diagnosed by the partial analysis, and their relative attractiveness shown up by the multi-sector analysis. The information thus obtained can help planners to allocate available funds efficiently.

An effort to integrate multi-sector analysis with partial sector analysis has been made in Tunisia. The multi-sector model developed for that country gives alternative development perspectives and indicates how investment funds are to be allocated to the large sectors, but it is not used to test the consistency of sector programs or projects. The emphasis is on the independent analysis and planning of the various sectors. The sector plans are being elaborated by the technical ministries which cooperate quite intensively with the planning office to avoid conflicts among the sector plans or between those and the national objectives (Zorghat 1977).

3.3 Sector planning and project planning

First, the functioning of the sector is assessed and its problems are identified by sector analysis. Next, solutions have to be found either on the sectoral or on the micro (project) level.

Programs developed on the sectoral level, referring to, for instance, credit schemes, marketing facilities, import duties on raw material, and subsidies on export goods, affect economic agents concerned with and operating in the sector involved. Furthermore, infrastructure works may be planned to boost the production of high-priority goods (farm-to-market roads).

On the micro level, production projects can be selected to achieve the goals set on the sector level, e.g., irrigation schemes for the cultivation of rice to make the country self-sufficient in its staple food.

The evaluation of development projects in the light of sectoral and national objectives is a very complicated matter, and many studies arguing for and against project evaluation by means of shadow prices have been devoted to the problem. We will not go into the theories and technicalities of evaluating development projects, but content outselves with the following brief description.

Sectoral plans set out the goals to be achieved and indicate the investment funds to be allocated to the sectors. Concrete development projects can then be placed in the framework drawn up on the sectoral level, evaluated in terms of the goals set, and approved by the development authorities, on the sectoral level. The projects can be ranked by their profitability and added to the selection until the funds available for development projects give out. The selected projects may have serious impacts on the calculations carried out on the sectoral or even the national level. If that seems to be so, the priorities among the sectors should be reassessed. In fact, on the project level development projects belonging to different sectors should be compared. The priorities given to sectors on the meso level will largely determine those on the micro level since the latter group should follow the same pattern. Moreover, development budgets allocated to the ministries concerned tend to be determined on the strength of the sectoral plans rather than on a ranking of development projects by their national economic profitability.

4. The Bottom-Up Approach

Several steps can be distinguished in a botton-up approach, some of them to be taken simultaneously, other successively.

The first step is to divide the national territory into regions, which may be done by various criteria. The most obvious choice is a division into areas coinciding with administrative regions, often the only ones for which data are available, and also offering the advantage of regional authorities to whom the responsibility for management and development can readily be assigned.

The second step is to draw up regional plans for the regions defined in the first stage. A regional plan assesses the region's agricultural, industrial, and mining potentials, as well as the quality of the social and technical infrastructure, and advises on the execution of concrete projects in the region. Project dossiers contain proposals for projects in all the fields referred to above. They present:

a. the consequences of each project, furing the investment stage, in terms of employment, demand on the budget, balance of payment, investment sum required, and deliveries from other branches of activity;

b. the consequences of each project, during the operation stage, in terms of employment, demand on the budget, balance of payment, operating costs, revenues, and deliveries to and from other branches of activity.

The third step, which in principle can be taken at the same time as the second, consists of drawing up detailed sector plans in which the development and future potentials of the sectors are analyzed on the national level. These plans take into account prospects on the national and international markets, export expansion, and import substitution on the national scale. Specific projects are defined and presented as in the regional plans.

The fourth step, which can be taken alongside steps 2 and 3, is meant to give an insight into the sectoral, regional, and national constraints with respect to, among other things, the market potentials of the sectors at home and abroad, and labor market by region and for the whole country, and, on the national level, the balance of payment and financing. It is at this stage that the link will be laid with the analyses on the macro and meso levels. The constraints can be determined either with the help of models or by partial analyses, the advantages and disadvantages of which we have already pointed out.

The fifth step, is the integration of the project plans thus evolved into a region-sector matrix. Two actions are needed:

a.   integrate regional and sectoral plans to obtain a set of plans by region and by sector;

b.   adjust the total set of regional and sectoral plans to existing constraints.

The following table (4.1) should elucidate the fifth step:

TABLE 1
SET OF REGIONAL AND SECTORAL PLANS (FOR INVESTMENT,
EMPLOYMENT, BALANCE OF PAYMENT, etc.)

Sector \ Region	1	2	..	..	r	S	Sectoral Constraint
1						S_1	$\bar{S}_1$
2						S_2	$\bar{S}_2$
. . . . .							
n						S_n	$\bar{S}_n$
R	R_1	R_2			R_r	N	
Regional constraint	$\bar{R}_1$	$\bar{R}_2$			$\bar{R}_r$		$\bar{N}$

The above matrix presents the projects initially proposed for the various regions and sectors. The following comments can be made.

1.   Projects are not independent from one another; clusters of (coherent) projects should be treated as such, aslo in the determination of priorities.

2.   National constraints (labor market, balance of payment, export potentials, shortage of capital, etc.) may prevent the complete N-set from being carried out (see step 4).

3. Regional constraints $(\bar{R}_1, \bar{R}_2,..., \bar{R}_r)$ referring to sales prospects, labor market, available skills, regional market volume, etc., may require adjustment of regional plans (see step 4).

4. Sectoral constraints $(\bar{S}_1, \bar{S}_2,..., \bar{S}_n)$ may restrict the execution of sectoral plans (shortage of suitable staff, market constraints, investment constraints, etc.; see step 4).

5. Some projects are not strictly associated with one region, either because they are footloose or because their activities, such as marketing services, are spread across the whole country; such projects will have to be placed in a separate column.

6. Matrices like the one above have to be composed for several aspects and repeated through time. One matrix may reproduce production by sector and by region, another the amounts invested by sector and by region. The former will contain constraints on sales prospects, the latter those springing from the scarcity of savings and other financial means.

Once regional and sectoral plans have been integrated, evidently the set of concrete projects can only be obtained by trial and error, consistency being achieved through sectoral, regional, and national constraints; there is no way to arrive at the final result by a succession of logical steps.

The sixth step will of necessity be simultaneous with the fifth, for it comprises ranking the projects by priority. Numerous aspects of the projects have been identified with step 2, and criteria are still being developed by which to assess the economic profitability of the individual projects. For the time being, however, a plausible priority list can be drawn up by weighing the parameters of the projects as calculated in step 2. It will be the planner's responsibility to point out to policy makers, who will have to decide on the ultimate ranking of attractive projects, the effects these projects will have.

The seventh step is the calculation of regional growth, growth by sector, and national growth, from the matrices drawn up with respect to investments, employment, income, balance of payment, and national budget.

In the eighth and final step, the outcomes of the exercises of step 7 carried out on the sectoral, regional, and national levels are set off against the assumed increases in demand and income from the proposed projects, and the project matrices corrected if and as required.

The final result is a set of mutually consistent projects producing collectively a certain well-considered growth by sector and by region.

Points to be observed in particular by the following:

a. The integration of regional plans should not be just the adding together of a couple of regional porjects; it should result in a set of projects for a system of regions. This

approach applies in particular to the planning of interregional infrastructure and interregional deliveries.

b.   When sectoral plans are integrated, deliveries among projects
     should be given special attention. Thus the foundations are
     laid for an input-output table that is more realistic than one
     with coefficients based on real projects following ex post
     from the analysis.

c.   Minimum constraints should be laid on regional plans. Not
     only projects within sectors but also projects within regions
     need to be weighed up. Minimum constraints ensure that not
     all the projects end up in a few privileged regions and that
     due attention is given to projects which may perhaps yield
     little economic profit but do push a certain region one step
     up towards development. This is one area where the social
     objective counts more heavily than the economic one.

5.   A Combined Approach for Indonesia

5.1 Introduction

The writers hope that the descriptions given in the previous
sectors have made it clear that there is another approach to
development besides the conventional top-down one, one that is probably
better suited to local and regional needs and possibilities. But would
it also fit the needs and potentials of large countriesμ The objection
cannot be that the projects in a large country are too numerous to be
included in the model, for that would be true whatever model is
chosen. The question is rather how to process a large number of
projects systematically. In this section we shall try to indicate how
the structure of the bottom-up approach can be adjusted to the size of
the problem, or reconciled with that of the top-down approach.

5.2 The difficulties of planning in a large country

The problems encountered in planning a large country are
special because of their very size. We have seen that the bottom-up
approach entails the difficult exercise of shaping, by trial and error,
the projects indentified by region and by sector into a consistent set
of projects that serves the national interest best. When the bottom-up
approach was applied in practice to the South American Republic of
Surinam, some 411 projects had to be ranked and ordered. For a country
like Indonesia, 511 times the size of Surinam, there will well be
211,111 projects. With such numbers, the trial-and-error method would
prove too much for the planners. A step-wise approach, logically
implying some decentralization of the planning procedure, would be more
appropriate.

If we divided Indonesia into 51 regions, the average population of
one region would still be ten times that of the whole population of
Surinam. Splitting up each region into sub-regions would bring a
bottom-up method within reach, particularly since the population of
some regions will be below average, and the regions with above average
populations are urban areas which need separate plans anyhow.

The problem is next reduced to giving each region a starting point for its planning which ensures that the integration of regional plans produces a consistent national plan. In that way a top-down approach could become the starting point for the bottom-up approach of the (large) regions.

5.3 Plan preparation in Indonesia

Indonesia has its National Plan, but knows no systematic regional planning, although quite a bit of planning is going on locally and in certain of the smaller regions. The Indonesian law on administration in the regions does, however, provide the framework required for the cooperation of regional and local bodies. The gaps should be filled, as indeed they have been recently, by activities of the Ministry of Public Works and in particular by the Directorate General of Urban and Regional Planning (Taka Kota dan Tate Daerah).

First, regions were delineated by determining how far and from where lorries are conveying freight, the outer boundary of their range being accepted as the region's boundary. Forty-three regions were formed in that way, most of them subdivided into an urban center and the surrounding countryside.

Next, efforts were made to develop (with the cooperation of one of the present authors) a regional model for the allotment of tasks; the result was the REMIND model (Regional Model Indonesia), the basic structure of which is reproduced in Figure 1.

5.4 The place of the model in Indonesian planning

REMIND is essentially a distribution model, trying to distribute among the regions, by macro-analytic means, within a given budget and on given levels of total production, the sectors and the money available for investments in such a way that within given constraints (for equity) the contribution to national income is maximized (for efficiency).

Since the regions involved are still quite large, and the sectors are large and complex, the results obtained with the model should be handed over to the authorities in the regions involved, who then have to try and divide the investment money to optimum effect among the regional objectives and translate the investment into specific projects. Perhaps they have projects of their own in mind that do not concur with the sector distribution suggested to them. They should have the opportunity to feed information about such projects back to the responsible higher authorities, who could use it to adjust the regional and perhaps even the national model. In that way the top-down and bottom-up approaches could be reconciled, and consistency achieved between national constraints and project potentials.

5.5 Intra-regional planning

In the previous section methods were proposed to arrive at realistic targets for each planning region, and a first step towards translating these targets into real projects was indicated. The question how to plan within each region (intraregional planning) was left open, however. In this section we shall try to get to "the bottom of the problem." The major objective of intraregional planning is to

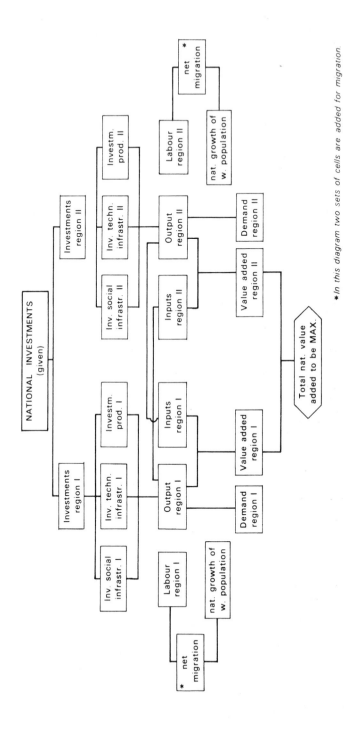

Figure 1.   Regional Model for Indonesia
(REMIND-Model).

*In this diagram two sets of cells are added for migration.

28

create an operational, interdependent, economic system of activities and of communication and transportation facilities. On the assumption that the activities to be developed emerge from regional exercises, their location within the planning regions is what remains to be settled. The location of agriculture, mining, fishery and forestry is mostly fixed, but that of manufacturing and services poses interesting problems. As service industries tend to locate near concentrations of manufacturing activities, the real problem is to find sites for the latter (to the exclusion of most of agricultural processing, which often takes place where the crops are grown). The basic strategy should be to select so-called growth poles, defined as centers with favorable development <u>potentials</u>. A city is said to have development potential if:

a. it has at least 111,111 inhabitants

b. it possesses a favorable economic structure, promising future growth

c. it is linked to other potential growth centers by an adequate infrastructure and communication system, or if good-quality infrastructure could be achieved at relatively low cost

d. its social intrastructure (facilities) is on a reasonable level

e. there are no major financial or physical obstacles to further growth

f. it offers good opportunities for industrial estates and housing schemes.

Growth poles ought to be selected on the national level. Secondary and agricultural centers should be selected on the level of planning regions. The secondary road network linking these centers among themselves and to the main growth centers should be gradually raised to the general standard of secondary roads as means become available. A priority scheme is nevertheless desirable. The principles of the systems of secondary and agricultural centers should be worked out regionally, but should be comparable to those mentioned above for large centers.

6. Conclusions

In this paper we have presented a planning technique which we hope is an improvement on both the top-down and the bottom-up approach. On the meso level, where the two meet, there is a choice of regional, sectoral, or functional aggregation. Should a regional aggregation be chosen, then the top-down part of planning consists of formulating targets by region, starting from the national level, and the botton-up part consists of using detailed inputs from the regional level based on local knowledge, information, existing plans, etc. The latter part of the planning process may give rise to a revision of the national targets and/or the adaptation of general sector plans, and thus to an adjustment of the national plan and the reformulation of the regional plans.

29

The authors are well aware that the combination of macro and micro approaches to development planning has not yet achieved a development methodology at once consistent, easy to understand, and reasonably simple to apply. They hope to contribute to such a methodology in the future.

References

Blitzer, Charles R., Peter B. Clark and Lance Taylor, (eds.), (1975). Economy-Wide Models and Development Planning, London: Oxford University Press, (for the World Bank).

Datta-Chaudhuri, Mrinal K., (1975). 'Interindustry planning model for a multiregional economy,' in Economy-Wide Models and Developing Planning, Charles R. Blitzer, Peter B. Clark and Lance Taylor, (eds.), London: Oxford University Press, pp. 235-57.

Fletcher, L.B. et al., (1971). Guatemala's Economic Development: The Road to Agriculture, Ames: Iowa State University Press.

Goreux, Louis M. and Alan S. Manne, (1973). Multi-Level Planning: Case Studies in Mexico, Amsterdam: North Holland.

Johnson, Glenn Leroy, et al., (1971). A Simulation Model of the Nigerian Agricultural Economy: A Progress Report to the Agency for International Development, East Lansing: Michigan State University Press.

Kornai, J., (1967). Mathematical Planning of Structural Decisions, Amsterdam: North Holland.

Kuyvenhoven, A., (1978). Planning with the Semi Input-Output Method with Empirical Applications to Nigeria, Boston: Martinus Nijhoff.

Mudahar, Mohindar S., (1971). A Dynamic Micro-Economic Analysis of the Agricultural Sector: The Punjab, Madison: University of Wisconsin Press.

Taylor, Lance, (1975). 'Theoretical foundations and technical applications,' in Economy-Wide Models and Development Planning, Charles R. Blitzer, Peter B. Clark, and Lance Taylor, (eds.), London: Oxford University Press, pp. 33-111.

Vaurs, R., P. Condos, and L. Goreux, (1971). A Programming Model of Ivory Coast, Washington, D.C.: World Bank.

Watanabe, Tsunehiko, (1975). 'Quantitative foundations and implications of planning processes,' in Economy-Wide Models and Development Planning, Charles R. Blitzer, Peter B. Clark and Lance Taylor (eds.), London: Oxford University Press, pp. IIV-28.

Waterston, Albert, (1977). La Programmation Sectorielle, Washington, D.C.: World Bank.

Zorghat, N., (1977). Plan et Projets: L'Experience tunisienne, Rome: Food and Agricultural Organization.

4 Towards new development concepts in relation to the energy crisis

ALBERTO NAEF

1. Introduction

"Living is nothing more or less than doing one thing instead of another." This sentence of Ortega y Gasset expresses, indeed, in a very realistic way the constraints of life. It indicates the limits we cannot trespass, because life itself has his own limits. Reality reminds us of these limits everytime we try to pass through them.

Considering these limits we intend to comment on the impact of the energy crisis on development strategies based on the transfer of technology from the industrial countries to the developing ones. We must consider whether the energy crisis represents a constraint in connection with development concepts. Our project does not intend to develop any ideologies, but will concern itself with empirical data.

2. The Challenge of the Energy Crisis

It may be useful to point out that the energy crisis is not a crisis in itself. The energy crisis would not exist, were there not a relationship between the availability of energy resources and the demand. The crisis is not one of energy, but an economic one. Energy becomes a factor of crisis in relation to growth, employment and inflation.

In the past the relationship between the increase of energy consumption and the growth of the gross domestic product has been considered in most countries a positive one. However, now the degree to which the economic sectors are mechanized has to be reconsidered. An expansion of man's ability to bring forth secondary products is, in fact, "useless unless preceded by an expansion of his ability to win primary products from the earth, for man is not a producer but only a converter and for every job of conversion he needs primary products. In particular, his power to convert depends on primary energy" (Schumacher, 1973).

A study prepared for the Swiss Commission for Energy Planning aimed at showing what would happen in Switzerland if there were a sudden shortage of oil in 1981 which would affect all consumer categories to the same extent. In the event of a 15Δ drop in oil supplies (based on normal oil consumption), the gross domestic product would decline by 7Δ, and 5Δ of the working population would be jobless. If the supply of petroleum were to sink by 25Δ, the gross domestic product would edge off by as much as 15Δ and there would be a 12Δ increase in unemployment.

3. Three Aspects of Energy Consumption

The energy consumption of industrial nations can be illustrated geographically and historically.

a. Geographical distribution of primary energy consumption, 1969 and 1979

The geographical distribution of energy consumption is represented in Figure 1.

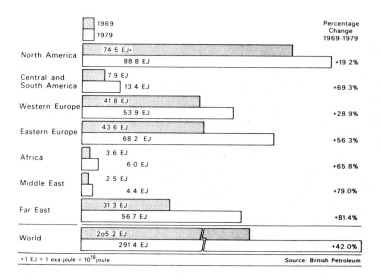

Figure 1. Geographical distribution of primary energy consumption in 1969 and 1979.

The difference of per-capita energy consumption became more evident when we compared some selected countries. The U.S. outdistances the rest of the world by a wide margin, though consumption figures for other industrial nations also lie above the world average (Fig. 2).

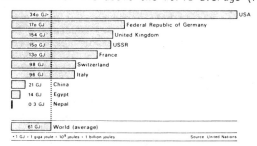

Figure 2. 1976 Per-capita energy consumption in selected countries.

b. Historic evolution of energy consumption

        In the course of history, there has never been such a huge
demand for energy as there is today. As shown in Figure 3, the
percentage of growth of energy demand due to the sharp acceleration in
the earth's population is only 9.8Δ. The remaining 91.2 Δ is a
consequence of industrialization, which requires energy to convert
primary goods.

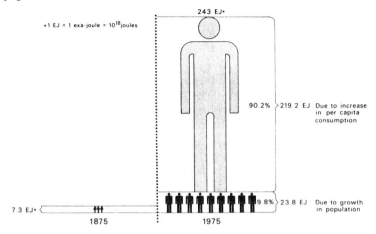

Figure 3. World energy consumption yesterday and today.

        Usually the growth of per-capita energy consumption is presented as
a consequence of rising living standards and requirements. It is also
considered as a result of increased welfare, i.e., either per-capita or
national welfare. Nevertheless today we must carefully examine the
real cost of this way of life. The consumption of unrenewable national
resources and the pollution of the environment is a consumption of
capital. Indeed, most of the energy sources used today are
non-renewable ones. Once they are exhausted, nature cannot replace
them, or at least not at a rate fast enough to match the consumption.
In effect, we are using up "capital" accumulated earlier. Oil, natural
gas and coal take millions of years to form. Population growth is not
as relevant as growth in industrial consumption.

c. Commercial - non commercial energy consumption

        Energy statistics have to be considered with some caution,
like all other statistics. First of all, the presented data do not
include energy sources of a local, non-commercial nature, such as wood,
dried dung or direct solar heating. It is estimated that up to 31Δ of
the world's energy needs are filled non-commercially. It is also
estimated that the domestic-energy consumption is higher in poor
countries than in areas where more sophisticated heating or cooking
systems are used, because the latter ones are more efficient in what
concerns the energy consumption per heating unit. If the developing
countries follow the way tranveled by the industrialized countries the
consequence will be the maintainance of the time gap existing between
them.

The question is this: must the developing countries follow the developed countries in their path to development or is there an alternativeµ The stupidity of the direct imitation strategy was already pointed out in a passage from the <u>Directives for Apostolic Vicars travelling in Tonking and Indochina</u>, written in 1695: "What could be more absurd than to bring to the Chinese France, Spain or whichever other European countryµ" (Brown, 1981).

4. Future-Oriented Planning

The least one can do is to start knowing and taking in full consideration the fundamental rules industrial development involves. For example, one cannot say directly: I will tell you to make an irrigation system. In contrast to such a concrete proposal the integrated process of regional development or physical planning appears nebulous. Even the implementation of plans is very intangible. The results are either not perceived or the perception is limited to the negative ones.

In contrast to this weakness, which is common to all planning processes, there are some very palpable facts to be considered. Unfortunately, there is space to present no more than a few suggestions. The development and detailed discussion of them must be left to more exhaustive studies.

As is shown in Figure 4, "The principal oil movements by sea in 1979," the reserves of traditional energy sources are spread very unevenly around the globe and in some cases, far from the consuming countries. This means that large amounts of energy have to be transported over long distances, which entails additional oil consumption and costs.

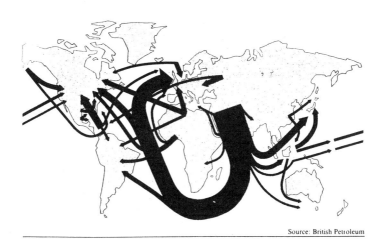

Source: British Petroleum

Figure 4. Principle oil movements by sea in 1979.

A second serious problem coupled with the uneven distribution of reserves arises from the dependence of consuming nations on specific regions or countries. The consequence is a high grade of vulnerability of the economies of the consuming nations. All oil-importing industrialized nations have experienced a worsening of their terms of trade and current account balances. In order to pay for the same volume of oil they have to export a larger volume of goods and services.

The oil price increase acts like a sales tax imposed on the world economy. Initially it goes into the cost-of-living index and adds to inflation. The inflationary impact is subsequently augmented by increases in the prices of oil-dependent goods. According to OECD estimates, a 11Δ oil price hike adds one-half of one percent to the cost of living. Thus a trebling of the oil price generates an inflation rate of 15Δ. Simultaneously higher oil prices take money away from consumers. Demand falls. Investment slows down. Economic growth is restricted. Unemployment rises. The primarily consumption-oriented economic approach of the past must therefore give way to one that lays greater stress on savings and productivity. This calls for a fundamental rethinking of the problem (Aeppli, 1981).

5. Implementation of Energy Consumption as a Factor in Development Planning

The first two strategies that should be used in developing energy-related plans are these:

1. choose solutions requiring less expense of energy

2. use the nearby available energy sources

In fact, so far as they are not developed in the sense of industrial countries, the economies of developing countries still have the chance to build up an economy that is less dependent on non-renewable foreign energy.

Some of the developing countries have their own energy resources: oil, gas, uranium, water, and solar energy. An integrated planning of all activities based on both low energy consumption and the nearby existing natural resources (maybe first of all the solar energy) should be able to improve the independence of developing countries from imported energy. Assuming this aim as a fundamental one, the following question is how to implement it in developing plans. In economic terms it means that energy consumption has to be internalized as a determinant factor in the evaluation of plans. The planning of housing is a good place to start.

a. Housing

Before dealing with some research results about the inter-action between settlements structures and energy demand for domestic supply, one should begin with the single home itself. A very impressive comparison was made by Makhijani (1978) between developing countries and the U.S. concerning the per capita use of fuels for cooking. In the U.S. the per capita annual use is about 3 million Btu's. In the countries of the "Third World" the annual use rises to about 5 to 7 million Btu. Makhijani states that "the open fires and stoves currently used for cooking are cheap, but generally inefficient." Even if one could hardly compare house-building in poor and rich regions, wherever they may be, one can waste less energy due to proper construction techniques and the optimal orientation of a house. Bliss points out that for every million Btu's saved at point-of-use there is, on the average, a lessened withdrawal of about 3 million Btu's at the 'point-of-origin.' By point-of-origin I mean the collection of oil wells, gas wells, coal mines, and uranium mines that supply not only the point-of-use energy but also all additional energy associated with refining, transportation, and conversion losses of the point-of-use energy (Bliss 1978).

   b. Settlements

      The result of research made about the more appropriate heating systems for different already existing or planned settlement types has to be mentioned. It has been recognized that the extent of economically sensible thermal protection depends decisively on the kind of heating system used. It varies about one hundred percent, being lowest for district- and block-heating systems and highest for electric storage heating (Roth 1981).

   c. Towards new urban sizes

      The above mentioned research is based on settlement struc- tures of industrialized countries. Possible changes of these structures are not evaluated, although there are some advertising and even studies relevating that the technological evolution, mainly in the field of telecommunication, could imply determinant changes in living and working conditions. Attending to this sensors the division between working and living places shall be confused more and more. There are some symptoms showing that work at home, even for sophisticated computerized operations, is expected to become a reality again. New forms of work at home, involving such industries as telecommunications and microprocessing, keep down the growth of metropolitan areas and all the energy consuming transportation costs. It seems relevant to consider the possibility of a change in the phenomenon of urbanization. It may be assumed that the development of the telecommunication technologies will have as a consequence a new urban network structure based on small or medium sized centers (Best 1976). One could not state the case better than by quoting Makhijani:

          The development of these technologies should be
          accompanied by the finest scientific and social
          thinking. Rooted in the realities of the country-
          side and drawing on the store of knowledge and
          experience of rural people, such research can
          produce technologies that, coupled with educa-
          tional and organization efforts, can deserve the
          adjectives "high" or "advanced." The commer-
          cialization of such technologies will not be in
          the building of factories but in the extension
          work in villages and towns. (Makhijani 1978).

6. The Third Dimension of the Planning Process

From what has been said it may be assumed that some very important changes are to be expected. From the smallest to the largest unit, planning has to consider the evolution which best fits the given territorial unit, be it at the local, regional, national or international level. These levels correspond to political and administrative territorial units. With some differences due to the organization of each nation, each level presupposes a public authority composed of politicians (either a parliament member and/or executive) and an administration. The administration is usually composed of different units, such as the police, military forces, education, health, industry and commerce, transport and communications, energy, agriculture, etc. Each unit has its own competences which have a direct or indirect influence on the living conditions and the land use of a territory. Therefore, there are material, i.e., sectorial, competences combined with territorial ones for a given geographical unit.

Each geographical unit has its own natural and socioeconomical characteristics. Planning decisions are made with these units in mind. The implementation of plans is delegated to the administration. The elaboration of plans, the decision taking process, and the implementation take time. The whole planning process has therefore three components: the natural and socio-economic elements, time, and the institutional dimension.

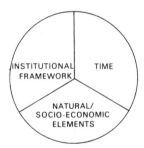

Figure 5.

The knowledge of the institutional framework is necessary for the whole planning process. Popular participation is a part of this framework. The implementation is also a duty of the institutional system, which also embraces the administration. It is important to emphasize the three dimensionality of the planning process because plans, particularly the integrated or the developing ones, should be prepared in order to fit with the decision taking process foreseen by the institutional framework.

In this study we have not tried to evaluate which public organization is more or less adapted for a planning process and its implementation. We are only presenting one reality of the planning process. This reality is at least as important as the natural and socio-economic reality. The knowledge about the existence of this reality and the way this reality works is important if we are to solve the problems we have, wherever we live, utilizing planning techniques and processes.

References

Aeppli, O., (1981). 'Oil, banks and the economy,' Banking Views, Vol. 8, pp. 7-9.

Best, R., (1981). Die Automation der Zukunft, Sandoz Bulletin, No. 57, p. 22.

Bliss, W. R., (1978). 'Why not just build the house right in the first placeµ' in Toward a Solar Civilization, Robert H. Williams, (ed.). Cambridge, Mass., M.I.T. Press.

Brown, quoted in: Hoffman, W.K.H., (1981). Vom Kolonialexperten zum Experten der Entwicklungszusammenarbeit, Saarbrucken.

Makhijani, A. 'Solar energy and rural development for the third world,' in Toward a Solar Civilization, Robert H. Williams, (ed.), Cambridge, Mass.: M.I.T. Press.

Roth, Ueli, (1981). 'Interaction between heating systems, settlement structure and urban planning at the local level,' in Research into Energy and Human Settlements Planning, Horsholm, p. 241 seqq.

Schumacher, E.F., (1973). Small Is Beautiful, A Study of Economics as if People Mattered, London.

5 Economic development, decentralization, and agglomeration

BRITTON HARRIS

In order to investigate problems of decentralization and agglomeration, in the less developed countries, I shall first outline a general view of the development process which will dwell on three principal topics. The first of these is the set of conditions leading to problems in development. The second is a brief review of the nature of development paths which have been pursued by other nations. The third is an overview of the spatial dimensions of urban and regional change and of national development. These three points will put the whole question in a perspective which is appropriate for a gathering of regional scientists, geographers, and planners.

Secondly, I shall pursue in an illustrative way some particular examples from my experiences in India and elsewhere of developmental problems which have important spatial ingredients. This portion of my remarks is based upon an unpublished memorandum entitled 'A Note on the Urban Rural Interface in India,' but represents an extension of these views into a somewhat more general context.

Placed in the most simple possible terms, the problem of the developing and underdeveloped areas is poverty. 'Poverty' implies in many ways a lack of resources both natural and human and a lack of productive capability. To put it this simply, is, however an understatement. I must constantly remind my friends and colleagues in more developed areas that the levels of poverty and deprivation which apply to perhaps three quarters of the world population are virtually unimaginable by Western standards. Whole families subsist in India on an income of less than $511 per year and frequently less than $211 per year. The whole of the Indian middle class lives at a level of income which is substantially below the poverty level in the United States. Without deprecating the problems facing the urban and rural poor in the West, it must be said that their conditions are better than those of the overwhelming majority of inhabitants in the Third World and will continue to be so for a number of years, if not decades. This is a situation which I regard as immoral and unacceptable for the world as a whole. Consequently, I have a vibrant interest in furthering the process of development and the solution of the problems of poverty.

Poverty is, unfortunately, not a simple or easily resolved problem. It can be divided into at least four distinct parts which interlock and interact with each other. First, there is the general concern of population growth, pressing against the resources of the earth. Second, there is the issue of agricultural productivity which is basic for the production of food and for the generation of surpluses in predominantly agricultural countries. Third, there is the area of industrial and post-industrial development, which involves the movement of workers out of agricultural and into other activities which will improve the quality of life and the well-being of the population as a whole. Finally, there is the question of the organization of non-agricultural production geographically, particularly in the form of urban places, which leads to innumerable issues regarding rural-to-urban migration and the provision of urban infrastructure and facilities. I will discuss each of these topics rather briefly.

The growth of population on the earth has already reached alarming proportions. It seems unlikely that the earth can sustain more than one or two more doublings of total population -- bringing us perhaps to the level of 16 to 21 billion people. Beyond that level the ability of earth's resources to support its population with food and energy, not to mention with available space, will be severely strained. This limit on the potential growth of population places a time limit on the period during which the problems of development may be solved. A neo-Malthusian position on the question of population might be thought to suggest that future limitation in the growth of population will arise out of war, pestilence, and famine. This, indeed, is not an entirely remote possibility even during the present generation.

However, it is now clear from the history of the Western world that limitations on the growth of population can rise out of beneficient advances toward higher levels of security, education, and income. Given both these higher levels and the security of the perpetuation of the family as the result of public health and public peace, it is not uncommon to find Western countries with relatively stationary populations and with the specter of unrestrained growth far behind them. It has been commonly thought that this type of limitation on growth is a consequence of urbanization; this, however, is not inevitably the case. More broadly considered, it should be evident that the state of natural control of population growth is a consequence of prosperity, security, and education, or of some combination of these factors. The devices which are used to achieve a stable population are relatively inconsequential, and means can be found by which this state can be achieved under almost any religious or cultural set of circumstances. This stable population size will not come automatically, and will require the development of policy at a national and regional level. Basically, however, although there are different policies which may be applicable in a given culture to rural and urban areas, the problem is not a regional, but rather a national one. Consequently, the problem of population (which will form a background for everything else that I have to say) does not arise explicitly as a problem of geographical and regional science.

The second major problem lying behind the poverty of the less developed nation is that of agricultural productivity. This problem is one on which I am not competent to discourse at very great length, but it has a number of interesting aspects which deserve comment. It is apparent, for example, that natural resources play an important role in development. It is, however, additionally obvious that the most important resource bearing on developmental problems is agricultural land. At the same time, from the ecological and environmental point of view, it is also clear on reflection that agricultural practices play perhaps the major role in man's modification of natural environment -- far outstripping the importance of mining and many other resource-based activities, with the possible exception of forestry.

Agricultural productivity plays a dual role in the development process. In the first place, it provides income to a large part of the population and alimentation for the population as a whole. Consequently, it can be regarded as a fundamental element in the health and well-being of the total nation. The existence or absence of an agricultural surplus plays an extraordinarily important role in the capability of a nation to generate new resources and to avoid the constant drain of foreign exchange which results from a deficit in food production. In addition to these two major direct aspects of agriculture production, the whole question of organization of agriculture and of land ownership plays an important role in the political and social fabric of the nation.

A third and possibly key issue regarding development is the promotion of non-agricultural activities as a basis for employment and for providing the ultimate necessities of civilized existence. A moment's thought might show that the basic needs for literacy in the form of books, television, radio, and movies, and for health in the form of antibiotics, drugs, and other aids are at any decent standard of existence still beyond the resources of the developing nations. If this is correct we could put aside all questions of conspicuous consumption and unlimited wants and address ourselves only to the basic requirements for health, welfare, and literacy. It is quite evident that most of the activities which are required to achieve these basic levels involve both manufacturing and service delivery, and that the technology for these activities, while accessible to the developing nations, is not entirely primitive and cannot be based on handicraft activities alone.

Thus it is necessary for the developing nations to find ways of increasing the productivity of the people through the provision of physical capital in the form of buildings and machinery and of human capital in the form of eduction and skills. There is a limited possibility that a developing nation may produce items of high labor and low capital content (such as tourist services and handicrafts) and highly standardized manufactures (such as textiles). These products can be exchanged for some of the more advanced products that are needed to satisfy the basic wants of a healthy and literate society. In the long run, however, this path is not completely productive and leads to a form of dependency which is bitterly resented by most developing nations.

It is at this point that important spatial considerations begin to enter the picture. The higher the level of technology involved in the production of goods and services for modern life, the higher the level of interdependence among the producers, and, consequently, the higher the economies which arise out of agglomeration and improved interaction. A combination of agglomeration economies and limited resources for development leads most developing nations into a formidable political paradox. Spreading the resources for development leads to a sacrifice of agglomeration economies and possibly to a defeat of development efforts, while a concentration of activities which captures the economies of agglomeration leads to geographical inequality and hence to a feeling of inequity and of political discontent.

A fourth principal problem of developing nations is perceived to be the very rapid growth of cities, creating as it does demands for infrastructure and services which strain national resources. Of course, this strain may be offset by the increased income generated in urban areas. Cities are natural centers for productive enterprise because they have larger markets, larger and more diversified work forces, greater availability of services, and a pool of entrepreneurial talent.

The growth of cities is obviously also fueled by the relative impoverisment of the rural population and its relative underemployment. This is exacerbated by any advances which may arise in agricultural productivity per person not accompanied by a similar increase in productivity per acre. The very large amount of tertiary and quarternary employment to be found in the cities of underdeveloped countries gives rise to the impression that these cities are parasitic on the body politic and the surrounding countryside. I believe, however, that a careful comparison of employment opportunities and income levels would show that the cities of India, China, and many other less developed countries provide better opportunities than the countryside, although these are opportunities which are parlous by Western standards.

Similarly, another source of the increase in urban populations is the unchecked rate of natural increase which would continue to lead to the expansion of the cities in developing areas and to their doubling every 15 years or so, even in the total absence of rural-to-urban migration. This rise in urban populations continues to occur despite the demographic changes seen in the West, because the nature of urban employment, urban production, urban culture, and urban education in developing nations is not yet such as to produce a stable environment for family planning. The consequence of urban growth as a result of both natural increase and rural immigration is an enormous stress upon the available infrastructure, including housing and public services, such as education and health. This stress is, however, partly a stress of rising expectations, since the level of services of the identical kinds which would be provided in rural areas are ordinarily not only below the expectations but also below the actuality of many urban areas. Once again this distinction is frequently overlooked in making rural to urban comparisons.

One consequence of this witches' brew of adverse circumstances is an exacerbated form of political instability. Many developing nations are starting from such low levels of resources, income, and capability that progress without sacrifice may be impossible, while sacrifice may be politically unacceptable. The unacceptability both of sacrifice and of the lack of progress may place decision makers and planners in such a bind as to lead them to believe that political stability is in no way achievable. Aside from questions of personal greed and lust for power, it seems likely that this conflict in development priorities and its consequent political destablization is the major cause for the prevalence of dictatorships in developing nations. This is not to say that these dictatorships can necessarily resolve the problems which I have discussed, but only that they can, at least temporarily, put a cap on the levels of political instability. This is a national and not a regional problem.

We now turn to the second major topic of my review: a consideration of the paths which have been pursued to economic development.

In reviewing this topic it is necessary to make a serious wrench in our thinking. There is, I believe, an anthropological fallacy of studying populations which have never progressed out of a relatively primitive state. The study of the Greeks, the Gauls, the Mongols and other societies which have achieved some form of modernity becomes the study of History rather than the study of Anthropology. Similarly, in the study of industrial development pure and simple, one might be tempted to examine small industries to find what conditions are necessary for their success. However, the examination of small industries assures that we will examine those who have not succeeded rather than those who have. We should prefer to examine medium and large-scale industries which were once small, and find out what conditions made it possible for them to grow and to be successful. Thus, if we wish to examine the conditions of economic development it is perhaps unwise to concentrate entirely on those nations which have not yet achieved it and continually wring our hands over their lack of success. It may be better selectively to examine those nations which have succeeded over the last 151 years in achieving advanced economic status and to examine the conditions under which this has occurred.

Actual development has followed a wide variety of paths and has been successful under a number of different conditions. The first wave of industrial development affected nations with major resource endowments in relation to population. (Similar conditions apply even today to the South American countries and for this reason their development problems are altogether different from those of South Asia and parts of Africa.) Great Britain, the United States, Western Europe, and even Russia had natural resource endowments which assured most of their populations adequate levels of subsistence into the 21th century. The poorest people in these nations have never in the past five hundred years been as poor in absolute terms as the populations of India and China are today. At the same time the existing conditions strongly influence the modes of development. The richest country in natural endowment, the United States, was able to make the most rapid progress once conditions of progress were established -- and this without major external conquests to fuel the development. Great Britain's resources lasted only perhaps to the passage of the Corn Laws in the 1841s and thereafter depended in a substantial way on foreign expansion. In most of western Europe the rapid catch-up development, which followed closely on the British example, was fueled by a strong new nationalism, and depended in part upon the growth of cartels and the suppression of trade unions. Russia's major development came at a very late date. It was fueled by a furious sense of national emergency lasting from 1917 until well into the 1941s, and occurred under the guidance of a powerful and perhaps unique political system. The Scandinavian nations and the Netherlands seem to have followed the path of Great Britain and Western Europe but with the tempering influence of a gulf stream of socialist humanitarianism.

In the current century, and outside of Western Europe, only a few nations have succeeded in rapid development. The most important of these is undoubtedly Japan, which has operated perhaps on the poorest resource base in relation to population of all large modern industrialized nations. Following very much in the footsteps of Japan are nations like South Korea, Taiwan, Singapore, and the crown colony of Hong Kong. All of these nations prodeded largely in the absence of a resource base, making use of industrial and commercial ingenuity and colossal national effort. Their problems are in sharp contrast to the nations of South America and to others in a similar position such as South Africa, Australia and New Zealand.

Perhaps it should be emphasized in connection with all of these developments, and in varying degrees depending on the level of resource endowments and of national resolution, that the working people of all developed countries have at one time or another paid a very substantial price in day-to-day sacrifice (whether voluntary or enforced) in the interest of the accumulation of national capital resources and productive capability. This should be taken as a caution with respect to the development efforts of those countries which are still undeveloped. Their present and past sufferings may have been due to a variety of circumstance, but in the nature of things this does not exempt them from future difficulties which will occur in the process of development. Outside assistance can undoubtedly help to speed the development process and to mitigate its sacrifices. Similarly, internal effort, good organization, resolution, and inventiveness can have the same effect as the development itself. Nevertheless, it would be a mistake to assume that development will ever proceed successfully without a very substantial effort and without withholding from the population as a whole some of the immediate benefits of production which might be directed to them in the short run.

Let me now summarize my conclusions under these first two major points. First, the basic need for long term development is a reduction in the rate of population growth, but this poses a problem of the chicken and the egg, since reduced population growth is unlikely to occur under conditions of low development except in the most dire circumstances. Second, there is immediate need for an increase in agricultural productivity per acre in order to expand the available resources for feeding the existing and future population in any given country. Third, an increase in agricultural productivity per worker is necessary to reduce the levels of rural poverty. However, increased agricultural worker productivity leads to rural underemployment, and this can not be absorbed by the economy without non-agricultural development. Thus, fourth, non-agricultural development requires investment in human resources, infrastructure, and productive capacity. The cost of this investment can be mitigated by foreign aid, but will depend ultimately upon the resources of the countries involved. This implies levels of sacrifice which are not readily contemplated in the political sphere. Fifth, the development of productive capabilities and the absorption of increased rural unemployment implies in most cases the development of urban areas, and this increases the burden of investment in infrastructure while at the same time increasing the productivity of investment and accelerating the creation of human capital through the educational experiences of the city. Sixth, and finally, there are many different paths of national development, with varying degrees of justice and injustice, varying degrees of social dislocation, and varying speeds and levels of accomplishment.

Let us now turn to some of the spatial aspects of this complex development process -- a process which indeed I have only begun to define.

It is almost a truism to say that where there is occupancy of space there must be separation of activities. Where there is separation of activities there is room for variation arising perhaps out of lack of contact. Where there is variation there arise separate cultures and concepts of identity. We therefore have a complex of factors arising out of the simple fact that human activities occupy space.

This space occupancy takes a number of forms. In the first instance, it is determined by what might be called production space, and primarily by the space occupied by agriculture. This is by far the most extensive use of space by humans in the productive sphere. Agricultural patterns depend in a complicated way on topography, drainage, soils, climate, and irrigation, and, as a consequence, there are regional differences in agricultural production. The history of large land areas such as India, China, Africa, and Latin America provide evidence that the separation of people owing to this concatenation of features leads to the development of regional languages and customs, and frequently to national or interregional distinctions which can be very persistent and long lived. The other side of these differences is found in an attachment of people to the land, from the community up to the regional and national level, which acts as a brake on intra-national migration and which means that the equilibration of the relationships between people and capital must be taken care of not only by the movement of people but also by the movement of capital.

The use of land for consumption in rural areas is a relatively minor matter. Villages are frequently built on marginal and submarginal land. In any event, the proportion of land used for dwelling is a small fraction of that used for agricultural production. In cities the situation is quite the reverse. More than half of the land area of cities is devoted to residential activities and if we include associated streets and residentially oriented trade and services, it seems likely that 75Δ to 81Δ of all land use is related to residential and consumption purposes. Even so, urban residential densities are by and large much higher than rural residential densities proper, even without reference to the gross density of population per square kilometer.

It might thus be thought that the separation of activities in the urban system is bound to be less than that in the rural system. There are, however, several features of urban life which militate against this simple concept. First, many urban centers interact with rural areas, and over a fairly wide span of distance. The more highly specialized the urban-rural services are, the larger the span of their reach. Second, cities are internally differentiated much more than are rural areas. The production and distribution activities of the city are more and more highly articulated with increasing city size, and the segregation of residence and work place also increases with city size. Thus the interaction between redicence and work place and the interaction among activities must overcome artifically created distances which cannot, however, be entirely eliminated. This friction of distance is intensified by urban congestion and by the lack of urban infrastructure. Finally, cities are differentiated among themselves, and there is a certain amount of inter-urban activity wherein one specialized city provides some of the needs of another. Thus the existence of a system of cities increases spatial separation and promotes interaction.

Let me now try to describe in rather brief form a sequence of problems which have developmental, social, and spatial dimensions which are incompletely understood. These problems could be profitable in regional science research, which would have the dual effect of increasing our knowledge and increasing the capability of the developing nations to act toward the resolution of their problems. The topics which I will discuss are largely suggestive, and it is perhaps self-evident that there are many other important and crucial topics for discussion.

First let me say a few words about rural development and rural-to-urban migration. Rural overpopulation or, alternatively, rural under-employment is a chronic problem of developing and even of developed nations. The attachment of rural populations to the land and to their way of life leads to a lag in adaptation, and this lag is accentuated by the lack of opportunities and lack of facilities for living in places of non-agricultural employment. This phenomenon is visible even in countries such as France, England, the United States and the Soviet Union. In the United States the rural poverty of Appalachia and the Ozarks is not easily eradicated. A cursory glance at Soviet population statistics suggests that there is an excess of rural population which may reflect either inefficient agriculture or sources of rural income which we do not fully understand.

From the point of view of minimizing social disruption, minimizing the cost of urban development, or both, there are two or three solutions to rural underemployment which might be preferred to migration to the larger urban centers.

The first solution would be the establishment of rural industries in agricultural villages or very small towns. The second possibility would be the development of non-agricultural employment opportunities in medium-sized cities in the range of about 111,111 people. This development might very well take the form of the provision of agricultural and other rural services which are not yet needed but which might become desirable in a future pattern of rural and agricultural development. A third possible form of development would be in the smaller of the large cities, in the population range, say, from 211,111 to 811,111 people, which would divert growth from the very large metropolitan centers of a million or more, but which would be essentially based on independent activities not directed exclusively towards the support of agricultural services in the urban hinterland.

At a later point I will discuss some of the agglomerative aspects of nonagricultural development which influence choices amongst these paths. At present, however, I wish only to emphasize the importance of social and economic linkages in influencing the pattern of rural-urban linkages at this level. In countries such as India even to the present and in China certainly before 1945, there exists an intricate structure of social and economic relationships in the countryside and small towns. These relationships involve not only social but also economic ties, having to do with land ownership, sharecropping, money-lending and the like. These relationships spill over into questions of class and caste, and politically into the question of party affiliation and voting rights. The well established and formalized nature of these relationships very strongly influences the willingness of rural surplus labor to accept employment in or migrate to nearby towns and centers. Frequently the desire to migrate out of the rural area is a desire to escape the entanglements of this economic, social, and political system. Since the market towns and most district centers are an integral part of the rural agricultural fabric and are dominated by the same groups, migration to nearby centers, regardless of their immediate relative economic attractiveness, does not provide the opportunity of escape which many migrants out of rural areas desire.

For this reason alone, Indian migration patterns, in particular, and Indian efforts to establish rural industry face serious problems. Aside from all other difficulties it seems likely that the establishment of rural industry in India will not solve some of the basic social problems reflected in the present system of land tenure and economic power. These problems have been resolved in a different way in the Soviet Union and China, and, to some extent, other things being equal, this provides better opportunities for the establishment of rural industry. In these nations migration may be somewhat more highly controlled and the social conditions and rural areas may not exert the same push that they do in India, but there is little reason to doubt that some of the same considerations apply and help to explain the continuing attractiveness of large urban metropolitan regions in all countries of the developing world -- whether capitalist, socialist, or mixed.

A second interesting issue on which I can only touch very lightly is the whole question of land law. Laws about the conversion, ownership, condemnation, and alienation of land are extremely important in the social fabric of all nations -- and especially of agricultural nations. At the same time they exercise great influence on geographical development in both rural and urban areas. Countries as diverse as India, Singapore, South Africa, Israel, and Canada have inherited a set of Victorian English land laws which to some extent seem to lack the ameliorative effects of British Common Law and which as statutes for regulation of modern economic and urban life are rapidly becoming outdated. At the same time both vested interests and inertia seem to make it very difficult to change these laws. As a result urban development in India for example is badly distorted by all sorts of innocent-seeming developmental restriction which frequently have perverse effects. As a simple example, it could be pointed out that the denial of urban services to areas which are developed without development permission is intended to preserve the public health and welfare by making such development impossible. In fact this is not the case. The developments take place in any event, and the integration of illegally developed areas into the metropolitan fabric becomes difficult as a matter of law. This is only one example of many difficulties which can be found in the writing and administration of legal restrictions on urban and rural development, but it serves as an indication of how these issues can become an important area of research and action in developing nations.

Two major issues of decentralization arise in most developing areas. One of these, and the most obvious for students of regional and interregional affairs, is the desirability of decentralizing the growth of employment in non-agricultural activities out of the major metropolitan centers. I now refer to this from the point of view of productive organization rather than from the point of view of the destination of migration, although obviously these two features of the problem interact strongly with each other. A second problem in most developing areas is that of decentralizing within urban and metropolitan sub-regions. Most cities in developing areas are very compact and have highly concentrated central business districts. In general, this compactness and concentration can be attributed to the necessity for face-to-face contact and the absence of economically affordable public transportation for the bulk of the work force. As we shall see, however, the problem is somewhat more complicated and deserves perhaps a different kind of attention.

By way of introduction to a general discussion of this problem I point to the wide discussion in the regional science literature (partly represented at this conference and in a session at the most recent North American Conference of the Regional Sciences Association) of the importance of agglomeration effects. In a different session of the RSA Conference, Thysse and Pappageorgiu referred to agglomeration as the 'glue' which holds together metropolitan regions. Agglomeration economies arise out of reciprocal productive activities and out of sharing of intrastructure, labor force, services, and other aspects of urban existence. Transportation costs aside (and in modern production these are becoming increasingly less important), no one would consider the establishment of a transistor factory at the headwaters of the Amazon. Similarly once established, a productive complex is extremely hard to disaggregate or deagglomerate because of the interdependency which has developed between the activities and their general environment, and which is in part established by the activities themselves. In the light of this general background let me consider the separate but related problems of regional decentralization and intrametropolitan decentralization.

An important issue in the planning of developing regions which appears to be especially provocative in India is the question of equality of income. Efforts to equalize income between rural and urban populations and between regions at the center and the periphery involve a number of complicated issues which cannot be fully discussed in this paper. The classical process of adjustment, which for many reasons does not always work, is an equilibration of the investment of capital and labor in various lines of activity and in various areas by means of the migration either of capital or of labor. Egalitarian views of development suggest that the migration of labor is for some reason undesirable and focus largely upon that migration of capital which might be needed to equalize the productivity of various parts of the nation.

It is a common observation that the establishment of modern industry in rural areas and in the less developed regions of a national economy is a difficult task. Once again the reasons for this are very numerous, but in the present context, two or three may be mentioned and singled out for special emphasis. There are certain threshold conditions which are necessary for the establishment of modern industry. These include the provision of infrastructure, for example, reliable electric power and elementary sanitation. Another form of infrastructure which may be important is the availability of human capital or an educated work force. In addition, since entrepreneurial capability is extremely important in the development of new industry, the social and cultural amenities of new locations for industry must be adequate to attract or retain managers and other key personnel who may be needed. Given all of these prerequisites, it is not surprising that the establishment of modern industry in remote locations can ordinarily only be accomplished by a very slow process of natural growth or by the establishment of large self-contained enterprises which are not dependent upon these environmental factors.

The question of accelerating regional development by decentralizing development from the more advanced portions of the nation can, however, be generalized in a somewhat different way. The prerequisites which have been mentioned before are in part the consequence of agglomeration. It is no accident that the development of urban infrastructure and other facilities in Bangalore has interacted with the establishment of a number of government and private enterprises of an advanced nature, nor is itaccidental that given these agglomerative economies these industries have been unwilling or unable to locate elsewhere in South India. Many of the agglomeration economies which are realized in large cities and developed regions arise out of the feasibility of face-to-face contact and the rapid delivery of a number of different kinds of services. In this type of interaction, questions of communi- cation and data transmission, as well as the delivery of documents and small parts, are extremely important. Thus in the process of industrial decentralization, communications play an important role in diffusing some of the economies of agglomeration.

It is therefore apparent that there are many obstacles to the necessary steps which would lead to equality of income across large nations such as India and China and across a continent like Africa. Some of these steps depend on the establishment of universal literacy and the availability of skills throughout a national environment. Others depend on the provision of infrastructure, and still others depend on physical economies of agglomeration. A very important part of these requirements, however, is the availability of good telecommun- ications which connect new industrial development with established centers of industry and government. These communication facilities are not widely available, and their absence creates a tremendous drag upon development.

Another problem in which agglomeration economies plays an important role is urban congestion. Large Indian cities have in addition to their industrial and transportation components considerable concentrations of service industries of various kinds where the principal requirements include office space, the assembly of clerical and similar labor forces, and in addition, under Indian conditions, face-to-face contact for the conduct of transactions. The requirement for face-to-face contact leads to very substantial economies of agglomeration which create high peaks of daytime employment. In addition, minor service industries having to do with food, shopping, and repair services, for example, lay a basis for the concentration of additional employment in providing services to the employees of the initial service concentrations. These high peaks of daytime employment (once again under the conditions of low development) require that workers live close to their employment, and this leads to high concentrations of residential density. The alternative to such concentrations in the case of highly focused urban employment is long and expensive transportation or transportation (e.g., by bicycle) which is costly of energy and not practical under all weather conditions. In short, therefore, the very high concentrations of population and employment and the low levels of residential space and amenity, together with the congested condition of streets and public transportation in large scale Indian cities, arise in the first instance out of the difficulty or impossibility of decentralizing employment.

Once again, it is highly probable that the need for face-to-face interaction and therefore the need for the high concentration of the larger service industries in Indian cities could be in part overcome by the provision of better telecommunications. This would enable the authorities to undertake more systematic decentralization of activities without the countervailing tendency of industry and services to move back into center cities in order to retain close interaction and realize economies of agglomeration. This fact is of major importance in planning for the decentralization of Indian metropolises, which would be a key to improving living conditions within them and to fostering further growth.

It is now appropriate to try to draw some conclusions from this discussion. It seems to me that regional and geographic analysis has an enormous role to play in improving the equity and effectiveness of developmental planning in countries such as India and China, since so many developmental issues are as closely related to the distribution and connection of activities as to the welfare of the population and its migration into new conditions of living. At the same time, there is a tendency to base policy recommendations in the regional field upon two disparate sources of influence without the requisite effort to bridge the gap between them. The first influence is a descriptive and somewhat aggregated view of development trends which reflect, in part, the general status of data collection and social science analysis in developing countries. The second influence is the goals and objectives of the people and their governments expressed in very general and somewhat idealistic terms.

Bridging the gap between these two views requires a very concrete understanding of the processes which govern development and consequently the processes which govern the success of productive enterprises, whether these are publicly or privately owned. Among those conditions are matters having to do with the behavior of entrepreneurs, managers, and work forces. In this paper I have talked about some of the influences on migration and some of the effects of agglomeration in both rural and urban development. This is a form of the country's attention to the linkage between objectives and actual conditions which needs an improved focus.

The next stage in the development of Regional Science in India will be based on efforts to measure the magnitude of the impact of different variables on the types of behavior which govern "industrial" location and "industrial" development -- taking "industry" in the broadest possible sense. This will represent a considerable advance beyond descriptive surveys and aggregated analyses and will extend work which is already in progress and which reflects the great potential of Indian social science.

6 Agglomeration economies and games of voluntary public good provision

THOMAS M. FOGARTY

1. Introduction

The principal purpose of this essay is to suggest and outline a connection between the economic study of agglomeration and the game theoretic analysis of public goods. The argument focuses primarily on those forms of agglomeration usually called localization and industrial complexes and uses a pure composite public good as a simple surrogate for more complex sets of pure and mixed public goods.

The geographic distribution of economic activity is highly non-uniform. The partial equilibrium conclusion toward which locational choices tend is that, given a pre-existing pattern of economic activity for N commodities and services, there exists some optimal point or set of discontinuous optimal points for each stage in the production and distribution of any N + l-st product. Generally, one expects there to emerge, from locational decisions within the market structure, a general location pattern for all aspects of economic activity which is (1) relatively stable, (2) characterized by gross production that is both high and efficient relative to other arrangements, (3) highly non-uniform, and (4) patient of characterization specific to industry and technology of production (Bos 1965; von Boventer 1962; Moses 1958; Tinbergen 1961).

'Agglomeration' is a term used to refer to three aspects of this process. It refers a) to those specific places where economic activity occurs with high relative intensity ('an agglomeration'); b) to the character of economic activity and the process by which it grows in those places ('agglomeration'); and c) to the multiple sources of economic advantages and disadvantages which accrue to locating a particular activity in a place where other economic activities of specific types have located or will locate ('agglomeration effects').

Agglomeration effects can be analyzed usefully by classifying them by the scale of organization at which their costs are internalized. The costs and benefits of scale effects realized by the expansion of a production process are largely internalized within a firm. Beyond simple technological economies, the costs and benefits of agglomeration accrue jointly to sets of actors and are not simply internalized. Where such agglomerations occur, therefore, they imply the successful provision of a range of pure and mixed public goods particular to the economic activities at issue (Kawaglima 1977; Isard and Schooler 1959; Fogarty 1980).

A commodity or service may be defined as a public good when, for that commodity or service, there exists a group of economic actors who cannot be excluded from consumption once the good has been provided in any amount and whose individual consumption in no measurable way diminishes the amount left for consumption by other members of the group (Samuelson 1954). The properties of non-excludability and joint consumption are analytically distinct (Head 1974) and distinguish the pure public good from its ideal contrary, the pure private good (Samuelson 1969).

Voluntary provision of a public good by the members of the group whose existence it defines is always problematic. This results from the fact that while production of the public good is costly, its consumption can be free. To provide a public good, the cost of production must be shared out among the members of its group and paid. Any member who evades contribution or who reneges on a commitment to contribute can consume for free what others provide at cost. Such a 'free rider' retains his share of cost and can apply it to the purchase of private goods. All free riders are better off than they would have been had they contributed. All members of the group can be free riders. Hence each member has an incentive to evade contribution, and coordination of voluntary provision is difficult.

Agglomeration economies beyond scale effects require the provision of specific public goods, i.e., they occur in contexts where the public goods problem has been solved -- at least to some extent. Often, public goods problems are solved through coercive provision involving governmental systems. Governments guarantee contracts in order to contribute among members and to coercively prevent evasion. To prevent misrepresentation of an individual's preferences, governments may themselves provide or supply public goods and allocate costs through taxation (Olson 1965; Weiss 1981). Neither system is generally adequate, however, to facilitate provision of any but the grossest and most wide-spread public goods. Governments lack information regarding more specific problems, and they lack a general welfare incentive to deal with problems restricted to relatively small sets of economic actors.

Problems of voluntary private provision have often been modeled as games among the members of the relevant groups (Hardin 1971; Davis and Whinston 1961, 1962; Axelrod and Hamilton 1981; Atkinson and Stiglitz 1981). It is the purpose of this essay to outline the manner in which such games are sensitive to the incomes or endowments of the players. As incomes or endowments increase, as is likely in the face of the realization of scale economies in production, many public goods games can become "easier" to solve successfully.

2. Agglomeration Effects

The effects of agglomeration are conveniently grouped into categories, according to the level of organization at which costs and benefits are principally internalized. Thus, for example, it is confusing to consider the increases in crime characteristic of large cities or their congestion and environmental degradation as agglomeration diseconomies at the level of the firm. Unless congestion results in notable increases in input delivery costs, or environmental degradation either lowers the quality or raises the price of production, these effects are largely invisible to the firm, except, possibly, in the form of higher taxation. The costs of congestion are principally internalized only at the level of the metropolis as a whole. Similarly, if agglomeration results in increases in the rate of technical innovation and invention, much of the benefit of such development is realized outside the agglomeration where it occurs and is internalized only at a regional, national, or, possibly, international level.

Agglomeration effects may be grouped in a variety of ways (Kawashima 1977; Fujita 1978). Here it will be useful to consider four levels of organization. (1) Production effects are those advantages and disadvantages internalized at the level of the firm, factory, or production process. (2) Localization effects are organized and internalized at the level of the local industry, i.e., the set of firms or factories producing locally the same approximate set of commodities or services. (3) Industrial complex effects refer to effects of agglomeration that accrue to the organization or coordination of firms or local industries producing different, but related, sets of commodities and services. (4) Higher level effects, such as congestion or innovation, which are internalized only at levels beyond the industrial complex.

Production effects are privately provided by the affected firm. They principally include gains to productivity associated with production for higher levels of demand, possibly occasioned by their location in or near populated centers.

Localization effects and industrial complex effects, on the other hand, require the solution of problems of coordination and organization between and among industries. Localizations of single product process retailers, for example, require that individual firms regularly make known their inventories and processing techniques to competing firms even in the face of the aggressive wholesale and retail competition which characterizes such localizations. High fashion garment manufacturers in New York's garment district, diamond cutters and merchants in Amsterdam, silk firms in Kyoto, insurance underwriters in London -- all provide instances where the mixed public good is well provided even though any single participant would do better to withhold information others provide. That Free Rider Problems are present is clear from the tendency, where scale economies develop, for localization to result in reductions in the number of firms or facilities and increases in average scale.

Industrial complex effects, similarly, require the provision of a similar range of mixed public goods among larger scale entities than firms or single facilities. Again, the conditions provided can usually be subsumed under the headings of coordination, organization, and information. Again, such mixed public goods are generally provided in contexts which are otherwise quite competitive.

3. Games of Voluntary Provision

The game called the Prisoner's Dilemma is generally familiar (Luce and Raiffa 1957). In its common two-person choice version it is defined as a game in which $_iX_{21} >_p {}_iX_{11} >_p {}_iX_{22} >_p {}_iX_{12}$, where $_iX_{jk}$ is the pay-off or outcome to the i-th player which results from his choice of the j-th strategy when his fellow player chooses the k-th strategy. Figure 1 illustrates the game in its "matrix" form and indicates the ordering of outcomes.

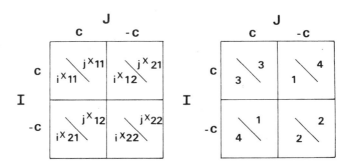

Figure 1. The Prisoner's Dilemma.

Prisoner's Dilemma has often been taken to be a natural and elegant paradigm of the problem of providing public goods on a voluntary basis (Hardin 1971). The outcome $_iX_{22}$ is taken to indicate the status quo. Each player has an endowment of private and public goods, and each has chosen -c, i.e., not to contribute any of his private good endowment to the provision of additional public good. Outcome $_iX_{11}$ is taken to be the result if each makes a contribution, and additional public good is provided. Since $_iX_{11} >_p {_iX_{22}}$, it must be the case that the public good provided in $_iX_{22}$ is sub-optimal.

Outcomes $_iX_{12}$ and $_iX_{12}$ result when one player contributes and the other does not. Since $_iX_{21} >_p {_iX_{11}}$, and $_iX_{11} >_p {_iX_{12}}$, each player has an incentive to be a free rider -- either by misrepresenting his preferences or by reneging on an agreement to contribute. The problem is particularly difficult since $_iX_{22} >_p {_iX_{12}}$. Not only does each player have incentives to renege; he faces a penalty if he contributes when the other does not. Voluntary provision is problematic.

To interpret the game further, it is necessary to structure the player's choices in a more detailed way. Many difficulties in voluntary provision of public goods arise because, in addition to the problems here, players differ in their evaluation of the public good or in their incomes. In order to abstract from such additional difficulties, assume that the game arises between players of equal incomes whose preferences are representable in identical ways.

The choices presented to the players, then, are -c, i.e., not to contribute, and c, which may be defined as an optimal fair contribution. Fairness is taken to mean that the possible contributions of equal players are equal. Given fairness and the presumption that the players have preferences which may be represented in the same form, the optimal contribution of one of two players to provision of the public good will be equal to what his optimal expenditure would be, were it a private good with price exactly half its actual cost (Fogarty 1982).

Figure 2 illustrates the game in the preference space of one of the players. Each player has an endowment of z_0 amount of a composite

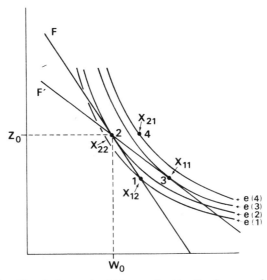

Figure 2. The Prisoner's Dilemma in the Preference Space.

normal private good. An endowment w_0 of the composite public good is
provided by nature or some unspecified source. Each player thus is
initially located at (z_0, w_0) or $_iX_{22}$.

The linear functions F and F' indicate the possible transformations
of z into additional w from (z_0, w_0). F represents the true production price of w in terms of z. F' represents the price the player
would have to pay if his fellow player agreed on contribution and
actually did contribute. F' transforms z into w at exactly twice the
rate of F, since w is a public good, and each player receives the
entirety of the quantity provided.

The outcome $_iX_{11}$ is the fair social optimum and is the point at
which F' just equals the marginal rate of transformation between w and
z generated by the player preferences. Outcomes $_iX_{12}$ and $_iX_{21}$
show the results, respectively, of "losing" and "winning" the game. At
$_iX_{12}$, the player loses, i.e., he contributes when the other does
not and discovers he has provided only one half the amount of additional
w he wished to have provided through joint action. At $_iX_{21}$, the
player "wins", i.e., he gets the benefit of the additional w provided,
but pays none of the cost. By the structure of the game, the equivalence classes generated by the player's preferences show the ordering
$e(4) >_p e(3) >_p e(2) >_p e(1)$. These are the ordinal payoffs of
Figure 1.

Figure 2 depicts a game which is highly impatient of solution. The
risk of becoming worse off if the other player reneges on a commitment
to contribute makes it unlikely that cooperation can occur in situations
where there are appreciable differences in the players' evaluations of
$_iX_{22} >_p {}_iX_{12}$.

Not all public goods games of voluntary provision are as severe as
the Prisoner's Dilemma. Figures 3 and 4, for example, show games which

are considerably more likely to result in cooperation.

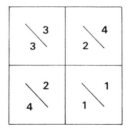 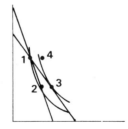

Figure 3. "Chicken" in the Preference Space.

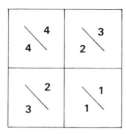 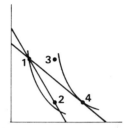

Figure 4. Fully Cooperative Game.

Figure 3 shows a game often called Chicken (Luce and Raiffa 1957). It has the ordering $_iX_{21} >_p {_iX_{11}} >_p {_iX_{12}} >_p {_iX_{22}}$. The Free Rider Problem remains obvious, but the possible penalty is removed. Either player is better off cooperating if he is sure the other will not. Each player is best off refusing to cooperate if the other makes a contribution.

Figure 4 displays a more benevolent game. Since $_iX_{11} >_p {_iX_{21}}$, neither player has any incentive, within the structure of the game, to avoid fair contribution.

The game of Figure 4 is benevolent. The game of Figure 3 is less so, but is more likely to lead to cooperation than the game of Figure 2. A maximin player, i.e., one who chooses that strategy which maximizes his worst possible result, would contribute in Figure 3, although he would not in Figure 4.

4. Relations Among Games of Voluntary Provision

Drawing the games of Figures 2, 3, and 4 is based on the assumption that the preferences of the players over z and w are of the usual type, i.e., they yield continuous convex equivalence classes of consumption combinations of z and w. Marginal rates of substitution and optimal choices are defined.

Generally it is extraordinarily hard to specify clear representations of preferences over sets of commodities which include public or mixed goods. This is so because economic actors have an incentive to misrepresent their true preferences and become free riders. True demand, therefore, for all the commodities is invisible: empirical demand for private goods is overstated; demand for public goods is understated.

This of course does not mean that preferences do not exist. Players presumably know what they want and act accordingly. Underlying preferences motivate players. If one assumed that a player's true relative preferences for the public good do not result from its being public, but only from its usefulness or desirability in consumption, then there is no reason not to expect that the underlying preference structure is of the usual type. Hence, one expects preferences to generate the continuous convex equivalence classes of Figures 2, 3, and 4.

The structural relationship among the games outlined earlier depends on what else one is willing to assume about the preferences of players underlying their actions (Fogarty 1982). Figure 5 illustrates this point.

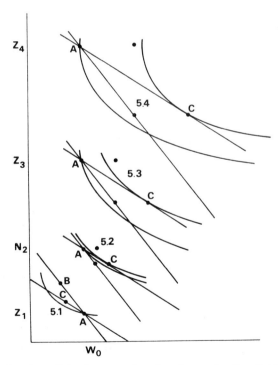

Figure 5.   Possible Progressive Development of a Public Goods
Game as Endowment Changes.

If one assumes that players' preferences show the public good to be normal (i.e., were it a private good, demand would show a positive income effect), then one can relate several games structurally. Formally one can show that any Prisoner's Dilemma at endowment (z_2, w_0) would have been a Problem of the Commons at some $z_1 < z_2$. Assuming convexity and normality, one knows that the optimal amount of w declines as income or endowment, i.e., the amount, z, declines. If (z_2, w_0) yields a Prisoner's Dilemma, then there exists some $z_1 < z_2$ where the players have too much w. Acting jointly, they would transform some w into additional z which they would distribute equally, re-locating themselves from A to C in Figure 5.1. Acting unfairly, each player would prefer to appropriate w, transform it into z for himself, and relocate individually to B. Assuming only normality and convexity, increases in initial z obliterate the Problem of the Commons and transform it into a Prisoner's Dilemma.

If one assumes additional properties on the structure of preferences, then there will exist $z_3 > z_2$ where the Prisoner's Dilemma is transformed into the milder game of Chicken with a Free Rider Problem. Additional and more restrictive properties would yield the existence of some $z_4 > z_3$ where Chicken is itself transformed into the benevolent game of Figures 3 and 5.4.

It is not the purpose of this short essay to outline properties of underlying preferences necessary to guarantee that a Problem of the Commons eventually becomes a benevolent game of voluntary joint provision. The point is that some structures of preferences will have those properties and some will not. If, for example, true underlying preferences were representable in the familiar Cobb-Douglas form, $u = z^a w^{1-a}$, all games would eventually progress to the form of Figure 5.3. If, additionally, $a = .5$, then the game becomes eventually asymptotically close to Figure 5.4. If $a < .5$, the game is transformed into Figure 5.4.

Preferences will ordinarily be sensitive to changes in income or endowment. They can be sensitive to income in ways that transform the Prisoner's Dilemma into less antagonistic games (e.g., cf. Schelling 1978).

5. Agglomeration and Public Goods

The result of Section 4 is easily extendable. Games among more than two players require only a large game matrix and a more complicated geometry. Games assuming players of different incomes require interpretations of the choice c. Games over mixed goods will lower boundary values in z.

The general thrust of the result is that, within the structure of a two-choice game, Prisoner's Dilemma, when it occurs, represents the mitigation of a previous more antagonistic game at a lower income and will itself be transformed into milder more cooperative games with increases in income for a variety of preference structures.

The application of the result to agglomeration effects at the level of localization and industrial complex economies is direct. Income effects generated at the level of production economies change what would otherwise be an antagonistic game of voluntary provision among the same or different economic actors into a game more patient of joint solution. The game changes most where income gains, actual or prospective, are most, i.e., in those agglomerations where production effects are most notably positive on net.

Figures 2 to 5 make it clear that actors may have in fact choices other than c and $-c$. More general analysis of the problem requires analysis of a wider range of choices in contexts of differing evaluations and incomes. The Prisoner's Dilemma has, nonetheless, proven a powerful paradigm in the analysis of voluntary public goods provision. The results presented here situate the Prisoner's Dilemma in the context of a wide range of similar games and suggest a relation between the sequence of games and observed processes of agglomeration.

References

Atkinson, Anthony B. and Joseph E. Stiglitz, (1981). <u>Lectures on Public Economics</u>, New York: McGraw Hill.

Baron, Mira, (1982). Doctoral Dissertation, Regional Science Department, University of Pennsylvania.

Bos, Hendriens C., (1965). <u>Spatial Dispersion of Economic Activity.</u> Rotterdam: Rotterdam University Press.

Boventer, E. von, (1962). 'Towards a united theory of spatial economic Structure'. <u>Papers</u> 10, <u>Regional Science Association.</u>

Davis, Otto A. and Andrew B. Whinston, (1962). 'Externalities, welfare, and the Theory of Games.' <u>Journal of Political Economy</u>, 70:241-62.

_____, (1961). 'Economics of urban renewal.' <u>Journal of Law and Contemporary Problems</u>, 26.

Fogarty, T.M., (1982). 'Prisoner's dilemma and other public goods games.' <u>Journal of Conflict Management and Peace Science</u>, (forthcoming).

_____, (1980). 'Agglomeration and de-centralization.' <u>Proceedings of the International Conference on Egyptian Needs in Local Government Administration and Local Development Planning.</u> Government of Egypt.

Fujita, Masahisa. <u>Notes Toward the Development of Location Theory.</u> Regional Science Department, University of Pennsylvania.

Hardin, R. (1971). 'Collective Action as an Agreeable n-Prisoners' Dilemma,' <u>Behavioral Science</u> 16.

Head, John G. (1974). <u>Public Goods and Public Welfare.</u> Durham, North Carolina: Duke University Press.

Isard, Walter and Eugene W. Schooler (1959). 'Industrial Complex Analysis, Agglomeration Economies, and Regional Development.' <u>Journal of Regional Science</u> 1:19-34.

Kawashima, T. (1977). Doctoral Dissertation. Regional Science Department, University of Pennsylvania.

Luce, Robert D. and Howard Raiffa (1957). Games and Decisions. New York: Wiley.

Moses, Leon N. (1958). 'Location and the theory of production.' Quarterly Journal of Economics 72:259-72.

Olson, Mancur, Jr. (1965). The Logic of Collective Action. Cambridge, Mass.:Harvard University Press.

Samuelson, Paul A., (1969). 'The pure theory of expenditure and taxation.' (In) Julian Margolis and H. Guitton, Public Economics. New York: St. Martin's Press.

_____, (1954). 'The pure theory of public expenditure.' Review of Economics and Statistics 36:387-89.

Schelling, Thomas C., (1978). Micromotives and Macrobehavior. New York: Norton.

Tinbergen, J., (1961). 'The spatial dispersion of production: A hypothesis.' Swiss Journal of Economics and Statistics 97.

Weiss, J.H., (1981). 'Ambivalent value of voluntary provision of public goods in a political economy.' (In) Michael J. White, Non-Profit Firms in a Three Sector Economy.

7 Policy analysis using an integrated multiregional model

WALTER ISARD AND CHRISTINE SMITH

1. Introduction

In the last few years, it has become increasingly evident to regional scientists that there is a high degree of interdependence involved in understanding and projecting the impacts of different policies, singly and in combination. The interdependence arises from the fact that each policy, say housing, energy, environment, or industrial development comes to affect the operation of any economic or other sector of a region and the region's welfare (state of affairs) which then influences how other policies may affect these sectors and the region's welfare. For example, it is obvious that any policy designed to maintain or improve the environmental quality of a developing region is highly dependent upon what energy policy is chosen, whether all-out nuclear, all-out coal, a combination of coal, oil, and solar, or something else. At the same time, the impact and effectiveness of an energy policy such as an all-out coal policy is highly dependent upon environmental regulations, regarding say allowable sulphur dioxide and particulate emissions since these regulations can significantly affect the cost of operating coal power plants. Similarly, it is easy to show how transportation, housing, urban land use, employment, industrial development, and other policies have impacts which can be projected only when we know the specific policies (and instruments) adopted in other policy areas.

In past decades, regional scientists have developed different kinds of models to understand and project the effects of different types of policy. For example, we have developed interregional linear programming to handle the implications of alternative energy policies; interregional input-output to get at multiplier effects of alternative industrial development policies; comparative cost and industrial complex analysis to gauge the impact of an across-the-board, nation-wide environmental regulation upon the cost of production in different regions and thus the relocation of industry; gravity and entropy-type models to project impacts of transportation development policies; factor substitution models to estimate changes in production practices from wage and price policies; and regional econometric and demographic models to estimate the impact of social welfare policy, unemployment compensation, etc., on migration. Now, however, when we have come to recognize the interdependence of the impacts of different policies, it is essential that we develop models which integrate several or all of the models mentioned above. It is essential that we do so if we are to project accurately the impacts of any policy,

64

whether we are considering a developed or developing region. That is, the impact or the effectiveness of any policy by itself cannot be examined without reference to what other policies are likely to be in effect.

Accordingly, the authors have developed in other manuscript an integrated multiregional model to help gauge better the impacts of several different types of policies upon a multiregion system for both developed and developing countries (Isard and Anselin 1982; Isard and Smith 1982a and 1983). As indicated in Figure 1, this model consists of the following modules:

1.   a national econometric module (NATLEC),

2.   an integrated comparative cost, industrial complex, input-output and programming module (CICIOP),

3.   a transportation module (TRANS),

4.   a demographic module (DEMO),

5.   a multiregion econometric module (REGLEC),

6.   a factor demand-investment supply econometric module (FACTIN),

7.   a multipolicy formation module (INPOL).

In a number of articles (Isard and Anselin 1982; Isard and Smith 1982a, 1982b, 1983, and C. Smith 1982a) and in a forthcoming dissertation (C. Smith 1982) we have established and developed most of the linkages, and, in part, the data base for the operation of such a model. We have also suggested the operation of a partially integrated model for situations often characteristic of developing nations where the data base is insufficient for the operation of a fully integrated model. However, we have yet to indicate in an effective manner the diverse approaches that might be adopted within the multipolicy formation module. Such approaches take into account the consequences of any mix of policies that might be proposed and lead to the identification of a best or most likely set of compromise policies. That is, in terms of Figure 2, we seek that set of compromise policies that might result after one or more sets have been fed into the aggregate of non-policy modules, indicated by the long, narrow, rectangular box designated "Use of the Non-Policy Modules of the Integrated Model" in the center of the figure, and the results examined. (The specific ways and exact points at which a given set of policies link to each module of the model, or of a partially integrated model, are discussed elsewhere) (Isard and C. Smith 1982b and C. Smith 1982).

In developing this paper, we also wish to point up how a specific compromise procedure (the method of determining group priorities a la Saaty) (Isard and C. Smith 1982, pp. 147-55, 165-68) can be used to identify (project) the most likely mix of policies to be adopted (Isard and C. Smith 1982b) in a given year of projection (say the year 2000). Because of limited space, we discuss only in general how other conflict management procedures (as systematically covered in Isard and C. Smith [1982] can be effectively employed to supplement the Saaty approach.

FIGURE 1

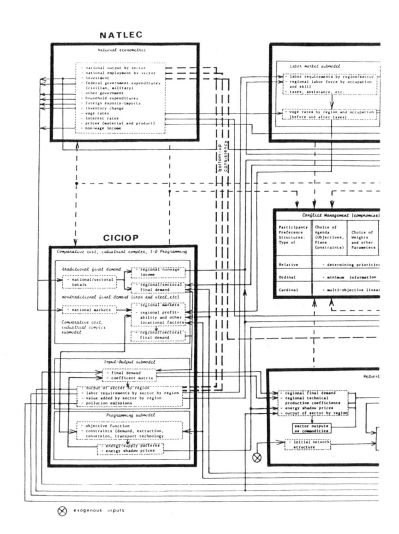

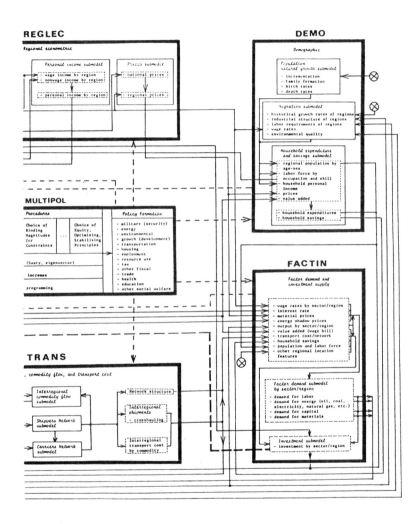

REGLEC

Regional econometric

Personal income submodel
- wage income by region
- nonwage income by region
- personal income by region

Prices submodel
- national prices
- regional prices

DEMO

Demographic

Population
natural growth submodel
- incrementation
- family formation
- birth rates
- death rates

Migration submodel
- historical growth rates of regions
- industrial structure of regions
- labor requirements of regions
- wage rates
- environmental quality

Household expenditure
and savings submodel
- regional population by
  age-sex
- labor force by
  occupation and skill
- household personal
  income
- prices
- value added
- household expenditures
- household savings

MULTIPOL

Procedures

Choice of Binding Magnitudes for Constraints	...	Choice of Equity, Optimising, Stabilising Principles

(Saaty, eigenvector)

incremax

programming

Policy Formation
- military (security)
- energy
- environmental
- growth (development)
- transportation
- housing
- employment
- resource use
- tax
- other fiscal
- trade
- health
- education
- other social welfare

FACTIN

*Factor demand and
investment supply*

- wage rates by sector/region
- interest rate
- material prices
- energy shadow prices
- output by sector/region
- value added (wage bill)
- transport cost/network
- household savings
- population and labor force
- other regional location
  features

Factor demand submodel
by sector/region
- demand for labor
- demand for energy (oil, coal,
  electricity, natural gas, etc.)
- demand for capital
- demand for materials

Investment submodel
- investment by sector/region

TRANS

, commodity flow, and transport cost

Interregional
commodity flow
submodel

Shippers Network
submodel

Carriers Network
submodel

Network structure

Interregional
shipments
- crosshauling

Interregional
transport cost
by commodity

FIGURE 2

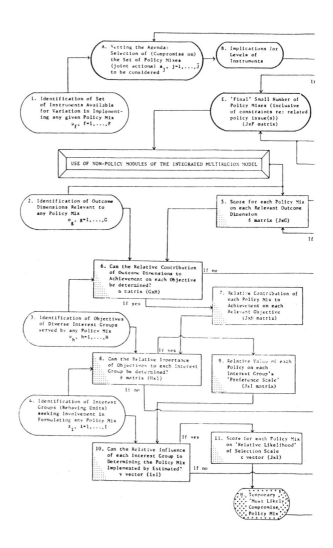

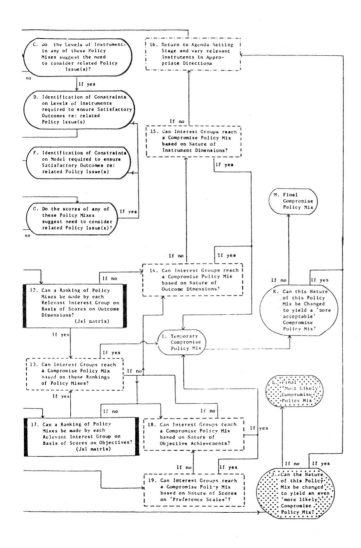

C. Do the Levels of Instruments in any of these Policy Mixes suggest the need to consider related Policy Issue(s)?
no — If yes

16. Return to Agenda Setting Stage and vary relevant Instruments in Appropriate Directions

D. Identification of Constraints on Levels of Instruments required to ensure Satisfactory Outcomes re: related Policy Issue(s)

15. Can Interest Groups reach a Compromise Policy Mix based on Nature of Instrument Dimensions?
If no — If yes

F. Identification of Constraints on Model required to ensure Satisfactory Outcomes re: related Policy Issue(s)

M. Final Compromise Policy Mix

G. Do the scores of any of these Policy Mixes suggest need to consider related Policy Issue(s)?
If yes — no

14. Can Interest Groups reach a Compromise Policy Mix based on Nature of Outcome Dimensions?
If no — If yes

12. Can a Ranking of Policy Mixes be made by each Relevant Interest Group on Basis of Scores on Outcome Dimensions? (Jxl matrix)
If no — If yes

K. Can this Nature of this Policy Mix be Changed to yield a 'more acceptable' Compromise Policy Mix?
If no — If yes

I. Temporary Compromise Policy Mix

13. Can Interest Groups reach a Compromise Policy Mix based on these Rankings of Policy Mixes?
If yes — If no

L. Final 'Most Likely' Compromise Policy Mix

17. Can a Ranking of Policy Mixes be made by each Relevant Interest Group on Basis of Scores on Objectives? (Jxl matrix)
If no

18. Can Interest Groups reach a Compromise Policy Mix based on Nature of Objective Achievements?
If no — If yes

J. Can the Nature of this Policy Mix be changed to yield an even 'more likely' Compromise Policy Mix?
If no — If yes

19. Can Interest Groups reach a Compromise Policy Mix based on Nature of Scores on 'Preference Scales'?
If no — If yes

2. The Basic Elements of a Policy Choice

We now list the basic elements in a policy choice by a given government unit (say, the Federal government):

1. Interest groups influencing the decisions of the given government unit $z_i(i=1,\ldots,I)$ (oval 4 of Figure 2),

2. Objectives of importance to one or more interest groups $v_h(h=1,\ldots,H)$ (oval 3 of Figure 2),

3. Outcome dimensions (as derived from the operation of the integrated model) $o_g(g=1,\ldots,G)$ (oval 2 of Figure 2),

4. Policy proposals (joint actions) a_j $(j=1,\ldots,J)$ (ovals A and E of Figure 2),

5. Policy instruments (specified in a form amenable for use in the integrated model) $\mu_f(f=1,\ldots,F)$ (oval 1 of Figure 2).

Given these elements, there exist many ways by which to evaluate the different policy mixes that may be proposed for the year 2000 in terms of their outcome implications as determined via the operation of the non-policy modules of an integrated multiregion model. With reference to Figure 2, one possible set of steps may be as follows:

Step 1: Selection of an Initial Set of Policy Mixes to be Considered

While many policy proposals (mixes or joint actions) may be considered, in practice only a few can be examined for outcome implications with the use of the non-policy modules of the integrated multiregion model. The activity involving the selection of these few proposals (which may be viewed as setting the agenda) via diverse compromises is depicted by the bold oval A where the political leaders, representatives of diverse interest groups and other behaving units, interact.

Step 2: Identification of Nature and Level of Instruments Required to

Implement the Given Policy Mixes
In bold ovals B, C, D, and E respectively

(i) We determine the set of instruments $\mu_f(f=1,\ldots,F)$ and levels of each required to effect each given policy mix (proposal) $a_j(j=1,\ldots,J)$;[2]

(ii) We consider whether the levels of instruments identified in (i) suggest the need to consider related policy issues not covered by these policy mixes.[3]

(iii) If there is such a need, we determine (identify) the constraints on the levels of the instruments required to ensure satisfactory outcomes regarding related policy issues;

(iv) We eliminate those policy mixes which cannot meet the constraints identified in (iii). This yields a JxF matrix recording level of the various instruments $\mu_f(f=1,\ldots,F)$ required to implement the final small number of policy mixes a_j $(j=1,\ldots,J)$ to be considered in subsequent steps.

Step 3:   Identification of Outcome Implications of Each Policy Mix

Each policy mix a_j can now be run through the non-policy modules of the integrated multiregion model indicated by the long rectangular box in Figure 2. This step is achieved by putting the set of relevant policy instruments at the corresponding levels identified in step 2. This yields a score for each policy mix (proposal) a_j $(j=1,\ldots,J)$ on a number of relevant outcome dimensions o_g $(g=1,\ldots,G)$.[4] See the shaded box 5 in Figure 2. We can then construct an outcome matrix (designated δ) of order JxG, with typical element o_j^g recording the score of policy mix j on outcome dimension g. That is:[5]

$$
\begin{array}{ll}
 & \quad\quad o^1 \quad o^2 \ \ldots\ o^g \ \ldots\ o^G \\[4pt]
a_1 \to o_1 & \begin{bmatrix} o_1^1 & o_1^2 & o_1^g & o_1^G \\ o_2^1 & o_2^2 & \ldots & o_2^g & \ldots & o_2^G \\ \vdots & & \vdots & & \vdots \\ o_j^1 & o_j^2 & \ldots & o_j^g & \ldots & o_j^G \\ \vdots & & \vdots & & \vdots \\ o_J^1 & o_J^2 & \ldots & o_J^g & & o_J^G \end{bmatrix} \\
a_2 \to o_2 & \\
\quad\vdots & \\
a_j \to o_j & \\
\quad\vdots & \\
a_J \to o_J &
\end{array}
$$

$$\text{JxG}$$

At this point we need to determine whether or not the outcome scores for any of these policy mixes suggest the need to consider implications for related policy issues not included in that policy mix.[6] See bold oval G. If not, we can proceed to step 5. Otherwise, we may need to change the levels of some of the instruments (bold oval D) associated with the given policy mixes. We may even need to impose other constraints [7] (bold oval F) which could result in the elimination of one or more policy mixes from further consideration. The integrated model must then be rerun for each non-eliminated policy mix under the new constraints, giving us a new δ matrix.

Step 4:   Identification of the Relative Contribution of each Outcome Dimension to Achievement on Each Objective[8]

The evaluation of these contributions can be done via the use of the Saaty procedure for determining group priorities. (See shaded box 6.) For example, for a given objective, v_h, we might (after consultation with relevant experts) obtain a pairwise comparisons matrix (GxG) in the following form:[9]

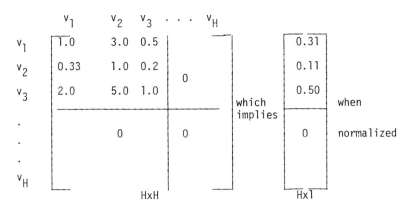

	o_1	o_2	o_3	$\cdots$	o_G		
o_1	1.0	2.0	3.0				0.540
o.2	0.5	1.0	2.0		0		0.297
o.3	0.33	0.5	1.0				0.163	when
.								normal-
.		0		0			0	ized
.							
o_G							

GxG   Gx1

As indicated above, this matrix yields a Gx1 vector of "weights" showing the relative contribution of outcome dimension o_g ($g=1,\ldots,G$) to the achievement of objective v_h.[10] For each of the H objectives a comparable Gx1 vector can be derived, and when these results are recorded in a single table this yields a matrix (designated α) of order GxH.

Step 5: Identification of the Relative Contribution of Each Policy Mix to Achievements on Each Objective

To identify these contributions, premultiply the α matrix of order GxH derived in step 4 (shaded box 6) by the δ matrix of order JxG derived in step 3 (shaded box 5) to obtain, as noted in shaded box 7, a JxH matrix. The typical element of this latter matrix gives the relative contribution of policy mix j ($j=1,\ldots,J$) to the achievement of objective h ($h=1,\ldots,H$).

Step 6: Identification of the Relative Importance of Each Objective to Each Interest Group[11]

This identification process can be done via the use of the Saaty procedure for determining group priorities. (see shaded box 8.) For example, for a given interest group z_i we might (after consultation with relevant experts) obtain a pairwise comparisons matrix (HxH) of the form:[12]

	v_1	v_2	v_3	$\cdots$	v_H			
v_1	1.0	3.0	0.5				0.31	
v_2	0.33	1.0	0.2				0.11	
v_3	2.0	5.0	1.0		0		0.50	
.						which		when
.		0		0		implies	0	normalized
.								
v_H								

HxH   Hx1

As indicated above, this yields a Hx1 vector of "weights" showing the relative importance of objective v_h ($h=1,\ldots,H$) to the interest group z_i.[13] For each of the I interest groups a comparable Hx1 vector can be derived, and when these results are recorded in a single table this yields a matrix (designated β) of order Hx1.

Step 7: Identification of the Relative Value of Each Policy Mix for Each Interest Group

We first premultiply the β matrix of order HxI derived in step 6 (shaded box 8) by the α matrix of order GxH derived in step 4 (shaded box 6) to obtain a GxI matrix which indicates the relative importance of each outcome dimension to each interest group. We can then premultiply this GxI matrix by the δ matrix of order JxG derived in step 3 (shaded box 5) to obtain, as noted in shaded box 9, a JxI matrix. The typical element of this latter matrix gives the relative value of policy mix $j(j=1,\ldots,J)$ to each interest group $i(i=1,\ldots,I)$.

Step 8: Identification of the Relative Importance (Influence) of each Interest Group in the Policy Formation Process[14]

This type of identification can be done via the use of the Saaty procedure for determining group priorities. See shaded box 10. For example, after consulting with experts on the policy formation process we might obtain a pairwise comparisons matrix of the form:[15]

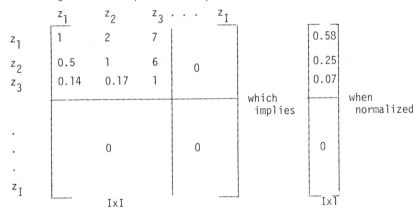

As indicated above, this yields a Ix1 vector of "weights" showing the relative importance (influence) of each interest group z_i ($i=1,\ldots,I$) in selecting the policy mix to be put into effect by the given level of government. We designate this vector the γ vector.[16]

Step 9: Identification of the Relative Likelihood of Adoption of each Policy Mix

We next multiply the JxI matrix showing the relative value of each policy mix to interest groups derived in step 7 (shaded box 9) by the γ vector of order Ix1 derived in the previous step (shaded box 10). As noted in the shaded box 11, this yields a Jx1 vector (designated ϵ) whose typical element gives the relative likelihood of selection (importance) of policy mix $a_j(j=1,\ldots,J)$ by the given level of government.[17] This is the desired outcome, and it may appear at first glance that we can now conclude that the policy mix (proposal) with the highest relative value be designated the 'most likely' compromise policy proposal. See the bold dotted oval H. However, we regard this conclusion as only temporary and suggest the adoption of one more step.

Step 10: Resetting of Agenda in the Light of the Results of Previous Steps

Next we may inquire (or the political leaders may consider) whether the nature of the most likely policy mix (identified in step 9) can be changed to yield an even more likely "compromise" policy mix. See the bold dotted oval J. If not, they accept the results in shaded box 11 as final, thus moving to the bold dotted oval L. If yes, they, in effect, return (via box 16) to the agenda setting stage (bold ovals A through E), introduce an adjusted policy mix, and go through the entire process again. However, if the Saaty procedure is once again employed some new problems and inconsistencies may arise. We cannot discuss these further here due to limited space.

Concluding Remarks

In this paper we have briefly sketched how one conflict management procedure may be employed together with the non-policy modules of an integrated multiregion model to forecast the policy mix most likely to be selected (in the sense of being a best compromise). There are many other procedures that can be employed, as we have suggested in the footnotes. Each procedure has its strength and limitations and for further discussion the reader is referred to Isard and C. Smith (1982) and references cited therein.

Footnotes

* The authors are grateful to the National Science Foundation and the University of Queensland for financial support of their research.

1 The policies selected for consideration are tariff policy, mineral development policy, immigration policy, foreign investment policy and the level and mix of federal government programs (inclusive of taxation).

2 For example, the policy mix may relate to military expenditures, energy resource development, low income housing provision, transportation network extensions, etc. In this situation the relevant set of instruments would include military procurement by region, employment on military bases by region, subsidies on oil shale installations by region, dollar expenditures on federal housing by region, and expenditure on mass transit by region.

3 For example, should the level of tariffs be reduced across the board by 25 percent in order to effect a trade policy, then we may need to consider the instrocution of a manpower planning policy to avert the undesirable employment implications of this tariff change.

4 Typical outcome dimensions would be regional employment and/or income levels, unemployment rates, air pollution levels, etc.

5 Note that each row represents the outcome vector corresponding to a given policy mix, and that each column has been normalized (i.e., converted to a common scale.

6 For example, examining the results recorded in the δ matrix may reveal that a given policy mix (say, a_{j1}) leads to an undesirably high level of unemployment in a given region (or for a particular class of workers). This unemployment situation may then suggest the need for the simultaneous adoption of a region- (or class-) specific employment development program.

7 For example, such constraints may relate to outcome dimensions such as oil imports, capital available for investment in housing and infrastructure, and disparities in regional per capital income. In some situations, political leaders (or their right hand men) may be unable to agree on a particular set of policy mixes to be considered, yet able to specify a minimum acceptable target score on each outcome dimension. The analyst may then be able to

identify a set of policy mixes which are each capable of meeting
these target scores.

8 If such relative contributions can not be identified using the
Saaty procedure, then we must consider other alternatives. For
example, (as indicated in boxes 12 and 13, respectively) should a
ranking of policy mixes (or proposals) be available (or able to be
constructed) for each interest group on the basis of the outcome
scores identified in step 3, then the analyst may consider the use
of rank-oriented conflict management procedures, which yield a
temporary compromise policy proposal, as indicated in the light
dotted oval I). Where such rankings are unavailable, the analyst
may focus on the outcome scores or instrument dimensions directly
and (via the use of one or more reasonable conflict management
procedures) reach agreement on a compromise set of
outcomes/instruments levels. These options are indicated in boxes
14 and 15, respectively. If successful, they too yield a temporary
compromise policy proposal (light dotted oval I). On the other
hand, should none of these approaches work, then the analyst will
need to return via box 16 to the agenda-setting stage (bold oval A)
and consider a revised set of policy mixes.

9 Note that the 3.0 in the cell o_{13} implies that o_1 makes a
"weakly more important" contribution to objective v_h than o_3,
and in particular in three times as important as o_3 when using
Saaty's scale and method. For a full discussion of the scale used
in making such pairwise comparisons, see Saaty and Khouja (1976)
and Isard and C. Smith (1982: 148-50).

10 For example, the 0.540 and 0.297 in the first and second rows of
this vector indicate that compared with a unit of o_2, a unit of
o_1 makes a (0.540/0.297) times greater contribution to objective
v_h.

11 If such relative importance cannot be identified using the Saaty
procedure, then we must consider other alternatives. For example,
(as indicated in box 17) should a ranking of policy mixes (or
proposals) be available (or able to be constructed) for each
interest group on the basis of the objective achievement scores
identified in step 5, then the analyst may consider the use of
rank-oriented conflict management procedures. (This yields a
temporary compromise policy proposal, as indicated in the light
dotted oval I). Where such rankings are unavailable, then the
analyst may focus directly on the objective achievment scores and
(via the use of one or more reasonable conflict management
procedures) reach a compromise set of objective achievements. This
option is indicated in box 18 and, if successful, it too yields a
temporary compromise policy proposal. On the other hand, should
neither of the above approaches work, then the analyst will need to
consider one or more of the options discussed in footnote 8.

12 Note that the 5.0 in the cell v_{23} implies that interest group j
considers that v_2 is of "strong" importance relative to v_3, and
in particular is five times as important as v_3 when using Saaty's
scale and method. For a full discussion of the scale used in
making such pairwise comparisons, see the references cited in
footnote 9.

13 For example, the 0.31 and 0.11 in the first and second rows of this vector indicate that for interest group z_i a unit of objective v_1 is regarded as (0.31/0.11) times more important than a unit of objective v_2.

14 If such relative influence (importance) cannot be identified using the Saaty procedure, then we must consider other alternatives. For example (as indicated in box 19 outlined by dashes), the analyst may consider the use of outcome-oriented conflict management procedures based on the relative preference values derived for each interest group in step 7. These procedures yield a temporary compromise policy proposal (light dotted oval I). If no acceptable outcome-oriented CMP's can be found, then one or more of the approaches discussed in footnotes 9 and 12 need to be employed.

15 Note that the 7.0 in the cell z_{13} implies that, for the given government unit, interest group z_3 is considered to have "demonstrated" influence relative to z_1 and, in particular, is seven times as important as z_1 when using Saaty's scale and method. For a full discussion of the scale used in making such pairwise comparisons.

16 In later manuscript, where we generalize the analyses to cover many government units $_d(d=1,\ldots,D)$, we obtain a η matrix of order IxD where each column gives the relative influence of interest groups within any given government unit. We then need to take the additional step of identifying a Dx1 vector showing the relative importance of each government unit in determining the nature of the policy mix adopted.

17 Mathematically, we may summarize the operations performed up to this point as $[\epsilon] = [\delta] [\alpha] [\beta] [\gamma]$.
 Jx1 JxG GxH HxI Ix1

References

Isard, W. and Anselin, L. (1982). 'Integration of Multiregional
    Models for Policy Analysis,' Environment and Planning A, 14:
    359–76.

Isard, W. and Smith, C. (1982). Conflict Analysis and Practical
    Conflict Management Procedures: An Introduction to Peace
    Science, Cambridge, Mass.: Ballinger.

Isard, W. and Smith, C. (1982a). 'Linked Integrated Multiregion Models
    at the International Level,' Papers, Regional Science
    Association, Vol. 50.

Isard, W. and Smith, C. (1982b). 'Explorations on an Empirical
    Framework of the Integrated Multiregion Model for U.S.A.,'
    Paper presented at North American Meetings of Regional Science
    Association, Pittsburgh, November.

Isard, W. and Smith, C. (1981). 'Incoroporation of Conflict and Policy
    Analysis in an Integrated Multiregional Model.' To appear in
    a book on the UMEA Conference, (forthcoming 1983).

Saaty, T.L. and Khouja, M.W. (1976). 'A Measure of World Influence,'
    Journal of Peace Science, 2, (1): 31–48.

Smith, C. (1982). 'Integration of Multiregional Models for Policy
    Analysis,' Unpublished Ph.D. dissertation, Cornell University.

Smith, C. (1982a). 'An Empirical Framework for an Integrated
    Multiregion Model for Australia,' Paper presented at North
    American Meeting of Regional Science Association, Pittsburgh.

8 Qualitative spatial input analysis

PETER NIJKAMP

1. Introduction

The division of the world into a rich and a poor part is to some
extent arbitrary, as it neglects the wide variety of welfare and
development patterns in both the developed and the developing
countries. Even in the ancient world individual countries displayed
rich and poor areas. The same holds true for our present world.
Several developed countries have also backward areas; while several
developing countries have also economically advanced areas. Though
there may be a big absolute difference between developed and developing
countries, the relative welfare differences in both the developed and
developing countries are much less significant. Clearly, it should be
taken into account that cross-national welfare comparisons are very
difficult due to inconsistent data, unrealiable information systems
(e.g., the measurement of the importance of the informal sector), and
different social and economic goals (cf. Chatterjee and Nijkamp 1981).

The urban and regional growth patterns in developing and developed
countries show many similarities, but at the same time also many
dissimilarities.

Similarities in urban developments between developing and developed
countries include inter alia:

1. Rapid changes in numbers of inhabitants and job opportunities
   leading to sometimes unpredictable fluctuations in urban
   growth patterns and in urban life cycles (cf. Norton 1979).

2. The existence of a dual (or, in more general terms, a
   segmentated) labor market for different socio-economic groups
   leading to unequal opportunities and to social and political
   frictions.

3. A decay in urban quality-of-life due to increased pollution,
   congestion, decay in the quality of dwellings, and social
   alienation.

There are also substantial differences in urban development
patterns:

1. The developing world is still displaying a continuing urbanization process (e.g., Mexico, Manila, Bombay), while in the

developed world new urban development stages have emerged
(urbanization   suburbanization   desurbanization   re-urban-
ization) (see also Klaassen 1978, and Nijkamp and Rietveld
1981).

2. A major part of the economic activities in developing
    countries takes place in the informal sector (characterized by
    small-scale activities), which usually falls outside the
    economic statistics; in the developed world, more reliable
    information systems are available (although here the so-called
    "black circuit" may lead to biased economic statistics).

3. Most developing countries are still displaying rapid
    demographic changes leading to permanent perturbations on the
    housing market, whereas developed countries have a more stable
    growth pattern of population; in the last mentioned countries,
    however, the rise in the number of single- and two-person
    households has caused severe frictions on the housing market
    as well (cf. Van Lierop and Nijkamp 1981).

As far as similarities in regional development patterns are
concerned, the following elements may be mentioned:

1. Interregional equity is a rigid phenomenon that can hardly be
    removed: despite the implementation of many policies, the
    economic gaps between regions have not drastically changed
    (for instance, Stohr and Todtling (1977) have demonstrated
    that the application of growth pole theory has not been
    successful in many countries).

2. In many countries (e.g., Belgium, Canada, Spain, India,
    Indonesia) there is a strong movement toward more autonomy of
    the regions (especially the less central regions); this will
    of course have strong economic repercussions for a whole
    spatial system.

3. In all countries, regional developments are hampered by the
    rise in energy costs (especially the regions with poor
    locational conditions), so that regional disparities are
    likely to continue in the future.

There are also many differences in regional developments in the
developing and the developed world:

1. Many developing countries (e.g., India) are still rural and
    agricultural in nature (cf. Friedmann and Douglas 1975),
    whereas the developed world is mainly oriented to the
    secondary, tertiary, and quarternary sector; consequently,
    problem areas in developing countries are mainly those areas
    which have not yet reached their first "take-off" stage
    (Rostow 1960), while problem areas in developed countries are
    mainly those areas for which the "drive to maturity" (i.e.,
    modern economic sectors) is hampered by locational and
    infrastructural bottlenecks.

2. In many regions in developing countries, infrastructure
    facilities (e.g., roads, railways, medical care, educational

facilities, public utilities) are unsufficient to stimulate regional growth, while in many regions in developed countries the basic infrastructural endowments are sufficient (see Nijkamp 1982).

3.   The information and data systems in many regions in developing countries are rather poor (leading to lack of insight into actual developments), while in many regions in developed countries extensive (computerized) information systems have been developed.

It is clear from the abovementioned examples that current urban and regional development patterns are extremely complex in nature, not only because of the complexity of the urban or regional system itself, but also because of the interactions between the national, the regional, the rural, and the urban system. An integrative framework for studying these developments requires a coherent spatial impact analysis based on a fine tuning with urban and regional data systems. This will be the subject of the next section.

2. Spatial Impact Analysis

The dynamic economic developments and fluctuations during the last decades have evoked the need of various impact analyses such as technology assessment, environmental impact analysis, social and economic impact analysis, spatial impact analysis, and so forth. In general, impact analysis aims at assessing all relevant foreseeable and expected consequences of external changes in a system within a certain time period. External changes may relate to both exogenous circumstances (e.g., rise in oil prices) and policy measures (e.g., construction of a new underground system).

Due to the pluriformity and complexity of most countries, coherent and balanced public policy strategies are usually fraught with difficulties. For instance, the integration and co-ordination of various aspects of physical planning problems (such as public facilities, communication and infrastructure networks, residential housing programs, industrialization programs, etc.) are often hampered due to administrative frictions, mono-disciplinary approaches, lack of information, and political discrepancies. In such cases, an impact analysis may be a meaningful tool for more integrated and co-ordinated planning strategies, as such an analysis describes systematically the effects of changes in external variables on all other components of a system (see Nijkamp 1979). Consequently, an impact analysis should pay attention to the variety, coherence and institutional framework of the levels of the system at hand. This implies that economic, spatial, social, and environmental variables are normally to be included as relevant components of the system.

It is clear that numerous effects can be taken into account. Therefore, a certain clustering is necessary in order to obtain a systematic impact analysis. The grouping of a variety of variables in an impact analysis may be based on similarities in effects (cf. Friedrich and Wonneman 1981). Examples of such effects are changes in: (1) spatial accessibility, (2) urban residential climate, (3) social structures, and (4) urban employment attractiveness. Such responses may emerge from stimuli such as urban housing programs,

energy conservation programs, construction of an infrastructure
network, etc.

Formally, the relationships between policy controls and the related
impacts may be represented by a (qualitative or quantitative) model
thatreflects the structure of the system at hand. In this way, all
indirect and multiplier effects can also be taken into account (cf.
Nesher and Schinnar 1981). When a formal model cannot be constructed,
easier methods have to be designed.

Given the pluriformity and variety among the elements of most
social and economic systems, a multidimensional profile approach is
often a meaningful analytical method for considering systematically a
wide variety of different aspects in such systems. This approach
implies that a certain phenomenon in the system at hand is
characterized by a vector profile with a set of different
(multidimentional) components or attributes. For instance, urban
quality of life is a multidimensional phenomenon that can only be
represented in a useful way by means of a vector with elements such as
quality, size and rent of dwellings; the types of medical, public, and
educational facilities: availability of parks and recreation areas:
traffic congestion: the quality and distance of urban facilities, etc.
(see Nijkamp 1980).

Sometimes it may be useful to employ an impact structure matrix
which reflects the effects of policy measures $(p_1,...,p_N)$ upon the
vector profiles $(c_1,...,c_I)$ (See Figure 1). Each cell of this
matrix reflects the effect of a policy measure on an element of the
urban welfare profile.

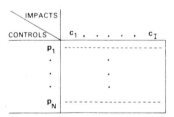

Figure 1. An Impact Structure Matrix

A spatial impact analysis focusses the attention in particular on
the spatial dimension of the abovementioned impacts. Such spatial
impacts may relate to regional, rural, or urban aspects of external
changes. The urban and regional dynamics may be caused by several
factors: endogenous growth processes (e.g., innovation), impacts of
urban and regional policies (e.g., housing programs), autonomous
developments (e.g., demographic growth), and exogenous circumstances
(e.g., rise in oil prices). In this paper particular attention will be
paid to the impacts of policy measures (Figure 1). This gives rise to
the following illustrative structure of spatial impact analysis (Figure
2).

It should be noted that one policy measure may have impacts on
several spatial (urban, rural, or regional) welfare profiles, while
there may also be mutual interactive effects among spatial welfare

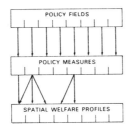

Figure 2.   Illustrative Structure of Spatial Impact Analysis.

profiles (indicated by means of the horizontal arrows in Figure 2).

During the last couple of years, in particular, urban impact analysis has drawn a lot of attention (see Glickman 1979, and Nijkamp 1981).Urban impact analysis is a specific kind of spatial impact analysis, as it focusses attention on the impacts of public policy measures on the urban welfare profile. The idea of urban impact analysis was born at the end of the seventies, when President Carter's National Urban Policy imposed on federal agencies the task to assess (prior to the implementation of new federal programs) the expected subsequent changes on various relevant urban variables (finances, housing, accessibility, etc.). In general, urban impact analysis does not aim at estimating the effects of urban policies themselves nor of exogenous (non-policy) shifts; it aims at measuring the impacts of non-urban policies (for instance, regional, national, or even international policies) on the urban system (Figure 3). It is clear, however, that the limitation of urban impact analysis to the effects of non-urban policies is restrictive and unnecessary. Therefore, in general, it is preferable to regard urban impact analysis as an analytical tool for assessing the effects of various kinds of external changes on the city.

Fig. 3.   Illustrative Representa-
          tion of Urban Impct
          Analysis.

Fig. 4. Illustrative Represen-
        tation of Rural Impact
        Analysis.

It has to be added that there is a wide variety of urban, regional and (inter) national policies: tax policy, energy policy, infrastructure policy, housing policy, health care, demographic policy, and so on. Each of these policy areas has a (multidimensional) set of relevant policy measures. Each measure may have a specific effect on the variables characterizing the urban system. As explained before, these variables can be grouped into more or less homogeneous or coherent urban welfare profiles (e.g., economic, social, infrastructural profiles).

In a similar way, one may also define <u>rural impact analysis</u> as an analytical method for estimating the consequences of external changes (e.g., regional policies, urban policies) on the welfare pattern of rural areas. An illustrative representation of such a rural impact analysis is given in Figure 4.

After this exposition, the use of spatial impact analysis may be defended on the following grounds:

1.   systematic assessment of all relevant regional, rural, or urban impacts of public policies may lead to more harmonious and balanced regional and urban policy decisions.

2.   An integrated impact analysis may prevent the neglect of (potentially) important indirect effects, especially as far as unintended effects are concerned.

3.   The presence of spatial spill-over effects and of interregional interactions requires a coherent insight into the complex mechanism of a spatial system.

4.   The hierarchical pattern of a national, regional, rural, and urban planning system requires a systematic impact analysis, by means of which policy effects at several levels can be estimated.

5.   A meaningful policy analysis requires also an analysis of spatio-temporal effects in a dynamic regional-rural-urban system (for instance, in relation to industrial innovation), so that public policymakers also receive meaningful information about the dynamics of a spatial system (cf. also Kelley and Williamson 1980, and Rogers 1977).

In conclusion, spatial impact analysis aims at providing an integrated (rather than a partial) picture of the consequences of a public policy plan (or of a set of such plans) for regions, rural areas, or cities.

Given the abovementioned concept of spatial impact analysis, the following requirements may be formulated for a meaningful spatial impact analysis:

1.   <u>relevance</u>: Impacts and indicators are to be associated with the objectives and instruments of urban, rural, and regional policies.

2.   <u>completeness</u>: All direct and indirect, intended and unintended impacts are to be included.

3.   <u>consistency</u>: The statistical and relational information should provide a coherent and non-contradictionary impact system.

4.   pluriformity: Impacts should reflect the variety and multidimensionality of a spatial system.

5.   comparability: Impacts should be comparable with analogous impacts measured at different places or in different points in time.

6.   flexibility: The information about impacts should be comprehensible for decision-makers and should be adaptable to new circumstances.

7.   data availability: Impacts should be measured on the basis of available data, so that no long-lasting research procedures are necessary: ordinal and soft information should not be neglected (see below).

8.   comprehensiveness: The successive steps in a spatial impact analysis should provide an integrated picture of all spatial interactions and effects (including distributional aspects).

9.   effectiveness analysis: Estimated impacts should allow a confrontation with a priori set policy goals.

10. feasibility: Urban impact analysis should fit in the prevailing pattern of urban, rural, and regional planning systems.

Given these methodological requirements, the question arises whether an operational and practical framework for spatial impact analysis can be designed. It will be shown in the next section that a systems approach may provide a meaningful perspective spatial impact analysis.

3. A Systems Approach for a Qualitative Spatial Impact Analysis

Given the need to obtain a comprehensive picture of all relevant (intended and unintended) spatial effects of policy measures, a systems approach may offer a practical frame of reference for spatial impact studies. In general, a systems approach aims at portraying the processes and relationships in a complex system that encompasses various components which are linked together by means of functional, technical, institutional or behavioural linkages and which can also be influenced by changes in parameters or controls from the environment outside the system itself (cf. Harvey 1969, and Klir and Valach 1967).

In general, a systems approach is based on a stimulus-response method. In the specific context of our paper, the stimuli are made up by policy measures, while the responses are made up by the various spatial welfare profiles (see also Figure 1). The following illustrtive representation of a stimulus-response model may be given (Figure 5):

The set of relationships and interactions between stimuli, interme-diate variables, and responses may include all kinds of relations: series, parallel, feedback, and component. The first-order intermediate variables represent the direct impacts of policy measures;

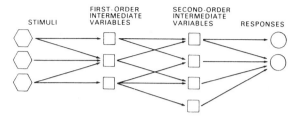

Figure 5.   An Illustration of a Systems Approach.

the secondorder intermediate variables, the indirect impacts, etc. In this way, a comprehensive representation of a complex spatial system can be obtained; hierarchical spatial systems can be represented in an analogous manner.

It is evident that an integrated spatial impact analysis requires data on the set of relationships between stimuli and responses. These relationships might be represented by means of a formal econometric model (estimated by means of time series or cross-section data) or by means of graphs or arrows (see Figure 5). The latter approach is more modest, as it does not require the construction of a comprehensive spatial econometric model: however, frequently, in this case, only qualitative statements regarding the responses of a spatial system to policy stimuli can be made. Especially in countries with a poor information system, the latter approach is extremely relevant.

The mechanism of this approach is essentially very simple. After the specification of the policy measures, the first-order impacts are assessed (via Fig. 5). Many of these impacts may be quantitative in nature, but qualitative impacts also have to be included. (Qualitative information refers to ordinal systems like "good," better," "best" or to nominal or binary systems like "high," "low"). Next, one has to follow the arrows of Fig. 5 in order to assess the second-order effects, and so forth, until finally the responses (spatial impact profiles) are assessed. Clearly, these profiles may contain both quantitative and qualitative information. It should be emphasized that qualitative information may not be neglected, as this may also include extremely important information.

Thus, a systems approach can be used to fill in the elements of the impact matrix. An operational use of spatial impact analysis requires fairly simple tools based on less detailed information. In respect to this, it has to be noted that in many policy problems a high degree of accuracy is not required: sometimes it is already sufficient either to indicate an order of magnitude of expected changes or to use a ranking of impacts. Even qualitative statements may be very useful. In such cases, an arrow scheme, illustrated in Fig. 5, may be extremely helpful, as it gives a systematic picture of the impact system and of all relevant profiles.

The successive impacts of policy measures can thus be assessed sequentially by means of a stage-wise effect analysis. The first-order impacts indicate the direct effects: the second-order impacts, the first sequence of indirect effects, etc., until all relevant effects have been considered. This sequential procedure may be terminated when the indirect impacts have become negligibly small, the information content is very unreliable, or the number of steps is fairly high.

In conclusion, spatial impact analysis may be an important tool in regional, rural, and urban policy analysis. In this respect, it may be meaningful to construct a set of profiles for the successive policy fields, such as:

1. economic (e.g., production, investments, consumption, labor market),

2. housing (e.g., quantity of dwellings, residential climate, rent),

3. infrastructural (e.g., accessibility via private and public transport, distance, mobility in terms of commuting and recreation),

4. financial (e.g., urban systems, subsidies, public expenditures, distributive aspects),

5. amenities (e.g., health care, culture, recreation facilities),

6. environmental (e.g., pollution, noise annoyance, water purification, density),

7. energy (e.g., consumption, insulation, tariff structure).

Clearly, for each specific policy problem a set of spatial welfare profiles has to be created. In general, the use of such multidimensional profiles fulfills the abovementioned conditions for a spatial impact analysis.

The abovementioned systems approach to spatial impact analysis may be an operational tool in a co-ordinated national, regional, rural, and urban planning framework, especially when this approach is extended with a policy scenario analysis and policy simulation experiments.

In many cases, it will be impossible to include in a spatial impact analysis all policy plans and instruments for all policy sectors in a certain area. Then it is very useful to carry out a scenario analysis, in which hypothetical, but coherent and consistent packages of public policy measures are treated. Each scenario can be composed on the basis of the policy impact structure illustrated in Fig. 5.

The way in which qualitative information can be considered is extensively described in Blommestein and Nijkamp (1982).

Thus, expecially qualitative spatial impact analyses are extremely important when the data base is insufficient to allow quantitative inferences. This is often the case in less developed countries. An empirical application of a step-wise spatial impact analysis including qualitative effects is contained in Nijkamp (1981).

4. Final Remarks

Spatial impact analysis may be a useful tool not only in the case of marginal changes or smooth transitions of a complex spatial system, but also in the case of perturbations of a system (for example, shocks caused by a sudden rise in oil prices). In that case, catastrophe-type models may be helpful to assess the impacts of policy scenarios (see also Van Dijk and Nijkamp 1980). As such jumps in a system are hard to quantify precisely, a qualitative impact analysis may be a useful tool.

It should also be noted that impact analysis may be important for complex decision problems where instead of one single decision-maker, a whole set of decision levels may be distinguished. In such cases, elements from conflict theory may be employed to arrive at compromise principles (see Nijkamp, 1979, 1980). Important tools for the application of conflict theory are multiobjective decision-making analysis and multiple criteria analysis. Also in this case, qualitative information from impact analysis and policy analysis can be dealt with.

After the assessment of quantitative and/or qualitative impact profiles, various statistical and econometric methods can be used to draw quantitative information from qualitative data inputs. Three types of analysis distinguish these methods:

1. statistical: based on ordinal correlation analysis (e.g., Kendall rank correlation analysis)

2. econometric: based on qualitative or ordinal estimation methods (for instance, logit analysis or scaling methods)

3. policy analysis: based on qualitative multiple criteria methods (for instance, dominance analysis).

An extensive description of these methods can be found in Nijkamp (1979, 1980), among others. Thus, one may conclude that, indeed, various methods do exist which are capable of treating qualitative information in an operational way so as to infer quantitative, valid final conclusions. In respect to this, spatial impact analysis may be an extremely important tool for treating all available information in a systematic and simple way, so that it may be a practical method in complex spatial planning problems.

References

Blommestein, H.J., and Nijkamp, P. (1982). 'Multivariate methods for soft data in development planning,' Urban and Regional Change in Developing Countries, (M. Chatterji et al., eds.) (forthcoming).

Chatterjee, L., and Nijkamp, P. (eds.), (1981). Urban Problems and Economic Development, Alphen a/d Rijn, Netherlands: Sijthoff & Noordhoff.

Dijk, F. van, and Nijkamp, P. (1980). 'An analysis of conflicts in dynamicenvironmental systems in catastrophe theory,' Regional Science and Urban Economics 10:429-51.

Friedmann, J. and Douglas, M. (1975). Agropolitan Development for RegionalPlanning in Asia, Nagoya, United Nations Centre for Regional Development.

Friedrich, P., and Wonnemann, H.G. (1981). 'Manual for identifying the effects of the settlement of a public office,' Locational Developments and Urban Planning (W.F.J. van Lierop and P. Nijkamp, eds.), Alphen a/d Rijn, Netherlands: Sijthoff & Noordhoff, 347-87.

Glickman, N.J. (ed.), (1979). The Urban Impacts of Federal Policies, Baltimore: The Johns Hopkins University Press.

Harvey, D. (1969). Explanation in Geography, London: Arnold.

Kelley, A.C. and Williamson, J.G. (1980). 'Modeling urbanization and economic growth,' Research Report 80-22, IIASA, Laxenburg.

Klaassen, L.H. (1978). 'Het desurbanisatieproces in de grote steden,' Economisch-Statistische Berichten, 63 (No. 3126), 8-10.

Klir, J. and Valach, M. (1967). Cybernetic Modeling, London: Ainsworth.

van Lierop, W.F.J. and Nijkamp, P. (eds.) (1981). Locational Developments and Urban Planning, Alphen a/d Rijn, Netherlands: Sijthoff & Noordhoff.

Nesher, A. and Schinnar, A.P. (1981). 'Neighbourhood and program multiplies of public funded community development activities', Locational Developments and Urban Planning, (W.F.J. van Lierop and P. Nijkamp, eds.), Alphen a/d Rijn, Netherlands: Sijthoff & Noordhoff, 389-406.

Norton, R.D. (1979). City Life-Cycles and American Urban Policy, New York: Academic Press

Nijkamp, P. (1979). Multidimensional Spatial Data and Decision Analysis, New York: Wiley.

Nijkamp, P. (1980). Environmental Policy Analysis, New York: Wiley.

Nijkamp, P. and Rietveld, P. (1981). 'Ordinal multivariate analysis,' Professional Paper PP-81-2, IIASA, Laxenburg.

Nijkamp, P. (1981). 'Urban impact analysis in a spatial context: methodology and case study,' Research Memorandum, 1981-5, Dept. of Economics, Free University, Amsterdam.

Nijkamp, P. (1982). 'A multidimensional analysis of intrastructure and regional development,' Structural Economic Analysis and Planning inSpace and Time, (A. Andersson, et al., eds.), Amsterdam: North-Holland Publishing Co.

Nijkamp, P. and Rietveld, P. (eds.)(1981). Cities in Transition, Alphen a/d Rijn, Netherlands: Sijthoff & Noordhoff.

Putman, S.H. (1979). Urban Residential Locational Models, Boston: Martinus Nijhoff.

Rogers, A. (1977). 'Migration, urbanization, resources and development,' Research Report, 77-14, Laxenburg.

Rostow, W.W. (1960). The Process of Economic Growth, Oxford: Clarendon Press.

Stohr, W. and Todtling, F. (1979). 'Spatial equity,' Papers of the Regional Science Association 38:33-53.

PART II
Urban and Metropolitan Growth Patterns

9 Technical assistance and national urban policies with special reference to Asia: a preliminary assessment

LLOYD RODWIN

1. Introduction

So far as I know there has been almost no examination of the exper-ience of the more developed countries (MDC's) and the international agencies with regard to technical assistance for urban and regional development in Third World countries. A fairly careful literature review has not led me as yet to a single study of such elementary questions as these: (1) How have the programs originated and evolved in Europe, Japan, and the United States, and what have been the differences between these policiesμ (2) How do these experiences compare with those developed by such international agencies as OECD, UN and the World Bankμ and (3) What, if any, were the learning experiencesμ The time I have had during the Fall and Spring (1981-1982) to delve into these matters and to do some checking in the field has been focused mainly on Japan, Sweden, France, Britain, The Netherlands, Germany and the U.S., and, to a lesser extent, the UN, OECD, and the World Bank. That is a lot of territory to cover. So what I can report at present is somewhat tentative, perhaps even a little hazardous. Still, what I have learned and what I can add in the form of personal recollections of relevant experiences over the past quarter of a century strike me as worth recording at least as tentative hypotheses or as first approximations of what we now know.

2. Claims and Assumptions of Technical Assistance

To place these questions in some historical perspective, consider first how the problems were viewed some 25 years ago when national urbanization policies and assumptions concerning technical assistance first became part of the political agenda of Western Europe and the United States. No doubt, historical characterizations will vary depending on who is doing the portrait. Even allowing for that necessity my impression is that a review of the policies of the period would confirm that the two dominant national concerns were how to achieve full employment and how to provide for some of the basic health, welfare, and housing needs and services for the poorest segments of the urban population. In the context of these issues two big area

---

*   Amended version of a paper prepared for the East-West Population Institute Conference on Urbanization and National Development, Honolulu, Hawaii, January 25-29, 1982.

development problems then loomed in the minds of the policy makers: how to deal with the diseconomies and the quality of life in the big cities; and how to cope with the low income and structural unemployment in the lagging regions (Rodwin 1981). The reformers on the physical planning side focused on the first of these problems, the economic planners on the second, and, for want of a better term, the "social reformers" on the third. Although the specialists spoke different lingos and were sometimes, perhaps even often, in conflict on ways of thinking about problems, they shared some common convictions. One was that the market economy, unaided, could not cope with these difficulties. Incentives and control mechanisms were deemed necessary and included an array of sub-national policies and programs especially for the less prosperous regions and segments of the population. These policies included area development plans, job creation strategies, the promotion of growth centers, the programming of infrastructure investments and the provision or improvement of a variety of local social and public services.

There was a striking similarity in the images of the area development problems of the Third World countries (TWC's) (Rodwin 1981, 139-44). The governments of these countries, most of them newly independent, with leaders and advisors often trained in the MDC's, tended to think of their urban and regional problems the way the governments did in the MDC's. Perhaps the main difference was that the problems were considered more critical and certainly more visible in the TWC's. The elite groups deplored the poor conditions of the capital or the primate cities, the poverty and scale of the "backward" regions, and the lack of elementary public services -- not to mention the inadequacies in addressing such basic needs as nutrition, health, water, sewage facilities, transportation, electricity, housing, and welfare services. Given the limited resources, experience, and trained staff, it was hardly surprising that TWC's looked for help on these matters from the MDC's as well as the international agencies (UN, OECD and the World Bank). It was taken for granted that the MDC's had the resources, that the international agency staff and the MDC specialists knew more or less how to address these problems, and that the problems could be tackled effectively within a reasonable period. In any case, there was a deep seated conviction that whatever the inadequacies of planning and the planner might be, they were far less serious than the inadequacies of the market.

These assumptions were understandable enough; but reasonable men might well have questioned whether the experiences were adequate or relevant, or that the planners had the necessary capabilities at the time these decisions were made. Certainly, the European experiences with these policies and programs, and, in particular, the experiences of Britain, France and Italy, were mixed and often negative. The control mechanisms proved inadequate, particularly in relation to small firms. The subsidies often helped the wrong economic activities (those particularly likely to move to the target areas) or failed to produce the intended effects. What was known about growth centers was shallow. The concept itself was spongy, there was little evidence that the growth would diffuse throughout the region, and it was a difficult policy to apply -- given the customary political pressures to spread the resources evenly between rural and urban areas and between all cities, big and small. In addition, the extent to which the ideas could be effective at all in any particular country depended not only on the amount of resources but also on the political will, continuity, and administrative capabilities, especially compentent, well trained civil servants and professional specialists. These were often lacking in many TWC's.

As for the U.S. experience in area development strategies, the thrust of the efforts there turned out to be even more diffuse and anything but successful. Japan's experience, too, and also Germany's, as latecomers to the field, did not count for much.

In other words, what was known at the time these technical assistance policies were embarked upon left much to be desired. Prior experience had not been really adequately assessed. Indeed, reasonably informed persons might well argue, despite an increasing number of studies by scholars and by the staff of public agencies during the past two decades, that this evaluation gap has still not be closed (Lo and Salih, 1978).

Finally, another group or critics, those with leftist or neo-Marxist views, argued that the problems were not really correctly formulated, and that too much emphasis was placed on the technical aspects of the problems. From their perspectives, significant solutions were unlikely until some more decisive structural changes occurred: changes, for example, in power, in the distribution of assets and in the control of institutions both within and between nations (Stohr and Todtling, 1978; Coraggio 1975; and Holland 1976).

What I am emphasizing here (instead of pressing the pros and cons of that situation) are the questions which might have been raised about the evidence and about the assumptions with regard to the national urban policies or of the technical assistance to promote these policies at the time these ideas were being advocated. I do so, I hasten to say, more as a proponent than as a hostile critic, and in this role let me also add the wry observation that these difficulties in pursuing urbanization strategies reflect almost inescapably the inadequacies of the paradigm of planning as well as the disingenuous ways planners as well as policy makers are generally obliged to present their views. I will cite only two examples.

Consider first how much the problems associated with national urbanization policies reflect the controversies about comprehensive and incremental planning. For some forty years (roughly between 1921 to 1961) the notion of comprehensive planning dominated the thinking of urban planners as the basic paradigm of the profession. Most of the professionals in the field, I believe, are now quite familiar with the sense of dismay, if not indignation, when these views came under powerful attack (Hirschman and Lindblom 1971; Altschuler 1965): (1) descriptively, on the grounds that that was not the way things happened; (2) in terms of feasibility, on the grounds that comprehensive planning wasn't possible, given existing resources, power and capabilities; and (3) normatively, on the grounds that even when possible it was not necessarily desirable as a way of getting things done.

No doubt, the doctrine of comprehensive planning, especially for area development, held sway for as long as it did because of the extraordinary problems associated with "ad hocery" and the undue

emphasis on sectors to the exclusion of complementary requirements.
There were countless examples of the failures to coordinate industry and
essential public services, to link jobs and housing, to relate housing
and community centers, indeed to take account generally of the secondary
effects of policies which have hamstrung or otherwise nullified explicit
area development policies. In short, there were good and substantial
reasons for decrying the limitations of incremental and sector planning
-- limitations which we still deplore today as tunnel vision and
bureaucratic laissez faire.

Nonetheless, in retrospect, notions of comprehensive and incremental
planning appear to be no better (or worse) than the kind of folk wisdom
which cautions us to look before we leap, yet warns us that he who
hesitates is lost. These admonitions are true enough in some circumstances. But, as is also true for such legal concepts as "reasonable-
ness" and "due process," they give us much too little help in
considering concrete cases.

The fact is that incremental and comprehensive planning are
inseparable polar categories, such as north and south, real and ideal,
the universal and the particular. One need only look closely to
discover that national urban policies fall squarely within the penumbral
zone between the incremental and the comprehensive. These policies must
take account of both the specific implications of sectoral policies on
incremental area development as well as of the inescapable
multi-sectoral requirements of area development. Because they must be
incremental in some respects and comprehansive in others, they are
subject to all of the critiques and dilemmas of incremental and
comprehensive planning. These questions fall into the category of
problems we must learn to live with. They are not, at least for the
present, problems we know how to solve.

Consider next the misleading way most of us think of planning. From
a perusal of most of the technical literature in the field, one might
gather that planning is essentially the art of getting agreement on
goals and devising means to realize them. This type of planning
presupposes that we know the goals and can spell them out easily at the
outset. Experience suggests, however, that goals are best formulated
towards the middle or end of most planning activities. We know far too
little to do more at the early stages of most significant problems.
This need to learn in the process of doing is another reason why
planning activities involve such erratic, expensive, and long term
processes.

Unlike many scientists, however, planners are not in a position to
speak candidly of their ignorance or failures. An immunologist or
carcinogen specialist might risk calling attention to the loss of
several hundred million dollars on research that turned out to be a dead
end. On the other hand, how prudent would it be for an area development
planner to tell a budget committee:

> We think technical assistance makes sense for all sorts of
> reasons, not just morally. But to be altogether candid,
> we really don't know much about the subject. It may take
> us two or three decades or more before we find out. It
> will require a lot of experimentation, and we are sure to

make many mistakes. In addition, it may be costly, although perhaps not more so than the failure to pursue such policies. But at the end of the period, perhaps — for there can be no guarantee — we may know a lot better what we need to do and how to do it.

Knowledgeable managers of area development might prefer such frankness, but how many are likely to practice it in most countries?

Lest what I am saying may appear cynical or overly critical of the field of planning, let me suggest that these problems hold — more or less — for other fields as well. Possibly the most well known example at this time is the blunt observation of that "enfant terrible," Mr. Stockman, Ronald Reagan's Director of the Bureau of the Budget, who acknowledged that no one involved in juggling the megabillions in the U.S. national budget quite understood what the changes in the numbers meant or implied. For this tidbit of refreshing candor, Mr. Stockman was given a "dressing down" by the President of the United States, and almost lost his job, although he undoubtedly gained some grudging admirers among intellectuals, liberal, as well as conservative.

Even more a propos and disconcerting may be the observation of the late Dr. Jacob Fine, once Chief Surgeon of Beth Israel Hospital in Boston and Professor of Surgery at the Harvard Medical School (one of the two or three most distinguished medical schools in the world). More than half (perhaps as much as 3/4), of the operations now performed by surgeons, Dr. Fine once told me, are based on false or inadequate hypotheses.

3. Experiences

So much for some of the aims and background of technical assistance with regard to urban development and some of the questions and uncertainties which characterized the claims and the assumptions. But I have only dealt with the subject from a technical point of view. One of the main differences, however, in our ways of thinking about urban strategies today as compared to the 1951s, is our greater sensitivity to the political issues. So perhaps we should consider how the perspectives and insights might be different if technical assistance were viewed from the perceptions of national interests of different countries and how these perceptions have shaped the patterns of technical assistance.

Before doing so, I must confess once again that my investigations to date have been far too limited to allow me to submit systematic evidence on these matters. All I can do at present is to share some of the impressions I have formed in the course of my interviews in Japan, Sweden, France, Britain, The Netherlands and Germany, impressions which have been supplemented or reinformed by documents examined while visiting these countries and by references to some of my professional experiences in a dozen other countries, including several (such as Portugal, Mexico, Turkey, Thailand, Korea, Taiwan, Malaysia and Indonesia) specifically referred to below.

In contemplating these political perspectives, it will be helpful to bear in mind the way the technical assistance processes operate or are supposed to operate as a rule. Developed over the past two or three decades, there are now many national and international programs of assistance. How these programs came into being cannot be dealt with here. All we need to note for our purposes is that TWC's must decide independently (or with assitance from advisors) in what areas and ways they need help. In turn, the donor countries must decide which items in the menu of possibilities they either will be able, or will choose to help. These "country programs," bilateral, and international, often involve complicated program formulations and negotiating processes on the part of all parties which may lead to amendments and/or substitutions in the policies and activities. The bargaining on the part of all of the parties requires skill and bluff as well as shrewd analyses of the relevant programs, interests, needs, and capabilities. Critics, depending on their political orientation, often take for granted that the TWC's or the MDC's are being unduly helped, hampered, or exploited; but in point of fact, the outcomes turn out to be less clear or certain than one might expect.

From the TWC's perspectives, no technical assistance program could go very far unless it was requested by them and likely to prove beneficial at least to some groups in the TWC. Host countries learn quickly enough what "goodies" are being offered or might become available and on what terms. They find out how they can take full advantage of the assorted assistance possibilities. Phisit Pakkasem of Thailand (Assistant Secretary General of the National Economic and Social Development Board, Office of the Prime Minister) recently regaled an audience of planners in Nagoya, Japan, simply by demonstrating how this game is conducted in his country (Pakkasem, 1981): how one donor country might be tempted to back a national urban strategy if another donor country or international agency turned out not to be interested; how padded costs by contracting firms could be shaved down by introducing competitive bidding; and how shoddy performance by contractors could be avoided or discouraged, etc. Pakkasem didn't mention -- for understandable reasons -- other less benign items such as how contracts might be obtained, and "pay-offs" or "shakedowns" arranged. There are negative as well as positive features in these games. But it is clear that, more often than one might suppose, the host country, if it has the will, can exert strong leverage to achieve its purposes.

It would be altogether unreasonable, however, to assume that programs which required substantial appropriations of funds would be approved or extended for many years without constant assurances that there would be significant advantages for the donor countries too. So, it is not surprising that one of the main beneficiaries, if not the principal beneficiary, would have to be the donor country or institution in order for the programs to prove stable and to continue functioning on a long term basis. As in trade relationships, both parties can be expected to benefit, but often one more than the other, and usually the one with more resources, information, power, and concern for immediate advantage.

So much for what one might expect in general. Now, how have technical assistance processes actually worked in specific casesμ

Turning first to Japan, I found surprisingly candid, albeit

unofficial acknowledgement that markets, raw materials, contracts, and spheres of influence were key considerations in the choice of countries and programs for assistance: this in Japan, which has benefited as much, if not more, than any other country from technical assistance. Although helping the LDC's is not a negligible criterion in Japanese technical assistance circles, as yet it appears to be almost an ancillary rather than a critical condition. This is one of the main reasons why most of the Japanese assitance (the scale of which is low in relation to its GNP and the contributions of other countries) is still mainly in southeast Asia. And that is why this assistance is also now veering towards the oil kingdoms of the Middle East and to some selected countries with rich resource endowments in Latin America (Economic Cooperation Bureau 1981). To be sure there are Japanese assistance projects in many other parts of the world, but most of them tend to be simply token acknowledgements of the assistance oblications. Offsetting this tokenism, moreover, is the growing reluctance of Japan -- amounting in some cases to outright refusal -- to provide technical assistance in certain fields such as steel making to potential competitors like Korea and Taiwan.

As for Europe and the United States, there is no reason, in most (not all) cases, to assume any lesser interest in markets, raw materials, contracts and spheres of influence. However, there are in these countries evidently greater commitments for assistance programs, including more unfettered assistance in industry, management, and research development programs; and often more sophisticated, or at any rate more flexible, ways of helping to make the programs effective. In part, the evidence I have in support of these impressions comes from the views of the officials in the host countries seeking assistance. These specialists comment mordantly on the lack of "openness" on the part of the Japanese in comparison with the relative ease with which useful information can be obtained in the U.S. and Europe. Even granting these differences, there can be little doubt that almost all countries try to guard their interests to some extent. The only countries I have found so far whose assistance funds appeared to be less "tied" initially to the purchase of goods and services in the donor countries appear to be Sweden and Germany and there are strong pressures in both which may well reverse the policy.[1] Interestingly enough, the United States has budged a little bit on the issue. It now allows the use of aid funds to obtain goods and services from other TWC's but not from other MDC's.[2]

If technical assistance is examined with specific reference to urbanization policies, still other differences are disclosed by comparative analysis. For instance, Japan's official views to date are quite negative with regard to assistance for urbanization strategies. The objection is that it takes too long to help develop urban and regional policies, not to mention national urban policies. The feeling is that

---

[1] These observations are based on talks with Ingvar Karlen, Swedish Commission for Technical Cooperation; Bjorn Sevenius, Vice President, SWECO; Jan-Olov Agrell, Chief Evaluation Unit, Swedish International Development Authority; and Bjorn Lundquist, VBB, SWECO.

[2] This change was called to my attention by the Assistant AID Representative in Thailand in November 1981.

these efforts do not help sufficiently to produce the desired credits, contracts, raw materials, or markets.[3]

In part, this lack of interest helps to explain why so little effort has been made to relate the Japanese experience in urban development (which is of interest to many countries) with the official programs designed for assistance, despite the fact that there is evidence of its relevance. One example is the conviction of Saburo Okita (former Foreign Minister and one of Japan's wisest and most respected development specialists) that Japanese development might have been far more socially acceptable not to mention less costly if there were more explicit and decentralized urban strategies (Okita 1981, 149-93, esp. 183-93). Another example is the carefully documented longitudinal research of Prof. Koichi Mera, focusing specifically on the Japanese experience with urbanization in relation to national and regional investment policies, and their effects on the national and regional distributions of income (Mera 1978). No doubt many features of Japan's development, because they are uniquely related to Japanese culture and institutions, are not transferable to other countries. Nonetheless, it would be premature, to say the least, to assume that none, or little, of this experience in one form or another had any relevance for other countries. Yet, to date, there appears to be far more interest abroad than in Japan in the implications of Saburo Okita's observations or in Mera's studies in official technical assistance circles.

Aside from the direct urbanization experience of Japan, there is still another, even more obvious example of this discrepancy between the knowledge of the urbanization experience of TWC's and Japan's official technical assistance policy. That is the very limited, in fact negligible, impact or influence on official Japanese technical assistance policies of the training and applied research programs of the U.N. Center for Area Development in Nagoya. This is all the more surprising because the Center is directed by Japanese specialists and is financed in the main by the Japanese government.

By way of contrast, U.S. technical assistance doctrines have been quite different on urbanization issues. These doctrines have been much closer to those of Britain and France despite the substantial differences between the urban policies of the U.S. and those of France and Britain. What is more, in comparison with Japan, the support of these doctrines in the U.S. was due in the main to technical considerations. Way back in the early 1961's when David Bell was the director of the Agency for International Development (AID, the principal technical assistance agency), there was much concern about the extraordinary proportion of the meager capital available for investments in LDC's which went into infrastructure rather than directly productive activities. Bell, in particular, was concerned with the evidence that many of these investments were made in questionable places and often

---

3   These views are based on conversations with a number of Japanese officials representing several agencies including the Overseas Economic Cooperation Fund, the Japan International Cooperation Agency and the International Development Center of Japan, as well as talks with Japanese professors specializing in the field of economic and regional development.

with dubious justifications. Although members of Bell's staff were skeptical on traditional grounds about investments in urban and regional programs, Bell decided to set up an advisory group to review the policy and issues.[4] The subsequent recommendations of this group reinforced Bell's decision to support national urbanization policies, primarily to encourage more explicitly and, hopefully more complementary, efficient and equitable programming of these infrastructure investments.

So far as I know, these reasons were also the main ones for the support by the United Nations of the urban and regional development strategies in Japan in the late 1951's; for the support in 1961 by the U.N. and the Organization for Economic Cooperation and Development (OECD) of the pioneering urban and regional development programs in Turkey; and for the subsequent World Bank support of the urbanization policies pursued in Mexico. Linked to these views in all of these cases[5] was the conviction that only a national urban policy was likely to offset the services, the market, and the bias of policy makers favoring the location of infrastructure investments in the capital city or the existing big cities.

Despite this history, AID now manages both to reject as well as to manipulate urbanization strategies to back up some of its diverse development assistance goals. The rejection reflects the disposition as of late in development circles to (1) de-emphasize growth and place more emphasis on employment and equity; (2) downgrade urban centers and to stress rural development and the informal sectors; (3) deplore concentration; and (4) applaud decentralization and participation. Partly on these grounds, AID officials informally vetoed a few years ago any proposals for an urbanization strategy in the late 1971's in Portugal, arguing that the main concerns of the agency had shifted to the needs of the poor and rural development. The same view was reaffirmed by AID officials in Thailand in 1981 despite the strong interest of Thai officials in a national urbanization strategy in order to counter the dominance of Bangkok. No doubt similar views became official AID doctrine in many other TWC's. Urban strategies seemed to be unacceptable except perhaps in the form of promotion of small town rural centers as a means of reinforcing rural development. It availed little to argue that a policy which ignored the capital city or large urban centers might turn out to be short sighted and ineffective, not least because of the powerful pressures which the interests in those centers could be expected to generate in order to reduce the congestion or the loss of productivity in those big cities.

There is some evidence, however, that AID has not altogether abandoned the support of national urbanization strategies when it might serve still other purposes. A current example is the case of Egypt where the government appeared determined to build new cities in the desert, a policy which AID officials have deemed costly and unwise in comparison with other urbanization and development alternatives. In these circumstances we find AID generously financing in 1981 national

---

[4] The author was a member of that committee.

[5] Directly or indirectly, the author had a professional association with these programs and most of the other programs discussed later in this paper.

urbanization studies in Egypt in the hope that the evidence justifying
less expensive urban policies might emerge. On somewhat the same
grounds, pressures are developing to enlist similar AID and World Bank
assistance for urbanization studies in several Latin American
countries. Even in Portugal there appears to be a possible change of
policy on urbanization strategies if pursued in the North.

This current tendency to deploy urbanization studies as a tool to
serve particular development aims has posed still another question, to
wit, the flexibility of the instrument and the uses to which it might be
put in varying circumstances. In Egypt, for instance, it is bruited
about that the firm or firms which would get the AID contract would need
to have the right views on new towns and urbanization if the studies
were to be continued beyond the initial stages and if the recommendations were to receive any effective implementation. Although the
innuendos may be exaggerated, it would be surprising if this prospect
were not taken into account by organizations which need such contracts.

Still another issue involves the trickiness of the diagnosis of the
appropriate conditions for the formulation and implementation of
national urban policies. A case in point is the experience of Indonesia
where there were many government agencies which regarded the formulation
and implementation of national urbanization policies as their
appropriate responsibility -- or at least one of their more important .
concerns. This was the view of (1) Bappenas (the central planning
agency which was concerned with the multi-level and inter-sectoral
government development policies); (2) the Ministry of the Interior
(which serviced and monitored local and provincial authorities); (3) the
Ministry of Finance (which was reexamining the handling of central local
government fiscal relationships); and (4) the Ministry of Public Works
(which sought an area development policy to guide the location of its
infrastructure investments -- investments equal to almost two thirds or
more of the total public capital formation).

Experience with national policies and programs in Indonesia
persuaded World Bank officials not only that the problems were real, but
also that the national intersectoral programs were not likely to be
within the administrative capabilities of the central government at the
time, at least on the basis of past experience. The consultant to the
U.N. and the government decided, however, (but not without some unease)
that the risks were perhaps reasonable in order to confront the
disproportions, misallocations, and conflicts generated by the absence
of such a policy. Therefore the proposal was made by the U.N.
Consultant to lodge this authority in a Directorate or sub-Directorate
within the Department of Public Works. That policy is now in the
process of being implemented. Whether it will succeed is difficult to
gauge at this point. But however dim or promising the prospects may be,
here too, we have evidence of the national urbanization policy being
initiated in the hope that it might provide an effective programming
tool to promote efficiency or equity. Once again, however, no one in
that situation has any clear perspective of how the different interests
and pressure groups may influence the use of that tool.

4. Conclusions

What conclusions, tentative as they might be, could one draw from this review of the experience of technical assistance and urbanization strategiesµ

Perhaps at the outset, in thinking of the role of technical assistance in relation to the interests of the MDC's and the TWC's, it might be useful to distinguish between what might be called "taking into account" and "serving the interests" of these two sets of countries. For even if there is a likelihood that technical assistance will be designed to take into account the interests of the MDC's, the grounds for the recommendations or the adoption of urbanization strategies tend in the main to be technical rather than political. There may be political pressures to act. There may even be inadequate knowledge or will to back up that action. Nevertheless, the evidence is that urbanization strategies were designed and advocated as technical solutions for problems of efficiency and inequality in the countries where they were developed.

Japan may appear to be an exception, but it is not. For even within Japan, urbanization strategies were adopted to serve the goals of efficiency and equalization. They have not been seriously considered by Japanese officials as appropriate technical assistance policies precisely because this tool did not lend itself readily to immediate or narrow political or economic exploitation by Japan.

At this time, moreover, it is not at all clear how Japanese policies on these matters may evolve in the future. One possibility is that Japanese policy may become less narrow, i.e., less oriented to immediate self-interest. There are, after all, Japanese leaders and specialists who are concerned with Japan's leadership role and image in the international scene. Frustrated by the current official policies, they are less concerned with the material advantage gained by technical assistance and more with the ways in which Japan may be helpful to others. They have a broader image of self-interest -- one based on the assumption that the growth and prosperity of TWC's are more likely to contribute to Japan's peaceful and prosperous development than the reverse. If these views were to prevail, there would be a much greater disposition to examine and to promote the elements of the Japanese and of the MDC's urbanization experiences which might serve these ends.

Another possibility -- one perhaps even more likely to be adopted in the short or intermediate term -- is that narrow policies of selfinterest will be pursued more in the private sector than in some aspects of the public sector. Most nations, not just Japan, may be reluctant to help other nations in ways that may entail serious risks or costs for their continued development. A policy which ignores self-interest is apt to be pursued more because of ignorance or misjudgments of the consequences: once the consequences become clear, it is unlikely to survive the shock of recognition. If these views are correct, dual policies may be pursued even by nations with relatively broad-gauged leadership. The tendency then would be to render assistance in areas where there would be relatively little clear disadvantage in sharing experience or knowledge with other nations, and a more cautious policy of assistance or non-assistance in other realms. TWC's would not necessarily be blocked in pursuing activities which might be fiercely competitive in the future, but the amount of assistance and the source of that assistance may be affected by these considerations. This model may be less flattering but a more realistic and workable basis for technical assistance. Were these policies to prevail, technical assistance for urbanization policies would be an example of policies in the public sector that might prove helpful in ways that would not compromise an MDC's significant economic interests.

However, the prospects of success in urbanization strategies are still dim because of the political and economic difficulties involved in implementing such strategies. On this subject the evidence is still quite indecisive. All we know at present is that success will not come easily under any circumstances. The necessary conditions, i.e., sustained will and administrative capability, are difficult to achieve in all countries, and all the more so in the unstable political environments of many TWC's. Despite these difficulties, urbanization strategies are not likely to be abandoned since the tool is too well known and, like the surgeon's knife, will be used, misused, or even abused in the course of efforts to cope with real and pressing problems. If this surmise is correct, it behooves us to learn more and as quickly as we can, about the different kinds of environments in which urbanization strategies have been deployed so that we can gauge better the circumstances in which different strategies may work -- or (if one prefers) do the least harm.

References

Altschuler, A. (1965). 'The goals of comprehensive planning,' Journal of the American Institute of Planners, 31.

Coraggio, L. (1975). 'Polarization, development and integration,' in Regional Development Planning: International Perspectives, ed. A. Kuklinski, Leiden, the Netherlands: Sijthoff.

Economic Cooperation Bureau, (1981). Ministry of Foreign Affairs, Japan's Economic Cooperation, 5 October.

Hirschman, A.O. and C.E. Lindblom (1971). 'Economic development research and policy making: some converging views,' in A.O. Hirschman (ed.), A Bias for Hope, New Haven, Yale University Press.

Holland, S. (1976). Capital versus the Regions, London: Macmillan.

Lo, F.C. and K. Salih (1978). Growth Pole Strategy and Regional Develop ment Policy, New York: Pergamon Press.

Mera, K. (1978). 'The changing patterns of population distribution in Japan and its implications for developing countries,' in Lo and Salih, op cit., pp. 193-215.

Mera, K. 'Population concentration and regional income disparities: a comparative analysis of Japan and Korea,' in N. H. Hansen (ed.) Human Settlement Systems: International Perspectives on Structure and Public Policies, Cambridge, MA: Ballinger, pp. 155-75.

Okita, Saburo (1981). The Developing Economies and Japan, Tokyo: University of Tokyo Press.

Pakkasem, P. (1981). Symposium on Implementation of Technical Assistance, International Conference on Local and Regional Development in 1981's, 11-16 November 1981, United Nations Center for Regional Development, Nagoya, Japan.

Rodwin, L. (1981). Cities and City Planning, New York: Plenum Publishing Corporation.

Stohr, W. and F. Todtling (1978). 'An evaluation of regional policies: experiences in market and mixed economies,' in N.H. Hansen (ed.), Human Settlement Systems: International Perspectives on Structure and Public Policy, Cambridge, MA: Ballinger.

10 Urbanization and development: a new policy perspective

VICTOR F. S. SIT

1. The Issue of Urbanization

Urbanization as a subject for academic examination is still very much in its youthful age, although as an important process in transforming human society, it may be dated back hundreds, or even over a thousand years, depending on different definitions.

In contemporary usage we normally reserve the term "urbanization" for the growth of cities after the Industrial Revolution. And, it is fairly well accepted that this process involves three major components: (1) an economic transformation whereby a basically agricultural economy is turning into a predominantly non-farm or manufacturing economy; (2) a spatial transformation in the distribution of population whereby cities grow in number and size and the relative proportion of the population living in cities increases, and (3) a social transformation whereby a formerly rural society is turning into an urban society whose individual members behave in such a way that they are qualified as "urbanites." Indeed, such a view of urbanization offers us a very good starting point for examining the process itself. The three components already put the vital ingredients of "economy" (achievement of material wealth), "people," and "space" together. These are not just the key considerations in regional planning, but are what governments should care about, above all things, in the governance of their respective countries.

Despite the rich and significant connotation of the process of urbanization, post WWII works on urbanization contribute little to our positive understanding of the full meaning of the process and pay little attention to the achievement of national development through urbanization. There have been, of course, a number of significant works done on world urbanization in general which gave us a much better grasp than before on the level and pace of urbanization in the regions of the world even down to individual countries. These works are typified by the numerous publications of Kingley Davis. (See Davis 1969, 1972). Another collection of urbanization studies accumulated over the 60s and 70s is primarily related to the demographic dynamics of urbanization and one of its major components, rural-urban migration.(Sovani and Eames, 1966; Eames, 1967; Robock 1968; Lewis 1965).

In his earlier work Kingley Davis (1954) attempted to relate urbanization with development. More serious and large-scale attempts in that regard by Goldstein and Sly were completed and published only in 1977. The Population Division of ESCAP is currently organizing yet another cross-country comparative study on urbanization which relates urbanization and economic development in the Asian Pacific Region.[1] It indicates a new movement toward more policy discussion.

Despite some recent developments, the main stream of urbanization studies, even up till now, has been busy with the grappling of statistics and the measuring of flows and levels of population movement. It has only weakly and timidly treated the process in policy discussions, whereas, in the real world, the process has been moving quickly, especially in the past two decades, to become the underpinning of many national economic, social, and political issues. Nor is the process within the confine of the urban arena. It is now an issue involving both the city and the country. It in fact works throughout the whole national space. Hence, understanding and mastering the basic laws of contemporary urbanization becomes an important key to national development and planning (see Friedmann 1973).

2. Urbanization in Developing Countries

Despite the positive contributions of previous studies to our understanding of urbanization, some analysts also exposed certain ungrounded fears and sometimes even misconcepts. Many of these fears, unfortunately, are related to the developing countries. One of them is the generally exaggerated imminent urban exposure of the developing countries. The other is that urbanization is quite often regarded as a negative process for the developing countries.

The lack of sufficient time series data and acceptable parameters maybe responsible for the sort of projections one often comes across in urbanization literature of the 60s and 70s. Between 1950-1970, the urban population of the world had increased 92%, an average rate of about 30 million persons a year. The projections for the period 1970-2000 indicated another 150% increase which would then push the overall urbanization level of the world to 51% (Goldstein and Sly 1977). The assumption was that world urban population would increase at an average rate of about 50 million a year. Besides, it was further assumed that the rate of increase in the developing countries would be 3 times the rate of the developed countries.

It is yet not possible to say pointedly that these projections are entirely wrong, since we still have 20 more years before we reach the year 2000, and since for many countries of the world, precise figures for the 1980 urban population are still unavailable. However, there are indications that the developing countries might have passed the prime rate in urbanization and population growth and are now moving at a much slower and more relaxed pace in both. Table 1, which covers the ASEAN (except

---

[1] This is the "Comparative Study of Migration, Urbanization in Relation to Development in the ESCAP Region". The first country report was published in 1980: ESCAP Migration, Urbanization and Development in the Republic of Korea, Bangkok, 1980.

TABLE 1

THE URBANIZATION PROCESS IN ASEAN
(except Singapore), 1950-1980

	1950	1960	1970	1980
Urban population as % of total population	14.5	17.1	20.5	22.5
% increase of urban population over 10-year period	--	48.7	51.6	35.0
% increase of population over 10-year period	--	26.5	26.2	23.00

Source: Computed from various sources

the city-state Singapore), may illustrate these possible new trends. The fastest rate of urbanization was found in the decade 1960-1970, during which the urban population of the region increased slightly over half. The immediate post war decade (1950-60) was also a hectic ten years, and the relative gain in urban population was only slightly lower than the following decade. However, the drop in the pace of urbanization in the 1970s was sizeable and obvious, although in general there was a gain in the level of urbanization. The decline of the pace of urbanization in the 1970s was significantly matched by an obvious drop in the rate of population growth. For these countries, we therefore have genuine reasons to doubt whether the pessemistic urban future predicted for the year 2000 will be relevant for them.

Secondly, the hectic pace of urbanization which formed the basis for many of our existing projections for the future, has indeed seldom been examined in its proper historic context. What people often pinpointed are its visually obvious ill-consequences, such as the lack of a başic urban infrastructure in the big cities to meet the sudden increase of urban population, and the resultant mushrooming of squatters and the expansion of unemployed and underemployed in the informal sectors. Nevertheless, no sufficient consideration has been given to two things which give us a better perspective of these phenomena. First, national independence and the initial national development drive immediately after independence logically bolstered the capital cities and hence attracted disproportionately large rural-urban migration towards them. Such developments, however, may experience a different turn when the national governments become established and more experienced and matured. Second, there seemed to exist a theoretical as well as a real limit to the amount of "excess" population in the countryside to sustain the level of rural-urban migration, given that technological innovations have not yet filtered down to the countryside of the developing countries. Rural-urban migration leads reduces the manpower required for maintaining the rural economy. It can only rise to a certain level, if that limit is reached, the overall pace of urbanization will be much constrained, since rural-urban migration has been the predominant factor for urban population increase, especially for the capital cities (Table 2).

TABLE 2

ESTIMATES OF MIGRANTS AS A PERCENTAGE OF RECENT
POPULATION INCREASES

City	Period	%
Abidjan	1955-63	76
Bogota	1956-66	33
Bombay	1951-61	52
Caracas	1950-60	54
	1960-66	50
Djakarta	1961-68	59
Istanbul	1950-60	68
	1960-65	65
Lagos	1952-62	75
Nairobi	1961-69	50
Sao Paulo	1950-60	72
	1960-67	68
Seoul	1955-65	63
Taipei	1950-60	40
	1960-67	43

Source: World Bank, Urbanization (Sector Working Paper), June 1972, p. 80.

However, it is often on the foundation of these superficial ill-consequences and the assumption of a continual sizeable rural-urban migration stream that post-war urbanization in developing countries has been given a negative connotation.

The situation of the ASEAN countries in the 1970's reinforced the above worries regarding the traditional wisdom on urbanization trends in the world in general, and that of the developing countries in particular.

3. New Perspectives in Urbanization Studies

The much cherished practice of the late 60s and early 70s in urbanization studies of relating and accounting for urbanization by pursuing changes in fertility rates, family size, medical and health situations, etc., has to be broadened out to include investigation into the interrelation between urbanization and the major national events of given time sections. Nor should we assess and measure rural-urban migration and hence urbanization on the basis of personal desires and wants of the individual alone. We have to pay heed to the collective will of the people, often expressed in the form of government plans and policies.

Indeed, we can find convenient examples in South East Asia that governments, especially since the 1970s, are becoming more and more involved in directing the course of development of the urbanization of their respective country. In the Philippines, a new ministry was set up in 1978, the Ministry of Human Settlements, which wants to work through a reasonable restructuring of the settlement hierarchy to achieve more equity and development for the nation. In Malaysia, the Urban Development Authority which was also created in the 1970s, is responsible to bring in a large Malay element into the urban centres to put the principle of "restructuring of society" into practice in the case of the urbanization issue. Thus there is no lack of evidence that urbanization has, in practice, been used as a significant policy tool for obtaining national goals of equity and development. And, perhaps this has produced the drop of the rate of urbanization in ASEAN in the 1970's as indicated in Table 1. Moreover, many of these policies and programmes have very strong "teeth," as they are in close alignment with major national development goals. When such governments are more on their feet, the effects of these policies would be enhanced. There is, consequently, an imminent need to direct urbanization studies towards goals of national planning and development, and to relate the present process to relevant policies and programmes.

In addition to the above reorientation, we may perhaps also need to breach the confine of some of our traditional concepts. For example, the ideal pattern and level of urbanization of a country at a given time may not be decided by its level of economic development. Inversely, it may rather conform with the national development goals of the time. And, as national development goals differ among nations (based on different ideological lines and difficult racial situations, etc.), it may equally seem appropriate to take the case study approach in urbanization studies.

4. Summary and Conclusion

We have said in the beginning that the term urbanization has a rich connotation, involving the elements of "economy," "people," and "space." Hence, logically, an ideal urbanization policy should try to achieve the "spacing" or clustering of people so that they will be conveniently supplied with jobs and services. The "economy" will also be so "spaced" to achieve efficiency (and hence growth) to sustain the increasing welfare of the population. The shift of focus in urbanization studies towards the testing of such goals is not only theoretically desirous (as it will bring a better understanding of the process), but it will at the same time make such studies much more meaningful and practical.

References

Davis, Kingley. (1969). World Urbanization, 1950-1970, Vol. 1, Berkeley: University of California Press.

_____, (1972). World Urbanization, 1950-1970, Vol. 2, Berkeley: University of California, Press.

Davis, Kingley and H.H. Golden, (1954). 'Urbanization and economic development of pre-industrial areas,' Economic Development and Cultural Change 3:1-13.

Eames, E. (1967). 'Urban migration and joint family in a North Indian Village,' Journal of Development Areas 1:2, 163-78.

Friedmann, J. (1973). Urbanization, Planning, and National Development, Los Angeles: Sage Publications.

Goldstein, S. and D. Sly, (eds.), (1977). Patterns of Urbanization: Comparative Country Studies, Vols. 1 and 2, Dolhain: IUSSP.

Lewis, O. (1965). 'Urbanization without breakdown: a case study,' in B.H. Dwight et al. (ed.), Contemporary Cultures and Societies of Latin America, New York: Random House, pp. 424-37.

Robock, S.H. (1968). The Rural Push for Urbanization in Latin America: The Case of Northeast Brazil, Occasional Paper No. 1, East Lansing: Michigan State University.

Sovani, N.V. and E. Eames (1966). 'Some notes on in-migrants in Indian cities,' in Urbanization and Urban India, New York: Asia Publishing House, pp. 142-55.

11 Spatial strategies and infrastructure planning in the metropolitan areas of Bombay and Calcutta

HARRY W. RICHARDSON

1. Introduction

This paper examines spatial planning strategies and their implications for the location and scale of intrastructure investments in
India's two largest cities, Bombay and Calcutta. In fact, the scale of
the analysis is that of the metropolitan region, namely the BMR (Bombay
Metropolitan Region) and the CMD (Calcutta Metropolitan District).
(See Map 1 and Map 2.) The BMR has an area of 4,350 km^2 and a
population of about 9.7 million, of which more than three-quarters live
in Greater Bombay. The CMD stretches north and south for nearly 70 km.
along both sides of the River Hooghly. Its population is close to ten
million, of whom about three million live in the City of Calcutta. In
1970, the GOWB (Government of West Bengal) established the CMDA
(Calcutta Metropolitan Development Authority) and gave it overall
responsibility for the planning, design and construction of public
works in the CMD. After some early problems, it has evolved into an
effective public works agency, though it has yet to become a successful
planning authority. BMRDA (Bombay Metropolitan Region Development
Authority) was established in 1975 to' coordinate the activities of
local authorities within BMR and to promote regional investment
planning. It has been much less successful than CMDA, due to a variety
of reasons including the strength of preexisting developmental agencies
(such as the Bombay Municipal Corporation), initial political mistakes,
and a small technical staff.

2. Economic Performance

Any comparison of spatial strategies and their implications for
infrastructure planning in Bombay and Calcutta must start from the very
different performances of their economies. The Bombay economy is quite
strong. Its economic base is oriented towards international and
national rather than regional markets, it has a vigorous and
diversified manufacturing sector (accounting for two-fifths of the
labor force), and the city is India's leading financial and business
center. With about one-twentieth of India's urban population, Bombay
generates one-tenth of the nation's industrial jobs, two-elevenths of
manufacturing value added and handles more than one-quarter of the
country's foreign trade. Despite a weak performance in 1974-5,
reflecting the city's openness and consequent vulnerability to world
recession, industrial production has been growing in recent years at a
rate of almost 7 percent, industrial employment by 2 percent and per
capita income by about 6 percent. Moreover, these gains have been

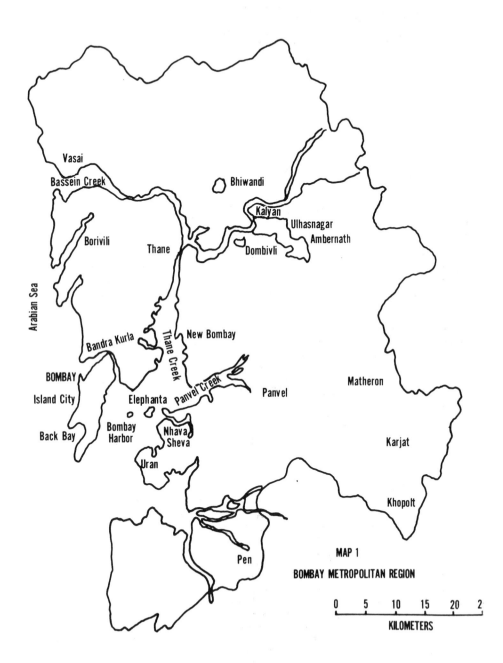

Vasai

Bassein Creek

Bhiwandi

Kalyan

Ulhasnagar
Ambernath

Borivili

Thane

Dombivli

Arabian Sea

Bandra Kurla

Thane Creek

New Bombay

BOMBAY

Island City

Elephanta

Panvel Creek

Matheron

Panvel

Back Bay

Bombay
Harbor

Nhava
Sheva

Karjat

Uran

Khopolt

Pen

MAP 1

BOMBAY METROPOLITAN REGION

0   5   10   15   20   2

KILOMETERS

114

MAP 2

CALCUTTA METROPOLITAN DISTRICT

NADIA

Bansberia
Kalyani
Kanchrapara
Halisahar

HOOGHLY

Hooghly-
Chinsurah
Naihati

Chander
nagar
Bhatpara

Bhadreshwar

Champdani
Garulia
N.
Baidyabati
Barrackpore

Barrackpore

Serampore
Titagarh
24 PARGANAS
Barasat
Rishra
Khardah

Konnagar
Panihati
New
Barrack
pore
Uttarpara
Kotrung
HOOGHLY
N. Dum

Kamarhati

Baranagar

Bally
Dum Dum
Kona
RIVER
S. Dum Dum
Howrah

Salt Lake

HOWRAH

Sarenga
Garden
Reach
CALCUTTA
CORPORATION
AREA

Bauria

Uluberia
Budge Budge
S. Suburban
Jadavpur

24 PARGANAS

Raipur

0   5   10   15
Kilometers

0   2   4   6   8
Miles

achieved with a negligible inflation rate by international standards. In addition, there is impressionistic evidence that some of the benefits of metropolitan economic growth have "trickled down," especially since 1975, though the improvement in living standards has been largely influenced by a dramatic improvement in the food supply situation.

The Calcutta economy, on the other hand, is quite weak, and has remained weak over a long period of time. Although Calcutta had recovered by the late 1950s from the loss of part of its natural hinterland by partition, it has more recently been plagued with many problems: power shortages, raw material limitations, shortage of capital, a reputation for labor troubles, and chronic excess capacity. The industrial structure is weak, dominated by traditional industries (e.g., textiles, heavy engineering, jute, rubber, and paper), many of them so "sick" that they have had to be taken over by the State government. Employment in the CMD has nevertheless increased very slowly because some service industries have continued to expand, although the largest source of service employment -- the Port of Calcutta -- has severely contracted its labor force. No major new industries have come into Calcutta in recent years, and the GOWB has reconciled itself to the view that CMD's industrial growth depends on the rehabilitation of existing industries, diversification of existing plants into new product lines, and the expansion of small-scale industry, especially outside the core areas.[1] Industrial stagnation is so severe that net inmigration into the CMD has dried up and living standards have probably declined, certainly in relative and possibly in absolute terms. The prospects for industrial revival, bleak in any event, are made even bleaker by national policies, such as the ban on new large- and medium-scale industry in large cities and measures that deprive West Bengal of its natural locational advantages, e.g., the nationwide steel price equalization scheme and coal freight rates that absorb freight costs for distant consumers.

The contrast in performance of the two metropolitan economies suggests somewhat different spatial planning implications. In Bombay's case, the growth of the economy, actual and potential, continues to generate pressure for decentralization. However, forcing the pace of decentralization by imposing negative controls in the Island City, such as F.S.I. (floor space index) controls, bans on new industrial firms and the prohibition of building development, could eventually threaten thestability of the central city and jeopardize the economic base of the metropolis and hence its prosperity. This argument implies that metropolitan planners should respond to spontaneous decentralization trends rather than push economic activities (and people) to places where they do not want to go. The choice of locations for planning actions in the BMR is made easier by the fact that some areas, especially the Kalyan Complex, have grown rapidly in the past and suffer from severe infrastructure lags.

The implications in the Calcutta case are not the same. The first

[1] M.G. Kutty, "Metropolitan Calcutta and Economic Action" (1979). Industrial production in West Bengal in 1977 remained 10 percent below the level of 1965, and the CMD accounts for more than 80 percent of the State's industry.

question is whether physical planning (and especially industrial infrastructure investment) can be undertaken in a way that stimulates industrial development. There is little ground for optimism here, since it
is unlikely that the availability of infrastructure will succeed where
incentives and market forces have failed. A second issue is how to
adjust the spatial strategy of the CMD to a steady state economy. The
most obvious point is that the prognosis for the economy does not favor
ambitious spatial extensions to the metropolitan region by opening up
new areas. A compact and congested metropolitan Calcutta may be consistent with the poor performance of the local economy and the low living
standards of the population.

3. Population Distribution in the BMR and the CMD

Tables 1 and 2 display some population distribution data for the
BMR and the CMD. The most important generalization from both tables is
that there has been spontaneous decentralization out of the central city
in both metropolitan areas (and this trend has probably accelerated
since the 1971 Census). In the BMR, the population of Island City
barely increased in the 1960s while the population of South Bombay
actually declined. Onthe other hand, the population of the suburbs
increased at an annual rate of 7 3/4 percent, that of Thane by 6 1/4
percent, and of the Kalyan Complex by more than 6 percent. None of the
peripheral urban areas, whether in the New Bombay or elsewhere in the
BMR, grew as fast as these three areas. In Calcutta, the share of the
Calcutta Corporation area fell markedly from 50 to 38 percent in the
twenty-year period 1951-71, while Howrah's share declined slightly.
The shares of some other municipalities increased sharply, including
Barrackpore, Panihati, Kamarhati, North and South Dum Dum, South
Suburban, Baidyabati, Rishra, and Uttarpara. Although the population
share of municipalities on the East Bank fell, this was because of more
rapid population growth in non-municipal areas rather than because of
population shifts from the East to the West Bank. The undeniable
growth potential of the West Bank municipalities is still held back by
the limited number of crossings over the River Hooghly.

4. Spatial Strategy for the BMR

From the perspective of Bombay's planners and policymakers, the
dominant issue in the metrpolis is the spatial distribution of population and economic activity. The Bombay Metropolitan Regional Plan of
1970 diagnosed most of the city's ills as a product of excessive spatial
concentration in South Bombay, and proposed a decentralization strategy
to combat this problem. This theme has continued to dominate the
thoughts and policies of local planners, for example in BMC's revision
of the City Development Plan and in the "Optimal Regional Structure"
document circulated by BMRDA in 1977. The idea, most clearly expressed
in the ORS paper, is to develop a policentric spatial structure based
on four major centers (South Bombay, Bandra-Kurla, New Bombay and Kalyan
Complex) to replace the monocentricity resulting from the heavy spatial
concentration in South Bombay.[2]

---

[2] The central argument of ORS is that the costs of providing housing,
water supply and transportation are much lower over the periods
1971-86and 1986-2001 with a policentric spatial structure than with
continued spatial concentration in South Bombay. The analysis

TABLE 1
POPULATION GROWTH IN THE BMR, 1961-71

| | Population ('000) | | Rate of Growth (%) |
	1961	1971	
Greater Bombay and Thane	4,257.2	6,163.4	4.48
South Bombay	686.8	671.7	-0.22
Rest of Island City	2,085.1	2,398.7	1.41
Suburbs	1,032.1	2,161.7	7.67
Extended Suburbs	348.0	738.5	7.83
Thane Agglomeration	105.1	192.8	6.26
Kalyan Comples	262.6	422.4	6.08
Dombivli	18.4	51.1	10.75
Kalyan	73.5	99.5	3.08
Mohone	7.3	11.3	4.47
Katemanivali	5.8	9.6	5.17
Ulhasnagar	107.8	168.5	4.57
Kulgaon	3.6	6.8	6.57
Badlapur	3.6	4.7	2.70
Ambernath	34.5	56.3	5.02
Kalwa	8.1	14.6	6.07
Rest of urban region	160.8	248.0	5.42
Bhayandar	7.0	10.6	4.24
Bassein	22.6	30.6	3.08
Manikpur	4.6	7.6	5.15
Sandor	5.6	6.7	1.81
Virar	9.4	12.7	3.05
Bhiwandi	47.6	79.6	5.28
Uran	10.2	12.6	2.14
Panvel	19.7	26.6	3.05
Neral	5.6	8.1	3.78
Matheran	2.8	3.4	1.96
Karjat	5.1	5.6	0.94
Khopoli	1.0	18.2	33.66
Alibag	9.9	11.6	1.60
Pen	9.5	--	--
Rasayani	--	2.0	--
Regional Rural	710.0	957.9	3.49
Total	5,551.4	7,791.6	4.03

TABLE 2

SHARE OF MUNICIPALITIES IN CMD POPULATION, 1951 AND 1971
AND POPULATION DENSITIES, 1971

	(%)		Density. 1971
	1951	1971	(per Km.2)
East Bank	69.91	63.06	--
Calcutta (Corporation)	50.25	37.79	30,278
Kanchrapara	1.06	0.95	8,684
Halisahara	0.65	0.83	4,839
Naihati	1.03	0.99	18,869
Bhatpara	2.51	2.46	17,120
Garulia	0.53	0.53	11,410
N. Barrackpore	0.60	0.91	9,066
Barrackpore	0.79	1.16	8,317
Titagarh	1.33	1.06	27.228
Khardah	0.35	0.39	8,325
Panihati	0.92	1.78	7,919
Kamarhati	1.44	2.03	15,457
Baranagar	1.44	1.64	19,219
Barasat	0.30	0.51	5,686
New Barrackpore	--	0.39	11,211
N. Dum Dum	0.22	0.77	4,094
Dum Dum	0.26	0.38	15,682
S. Dum Dum	1.14	2.09	11,477
Garden Reach	2.03	1.86	11,962
Budge Budge	0.60	0.61	6,569
S. Suburban	1.94	3.27	8,973
Rajpur	0.30	0.41	1,639
Baruipar	0.17	0.25	2,260
West Bank	15.49	15.97	--
Howrah (Corporation)	9.25	8.86	11,998
Bansberia	0.57	0.74	12,608
Hooghly-Chinsurah	1.06	1.26	6,722
Bhadreshgar	0.68	0.55	7,046
Champdari	0.58	0.70	9,057
Baidyabati	0.46	0.65	5,975
Serampore	1.38	1.22	17,351
Rishra	0.51	0.76	19,594
Konnagar	0.38	0.41	7,950
Uttarpara	0.58	0.81	9,320
Non-municipal areas	14.60	21.97	--
Total	100.00	100.00	

Source: CMDA, Development Perspective and Investment Plan (1976), p. 1-13, 1-14, 1-16.

This objective is pursued with the aid of several policy instruments such as the location of industry controls embodied in the State's location of industry policy developed after 1974[3] and the F.S.I. land use controls imposed by BMC and reinforced by BMRDA.

The important question for the outside analyst is whether the perceived problem is the real problem. The answer is not clear. Undoubtedly, there are congestion effects (e.g., traffic congestion) resulting from the spatial concentration of jobs in South Bombay and exacerbated by the geography of the Island City which forces both people and commodity flows through a very restricted number of North-South arteries. However, spontaneous decentralization trends have been evident since the 1940s.

The experience of Western countries suggest that it is very difficult to "fine tune" city control strategies. There is a danger that decentralization policies may be implemented so strongly that the decline of the urban core becomes cumulative. It is difficult to carry out an effective decentralization strategy since no one has been able to determine an optimal rate of decentralization.

On the other hand, there are arguments to support the case for a policentric less centralized metropolitan spatial structure. Land constraints in South Bombay make it difficult to expand the transportation system, to strengthen the city's industrial base[4] and to improve the housing situation except by investments on the periphery of the metropolitan area. Also, certain types of urban infrastructure (e.g., a water supply system) may be cheaper to build outside the central city than in the urban core. Of course, demonstrating the benefits of a decentralized spatial structure does not imply that policymakers should attempt to force it rather than allowing it to happen naturally.

The most reasonable position is that the spatial distribution issue in Bombay does merit the attention of local planners, but it does not justify their almost total preoccupation with the matter. A major explanation of its importance is that alternative spatial strategies

---

2 (continued from page   ) suffers from poor assumptions, such as the rapid growth of New Bombay, inadequate allowance for rising land costs, and neglect of the benefits side, especially the economies of agglomeration in South Bombay.

3 This policy has been more effective in controlling the growth of large- and medium- than of small-scale industry, and it has been more restrictive in the Kalyan Complex and the suburbs than in Island City. The explanation is that some industries would have decentralized in the absence of the policy because it was efficient to do so and that the manufacturing sector in South Bombay is small (only 7.2 percent of Greater Bombay's manufacturing labor force). Also, a major industry in Island City (the cotton textiles industry) is exempt from the controls.

4 Manufacturing industry has a preference for suburban sites if they are served with adequate infrastructure.

imply different sectoral investment decisions. For instance, attention to the office sector implies an emphasis on New Bombay or Bandra-Kurla rather than the Kalyan Complex.[5] Conversely, emphasis on manufacturing favors the Kalyan Complex or New Bombay rather than Bandra-Kurla. Moreover, choosing a particular decentralization strategy involves a decision to invest either ahead of demand (i.e., at New Bombay) or in response to existing demand (i.e., the Kalyan Complex). Similarly, it is difficult to formulate a regional transportation plan without taking a stand on the most likely (or most feasible) spatial structure for the metropolitan region. Finally, a decision to go ahead with certain key investment decisions, such as the Nhava Sheva port or the Thal fertilizer plant, has certain consequential implications for the rate and pattern of regional infrastructure investment. Thus, since major sectoral investments have direct locational implications, the question of spatial distribution cannot be ignored. The only issue is how strongly planners should intervene to guide the pattern of decentralization in a desired direction or whether it would be more efficient to respond to spontaneous decentralization trends. If planners choose the first alternative, and if it involves measures to control the expansion of economic activity in the central core (i.e., in South Bombay), the decentralization strategy may incur a high penalty in terms of lost economic growth.

A brief discussion of the growth potential of the three main candidates for decentralization is appropriate. Nhava-Sheva becomes a fourth candidate as the port project goes ahead. Bandra-Kurla is a secondbest option, since its relief to congestion in South Bombay would be marginal and because reclamation and land development costs are high. The Kalyan Complex is already booming, but its continued growth is severely handicapped by the lag in housing, urban and industrial infrastructure, and

---

[5] If congestion in Island City in general and South Bombay in particular is a problem, the concentration of office employment is much more serious than the concentration of manufacturing employment. Office jobs account for one-fifth of Greater Bombay's labor force, but 82% of these are in Island City, 62% in South Bombay, and 47% in A Ward. Much of the concentration in the CBD is accounted for by the quaternary sector-finance, banking and insurance, business corporations, and government. Nevertheless, there is some evidence of office decentralization into the suburbs, though most of the offices involved are small, commercial establishments. A stronger decentralization of offices would have a marked impact in reducing congestion in South Bombay, but the forces of agglomeration remain powerful. The effective method of inducing decentralization is to persuade a cluster of major employers to relocate simultaneously. The state government has refused to relocate to New Bombay, though some quasi-governmental agencies are interested in the shorter move to Bandra-Kurla. The strategy of using F.S.I. controls as an instrument for influencing the location of private offices is dangerous because, in the absence of the offer of equally attractive locations, negative controls impede the efficiency of the metropolitan economy. The use of subsidies and tax concessions might be more effective if the necessary financial resources could be mobilized. Fiscal disincentives might also be considered, but they could lead to higher operating costs rather than to relocation.

social services. Its municipalities have weak fiscal bases, and the transport services linking the towns in the complex are poor. There is an immediate need for major public investments in the area, and the high proportion of population in the EWS and LIG categories suggests that policies to increase the Kalyan Complex's absorptive capacity would impact favorably on the urban poor. The ambitious New Bombay project shows few signs of taking off. Its progress has been hampered by the failure of offices to relocate there, the lack of social infra-structure (e.g., schools and hospitals), and the precarious financial situation of its sponsoring agency, CIDCO. To make it succeed on something close to its original scale would require a massive and sustained injection of public capital. It would be wiser to abandon the idea in favor of a modestly sized Vashi New Town, where some infrastructure investments are in place. Wholesale markets are being relocated there, and there are some prospects for an inland water terminal.

The policymakers' priority rankings among the decentalization nodes are New Bombay, then Bandra-Kurla and finally the Kalyan Complex. On pragmatic grounds, Bandra-Kurla may be assuming the first priority because its scale is more manageable and there is evidence of an effective demand for its sites. Yet a commonsense ranking of priorities would reverse this sequence: the Kalyan Complex is a natural and vigorous growth center, New Bombay is faltering and the Bandra-Kurla project is not yet under way. The policymakers' preferences can be explained in terms of the self-financing potential of investments in New Bombay and Bandra-Kurla compared with those in the Kalyan Complex. The office sector favors Bandra-Kurla because of New Bombay's lack of infrastructure and the Kalyan Complex's heavy industrial base.

As for the minor candidates, Nhava-Sheva port, and to a lesser extent the fertilizer plant at Thal, will provide the nucleus for secondary centers. However, the decision to proceed with these projects has been taken on national economic grounds without consideration of their consistency with a decentralization strategy for the BMR. In fact, although they would attract substantial auxiliary activities, it is unclear that these projects would help very much in decongesting population out of South Bombay. Instead, they may attract population from the rest of the BMR, elsewhere in Maharashtra, and from other states. In other words, they may promote further growth of the BMR much more than the spatial restructuring of the metropolitan region.

The major growth centers are competitive rather than complemen-tary.[6] The development of Bandra-Kurla will undercut the office potential of New Bombay. Aothough expansion of the Kalyan Complex is so expensive that it would absorb public investment resources that might be used to promote New Bombay, it is a sounder decentralization prospect because the case for industrial decentralization is stronger than the case for office decentralization and because it is easier to identify beneficial impacts on the poor. Offices can be decentralized on any major scale only in the long run, and probably only to New

---

[6] A qualification is that the decision to build Nhava-Sheva port should encourage a more rapid expansion of New Bombay.

Bombay. Their continued concentration in South Bombay may be for the present both efficient (due to the economies of agglomeration) and more equitable. Higher congestion and operating costs may be passed on to clients and consumers who are not the urban poor while the time costs of congestion are higher for the well-off.

5. Spatial Strategy for the CMD

The spatial strategy recommended in the Basic Development Plan (BDP) for 1966-86 was that of a bipolar metropolitan structure with the promotion of Kalyani-Bansberia in the north of the CMD as a counter-magnet to the Calcutta-Howrah core. In spite of substantial infra-structure investments to promote Kalyani in the years that followed, development there never ":took off" on the required scale.[7] The Development Perspective and Investment Plan (DPIP) of 1976 recognized this, and the bipolar strategy was formally abandoned. This was a wise decision, because a bipolar approach is theoretically and practically unsustainable (since no second center can compete effectively with the original CBD and central core). If conditions permit a change in urban spatial structure from a monocentric pattern, the appropriate replacement is a policentric structure with the emergence of several satellite subcenters at a distance from the core. These subcenters are presumed to serve the peripheral areas of the metropolitan region at lower cost than the central core, because of lower rents and distribution costs and a lesser degree of congestion. However, the central core remains dominant for activities where economies of scale and agglomeration are greatest, e.g., high-order quaternary functions.

The DPIP, not unexpectedly, came out in favor of a "multicentric" or "polynodal" strategy aimed to achieve "a more balanced spatial distribution of population and desired dispersal of economic and employment opportunities within the CMD."[8] These nodes would be based on "community groupings" of 60,000 and would be linked by a network of linear transport corridors.[9] A large number of centers are envisaged. Work is already under way in Kalyani and Salt Lake, and more recently at West Howrah and East Calcutta. These are the priority areas. In addition, another 18 centers were identified, nine on each bank of the River Hooghly.[10] A major objective of the strategy is to counteract the dominant North-South axis (on both sides of the river)

---

[7] The completion of the Kalyani Expressway and the designation of Nadia as a "backward" district in the State's industrial incentive scheme may at last help to turn Kalyani around.

[8] CMDA, Metropolitan Development Programme: 1982 to 1987, (1979), p. 21.

[9] CMDA, DPIP (1976), p. 1-36.

[10] On the West Bank the other centers are Bansberia, Hooghly-Chinsurah-Bandel, Chandernagar, Bhadreswar-Champdani, Serampur-Rishra, Uttarpara-Konnagar, Dankuni-Bally, Andul-Sankrail, and Bauria. The centers on the East Bank are Naihati-Halisahar, North Barrackpore, Barasat, North Dum Dum, Rajarhat Dum Dum, South Suburban, Budge Budge, Rajpur and Baruipur.

of the CMD by promoting an East-West axis, based on Salt Lake and East Calcutta in the East and on West Howrah and Kona in the West. There would also be secondary east-west links at Bansberia-Kalyani, Serampore-Barrackpore, Bally-Dankuni-Dhakhineswar, and Bauria-Budge Budge.

There are some problems with this policentric strategy. Strengthening the East-West axis appears logical, but its value as a means of relieving metropolitan congestion is doubtful. The promotion of Salt Lake Metro-Sub-Center as a focal point for government activities and other office developments and the promotion of Kona (in West Howrah) Business Center as a transportation and wholesale facility would create substantial traffic. Traffic could increase faster than the capacity to move it across the river, even after taking account of completion of the Second Hooghly Bridge at Princep Ghat and construction of another trans-river connection at Sovabazar. The introduction of tolls on all crossings might dampen traffic demand but probably not to the level that would relieve traffic congestion to a substantial extent. If an East-West strategy is to be successful, the feasibility of introducing multiple low-cost river crossing links (e.g., ferries) throughout the length of the CMD would have to be considered seriously.

Implementation of the multicentric strategy requires substantial infrastructure investments in many of the proposed subcenters. These investments are called New Area Development Plans (NADPs). They have absorbed no CMDA investments in the past. They currently account for 7% of the total, and CMDA recommends that this share be raised to 10%.[11] Although the proposed share remains small, marginal shifts out of other programs could squeeze them and reduce their impact. An undoubted appeal of NAD is that the constraints on development (e.g., problems of public land acquisition, land use conversion, and political and institutional obstacles) are much less severe than in the central core.[12] However, these are strong grounds for moving ahead very cautiously on the NADP program. These are based on the argument that a policentric pattern of development typically develops during conditions of rapid metropolitan growth. Calcutta is growing so slowly that the pressures for subcentring are quite weak. Emergence of a policentric structure is most effective when it develops spontaneously, with a modest degree of public sector guidance. If the metropolitan authority attempts to promote subcenters in advance of the market, there is a severe risk of wasted public investments. Such a risk is not worth taking in Calcutta because of extreme pressure on scarce capital resources.

Of course, in a world without resource constraints, there would be some virtue in reducing the high densities of Calcutta's central core.

---

[11]CMDA, "A Note on Some Basic Issues Relating to the Development Strategy for Future CMDA Programme", (January 1980, p. 13). See also Table 5.

[12]On the other hand, CMDA proposes raising the Integrated Area Upgrading Plans (IAUP) component from 22% (previously 15%) to 35% of total investments. Although most of these areas are centrally located deteriorating areas, some are peripheral areas with growth potential.

But a strategy of suburbanization and decentralization is not justified in current economic conditions. The costs of redeveloping the central areas are too high, and there is little prospect that many households would relocate in the absence of the creation of new jobs and the provision of affordable housing at the proposed new subcenters. Certainly, there are insufficient stimuli from outside Calcutta (i.e., the entry of new firms and the arrival of new immigrants) to supply a base for subcenter growth. Moreover, rising energy and transportation costs increase the relative efficiency of a very compact metropolitan area compared to a highly decentralized metropolitan region. The gains from decentralization are too speculative to justify departing from a minimum investment strategy by expanding the NAD program.

6. Investment Planning and Resource Availability in the BMR

There is no regional investment planning in the BMR. The so-called "Regional Investment Plan" (RIP) developed for 1978-83 by BMRDA (see Table 3) is not a plan at all but rather the aggregation of the projects under consideration by the various public agencies. Some of these projects may not be implemented, or even started, during the Sixth Plan period. Also, the RIP is limited to four main sectors: housing and urban development, industrial area development, environmental infrastructure (predominantly water supply), and transportation. Important excluded sectors are power, telecommunications, social welfare, agriculture and animal husbandry. It does not reflect any attempt to prioritize projects across sectors, because BMRDA has no authority, or even influence, over the sectoral agencies. Five sub-sectors -- urban water supply, slum improvement and repairs, housing, mass transit, and roads and bridges -- absorb about 70% of the intended expenditures.

Many of the projects included in the RIP would help to promote decentralization out of Greater Bombay, and the areas outside Greater Bombay would reveive 30% of total investments. This reflects the fact that most public agencies have accepted the decentralization goal, so that a degree of consistency has been attained even without a coordination mechanism. However, the two main projects in RIP financed by the World Bank (the Bombay water supply and urban transportation projects) reinforce centralization in Greater Bombay. RIP implies almost a 300% increase in the nominal value of the same sector investments in the Fifth Plan, and the scale of this increase raises the question of how the investments might be financed. Since the shares of the central government (11%) and the State (14%) are quite small, (see Table 4) the burden of the plan would fall on internally generated resources and long-term loans. With respect to the latter, World Bank loans account for most of the needs under water supply and urban road transportation, but there is a major loan gap in the housing and urban development sector. The goal is to increase the share of internally generated resources, but the task is very difficult.

The problems of resource generation remain critical. For instance, the commitments of Bombay Municipal Corporation (BMC) to implement its Development Plan amount to about Rs. 1,000 crores, but its expenditures on the plan have been only Rs. 12.5 crores per year over the last decade. Its present revenues and loan-raising capacity amount to a maximum of Rs. 20 crores per year, but the Development Plan would require Rs. 50 crores (constant prices) each year up to the year 2000. The discounted value of the least-cost scenario of Optimal Regional

TABLE 3

REGIONAL INVESTMENT PLAN, 1978-9 to 1982-3
(Rs. Crores)

| Sector | Zones | | | | Total | Percentage Distribution |
	GR. Bombay	New Bombay	Kalyan Complex	Rest of Region		
Housing and Urban Development	515.79	94.42	75.79	18.30	804.30	41.7
(Zonal Distribution %)	(64.1)	(11.7)	(9.5)	(2.3)		
Housing Public and Private	179.81	37.92	46.46		264.19	13.7
Slum Improvement	113.98	1.50	5.83	2.80	124.11	6.4
Repairs and Construction	155.00	--	--	--	155.00	8.0
Village improvement	2.00	1.50	2.00	3.00	8.50	0.4
Growth centers	65.00	38.50	9.00	--	112.50	5.8
Urban social infrastructure	--	--	--	--	100.00	5.2
Establishment of 2 Corporations	--	--	12.50	12.50	25.00	1.3
Relocation of wholesale markets	--	15.00	--	--	15.00	0.8
Industrial Area Development	2.12	20.03	8.23	68.67	99.14	5.1
(Zonal Distribution %)	(2.1)	(20.2)	(8.4)	(69.3)		
Environmental Infrastructure	371.51	14.35	89.05	64.34	540.00	28.0
(Zonal Distribution %)	(68.8)	(2.7)	(16.5)	(11.9)		
Water Supply and Sewage	341.24	9.67	80.33	5.81	437.05	22.6
Rural Water Supply	--	--	--	7.46	7.46	0.4
Water Resource Development & Irrigation	28.96	--	6.98	51.02	87.46	4.5
Environmental Protection	1.31	4.68	1.74	0.05	8.03	0.4

TABLE 3 (continued)

Sector	GR. Bombay	New Bombay	Zones Kalyan Complex	Rest of Region	Total	Percentage Distribution
Transport and Communication	360.00	69.60	12.20	40.60	487.40	25.2
Zonal Distribution%	(73.9)	(14.3)	(2.5)	(8.3)		
Roads and Bridges	145.90	10.10	5.10	13.60	174.70	9.0
Mass Transit (Rail)	108.30	10.00	--	2.70	121.00	6.3
Mass Transit (Road)	53.70	11.40	4.00	7.00	76.10	3.9
Goods Transport (Rail)	9.30	4.00	3.10	17.30	33.70	1.7
Goods Transport (Road)	1.00	--	--	--	1.00	0.05
Inland Water Transport:						
Infrastructure	--	8.60	--	--	8.60	0.4
Mass Transit	0.50	0.50	--	--	1.00	0.05
Port	41.30	25.00	--	--	66.30	3.4
Surveys and Research	--	--	--	--	5.00	0.4
Total	1,249.42	198.40	185.36	191.91	1,930.84	100.0
Zonal Distribution%	(64.7)	(10.3)	(9.6)	(9.9)		

Source: BMRDA, Regional Investment Plan for BMR, 1977-8 to 1982-3 (1978), pp. 17-19.

127

TABLE 4

SOURCES OF FINANCING FOR REGIONAL INVESTMENT PLAN
1978-9 to 1982-3
(Rs. Crores)

Sector	Internal Resources	Long-term Loans	Central Govt.	State Govt. and other public bodies	Total Investment
Housing and Urban Development	365	337	---	138	840[1]
Industrial Area Development	77	15	---	7	99
Water Supply, Sewerage and Environmental Protection	147	288[2]	---	105	540
Transportation	163	733	217	34	487
Total	752	723	217	284	1,966
Percentage Distribution	38.3	36.8	11.0	14.4	100

Source: BMRDA, Regional Investment Plan for BMR, 1977-8 to 1982-3 (1978), p. 89.

[1]This does not match the Rs. 804.3 crores given in Table 3 , because the housing component here represents Rs.300 crores rather than Rs. 264.2 crores. The difference is due to a surplus generated through land disposal.

[2]World Bank loan component is Rs. 288 crores.

[3]World Bank loan component is Rs. 41.3 crores.

Structure is about Rs. 2000 crores.

There is little scope for financing these programs by more assistance from the Central and State governments, because their priorities (power, irrigation, agricultural development, and provision of minimum needs) are likely to accelerate the shift from urban or rural investments. The shares of the urban-oriented sectors (industry, transport, social services) have declined in the Sixth Plan.

In view of this situation, there is a pressing need to increase the revenue potential of local governments and other public agencies. The small municipalities in the BMR (e.g., those in the Kalyan Complex) have very limited financial resources, aggravated by the tendency of large industrial firms to locate outside municipal boundaries. CIDCO is handicapped by having to borrow 15-year loans on the open market and the laggardly sale of developed land in New Bombay. The two key agencies operating in the BMR are, of course, BMRDA and BMC. BMRDA has several sources of finance available under the BMRDA Act, but the constraints on their use have inhibited spending. The originally intended land developmental role has been abandoned, except in Bandra-Kurla. BMC has adopted conservative fiscal policies and has consequently maintained a sound financial position. With little grant income, the Corporation has relied on outside borrowing (up to 20% of total revenues), expecially for transport and water supply. The budget has remained in surplus, with the surplus (and revenue generated from increasing user charges) used to meet capital expenditure commitments. The contributions of tax revenues and user charges are approximately equal, but tax revenue growth has been very sluggish. The property tax yield is low because of rent control and statutory limits on the tax rate, and the octroi yield has been affected by industrial decentral-ization. Revenues per capita remain low, and the provision of services has lagged behind population growth.

7. Investment Planning and Resource Availability in the CMD

The Basic Development Plan (BDP) of 1966 provided the overall policy framework for planning in the CMD and included Sectoral Master Plans for water supply, sewerage and drainage, and traffic and transportation. These plans provided the base for the CMDA investment program that began in 1970. This program consisted of Rs. 150 crores of investment, covering about 100 projects in water supply, sewerage and drainage, traffic and transportation, bustee improvement, garbage disposal, housing redevelopment and other sectors. In 1973 IDA (International Development Association, a subsidiary of the World Bank) agreed to provide financial assistance for 44 (later trimmed to 39) of the projects with a credit of Rs. 26 crores (IDA-I). This loan, originally intended to be spent by June 1977, was extended until December 1979. In 1976 the Development Perspective and Investment Plan (DPIP) was prepared to update the 1966 BDP. This has generated a five-year investment plan of Rs. 277.74 crores, including a second IDA credit of US $87 million (IDA-II).[13]

The key features of the DPIP are as follows:

---

[13] See the first row of Table 7 for the distribution of spending under this plan over the five years.

a)   A relative shift in attention from the provision of primary infrastructure to the upgrading of mainly older area (Integrated Area Upgrading Plan-IAUP) and the opening up of new areas (New Area Development Plans-NADP).

b)   The explicit abandonment of the bipolar strategy endorsed in the BDP in favor of promoting a policentric spatial structure with the eventual development of 22 centers considered to have growth potential.

c)   Priority to projects that would facilitate the "trickling down" of benefits to the urban poor, especially the EWS group.

d)   Related to b., measures to disperse economic activities and population out of the central core, not only to the strong centers but also to the non-urbanized and less developed parts of the CMD.

Since CMDA is not an economic planning agency but is primarily a public works agency, it has not developed policies that induce metropolitan decentralization. Nor has it designed projects that explicitly include an equity component, though it has suggested a "minimum standards" approach to infrastructure investment which would maximize the number of beneficiaries. Hence, its most clear-cut action to implement the objectives of the DPIP has been a shift in the pattern of its investments away from primary infrastructure in favor of area upgrading and opening up of new areas. This trend is illustrated in Table 5. In fact, there has been some redistribution in primary infrastructure investments away from water supply and roads in favor of sewerage and drainage and solid waste management. But the major shifts, already reflected in current operations but intended to be reinforced, are the expansion of IAUP and the introduction of NADP. The latter is the most dangerous aspect of the shift. Although actions are presently limited to East Calcutta, Salt Lake, West Howrah and Baishnabgahta-Patuli, extension of the NAD program to other areas, as suggested above, might waste investments and promote an excesssively dispersed pattern of metropolitan development that is not consonant with current economic conditions.

The sectoral distribution of CMDA investments during the period of the Sixth 5-year Plan is shown in Table 6. The three major sectors (water supply, traffic and transportation, and sewerage and drainage) remain dominant, accounting for more than 56% of total investments. However, area development and bustee improvement also figure prominantly with 16.0 and 10.7% of the investment program. Probably, bustee improvement and municipal and anchal development have been particularly cost-effective, and hence successful, investment programs. It is interesting that the IDA share is especially large in these two sectors, as well as in other areas where programs are relatively "soft," e.g., education and health. There is scope for the World Bank to influence the future direction of CMDA investments, hopefully by nudging them into capital-saving types of activity. Since IDA accounts for the majority of the CMDA investment program, the World Bank's ability to

TABLE 5

PATTERN OF CMDA INVESTMENTS

	Past	Present	Recommended
Primary Infrastructure	85	71	55
of which: Water Supply	32	23	10
Roads and Streets	29	22	10
Sewerage and Drainage	20	18	25
Solid Waste Management	4	8	10
Integrated Area Upgrading Plans (IAUP)	15	22	35
New Area Development Plans	0	7	10
Total	100	100	100

Source: CMDA, "A Note on Some Basic Issues Relating to the Development Strategy for Future CMDA Programme", Report 109, (1980), p. 13.

influence the sectoral distribution of future investments should be recognized.[14]

Since the five-year investment program is much larger than CMDA investments in the past (amounting to more than Rs. 342 crores after allowing for interest, sinking fund payments, and maintenance) the question arises as to whether the necessary resources are available. Table 7 sheds some light on this issue. About 56% of available resources will be in the form of government grants or transfers (mainly from the State government, and including the IDA credit), 21% will come from market borrowings, and 23% from the octroi yield. The last is the main internal resource, since 50 percent is distributed among the municipalities. The CMDA's share of octroi in 1979-80 is now expected to generate Rs. 18 crores as a result of a hike in octroi rates, and this will improve the resource deficit shown in Table 7. Nevertheless, even if the resource gap is reduced from the Rs. 83 crores suggested by the data of Table 7, it is unlikely to fall below 50 crores. Thus there is a need for additional resources, either from GOWB/GOI or from internal resources within CMDA. The prospects for the latter are relatively dim since there has been negligible cost recovery from past investments and probably only modest revenues from current and future projects (e.g., from water tariffs). Although attempts should be made to increase cost recovery, there is a conflict between the objective of

---

[14] The critical sector missing from Table 6 is, of course, power, but this is the responsibility of the Union and State governments and has been given the maximum priority in the Sixth Plan.

TABLE 6
SECTORAL DISTRIBUTION OF CMDA INVESTMENTS, 1978-1983

Sector	Investment (Rs. Crores)	Percentage Distribution	IDA Share (%)
Area Development	36.30	16.0	42.1
Bustee Improvement	24.19	10.7	79.1
Schools	2.46	1.1	87.4
Health	0.20	0.1	100.0
Water Supply	48.87	21.5	42.0
Sewerage and Drainage	36.20	16.0	59.6
Solid Waste Management	10.36	4.6	80.7
Environmental Hygiene	5.54	2.4	63.9
Traffic and Transportation	42.47	18.7	55.5
Technical Assistance	8.85	3.9	66.2
Municipal and Anchal Development	10.02	4.4	79.7
Parks	1.50	0.7	0.0
Sub-Total	226.95	100.0	56.5
Design & Supervision	28.16		34.3
Contingency	22.63		100.0
Total	277.74		57.8

TABLE 7

CMDA INVESTMENT PROGRAM AND AVAILABLE RESOURCES, 1978-83
(Rs. crores)

A. Expenditures	1978-9	1979-80	1980-1	1981-2	1982-3	Total
Project Expenditures	33.25	59.86	61.92	63.94	58.70	277.74
Interest	6.80	7.53	8.28	9.02	9.76	41.39
Sinking Fund	3.61	3.61	3.61	3.61	3.14	17.58
Maintenance	2.00	1.50	1.00	0.50	0.50	5.50
Total Expenditures	45.66	72.50	74.81	77.07	72.10	342.21

B. Resources						
Grants:						
GOI	10.47	-	-	-	-	10.47
GOWB	16.05	14.90	14.90	14.90	14.90	75.65
Additional Transfers from GOI via GOWB	-	18.62	18.13	18.62	-	55.37
Market Borrowings	11.00	11.00	11.00	11.00	11.00	55.00
Octroi	9.78	12.00	12.00	12.60	13.20	59.58
Total Resources	47.30	56.52	56.03	57.12	39.10	259.07

C. Gap	+ 1.64	-15.98	-18.78	-19.95	-33.0	-83.14

Source: CMDA, Five Year Investment Plan (1978-9 to 1982-3), Report 103 (1979), p. 12.

attaining financial viability and that of reaching the poor. In some cases, these objectives may be reconciled with cross-subsidization schemes.

The resource constraints reinforce the merits of a minimum investment strategy. CMDA has raised the issue of whether the next five year plan (1982-3 to 1986-7) should be prepared for an investment budget of Rs. 350 crores (assumed to be of similar scale to the 1978-83 Plan after allowing for inflation), Rs. 450 crores, or Rs. 550 crores. The case for the smallest budget is very strong, particularly since the expansion of the infrastructure stock will generate a need for higher maintenance expenditures.

8. "Minimum Investment" Strategies

An important guideline, especially useful in the Indian case where capital (material as well as monetary) is so scarce and where the problems of resource generation are so difficult, is caution in embarking on large-scale single-sector projects. Such a course has many pitfalls. If the project is covered by an external loan, the match requirements may distort local budget priorities, and starve other important sectors of resources. Many sectors are closely interdependent, and beneficial impacts may be maximized by the sharing of available investible resources among several sectors in a program package. Of course, multisectoral projects are more difficult to manage and the involvement of many local agencies in such a program makes coordination troublesome. Nevertheless, this practical problem is frequently outweighed by the benefits to be gained from a multi-sectoral program of projects. These benefits include: avoidance of imbalances in the public investment portfolio; recognition of the fact that most cities have many problems and infrastructure deficiencies, not merely one; and making sure that the full effectiveness of public investments in one sector is not blunted by a neglect of other sectors that are interdependent with it. For example, a housing project may need to be supported by a water supply and sanitation project and by a health project for maximum effectiveness.

An obvious means of counteracting the dangers of large projects in a capital-scarce environment is the substitution of policy innovation and institutional changes (i.e., "soft" options) for massive infrastructure investments (i.e., "hardware" projects). This implies the need to make better use of existing facilities. Examples include better management and regulation of traffic rather than building new highways, or making maximum use of the existing CBD rather than investing in expensive new subcenters (e.g., New Bombay). The latter example suggests the possibility that a decentralization strategy may be too expensive compared with maintaining the existing spatial structure.[15]

In Calcutta the minimum investment approach implies a "go slow" in for policentrism are currently weak rather than strong: the modes rate of population with possibly zero net migration; the relative economic stagnation of the metropolitan industrial base; the resource limitations; relocation costs that are relatively high with regard to the low living standards; and rising transportation costs favoring continued reliance on a compact metropolitan core. (Footnote 15 on next page).

134

There are several justifications for the minimum investment
strategy proposed here. First, the resource constraints make it
obligatory in any event, and they offer an opportunity to create a
virtue out of necessity. Second, it is doubtful whether the obstacles
to economic development, on which welfare levels ultimately depend, can
be broken down by infrastructure investments (the electric power
problem in Calcutta may be a partial exception to this generalization). Third, on similar lines, many of the metropolitan problems of
Calcutta and Bombay can be attacked with political, institutional, and
management remedies more effectively than through infrastructure
investments. These problems include public land acquisition, urban
redevelopment, housing maintenance, the promotion of small-scale
enterprises, traffic movement, the reduction of poverty, and preservation of environmental quality, among others. Another implication is
more attention to the political process that creates the environment
within which institutional reform and new policies can be introduced.
From some points of view, this is more difficult to carry out
successfully than an infrastructure investment strategy. It is
especially difficult in India where metropolitan interests are
underrepresented in both State and the Union governments, and where
dogma inhibits policy changes that might be considered desirable if
examined pragmatically (e.g., the abolition of rent control).
Obviously, a shift from hard to soft strategies implies a parallel
broadening of the functions of CMDA from its dominant public works role
to include metropolitan policymaking. This shift would require
organizational restructuring and the recruitment of new, and a
different type of, staff. Policy innovations are harder still in
metropolitan Bombay, because BMRDA is not a policy-making body and
lacks the political muscle to become one. Recognition of the value of
"soft" compared with "hard" strategies is important psychologically
because it helps to wean policymakers from the false doctrine that
metropolitan problems can be resolved by public investments, if only
the scale of investing is large and broad enough. On the other hand,
it is equally important to stress that "soft" strategies are not free;
they often require investment in human resources and if they involve
controls they may have a substantial efficiency cost.

In some situations, a response to the problems of a particular
sector will require investment in physical facilities. Even in such

---

[15]This argument appears to conflict with ORS strategy. However, that
strategy compares the cost of new investments in the suburbs with new
investments in South Bombay not the costs and benefits of investing
in the suburbs with a minimum investment strategy in South Bombay.
the NADPs. It could be argued that the New Areas of Development are
a diversion from the more critical problems in the existing
metropolitan core, since investing in new places is so much easier
than restructuring the old. Unless the pressures of demand
(population and new economic activities) are very strong, new area
investments may squander resources in the wrong places at the wrong
time. This plea for caution is not an argument against a policentric
structure for the Calcutta metropolitan region. However, such a
structure should be allowed to emerge spontaneously with planning
following rather than forcing the market. There are grounds for
believing that the forces

cases much can be done to hold down costs. In a country such as India it is vitally important that policymakers should search for low-cost solutions; improvements in existing roads rather than building new highways; sites and services rather than public housing supply; low-cost sanitation technology rather than main trunk sewer lines; improved maintenance of existing capital rather than continual investment in new facilities; and critical investments that are complementary to primary infrastructure investments already in place rather than independent of them. Of course, a focus on minimizing investment costs implies a reduction in design standards, an aim which may require policy changes to revise housing and health code standards. However, this is usually justified, since average levels of service areso low that the gains from reaching many more people outweigh the costs involved in relaxing standards. Little is known about what constitutes minimum urban service needs and what investment costs are involved in satisfying these needs, but the cost-effectiveness of following this type of strategy is hard to challenge.

Of course, there are several kinds of "soft" policy. In some circumstances controls are needed; traffic regulation and building codes are obvious examples. However, in general controls can be very costly because they hamper efficiency in resource allocation. In Bombay, the F.S.I. controls, to the extent that they are effective, may have damaged the growth of the quaternary sector, an important component of Bombay's economic base. In both cities rent controls have over a long period inhibited the growth of the housing stock and contributed to its severe undermaintenance. Industrial location controls have probably had only a moderately adverse impact in the central cities, but they have inhibited industrial expansion in the suburbs, at least in Bombay (especially in the Kalyan Complex).

Reliance on user charges have the advantage that they improve allocative efficiency rather than distort it. They help to reduce excess demand and to contribute to recovering the cost of new projects. Nevertheless, their extension in India has to be handled cautiously. The high proportion of low-income households in the population implies a danger of regressive impacts, unless cross-subsidization elements can be incorporated in new user charge schemes. Also, there may be political objections to a widespread adoption of user charges (especially in West Bengal, given the political complexion of the State government). These have to be handled delicately by treating them not as an ideologicsl instrument but as an effective and practical solution to the problems of resource generation.

Useful pricing strategies include the following measures: promoting tax-subsidy schemes as an alternative to industrial location controls; raising transit fares (since artificaly low fares comprise an implicit subsidy to centralization); providing market incentives and facilitating self-help in housing as an alternative to expanding public housing supply; and raising water tariffs to their marginal cost level and incorporating cross-subsidies to permit the extension of piped water to deprived groups.

Institutional and organizational charges are even harder to implement. One possibility is to generate new revenue sources (or to improve the yield from existing sources). For instance, octroi (though not a very efficient tax) has been a primary internal revenue source for CMDA, but has not been available to BMRDA. Property tax yields have been unacceptably low, partly because of poor collection procedures, but mainly because the basis has been imputed rental income which is artificially low as a result of rent control. The land market is a potential source of public revenue that has not been successfully tapped, largely because of the failure of the 1976 Urban Land (Ceiling and Regulation) Act and other legislation.

9. Conclusions

1. Bombay and Calcutta are spatially extensive metropolitan regions each with about ten million population. The problems of their most efficient spatial structure and infrastructure priorities are by no means trivial. Also, they are inter-related. In particular, there may be a trade-off between promoting spatial decentralization and making up the major public service deficiencies.

2. The Bombay economy is relatively strong whereas the Calcutta economy is stagnant and weak. The implication is that a decentralization strategy is more appropriate in Bombay, although even there it should be guided very cautiously rather than forced. The greatest risk in both metropolises is to squander scarce infrastructure investments in undeveloped, sparsely populated areas.

3. In recent decades there has been a degree of decentralization in both the BMR and the CMD. The central cities' share of metropolitan population has dropped markedly while some suburban areas have expanded rapidly. This redistribution of population has occurred largely as a result of spontaneous market forces rather than because of specific policy interventions.

4. The ORS (Optimal Regional Structure) document of BMRDA in 1977, an updating of the Bombay Metropolitan Regional Plan of 1970, recommended a policentric spatial structure based on four major centers (South Bombay, Bandra-Kurla, New Bombay and the Kalyan Complex) to replace the monocentricity resulting from heavy spatial concentration in South Bombay. Although there are some arguments in favor of a more decentralized pattern (land constraints, cheaper infrastructure costs, promoting jobs and low-cost housing in close proximity to each other), Bombay's policymakers have become obsessed with decentralization. It would be more efficient to respond to decentralization rather than to force it, since the latter policy might incur a high penalty in lost economic growth.

5. Policymakers favor New Bombay or Bandra-Kurla over the Kalyan Complex as the dominant subcenters. However, there are few signs that New Bombay will take off in the absence of a commitment by the State government to relocate a large number of public sector jobs there. Bandra-Kurla is too near to South Bombay to relieve congestion to any major extent. The Kalyan Complex deserves more attention because of its infrastructure lags, population pressure, and high incidence of poverty. Nhava-Sheva could also be a

development as the construction of the new port goes ahead.

6.　In Calcutta the DPIP (Development Perspective and Investment Plan) of 1976 recommended the substitution of a policentric structure with the eventual development of 22 centers for the pipolar strategy (Calcutta and Kalyani) suggested in the BDP (Basic Development Plan) ten years earlier. Although the bipolar strategy was misguided (no second center can compete with the CBD), a vigorous push of decentralization to many subcenters is not justified at this time because of the economic stagnation of the Calcutta metropolis. The reallocation of infrastructure investments to the NADs (New Areas of Development) will squeeze other investment programs and represents a way of avoiding the institutional and political problems associated with tackling the problems of the central core.

7.　The RIP (Regional Investment Plan) of the BMR for 1978-83 aims to undertake 30% of investments outside Greater Bombay. However, the scale of the increase over the Fifth Plan and the small contributions of the Union and State governments will make it difficult to achieve the planned investments unless resources are generated internally. The housing and urban development sector will be squeezed most since World Bank loans meet most of the requirements in urban transportation and water supply.

8.　Although the CMDA investment program is smaller than that in Bombay, more than one-half (58%) is being financed by IDA-credits. Since 1976 there has been some shift away from primary infrastructure investments to what are described as Integrated Area Upgrading Plans (IAUP) and the opening up of new areas (the NAD Plans); this shift is expected to continue, even to accelerate. Although three sectors (water supply, traffic and transportation, and sewerage and drainage) remain dominant, area development and bustee (slum) improvement are also important. The fiscal resource gap is narrowed by the growth in octroi yield, but there remains a need for internally generated resources. However, there has been negligible cost recovery from past investments and the case for a minimum investment strategy remains overwhelming.

9.　In large Indian cities, and especially in the Calcutta case, there is much merit in the substitution of "soft" policies and institutional change for massive infrastructure investments (a "hardware" approach), e.g., traffic regulation and management rather than building new highways, maximizing the use of the CBD rather than investing in new subcenters. "Soft" policy options include controls, pricing strategies and institutional change. A minimum investment strategy will economize on scarce capital resources and will force policymakers to address the more difficult policy problems such as public land acquisition, urban redevelopment, housing maintenance, the promotion of small-scale industry, improving environmental equality and reducing poverty. Such a shift of attention implies a broadening of functions and staffing requirements of

the regional planning authorities, BMRDA and CMDA. Where
metropolitan policies involve public investments, searching
for low-cost solutions and aiming for minimum service
standards require vigilance.

12 Policy development in urban and regional planning: an inquiry into the nature and process of problem solving in metropolitan Lagos

H. S. COBLENTZ AND AYODEJI FAKOLADE

1. Introduction

This paper attempts to demonstrate how given the existing structure in and processes for policy development in urban and regional planning in metropolitan Lagos, Nigeria, the search for a responsive and lasting solution to the diverse problems of urbanization and peoples in Lagos is elusive. The emphasis is placed not so much on individual substantive planning issues, but on policies and procedures for problem solving. Conversely then, any attempt to improve the product of planning should first disengage itself from "the-more-and-better syndrome" (i.e., more planning is good) and address itself to the question of what kind of planning and for what ends it is being done. Such a reevaluation impells the need for realignment of institutional planning activity with the spontaneous actions and circumstances of the mass of the people. This realignment calls for profound changes in the structure and process of planning. It implies a need for broad democratization at all stages of the planning process, especially through involvement of all citizens.

The first section of this study reviews the characteristic features of urbanization and societal governance in Nigeria and Lagos. These features have in part been derived either intentionally or unintentionally from the policies or lack of policies in national and metropolitan (Lagos) development processes, respectively. Of greater importance, however, is the fact that these features constitute the environment within which future policies will be generated. The next section conceptualizes what the writers believe are the major problems in the policy realm of Lagos's urban and regional government. Based on this perspective, the various dimensions and scope of the review are defined.

2. Urbanization in Nigeria

An important feature of urbanization in Nigeria as with many other developing nations is its rapid rate of growth. In Nigeria, the total population of which grew from 30 million in 1952 to 55 million in 1963, there has been a burgeoning of urban centers over the past thirty years, a phenomenon which (Rosser 1973) dubs as "exploding cities in unexploding economies." The intercensal increases of total versus urban population were thus 46.4 and 83.1%, respectively. In 1953 there were only 56 cities of more than 20,000 people but by 1963 the number had risen to 183.

Underlying such high rates of urbanization are high rates of rural-urban migration encouraged by the urban orientation of planning and development. Federal and state government expenditures have concentrated on the urban areas. An in-depth examination of structures, policies, and processes in education, agriculture, industry, and social development reveals a definite growth policy in favor of urban areas. For the migrants cities represent a real or perceived opportunity. Such migrations generate the paradoxical condition of severe unemployment, poverty and congestion in cities; and a labor and food deficit, poverty, misery and desolation in rural areas. The associated wide disparities between rural and urban areas and between the rich and the poor are further accentuated. Everywhere, wealth gravitates from the rural to urban areas (Green and Milone 1971) and within the cities themselves wide and deepening disparities exist between different sections and individuals.

Most Nigerian cities seem to have outgrown the capacity for planned development. Unplanned large urban centers reveal a jumble of structures and functions. Factories, markets, shops and houses exist side by side (Adedeji and Rowland 1973).Physical infrastructures and social services are inadequate. There is an acute shortage of housing, and rents are high. There is an associated concentration of housing investment and ownership in a few hands. Coupled with these physical inadequacies are the grave social problems of high unemployment, crime, and gross inequities.

In spite of these problems the cities, particularly Lagos, represent opportunity for upward social and economic mobility and offer a chance of a dramatic, if not abrupt, break with the past -- a vindication of the failure of progressivism or gradualism, or of the hidden hand of the marketplace to deliver optimal opportunity for the improvement of living conditions. Even when such opportunities are only hopes, people seem prepared to suffer and hold on for several years in expectation of the one big chance (Fakolade and Coblentz 1981).

As indicated earlier, the growth and rate of physical, social and economic changes have outpaced the capacity of constituted authority to control or guide the development process. This attenuation of authority is itself aggravated by the ineffectiveness and poor orientation of the controlling mechanisms. There is widespread resentment and confrontation with the introduction of a new piece of policy legislation. Public dissatisfaction with the process and product of governance has become increasingly vocal and articulate of the past few years, and such resentment results from conflicts between governmental programs and the demands of its citizens (Turner 1968).

3. Features of Urban Development in Metropolitan Lagos

Lagos is the capital[1] of the Federal government of both Nigeria

---

[1] A new inland capital site has been chosen and will probably be built in the next few years, although Lagos will continue as the capital of Lagos state and probably still be the dominant center of commercial life in Nigeria.

and Lagos State. Its population was about 3.5 million in 1976 with a growth rate of about 10.6%, one of the highest in Nigeria.

Migration accounted for about 62% of the growth between 1953 and 1976; in fact two-thirds of Lagos' inhabitants are relative newcomers, arriving from all over the country. The land area of the city has not grown correspondingly because of swamps, lagoons, and the nature of the soil. This high growth rate has created high population densities, particularly in the 'indigenous' areas of the city. Adjoining these areas are the high quality, low density government residential area.

In 1976 Lagos was estimated as having 4.3% of Nigeria's population. Nevertheless, it handles 80% of total cargo passing through Nigeria's ports, has 34% of the trade turnover, and accounts for 43% of employment in the modern sector. In 1973, it had 28% of the manufacturing establishments, 47% of the employment, 58% of the wages and salaries, 59% of value added and, 73% of net capital expenditure of the country. There are thus not only more and larger firms, but higher productivity and better salaries for employees in the modern sector. So the trend towards concentration has been increasing in recent years, and this concentration of federal, state, and private projects continues to draw more and more people. But such statistics do not reveal the extent of unemployment, poverty, and misery in Lagos; the majority of its population live in bad conditions. So, as in other large third world cities, the poor of Lagos are being edged out of the good life.

4. The Problems/Policy Issues

As mentioned earlier, the grave physical, social, and economic problems of Lagos seem to be increasing rather than decreasing, despite the huge resources, money, time, and effort committed to its planning. Public dissatisfaction with the output and process of planning is becoming increasingly vocal and articulate. Examples of widespread confrontations between the masses and official policies include those for "street trading," the "odd and even" number traffic rule, taxi-meters, rent control, and land use decree. These problems have often been wrongly diagnosed as arithmetical; however, putting in more planning agencies, strengthening existing ones, making more master plans, training or borrowing more planners, will not solve the problems. While recognizing the need for some of these measures, people now realize they beg the real issue: how to correct the structure, philosophy, and process of societal guidance in Nigeria. The growing resentment created by planning results from a fundamental disfunction in the policy-making system which transcends whatever relief increasing numbers can confer. We contend that much of what happens or does not happen in metropolitan Lagos is not the result of explicit, well-structured, noncontradictory and responsive governmental programs or plans of action but instead, the residue of a curious mixture of planned action, iteration, coalescence, coalition, and (oftentimes) conflict of public and strongly vested private interests, interdepartmental power groups, and technocratic forces. The prominent non-involvement of the key beneficiaries or victims of the outcomes is noticeable. In particular, overlapping and discordant activities of government agencies contribute to the problem rather than its solution. The task is to analyze how the policy-making system functions, how it is supposed to function from the perspective of the various actors, what bottlenecks exist, and how the system can be made more responsive to the human ends it is supposed to serve. This procedural approach throws the emphasis not on finding the "right" answers, if they in fact exist, but upon finding appropriate and relevant processes for reaching so-called answers: the ends may be rational, but the means may never be. A part of this "process-problem" is the generally wide distance existing between problem-solvers and clients -- the many publics of metropolitan Lagos. Such gaps create distortions and misperceptions not only of the needs, but of effective prescriptive measures. They also generate alienation and withdrawal on the part of the publics and a consequent lack of identification with the problem-solving process.

5. Operationalization

This section examines what policy is, evaluates the imperatives of effective policy-making, and delineates the scope of urban and regional planning.

(a) Policy is defined by one source as the authoritative allocation of values in society. The perception of policy thus connotes a distributive/redistributive orientation. In real terms, a policy gets translated into specific guidelines for action or inaction in a variety of ways in different societies. Accordingly, its means and scope differ among individuals, groups, and whole societies. Rose (1968,4), in enunciating a basis for Canadian housing policy evaluation, suggests that any policy should include legislation, financial resources, responsibility for action, and appropriate administrative arrangements. Only when all these elements are present can there be said to be policy. His conception of policy thus stresses comprehensiveness.

Policy is also described as a set of guidelines for human behavior. Customs may be viewed as informal policy. Dror asks the debate on policy to address not what it is, but what it does. For Dror public policymaking is no more and no less than an instrumental activity. Evaluation must have as its focus neither the policy nor its feasibility, but rather its substantive effects on a real social situation (Dror 1968,36). However, we suggest that if the "substantive effect on real situations" is to come out of a deliberately fashioned, as opposed to iterative process, then policy substance must not be put aside.

It can therefore be seen that conception of policy, as well as its scope and level of articulation, vary significantly. The scope, detail, and articulation of any policy will depend on the existing state of affairs in a society or community. In Nigeria it could be governmental legislation published in the official gazette, White Paper, or other official organ and backed by a high or low level study of the phenomenon it concerns. A formidable task of policy evaluation is knowing what the policy is, and this task is in part the reason why so many studies in Nigeria deny the existence of policy. They conclude by calling for a policy, whereas what they should be doing is calling for refinements of extant policy. In this study, policy is construed in a broad perspective and will include legislation or define procedures when they exist. However, it will also include written as well as unwritten statements which constitute key guideposts for action. These fluid and loose elements make the term policy in this context more appealing than the idea of planning, plan, or plan-making which tends to invoke the notion of an ordered, consciously-designed and well-structured program of decision-making or guidance.

A policy could be designed to achieve either one or a combination of these effects:

1)   enabling behavior to happen which would be difficult or even impossible without policy

2)   regulating behaviour into routine patterns

3)   inhibiting behaviour that would be widespread without policy

Yet mere enunciation of policy does not guarantee that the behaviour will be significantly responsive. An effective policy is one that guides the behavior of stakeholders in the manner incorporated in the provision of the policy. Warfield (1975) suggests that for a policy to be effective,

1)   The stakeholders must understand the provision and what is expected of them.

2)   The policy must be acceptable to the stakeholders. In the case of unpopular policies, the need must be clearly demonstrated.

3)   There should be power to enforce. In itself, this does not constitute good or bad policy, but only emphasises the need for effective coverage.

4)   It should be feasible and easy to obey by making it relevant to the stakeholders' circumstances and by obtaining their significant input into its formulation and implementation.

Effectiveness is only one and indeed a narrow measure of policy and does not necessarily measure quality or desirability. Several central questions must be asked: Who benefits from the policy, and when? Is the policy effective? Has the policy led to unexpected consequences? Are such unexpected consequences good or bad? (Whether a policy is good or bad is an oversimplification of a complex construct, and pertinent concerns should revolve around whether or not existing policy should be changed and why.) Other questions will follow: What is a good policymaking process, and why? Is policy A better than policy B, and if so, why? Is "no policy" better than a policy? Why or why not? These concerns shift the debate from substantive matters to procedural issues and they also stress the need for conceptualizing policymaking and evaluation as a continuous, on-going process rather than a single-shot attempt at attaining perfection.

(b) Urban and Regional Planning. Planning in this context should be synonymous with policymaking or decision-making. Friedmann (1973), with whom we share common views, takes it to include any activity that involves the linking of knowledge to organized action. Thus, the range

of activities covered by urban and regional planning would include all
actions that have a significant impact on multi-activities, people and
space. It will include at its center all the items which dealt mostly
with land-use and land-related matters included in the Nigerian "town
and country planning" ordinance of 1946 and at its periphery all those
actions that can impact directly on that realm or on the peoples
inhabiting such areas.

6. Organizational Structure of Planning in Lagos

A prominent feature of planning in Lagos is the fluid and changing
organizational structure. There are also curious relationships and
involvements of various levels of government in developmental
activities. The 1917 Township Ordinance (29 of 1917) made Lagos
(Island) into a "firstclass" township administered by a Town Council
which had planning jurisdiction over what is now the Lagos Island area
of metropolitan Lagos. The work of the Town Council was primarily
related to sanitation. Later it became the Lagos City Council with
broader powers on a range of developmental issues. The Lagos City
Council area belonged to the Federal Government of Nigeria and was
administered on its behalf. At that time, the mainland areas of
Mushin, Ikeja and Agege belonged to the jurisdiction of the Western
Regional Government. The latter areas were hurriedly developed, with
disregard for the overall need for metropolitan-wide planning and
growth.

It was significant that the 1917 ordinance applied to the creation
and operation of European Reservation Areas, whereas the native areas
were unaffected except for sanitary concerns. In 1967, twelve states,
including Lagos, were created out of the existing four regional
governments. Lagos was made a "special area" and was both the capital
of the Federal Government and Lagos State. The Federal Government
continued to operate in the former Lagos City Council area while the
Lagos City Council, itself part of, and responsive to the Lagos State
government, continued. The Lagos State government subsequently shifted
its capital and secretariat to Ikeja on the mainland. The Lagos State
government became the sole authority for urban and regional planning in
the whole of metropolitan Lagos, including the Federal government
occupied areas. This authority is vested in the Lagos State Ministry
of Works and Planning (LSMWP); the Physical Planning Division of this
ministry is responsible for the processing and approval of layout
plans, while the Development Control Division is responsible for
monitoring and development control. In spite of this arrangement, the
Master Plan Project Unit (MPPU) of the Ministry claims that "plan and
project implementation or commitments are carried out by some agencies
without approval of the Physical Planning Division. It further claims:

> Almost all the issues, with few exceptions, related to
> the urban development and management in Lagos, have its
> parts connected to different levels of the administra-
> tive mechanism, which necessitates great efforts of
> coordination. This creates a complicated network; in
> some cases a confusion or duplication of rights and
> responsibilities between various agencies exist, all
> mainly due to the lack of required coordination.
> (MPPU 1976, 25)

The Local Government Reform of 1976 has strengthened, albeit crudely, the responsibility of local governments five units of which are in the metropolitan Lagos area. The powers of the local governments, elected by citizens, are ill-defined, but their area of operations includes maintenance of some roads, market places, and local services, and provision of low-income housing. Autonomous Federal activities, such as the Ministries of Works, Transport and Housing, and Environment: Nigerian Railways; and the Nigerian Ports Authority, have broad powers within metropolitan Lagos.

At the state level, the various ministries (e.g., Agriculture, Lands and Survey, Local Government and Chieftaincy Affairs, Finance), and agencies (e.g., Lagos State Transport Corporation, Land Use Allocation Committee, Lagos State Development and Property Corporation) all carry on a number of activities whose functions overlap. There are no adequate mechanisms to deal with the resulting conflicts in jurisdiction and operations.

The power to plan, under the 1973 Town and Country Planning Law, is vested in the State Ministry of Works whose responsibility is to make official plans for all towns and cities in the State as well as to monitor all developmental activities.

The Master Plan Project Unit is responsible for making or commissioning master plans throughout the State. The master plans for Epe, Badagry and Ikorodu were contracted out to private consultants. In 1975 with the United Nations Office of Technical Assistance, the unit began the preparation of a master plan for metropolitan Lagos which it completed in 1980. The Lagos Executive Development Board (LEDB) was created in 1928 as a result of an outbreak of bubonic plague in order to eliminate filth and unsanitary conditions. The Board became famous for its urban renewal scheme in Central Lagos wherin it destroyed one of the worst slums and resettled, though ineffectively, the residents in a housing scheme in Surulere (Lagos mainland). In 1972 the LEDDB was dissolved and recreated as the Lagos State Planning and Development Commission (LSDPC). Its activities are similar to, but broader in scope than those of the LEDB. In addition, they include the entire State. The immediate implications of this curious division and alliance of powers in metropolitan Lagos is that effective and responsive taxing structures are not developed to tap financial resources that could result from economic growth "at-source." The various planning and control mechanisms are operated from grants and budgets provided from State Federal governments. The local government lacks not only the legislative power, but the financial resources to undertake its functions. As a result of the confusing and conflicting nature of planning jurisdictions and powers many problems are not dealt with. Partly, in a response to the "unmanageable" problems and Lagos' locational disadvantage, and partly in response to national political pressures, the Federal government has committed itself to shifting its capital to Abuja, a more inland, virtually uninhabited, location. After the move, which is expected to be completed in a few years, there will be changes in the organizational structures for planning in Lagos in terms of who is involved. But the form and impact of the move can only be a conjecture at this time, especially since it hinges on what will become of the various federal agencies and departments in the present location.

Conventional planning activity for all parts of Nigeria is based on the Town and Country Planning Ordinance, 1945 (no. 4 of 1946). The ordinance provided for the "replanning, improvement and development" of different parts of the country by means of "planning schemes" administered by "Planning Authorities." It empowered the Governor to appoint a "Planning Authority" vested with executive authority for the planning and carrying through of any scheme under its area of jurisdiction. A planning scheme was designed

to control the development and use of land, securing proper sanitary conditions, amenities, and convenience, and of preserving buildings and other objects of architectural, historic or artistic interest and places of natural interest or beauty, and generally of protecting existing amenities whether in urban or rural portions of the area.

A further example of planning dilemmas is the self-supporting commercial bent of the planning authorities' housing programs which were directed at middle and upper income groups. This bias resulted in the emergence of low-income "shanty" settlements outside the planning areas defined by the Authorities, but near enough to take advantage of the infrastructure and services provided for upper and middle-income housing. Such settlements not only have the highest residential densities, but also the highest unemployment rates and worst conditions.

The Lagos State Town and Country Planning Law Cap. 13 of 1973, the instrument for contemporary planning activity in Lagos State, is strictly modelled after the 1946 Ordinance. Responsibility for "town and country planning" is placed with the Ministry of Works and Planning and specifies that its responsibility shall include "the preparation of master plans as well as the control of development of all areas of the State." However, the preparation, adoption, and submission for ministerial approval of official plans is not made mandatory under the Act. When prepared, master plans will be approved by the Executive Council of the State. Any unapproved development shall be liable to a fine of N,1000 (about $1800), and the Ministry may order the demolition of buildings erected without approval. The Lagos City Council will continue to perform its functions under sections 126, 128, and 129 of the Local Government Law, subject to such conditions as the Ministry may direct. All planning powers by any other body or authority are thereby abrogated and vested in the Ministry.

The several planning Acts preclude the inclusion and consideration of social and economic objectives and consequences in plan-making and evaluation. Neither the 1946 Ordinance nor the 1973 Act address the need for vertical relationships in planning, such as the relationship of local federal levels to the Lagos State Ministry of Works and Planning. There is also no mention of horizontal relationships between the Ministry of Planning and other Lagos State ministries.

A salient feature of both pieces of legislation is the high degree of centralization of powers and structures for planning. Such centralization prempts local initiative and participation in planning. The 1946 Ordinance placed overall wisdom and capability in matters related to plan ("scheme") making and implementation with the Planning Authority, which was appointed by the Governor. Even when objections

are raised by individuals affected by the Authority works and
decisions, the sole authority for arbitrating and dealing with
dishoused persons rests with the Authority itself.

There is no provision for citizen-involvement in planning or in the
preparation of master plans and furthermore there is no discussion of
the legal effects of an official plan, whenever one is prepared.

The 1973 Act perpetuates a haphazard and uncoordinated perspective
in planning in metropolitan Lagos since the total defined area of the
severed communities do not cover the whole of metropolitan Lagos.

7. Processes and Procedures of Planning

As mentioned earlier, there are many agencies that perform a range
of functions which could be tagged "planning" although officially the
power to plan rests with the Lagos State Ministry of Works and Planning.

The Master Plan Project Unit of the ministry, in conjunction with
the United Nations Office of Technical Assistance has been responsible
for preparation of the master plan for metropolitan Lagos. Some
background studies were sub-contracted out to local and foreign
consultants. The Ministry's staff undertook a land use inventory in
1975 and prepared a land use map. The staff were divided into various
task groups made up usually of two to four persons charged with
carrying out field surveys and preparation of position papers on topics
including administrative, legal, and recreational needs of metropolitan
development. Staff findings and reports will be incorporated into a
master plan for the city. For the series of field inquiries which
could bring a staff in contact with the local citizenry, the whole
exercise was an exclusive "desk and drawing board" affair. The whole
process was highly centralized and detached. The master plan, when
finally prepared, will presumably descend on the people like a sort of
holocaust, and if the plan is to be taken seriously in terms of
effects, it is most likely to lead to major confrontations with the
people as have other States policies. On the other hand, the plan may
be ignored. Was it all worthwhile considering the time and effort
spent on its preparation?

8. Summary: Elements of the Present Public Policy-Making System

From the discussion thus far, it is pertinent to summarise the main
features of the public policy-making system as follows:

1. Muddling-through/disjointed incrementations, iteraction,
    ad-hocracy, and ego-involvement/after-the-fact reactions/panic
    measures (cures for symptoms rather than causes)/expensive
    side-effects of program and public programs exploited by
    groupsirresponsiveness and ineffectiveness/short-range
    orientation/non-complementary and, most often, contradictory
    policies and programs.

2. Technical conceptions of efficiency and public interest
    dominate.

3. A great schism exists between policy-makers (planners) and
    victims or beneficiaries of policies.

4. Commitment on the part of policy-makers to maintain or reinforce existing power relations and the use of policy instruments to stabilize power relations are counter-productive.

5. Umbrella or omnibus legislation fosters manipulation and self aggrandizement on the part of policy-makers and implementors.

9. Scenario: Towards a New Approach to Public Policy-Making in Metropolitan Lagos

We have attempted to show the extent to which the nature and structure of the policy development process is fraught with inherent problems that make the search for responsive answers to societal problems an elusive task. It is pertinent at the present juncture to review in outline the major elements of an improved policy-making system based on the problems diagnosed earlier.

1. Making goals and objectives of public policies and programs explicit:

    - improved communication in planning
    - more learning feedback
    - more elaboration of operational goals

2. Setting up a systematic process for making decisions:

    - much more systematic and explicit determination of policy strategies
    - emphasis on procedures rather than end states
    - some elements of routinization (can't be pushed to far) to remove problems of manipulation, iteration, and personalization of procedures

3. Citizen-participation in the planning process:

    - "opening" up organs of governance
    - relevance of diagnosis and solutions of peoples' problems
    - greater commitment to implementation

4. Weighing the consequences of alternatives carefully:

    - concern with distributive and redistributive impact of public policies and programs
    - more rigorous search for alternative ways of perceiving and problem-solving

5. Structural shifts in policy-making system. Existing policy-making structure seriously lags behind pervading realities and needs. This lag results in the policy crisis, which has been self-evident over the past years:

    - re-evaluation and re-designing of policy-making systems
    - re-alignment of institutional capacity and performance with peoples' circumstances
    - decentralization of structures

6. Improvements in planning legislation

10. Achieving the Desirable Future

Structural shifts in organization and procedures for policy-making
are never neutral in terms of the balance of powers and resources in
society. The critical question is whose interests in society are
served by such shifts. If we assume the changes will serve the larger
interests of the mass of society much more effectively and
responsively, the critical question again is one of initiative. Who
takes the initiative for change and redirection, especially given the
fact that the most resourceful groups, the policy-makers and
establishment-groups, are those who benefit most from the present
arrangement and who are therefore most committed to the status quo.
Change then becomes an open-ended question. It is also one of whether
or not the society is willing and able to facilitate meaningful
incremental change effectively and smoothly within a reasonable span of
time or face up to an inevitable convulsive and cataclysmic change
seeded by the contraditions and injustices of the present policy-making
system. The view of this paper is that change is better through the
former route. Based on this, a discussion is offered here about the
tools which could and should be used to make the policy-making system
more responsive and relevant to societal needs in Lagos.

a) Organizational shifts in planning

At present, there are wide distances between the governmental
units that make policy (including plans) and those affected by such
policies. We suggest that it is counter-productive that planning at
the scale of metropolitan Lagos be done by the State Ministry. What is
needed therefore, is an immediate placing of responsibility for
planning in the local governments of which there are five in
metropolitan Lagos. To carry out this task, the local governments
should be strengthened financially, administratively, and technically.
The local governments must have the authority, particularly through
taxation and surcharges for services, to generate their own revenues.

State involvement in planning should be confined to matters of
policy and strategy setting, and of providing a supportive role for the
local governments. Such a supportive role should include the operation
of a State Statistical Center, which should receive copies of all local
government and State statistics, issue a periodical inventory of
statistics and statistical summaries within the State, and foster
measures for standardization of data collection systems between local
governments and subsequent geocoding of all collected data. The State
support for local government planning should also include the operation
of a research program to prepare and maintain an index of research
projects relevant to planning. Finally, the State's role in local
government planning should include the setting of social and environmental development objectives, and studies of the impact assessment of
the consequences of planning in the State and in particular of Federal
government projects in the State.

b) Plan-making and approval

The local governments should have planning boards, which are
charged with the responsibility of preparation of local government or
municipal plans. The plans originating from the planning boards,

should be approved by the elected local government council. Ultimate approval of the plan will rest with the Minister in charge of planning in the State to ensure that local government or municipal plans conform with the State structure or policy plans.

There should be statutory provision for citizen-participation at all stages of the plan-making and approval process. In particular, both local government and State structure plans should undergo a statutory process of public hearing, adoption, and review. Access should be provided for persons and groups affected by either plans or the planning process to have access to impartial hearings and adjudication by a body other than the Minister and similar bodies connected with the planning process.

c) Planning education

The previous discussion has shown that the conception and operation of planning in metropolitan Lagos as well as for Nigeria is predicted on land-use issues and a detached, non-activist role for the planner. It has also stressed the need for a re-alignment and broadening of planning to embrace non-land use issues, concepts of citizen-involvement, as well as accountability of the planning process. Most of the present planners are ill-suited to operate in the conception and structure of this type of planning.

4. Citizen-participation in planning

Citizen-participation is fundamental to a realignment of institutional capacity and performance and has to be incorporated into the Planning Act. Where mass illiteracy and apathy exist in a society, planning has a herculean task to foster meaningful citizen-involvement. Planning documents need to be made available in major Nigerian languages as well as in English, They should also be readily available throughout the community.

11. Conclusions

This study has attempted to show that problems of planning in Lagos cannot be solved solely by technical or quantitative means. Declaring "any plan is better than no plan" is not sufficient, for there are basic problems with the structure and process of planning in Lagos. Improvements in planning and its process will require the realignment of institutional power and structure as well as a broad democratization of the planning process through active and real citizen involvement. Above all, political will and commitment to change is a prerequisite to any effective reorientation of planning in Lagos.

References

Adedeji, Adebayo and Rowland, L. (eds.) (1973). <u>Management Problems of Rapid Urbanization in Nigeria</u>. Ile-Ife: University of Ife Press.

Dror, (1968). <u>Public Policymaking Re-examined</u>. Scranton, PA: Chandler Publishing Co.

Fakolade, A., and Coblentz, H.S. (1981). 'Citizen participation in urban and regional planning in Nigeria: A preliminary enquiry," <u>Community Development Journal</u>, 16 (2) 119-29.

Green, Leslie, and Milone, Vincent. (1971). <u>Urbanization in Nigeria: A Planning Commentary</u>. New York: Ford Foundation.

Master Plan Project Unit. (1976). <u>Characteristics and Problems of Urbanization in Lagos</u>. (Lagos: State Min. of Works and Planning.

Rose, A. (1968). 'Canadian housing policies.' Background Paper, Canadian Conference on Housing, October 20-23.

Rosser, Collin. (1973). <u>Urbanization in Tropical Africa: A Demographic Introduction</u>. New York: Ford Foundation.

Turner, J.F.C. (1968). 'Housing priorities, settlement patterns and urban development in modernizing countries'. <u>Journal A.I.P.</u> 354-63.

Warfield, J.N. (1975). <u>Improving Behavior in Policy Making</u>. Columbus, Ohio: The Academy for Contemporary Problems.

13 Rapid urban growth and urban environmental problems: the case of Ile-Ife, Nigeria

JOSEPHINE OLU ABIOUDUN

1. Introduction

The use of public institutions, particularly an educational establishment, to induce growth and development in an otherwise backward area (especially a less developed country) is not often highlighted in the literature. The establishment of the University of Ife in Ile-Ife in 1967 provides a case study of the potential impact which such a public institution can have in stimulating growth and development in the town of its location as well as in the surrounding areas, i.e., in generating a type of growth center. Prior to 1963, Ile-Ife had a population growth rate of about 1.6 percent per annum. However, this rate accelerated to an estimated 5 percent per annum after 1967 (Olayemi 1977, 140), consequent to the advent of the University in the town. The associated impact on the physical growth and expansion of the town, as well as the attendant problems of pressure on residential environment, is examined in subsequent sections of this paper. Suggestions are also offered which could assist in ameliorating the observed problems.

2. Pre-1950 Growth of Ile-Ife

Although Ile-Ife is reputed to be of great antiquity, the founding of the town having been dated at about 350 B.C. (Ozanne 1969) or between the 7th and 10th centuries A.D. (Biobaku 1955). However, its built up area remained unimpressive. Up to 1950 the town itself remained encompassed within the town wall (Figure 1). The stunted growth of the town at that period could be ascribed to the generally low level of economic activities in the town relative to other towns in Nigeria which were located along major trade routes or along major lines of communication (e.g., Ibadan, which is located along the north-south railway line) during the colonial period. Although the introduction of cocoa into the Ife region during the 1930a and trade in kolanuts brought some income, most of it was invested in property development. The impact was very limited, and very little spatial expansion of the built-up area occurred. By the end of 1950, the refugee settlement of Modakeke which came into existence in the 19th Century still remained distinct from the host settlement Ile-Ife (Figure 1).

3. The Period From 1950 to the Present

Between 1950 and 1981 the built-up area of Ile-Ife expanded more than three times its pre-1950 extent. In the process, both Ile-Ife and Modakeke have merged into one urban unit (Figure 1). The single most important factor in this dramatic change in the built-up area of the town has been the advent of the University of Ife in the town. The University moved from its temporary site in Ibadan, to its permanent site in Ile-Ife in 1967. The location of the University outside the town wall gave rise to land speculation and expansion of the built-up area toward the University (Figure 1). It is significant to note that while the University of Ife started with a student population of 244 in.1962, by 1972 it was just under 4,000 students and by December 1980, the student population in the main campus in Ile-Ife was 9,000. If students in other campuses of the University, but outside the town were included, the figure was over 11,000. This was an increase in student population of over 40 times in less thantwenty years. Whereas in 1962 the University had an academic staff of only 80, by 1980 there were 1,092 on the teaching and research staff in the University, an increase of more than 13 times in 18 years. These penomena have significant ramifications in the process of change and modernization in Ife town.

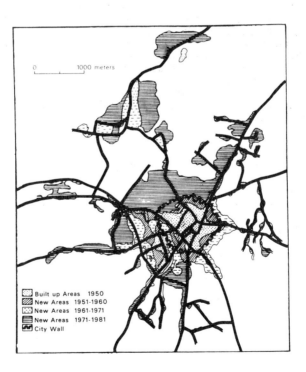

Figure 1.   Ile-Ife: The Expansion of the Build-up Area.

First, the presence of the University in Ife since 1967 has changed
the town from a predominantly farming settlement to a modernizing and
fast expanding University town. With a population of 110,790 in 1952,
the town grew to only 130,050 in 1963. Today, it is estimated to have
attained a population of 350,000. As noted earlier, prior to 1963, the
population growth rate in the town was only about 1.6 percent per
annum. This rose to an estimated 5 percent per annum after 1967
(Olayemi 1977, 140). There has been an unprecedented influx of
population into the town in response to the demands of the University.
Apart from the phenomenal increase in both academic staff and student
population mentioned above, the University employs a substantial
population of administrative, technical, and other supporting staff
whose population has risen considerably since 1967. Added to these
numbers are the dependent families of those University employees who
invariably move to the town. Moreover, there are those who are
attracted to the town in the hope of securing wage employment. It is
significant to note that this latter trend is a reversal of the
prevailing situation in the town prior to 1967. At the time Ile-Ife
had the occupational characteristics of a typical small Yoruba town.
As Lloyd (1959, 50) observed, most Yoruba towns have, until recently
"had few opportunities for school leavers and almost all of these
youths have found jobs in Lagos or Ibadan." Today, the University, as
the single most important employer of labor in the town, is providing
wage-employment opportunities for both the indigenous people of Ile-Ife
as well as migrants and immigrants to the town. Moreover, the town has
become more heterogeneous in its population composition, with the
presence of highly skilled University staff of varied nationalities as
well as migrants from the various states within Nigeria.

There has been significant changes in the occupational structure of
the town since 1967. Although the absence of any up-to-date data
precludes a detailed analysis of the occupational structure of the
town, say, by sex and place of origin, there is no doubt that an
increased diversification in the occupational structure of the town has
occurred since 1967. In addition, several changes had taken place in
both the level and the variety of social and economic facilities
available in Ile-Ife. For example, prior to the mid-1960s, Ile-Ife,
with a population of more than 100,000, had only two commercial banks,
three outposts of big commercial firms [G.B. Olivant (established in
Ife in 1920), Patterson Zochonis (1925), and N. Zard (1950)], and one
Post Office. Today, there are five different commercial banks with
nine offices, three of which are located within the campus of the
University. There are three Post Offices (including one on the
University campus) and many modern retail stores. Similarly, while in
1973 there were in the town eight secondary Grammar Schools and one
Technical College, in 1981 there were twenty-five secondary Grammar
Schools, one Technical College, and one Higher School (intermediate
between the Grammar School and the University level). The first
hospital, Seventh Day Adventist Hospital, was established in 1946.
Now, in addition, there are the General Hospital and the University of
Ife Teaching Hospital Complex. The latter, while using already
existing Hospital establishments in Ile-Ife and the neighboring town of
Ilesha (pending the construction of a full-fledged Hospital unit),
provides the population with highly sophisticated and modern health
care facilities which otherwise would have been unavailable.

A major area of striking change has been in the field of housing.

One important impact of the University on residential accommodation in Ile-Ife town emanates from its policies with respect to housing for its staff and students. Initially, efforts were made to provide houses for both staff and students on the campus. However, with the pressure of numbers, the University had to solicit the co-operation of private entrepreneurs who could build modern housing facilities for rent by its staff in the town. Such efforts produced the Sijuwade and Ajanaku housing estates. At present, contrary to its previous practice, the University now offers its staff on initial appointment, a stipulated monthly allowance as rent subsidy and requests this staff to acquire accommodation in the town. Similarly, as a matter of policy the University undertakes in principle to provide accommodation to all its students except the male students in the second year of the under-graduate program. The latter category of students are expected to find private accommodation for themselves in town. Added to this housing demand is the one created by hard-pressed migrants who invade the town in increasing numbers. The latter category tends to invade the older wards.

The latest estimate of available housing stock in Ile-Ife was in 1976. This gave a figure of 14,110. On the basis of a population of 250,000 for that year, this gave an average of 18 people per house (or a people to house ratio of 21:1, if the population estimate of 302,000 is accepted (Olayemi, 1977 p. 140)). The average figure however masks the generally high residential population density. The emergence of continuous stretches of rooming houses on the outskirts of the town and along certain main traffic arteries tends to diminish the housing congestion in those areas, but a situation of great congestion still prevails in the old wards.

4. Component Analysis Questionnaire

In order to further investigate changes in the spatial structure as well as the attendant problems in the residential district in Ile-Ife, the town was divided into 15 residential units (Figure 2) based on the existing ward demarcations, as well as taking into consideration the period when specific localities became built-up. Questionnnaires were used to investigate both the spatial variations in housing and the environmental characteristics of the town. The 33 variables used are listed on Table 1. A systematic sampling procedure was adopted. First, the number of streets in any residential unit was counted. Then, every third, fourth, or fifth street was scheduled for survey. Along each street, the head of the household in every fifth house was interviewed. The total sample (450 questionnaires) was analyzed using the multivariate technique of component analysis.

6. Discussion of the Results of the Questionnaire
A look at Table 1 reveals some interesting facts about Ile-Ife. For example, the mean percentages for each of the variables show that 10 percent of the surveyed household heads were employed by the University while 17.4 percent were self-employed farmers. The latter

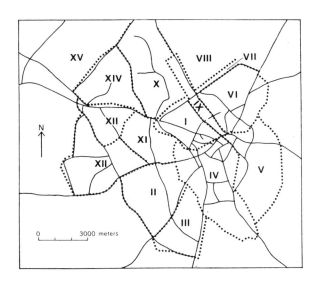

Figure 2. Ile-Ife: The Fifteen Residential Areas.

TABLE 1

THIRTY-THREE VARIABLES FOR FIFTEEN RESIDENTIAL UNITS IN ILE-IFE

Variable (in %)	Mean	Standard Deviation	Range Minimum	Maximum
1. Single Family Household	48.2	23.2	10.0	85.0
2. Multi-Family Household	51.8	22.8	12.5	90.0
3. 1 - 3 Household Size	9.4	12.3	0.0	47.0
4. 4 - 6 Household Size	37.0	18.7	5.0	66.7
5. 7 or more Household Size	54.5	23.0	15.8	95.0
6. Employment with the University	10.0	20.0	0.0	75.0
7. Employment in town but not with University	37.0	20.3	5.0	54.8
8. Employment outside town	17.4	12.3	0.0	35.0
9. Self-Employed (farmer)	15.4	14.3	0.0	50.0
10. Self-Employed (others)	33.0	18.5	0.0	72.0
11. Primary School Education	25.0	15.5	0.0	46.7
12. Secondary School Education	13.5	12.7	0.0	47.0
13. Post Secondary School Education	22.0	27.0	0.0	100.0
14. Illiterate	42.4	22.8	0.0	80.0
15. Place of Origin - Ife	79.4	18.9	44.0	100.0
16. Place of Origin outside Ife but in Oyo State	10.0	15.4	0.0	46.0

Table 1 (continued)

Variable (in %)	Mean	Standard Deviation	Range Minimum	Maximum
17. Place of Origin outside Oya State	11.0	12.0	0.0	36.8
18. Wall: Mud Plastered with cement	48.0	35.1	0.0	95.8
19. Wall: Cement/Brick	45.3	34.9	0.0	
20. % Household with flush Toilet	25.5	32.7	0.0	100.00
21. % Household with pit latrine	63.4	30.7	0.0	90.0
22. % Household without Toilet	10.8*	12.06	0.0	40.0
23. % Household with Pipe-borne water	32.1	35.7	0.0	100.0
24. % Household with no pipe-borne water	38.0	35.6	0.0	100.0
25. % Dwelling with Electricity	82.0	16.7	50.0	100.0
26. % Dwelling without Electricity	17.9	16.7	50.0	100.0
27. Refuse Disposal in Public Dustbin	14.2	20.9	0.0	52.9
28. Refuse Disposal by Burning	12.3	18.5	0.0	52.9
29. Refuse Disposal in the Bush	67.4	34.8	10.0	100.0
30. Other Means of Refuse Disposal	5.8	12.1	0.0	36.0
31. Good Tarred Road	8.2	25.6	0.0	100.0
32. Good Untarred Road	21.6	23.5	0.0	47.0
33. Poor Tarred/Untarred Road	70.0	30.1	0.0	100.0

Source: Author's fieldwork.

* The percentages as recorded in column 1 of variables 20, 21 and 22 do not add up to 100 because of rounding errors.

figure succinctly reflects the predominant occupational characteristics of the twon prior to the advent of the University. It also contrasts with the accepted Western concept of a town as articulated by Dickinson (1947), who asserts that an urban center is "a compact settlement engaged in non-agricultural occupations." Another point worthy of note is that more than 50 percent (in fact, 54.5 percent) of the surveyed households had seven or more people. This is a reflection of the extended family system which is prevalent in this area. Variables 16 and 17 reveal that 21 percent of the surveyed household had migrated to the town -- 10 percent from within Oyo state in which Ile-Ife is located and 11 percent from outside the state. No doubt, these latter elements are attributable to the attractive pull of the University.

Another aspect of the survey reveals that 10.8 percent of the house-holds have no toilet facilities whatsoever. Such respondents made known that nearby bushes and "dung hills" were generally used as conveniences. With the continued disappearance of unbuilt plots within the town, a crisis in sanitation facilities is gradually emerging. Another 63.4 percent have pit-latrines, while only 25.5 percent have flush toilets. No pipe-borne water supply exists in 68.0 percent of the households. Public water taps (which often remained dry) and wells were the sources of domestic water supply. The health hazards associated with this situation are quite obvious. There is the possibility of seepage from the pit latrines to the wells. In addition, only 14.2 percent of the households disposed of their household refuse in public dustbins. 67.4 percent used nearby bushes for refuse disposal, and 12.3 percent burnt their household refuse themselves. It is significant to note that with the increasing rate of land development for residential purposes within the last decade, available bush for refuse disposal continues to shrink. In consequence, households are experiencing considerable pressures with regards to refuse disposal. Finally, the table indicates that 70 percent of the households in all the residential units are served by poorly tarred or untarred roads.

From the above analysis it is obvious that the phenomenal rate of growth and expansion of the town in recent years has been accompanied by increasing problems in the provision of basic infrastructural facilities to all the residential areas. In many cases, houses are built at the periphery of the town well in advance of the provision of either pipe-borne water or electricity. Moreover, the extremely limited personnel at the Town Planning Office in the town had been unable to keep pace with the need to monitor the construction of new housing units and control environmental standards. In consequence, environmental deterioration particularly in terms of neighborhood hygiene becomes noticeable in certain residential areas within a decade of their being built-up.

7. Spatial Variations in Residential Areas

In order to further examine the variations in the level of environ-mental deterioration among the different residential districts the original 33 primary variables observed for the 15 residential areas were subjected to the multivariate technique of component analysis. From the original primary variables 14 components were extracted which completely describe the variability among them. Of these new components eight account for 91.1 percent of the total variability as shown in Table 2. The ensuing discussions are therefore based on these eight components which are adjudged to describe the problems adequately.

The scores of each residential area on these components were analyzed, and Figure 3 shows the pattern derived. This figure depicts the degree of residential and environmental pressure along with deterioration in the different residential areas in Ile-Ife.

As would be expected the locations with the greatest pressure are the residential areas (I and IX) in the traditional core of the town (Figures 2 and 3). However, the pressure does not appear as a circular shape; it occurs as sectors within the town. In addition, both

TABLE 2

COMPONENTS DERIVED FROM THE ORIGINAL 33 PRIMARY VARIABLES

Component	Eigenvalue	% of Variability	Cummulative Percentage
1	11.80	35.8	35.8
2	4.68	14.2	50.0
3	3.51	10.6	60.6
4	2.85	8.6	69.2
5	2.36	7.2	76.4
6	1.84	5.6	82.0
7	1.66	5.0	87.0
8	1.35	4.1	91.1

residential areas I and IX are adjacent to the Afin, the palace of the Oba (the Ooni of Ife). Residential and environmental pressure and deterioration tend to decrease outward from these traditional areas to

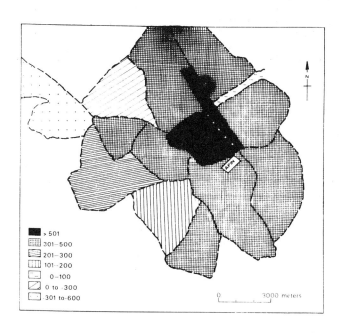

Figure 3.   The Spatial Pattern of Residential and Environmental Pressures in Ile-Ife.

the periphery. By contrast, the most recently developed areas in XIV and XV recorded the least level of environmental pressures as indicated by the negative scores of these areas.

8. Suggested Strategies for Solving the Observed Residential Problems

The problems identified in this study relate to those attendant on the rapid rate of growth and expansion of an urban area consequent upon increased level of social and economic activities. The influx of migrants from the rural areas as well as the inflow of personnel from various parts of Nigeria and from abroad in response to the needs of the University create great pressure on infra-structural facilities. Also, existing housing stock remains inadequate and unimproved while the rate of growth of new housing units remains very low. In recognition of this problem, the Oyo State Property Development Corporation (an agent of the State Government) is currently constructing a housing estate in the town. However, this effort needs to be greatly supplemented by private enterprise, possibly through government incentives such as easier access to mortgage loan.

With regards to sub-standard neighborhoods, a wholesale demolition of existing housing units is not recommended since such exercises, in the Nigerian experience, had tended to create more social problems than were solved. Moreover, adequate financial resources for such an exercise is unlikely to be forthcoming. However, it is possbile, through some form of aided self-help program, to assist individual landlords in improving existing structures.

The problems of low environmental standards may, in the final analysis, be attributed basically to poverty and low environmental perception. The former may be addressed by stimulating small-scale enterprise, which could provide increased income for the urban poor. The latter could be tackled through a program of community health education. Incidentally, certain interested staff at the University of Ife Faculty of Health Sciences are currently initiating a program in this direction.

The need for improved urban management institution is imperative. At the moment, two distinct authorities, the Local Government Council and the Town Planning Authority, are responsible for the management and planning of the town. There is a need for greater collaboration between these institutions to achieve greater efficiency. Also the lack of skilled personnel hampers the effective control and monitoring of urban growth and expansion by the Town Planning Authority. There is an urgent need to rectify this deficiency.

9. Conclusions

This study has highlighted the role of a public institution, an educational establishment, in inducing growth and development in an otherwise relatively stagnant urban area. Emphasis in this study has been on the growth and expansion of the built-up area of the town and the associated environmental problems. It has been found that while prior to 1967, when the Univeristy moved to Ife, the town experienced a slow rate of growth both in population and in the built-up area. Between 1967 and 1981 the population growth rate had increased from 1.6 percent per annum to an estimated 5 percent per annum. Similarly, the built-up area had increased more than three times. Such a rapid growth

rate had brought in its trail a considerable pressure on basic infrastructure and on housing facilities. Neighborhoods which are
experiencing considerable environmental pressure and deterioration are
identified.

The need for stimulating the provision of more housing units in the
town is recognized, and, apart from the on-going effort by the
government, easier access to mortgage facilities could assist the
private sector in making its own contribution. There is also a need to
strengthen the economic base of the town by stimulating the emergence
of more smallscale enterprises to provide increased income for the
urban poor. The gross inadequacy of basic infrastructural facilities
can be solved through improved urban management institution. In this
regard, greater collaboration between the Local Government Council and
the Town Planning Authority is desirable. In addition, a program on
community health education is suggested as a strategy for improving the
environmental standards within the town.

References

Adepoju, Aderanti (1975/76). 'Urban migration differentials and selec-
tivity: The example of Western Nigeria'. African Urban
Notes, Ser. B, Vol. 11, No. 1, 1-24.

Bascom, W.R. (1959). 'Urbanism as a traditional African pattern.'
Sociological Review, 7:29-43.

Dickinson, R.E. (1947). 'City, Region and Regionalism'. London:
Routledge and Kegan Paul.

Probenius, Leo (1913). The Voice of Africa. Vol. 1, New York:
Benjamin Blom, 105-26.

Galletti, R., K.D.S. Baldwin and L.O. Dina (1956). Nigerian Cocoa
Farmers. Oxford: Oxford University Press, 744.

Lloyd, R.C. (1959). 'The Yoruba town today'. Sociological Review, New
Ser., Vol. 7, (1):45-63.

Ojo, G.J.A. (1970). 'Areas of influence of Ife'. in S.A. Agboola
(ed.), The Ife Region, Department of Geography, University of
Ife, Monograph, 1-20.

Ojo, G.J.A. (1968). 'Hausa quarters of Yoruba towns with spatial
reference to Ile-Ife'. Journal of Tropical Geography,
27:40-49.

Olayemi, A.O. (1977). 'Problems of the planning administration,'
Ile-Ife, Nigeria. EKISTICS, 262, September, 140-43.

Oluwasanmi, H.A. (1980). 'The university of Ife in the 21st century'.
1980 Convocation Lecture, Ile-Ife: University of Ife,
December, 1, pp. 1-24.

Ozanne, Paul (1969). 'A new archaeological survey of Ife'. ODU New
Series, No. 1:37.

PART III
Population, Housing and Land Use:
Problems and Policy

14 Growth and spatial patterns of population in Indian cities

JOHN BRUSH

1. Introduction

It is taken as an axiom in geography and planning that growth of urban population, both in actual numbers and percentage share of a nation's total, is concurrent with economic development in any country. We know that such an urbanization process cocurred during the 19th and 20th centuries in all Western European and some American countries, which are now considered to comprise the principal parts of the More Developed World. It has also occurred in Japan and is still under way in the U.S.S.R. and many other countries, including India. In relative terms this process involves a shift of the population from 10 to 20 percent or less urban to 60 or 70 percent and more urban. On such a scale India is low in 1981 with between 23 and 24 percent of the total population being classified as urban.

The trend of urbanization in India clearly has been accelerating, especially in the last three decades (see Table 1). In 1951 there were 61 million people in India's cities and towns, or 17.6 percent of the total. In 1981 there were 156 million in the cities and towns, or 23.7 percent (exclusive of Assam and Kashmir and Jammu). In the last decade alone the number of urban dwellers has grown by more than 49 million, absorbing about two-fifths of the total population growth in India. The urban population increase from 1971 to 1981 is 46 percent; or, if one were to include the two uncensused states (Assam and Jammu and Kashmir), the urban increase would be 46.12 percent, based on an estimated urban population total of 159 million in the whole of India as of 1981.

Procedures for classification of urban population used by the Census in 1981 may have caused some exaggeration of the growth. The Census includes in the counts of urban many new areas of out growth (non-municipal areas) such as formerly rural villages, adjacent to municipal areas, as parts of urban agglomerations. Another problem of comparability of 1981 data and that of 1971 or 1961 is the changes in status Class IV, V and VI census towns (Premi, et al., 1977).[1] However, should we exclude some nine million of the urbanpopulation reported in 1981, who were living in places not classified urban in

---

[1] Personal communication with Dr. M.K. Premi, Jawaharlal Nehru University, New Delhi, November 6, 1981.

TABLE 1

TREND OF URBANIZATION IN INDIA

Census Year	Urban Population (Millions)	Percent Urban
1901	25.62	11.00
1911	25.58	10.40
1921	27.69	11.34
1931	32.98	12.18
1941	43.56	14.10
1951	61.63	17.62
1961	77.56	18.26
1971	106.87	20.22
1981	156.19	23.73

Source: Census of India 1981. Series 1-India. Provisional Population Totals. Paper-2 of 1981, Rural-Urban Distribution. Statement 3, p. 24. Excludes states of Assam, Jammu and Kashmir.

1971, the total would be reduced to some 47 million. The urban population increase would appear to have been only about 40 million, instead of 49 as reported.

Without question there has been massive growth and migration into Indian cities during the last decade and this growth has occurred mainly in the cities of 100,000 and over (1981) which now comprise 94.3 million, or 60.4 percent of the total urban population (Census of India, 1981). Such concentration in the largest cities continues a progressive shift in the locus of urbanization which has been going on in India since 1901 (see Figure 1). Look at the trends of growth in cities of different size groups. These trends of change illustrate a world-wide phenomenon, observed in almost all countries of the Developing World.

There are now twelve large cities in India where at least one million inhabitants are recorded as of March 1, 1981 (Census of India 1981, Table 4, p. 65). It is to be noted that with one exception -- Lucknow -- their growth exceeded 30 percent in ten years, which is more than the overall national population growth rate of 24.43 percent, excluding the states of Assam and Jammu and Kashmir. (Table 2). Growth of the Calcutta Urban Agglomeration lags in comparison with Greater Bombay and particularly in comparison with the Delhi Urban Agglomeration which grew more than 56 percent, gaining more than 2.1 million. The Bangalore Urban Agglomeration shows the most outstanding growth rate, followed by Jaipur which entered the group of "One Million Plus" cities since 1971. Nagpur and Lucknow also qualified for this group for the first time in 1981. Otherwise, the most rapidly growing centers are Pune, Ahmedabad and Hyderabad. But Hyderabad lost its position among the metropolises of India to Bangalore, now the fifth

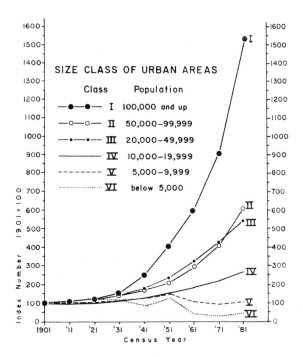

Based on Figure 5. *Census of India 1981. Provisional Population Totals. Paper-2 of 1981. Rural-Urban Distribution.*

Figure 1.   Growth of Urban Population by Size of Urban Areas
in India, 1901-1981.

largest urban agglomeration in India.

The concept of urban agglomeration has been used by the Census of
India in recognition of the fact that urban growth usually extends in
several geographically associated jurisdictions. This growth is a
continuous process, requiring adjustments in successive censuses to
take account of newly urbanized areas, some of which remain
non-municipal. Some of the apparent growth of population in India's
large cities, thus, is a statistical artifact because of changes in
areas from 1971 to 1981 which add a component of increase attributable
to inclusion of formerly rural villages and outlying towns. The
Calcutta Urban Agglomeration takes in not only the satellite city of
Haora (Howrah), but also 105 other smaller municipalities and
non-municipal areas located in the suburbs and industrial towns along
the Hooghly Riverfrontage. The Calcutta Municipal Corporation alone
has some 3,291,000 inhabitants, only 36 percent of total in the urban
agglomeration. Greater Bombay, on the other hand, is a single
municipal jurisdiction and does not include Thane, "New Bombay" or any
other nearby municipalities on the mainland. The ten other Million
Plus cities listed include areas outside of the jurisdiction of the
central city and their territorial bounds in 1981 are probably
different than in 1971. It is impossible at this time for me to

TABLE 2
URBAN AGGLOMERATIONS OF ONE MILLION PLUS IN INDIA

Rank	Urban Agglomeration or Municipal Corporation	Population 1981	Percent Change 1971-81
1.	Calcutta Urban Agglomeration	9,165,560	+ 30.35
2.	Bombay Municipal Corporation	8,227,332	+ 37.80
3.	Delhi Urban Agglomeration	5,713,581	+ 56.66
4.	Madras Urban Agglomeration	4,276,635	+ 34.91
5.	Bangalore Urban Agglomeration	2,913,537	+ 76.17
6.	Hyderabad Urban Agglomeration	2,528,198	+ 40.74
7.	Ahmedabad Urban Agglomeration	2,515,195	+ 43.53
8.	Kanpur Urban Agglomeration	1,688,242	+ 32.39
9.	Pune Urban Agglomeration	1,685,300	+ 48.48
10.	Nagpur Urban Agglomeration	1,297,977	+ 39.50
11.	Lucknow Urban Agglomeration	1,006,538	+ 23.66
12.	Jaipur Urban Agglomeration	1,004,669	+ 57.78

Source: Census of India 1981. Series-1, India. Provisional Population
Totals. Paper-2 of 1981, Rural-Urban Distribution. Table 4,
p. 65.

analyze the changes because maps are not yet available. It is to be
hoped that the final census reports will contain sufficiently large-
scale maps to allow comparative study. If the Census Commissioner
could fix consistent boundaries of divisions or any other geographical
data base it would be helpful for the purposes of planners, geographers
and other social scientists.[4] There is, or course, no way to avoid
the necessity of revisions of the outer limits of urban areas in
successive censuses. Indeed, growth on the fringes of India's
metropolitan cities may be expected to accelerate as resources become
available for expansion of housing, improvement of transportation and
extension of basic utilities and services.

2. Spatial Patterns of Population

It should come as no surprise to anyone who has been observing the
course of urbanization in India, if I state most of the urban growth
has been accommodated through concentration rather than sprawl. The
result has been progressive crowding of more and more people into the
cores of cities. Densities have risen in some cities to levels which
are twice what they had been at the beginning stage of the current
growth trend. Such a centripetal tendency is contrary to the usual
growth pattern observed in Western Europe and North America, where in
the past four or five decades central densities have decreased while
peripheral densities have increased (Brush 1970). I have identified
four distinct types of urban spatial structure in India, reflecting the
economic and political circumstances of urban development (Brush
1968). Although the tendency towards concentration is not equally
strong in each of the four types, the dominant pattern until 1971 was
concentration rather than accretionon the margins. I anticipate,

however, on the basis of spatial processes at work that density change in India would ultimately conform to the general model of central decline concurrent with peripheral growth (Brush 1973).

Measurement of spatial change in population distribution requires information on the areas and numbers of inhabitants for each of the census divisions within the municipality and determination of the mean geometric distance of each of these units from the center of the city. If the logarithms of the densities and respective distances of these units are treated as variables in simple regression, the result of the computation is found to be a negative exponential relationship which will show a statistically significant correlation in nearly all instances. The regression appears as a straight line with negative slope on a semi-log graph (see gradient A, Figure 2). If growth in successive time periods has occurred by central increase as well as peripheral increase the gradients will rise with more or less the same slope (see B 1, 2 and 3). If growth occurred only by peripheral increase, the gradients will be reduced in successive time periods (see C 1, 2 and 3). If there has been central decrease with peripheral growth, the gradients will decline through both downward shifts at the center and upward shifts at the periphery (see D 1, 2 and 3). The dominant pattern in India until 1961 is illustrated by B. But pattern C has begun to appear and there was no evidence of D as yet. In 1971 and 1981 I find that pattern D occurs in two major cities: Bombay and Delhi.

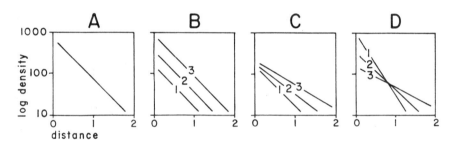

Figure 2.

3. Case Studies

Gaya, a small city of less than 200,000 (1971) in South Bihar, will serve to exemplify the basic spatial pattern I have found in Indian cities (see Figure 3). It will be noted that in 1931 to 1951 that the general gradient moved upward in parallel fashion as illustrated by B (Figure 2). But in the period 1951 to 1971 there was little change of the central density levels, as determined by regression, while there were progressive upward shifts of the densities on the periphery as illustrated by C (Figure 2). A more accurate portrayal of Gaya's density profile is obtained by averaging the wardwise densities

---
4   In Patna recently I was shown a map, prepared by the Bihar Census Directorate, which shows the "Standard Urban Area" of Patna and includes associated municipalities and adjacent or intervening agricultural villages. It represents the area which may be expected to come under Patna's metropolitan influence in future.

according to distance increments of one half mile. The adjusted
gradient now appears as a curved profile line, bulging above the
general regression line in the second and third half-mile increments.
It would seem that the center of the city was approaching saturation in
1961 and reached this condition in 1971. In fact, the ward comprising
Gaya's central bazar registered a slight decrease of residential
population between 1961 and 1971.

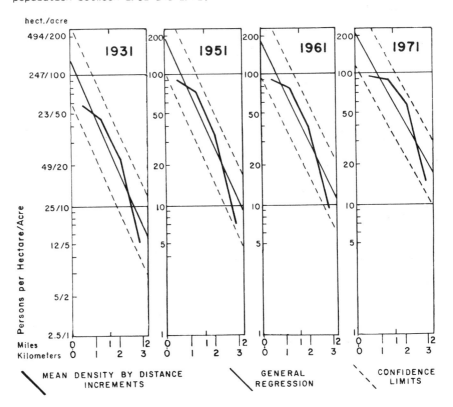

Figure 3.   Change of Gross Density for Gaya Municipality,
            1931-1971.

     Bombay and Delhi exemplify the patterns of change, illustrated by D
(Figure 2), which may portend the future spatial changes to be expected
in other Indian cities. In both cases central density increases
occurred until the 1961 census as in other Indian cities generally.
But central density decreases began in 1971 and in 1981 the areas of
decline were enlarged, while growth continued in the intermediate and
outer areas. Thus, 1961 was the turning point in change of the spatial
structure of population growth in two of India's largest and most
rapidly growing metropolitan cities.

     In the case of Bombay, the density of population according to
distance from the central business district always has exhibited a
convex profile like that observed in the big Western cities. The

original Bombay Fort, the walls of which were removed in the 1860s has
been dominated for commercial non-residential land use for a hundred
years (Kosambi 1980) resulting in relatively low population density of
less than 100 persons per hectare in 1961 as compared with the former
"Native City" (outside the walls) where mixed commercial and
residential land use produced over 1,000 persons per hectare and the
maximum gross residential density in India of 3760 per hectare existed
in 1961. In the 1971 census, for the first time since regular counts
became available in 1881, decreases were reported both in the area of
the "Fort" and the "Native City." In 1971, 15 census sections showed
decline; in 1981 not only did the same sections show continued decline,
but decline also occurred in 9 additional sections (see Figure 4). It
has become clear that office and other non-residential land uses are
now dominant in the main central business district around Flora
Fountain, spreading to Churchgate and Nariman Point, while commercial
uses are displacing residential use along Marine Drive to Chowpatty, as
far north as Dongri on the Harbourside and towards the industrial heart
of Bombay Island as far as Tardeo, Nagpada and Kamathipura. If a line
were to be drawn across the Island from Mahalaxmi Temple on the Arabian
Sea to Mazagaon Railway Station on the Harbour Line, it would be seen
that the only census sections with growth recorded from 1971 to 1981
are in the Byculla area and in the sections containing Cumballa and
Malabar Hills and Colaba Point from the Gateway of India southward.
North of this line four sections showed population losses from 1971 to
1981: on Bombay Island in Parel, Mahim and Matunga (the latter began
its decline in 1961-71) and in the Western Suburbs in Khar-Pali.
Greater Bombay's decadal population increase of some 2.2 million has
been absorbed partly in the mill and warehouse or dock sections and in
the residential sections along the Seaface and the Back Bay reclamation
near Colaba Point, while growth has been largely accommodated in the
Eastern Suburbs on Salsette and Trombay. Observers of this process of
centrifugal growth agree that it represents displacement of residential
space and expansion on filled land by retail and wholesale trade,
personal and professional services, banking, governmental administration and transportation. The continued concentration of working
population of lower Bombay has increased the daily movement of people
on railways, buses and cars, producing more traffic congestion, higher
intensity of land use and enhanced land values. These areal phenomena
are familiar in the urban areas of the More Developed World. It seems
doubtful that plans for development of New Bombay as a satellite city
and the construction of the Trans-Harbour Bridge or Bridge-cum-Tunnel
to a new port on the mainland will reduce the centralization of
business and service functions on Bombay Island.

In Greater Delhi (or the Delhi Urban Agglomeration according to the
Census of India classification) the population density profile in 1971
tended to be concave and the gradient was very sharp beyond the limits
of Shahjahanabad, the 300-year-old Walled City. The peak of density in
1971 was 1665 persons per hectare near Chandni Chowk, the principal
bazar street and around the Jumma Masjid, and ranged upward from 500
per hectare in many of the census charges located "inside the walls" or
nearby in Paharganj and Subzi Mandi. Outside the former walls,
densities fell rapidly to 150 per hectare and dropped lower than 70 in
New Delhi Municipality, Delhi Cantonment and other outlying areas. A
secondary clustering with density between 150 and 500 per hectare
existed on the south fringe of New Delhi and the adjacent sector of the

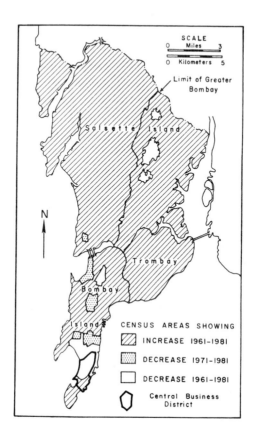

Figure 4   Population Changes in Greater Bombay,
1961-1981.

Delhi Municipal Corporation. The distribution of population in Greater
Delhi in 1971 remained basically as it had been in 1961, but it was
evident that most of the growth was being absorbed in the vast reaches
of the Delhi Municipal Corporation, extending west and south as well as
across the Yamuna River, while the Walled City had already begun to
decline (see Table 3). Provisional results of the Census of 1981
showed that decline in the old city has been accelerated, reducing the
number of inhabitants to less than that recorded in 1951. New Delhi
Municipality lost 10 percent in the decade 1971 to 1981. Planning
Division 'A' lost 8 1/2 percent of its 1971 population by 1981, while
population in the remainder of the Municipal Corporation grew 85
percent.

TABLE 3

GREATER DELHI: CHANGES IN POPULATION DISTRIBUTION

1951-81

Area	1951	Population (100,000's)		
		1961	1971	1981
Old "Walled" City	3.81	*4.20 (+10.24%)	4.09 (-2.62%)	3.62 (-11.49%)
Planning Division 'A'	5.38	6.50 (+20.81%)	*6.80 (+4.62%)	6.22 (-8.52%)
Total: Delhi Urban Agglomeration	14.37	23.59 (+64.17%)	36.47 (+54.57%)	57.14 (+56.66%)

* Maximum density. ( ) Figures in parentheses give decadal variation in
         percent.

Source: Census of India 1971, Series 1-India, Part II-A (i), General
         Population Tables, Table A-IV; Census of India 1981, Series -1
         India, Paper -2 of 1981, Provisional Population Totals,
         Rural-Urban Distribution, Appendix II. Details for the Walled
         City and Planning Division 'A' taken from the Delhi
         Development Autority, Perspective Planning Wing, "Policies for
         Delhi - 2001 - Shelters," Seminar Paper No. 2, Part IV, p. 4,
         courtesy of Mssrs. V.S. Ailawadi, Chairman, Steering
         Committee, E.F.N. Ribeiro, Planning Commissioner and J.C.
         Gambhir, Secretary of the Steering Committee.

     Thus, the spatial growth process has become centrifugal in Delhi's
rapid expansion, producing a flattening of the population profile and a
downward shift of the gradient. One observes this change of land use
not only in Old Delhi in Daryaganj near the Red Fort and along Chandni
Chowk but also in New Delhi around Connaught Place and along the
thoroughfares leading to old Delhi to the Railway Station and to the
Parliament. In New Delhi there is the added factor of the increasing
requirements of the Central Government for administrative functions.
While metropolitan Delhi in comparison with Bombay is much less crowded
and has spread readily by virtue of the less restricted site, it can be
anticipated that both Old and New Delhi will lose residential
population while gaining commercial and service functions. Because
Delhi has been lacking good rail and bus transit systems, secondary
office centers, such as Nehru Place in South Delhi and Rajendra Place
in West Delhi, have developed rapidly in the last decade. The trend
towards residential sprawl which has long been evident in the southern
sector of metropolitan Delhi is now becoming stronger in the western
and northern sectors and across the Yamuna in Shahdara. Planners
project the future pattern of transportation in

the Delhi region as a vast network of radial axes and concentric rings with improved access to the core as well as the periphery. It is doubtful if a good transit system will counterbalance the shift to non-residential uses in the core areas or eliminate the preferences of the urban elite for suburban housing colonies. If the population of Greater Delhi should double in the next two decades as anticipated, development of the transportation system can not be expected to reduce the congestion of transport or lessen the pressure of rising land values in the urban core.

4. Conclusions

My tentative conclusion, based on further analysis of the 1971 census data for twelve other Indian cities, together with the foregoing evidence from the Census of 1981 in Bombay and Delhi, is that urbanization in India is entering a new phase of growth. There is no doubt that Indian cities are rapidly gaining population and spreading outward more than ever before. Density of population in central commercial areas of many smaller cities may be expected to stabilize and eventually decline. Centrifugal tendencies will dominate future growth of urban areas.

The 1981 census results are still being tabulated and will not be available, as I understand, until after March 1982. At that time it is to be hoped that the counts will be issued for municipal wards, or other census divisions and non-municipal areas, accompanied by large-scale maps sufficiently accurate to identify the areas to which the census data pertain. We can expect that the size and complexity of urban areas will increase and the problems of securing good base maps will persist. I hope that it will be possible for planners and others to pursue detailed geographical analysis in order to gain a clearer understanding of the spatial processes of population change in urban India.

References

Brush, John E. (1973). 'Application of a model to the Analysis of population distribution in Indian cities,' Urban Geography in Developing Countries, (ed.) R. L. Singh, Varanasi: National Geographical Society of India, pp. 28-49.

_____. (1970). 'Some dimensions of urban population pressure in India,' in Geography and a Crowding World, (ed.) Wilbur Zelinsky, L.A. Kosinski and A. Mansell Prothero, New York: Oxford University Press, pp. 279-304.

_____. (1968). 'Spatial patterns of population in Indian cities,' Geographical Review , Vol. 58, pp. 362-91.

Census of India 1981. Series-1, India. Provisional Population Totals. Paper-2 of 1981. Rural-Urban Distribution.

Kosambi, Meera (1980). Bombay and Poona: A Socio-Ecological Study of Two Indian Cities, Stockholm, Sweden: Department of Sociology, Ph.D. dissertation.

Premi, M.K. et al. (1977). 'The concept of urban areas in the 1961-1971 census,' in Population Statistics of India, ed. by Ashish Bose, D.B. Gupta and G. Raychoudhuri, New Delhi: Vikas Publication House.

15 Technology choice in the construction sector of developing countries

LATA CHATTERJEE

1. Introduction

The remarkable growth in per capita real income in the last two decades in the developing world has been accompanied, in most instances, by increasing income inequalities and poverty. Consequently, alternative development strategies, that combine growth with equity objectives have been proposed by several analysts (Chenery et al. 1974, Streeten 1979). The assessment of such development strategies, that can increase both production and consumption in developing countries, is currently a major item on the analytical agenda of development planners.

The distribution of real income in a country or region is dependent on two components: primary income, which derives from payments received for production (employment), and secondary income which results from transfer payments made from the primary incomes. Transfer payments have been viewed as a viable means for improving the income distribution in affluent economies and there is a difference between the primary and secondary income distributions in advanced economies. However, the feasibility of income transfer for improving the primary income distribution in low income developing countries is limited and the efficacy of transfer payments for improving income distributions decline with income of the country. This difference between the advanced and developing countries results partly from the latter's weak resource base (from which transfers can be made between the sectors and the income groups), and partly from the political/social forces that divert the limited resources available for transfers, to upper income groups. In many developing countries, income transfers have been regressive and have accentuated, rather than diminished, inequality. This is particularly true in the construction sector, where income transfers through subsidized infrastructure and housing investment have benefited the elite.

If development policy is to improve income distributions, production policies should be evaluated in terms of their impact on the primary income distribution. The primary income distribution is dependent on two interacting systems: the political/institutional system that sets rules for governing payments to factors of production (i.e., wages, interest, profit) and the technological/economic system that determines (through the type of, access to, and ownership of these factors of production) the manner in which these rules are expressed in the actual income distribution (Sen 1975). It is the combination of

178

these two payment systems that governs technological choice in the developing world. It is argued here that both payment systems have consistently encouraged the adoption of modern technology and thus have increased income inequalities, unemployment and poverty. This paper uses the construction sector to illustrate the issues raised in the theoretical literature on technology choice and to suggest policy alternatives for that sector.

The reasons for adopting modern technology have received widespread attention from economists. Three types of consequences of the indis-criminate adoption of modern technology have been noted. All these consequences have converged toward generating and sustaining inequal-ities. First, modern technology is designed for advanced capital rich economies and has high capital labor ratios (K/L ratios.) It absorbs a small proportion of the labor force and invariably benefits the small minority who find employment in the high wage modern sector. Second, capital intensive technologies produce commodities suitable for the consumption of higher income groups and ignores basic needs items appropriate for meeting the consumption needs of the poor. Consequently there is a chronic shortage of items of consumption necessary for the survival of the majority -- leading to rapid inflation in the economy, and underconsumption of the majority. Third, modern technology requires large infrastructure investments for its effective functioning. Concentration of such infrastructure investments in a few large cities works to the detriment of the majority -- causing paucity of infrastructure in the remainder of the country (e.g., smaller urban areas and rural areas) -- noted as the urban bias in development (Lipton 1977). In summary, excessive concentration of investment in the modern sector distorts consumption and production patterns and worsens the income of the majority who are neither employed in that sector nor consume its output.

In the light of these observations, there is a burgeoning literature on technology choice. Strong pleas have been made for the adoption of appropriate (or intermediate) technology i.e., technology that is consistent with the factor endowments of the country. In the context of labor surplus economies, such as India, it implies the adoption of improved labor intensive technology that increases output without sacrificing employment -- thereby maximizing social welfare. In spite of these analytical arguments there is little practical response to these pleas. A case in point is the allocation of construction materials and funds for the Asian games in New Delhi, (to the detriment of regional infrastructure investments and lower income housing).

The objective of this paper is to explain the forces leading to capital intensity as they unfold in developing countries and to point out some strategies that can contribute to more equitable development. In Section II, the conventional arguments for this bias will be briefly reviewed. In Section III an alternate explanation is provided. In the concluding Section possible contribution of the development geographer, to this controversial issue will be highlighted.

2. Factors governing the Capital Intensive bias

While developing countries have labor surplus economies, with

elastic labor supply curves and low wages, the development of the
construction industry (in common with manufacturing and transport) is
increasingly becoming capital intensive. In a situation of capital
scarcity in the economy (relative to "need") and labor surplus
(relative to available employment) the scarce factor is being used in
increasing quantity in relative and absolute terms, (leading to
increasing dependence on a world capital market). What are the reasons
behind this paradox? The conventional arguments provided for the
capital intensity bias can be divided into 4 broad classes:

a)   factor price distortions in the market;
b)   technological determinism resulting from lack of development
      of efficient labor intensive technologies;
c)   technocratic behavior resulting from the preference of
      planners, engineers, bureaucrats for capital and import
      intensive modern technology;
d)   consumer's preferences for modern sector output.

The strongest arguments made for the capital intensity bias stem
from the neoclassical argument of distortions in relative prices of
factors of production in the market. It has been observed that capital
goods prices do not reflect the scarcity of capital and are kept
artifically low by national planners through regulation and control of
exchange rates and interest rates. This artificial undervaluation of
capital acts as a deterrent to the maximum use of the abundant factor
-- labor and complementary domestic resources. It encourages the use
of capital intensive equipment such as earth movers, caterpillars, etc.
in construction. The usual recommendation has been to correct this
capital intensive bias and to provide appropriate price signals in the
factor markets so that scarce factors are economized and abundant
resources are more utilized.

The technological determinism argument states that the best
available technology is capital intensive since Research and Development
(R & D) is carried out in advanced economies, where labor is scarce and
expensive relative to capital. Therefore new technological developments
are suited to factor endowments different from those that prevail in
developing countries (Eckaus 1955, Singer 1973). Where older vintage
technology with higher labor components are available, spare parts
become unavailable (Baer and Herve 1966). Since developing countries
lack their own capital goods industry this situation is likely to be
perpetuated (Stewart 1978, Bhalla 1975). The policy recommendations in
this case call for the stimulation and subsidization of R & D of labor
intensive efficient technology by supporting appropriate technology
institutions and research on intermediate building technology. Research
on building materials (such as mudcrete instead of concrete, manually
operated mixers and like) illustrate this approach.

The third approach eschews the simple "no choice" view of
technology choice and suggests that institutional factors at the
engineering, managerial and bureaucratic levels, occurring at each
stage of the production process, are responsible for this capital
intensity bias. They note the availability of a wide range of
efficient technologies. Actually, the adoption of technology depends
on the decisions of the technicians-engineers, planners and managers
and they make the high K/L choice due to their own attitudes and
preferences. Some of these attitudes partly result from:

a) their own "scientific expertise" and familiarity with modern methods of production;
b) from status values imputed through the educational and socialization process; and
c) from their desire to maximize control, meet production deadlines, minimize labor relations and so on (Picket 1974, Hawrylshyn 1978).

Housing technology choices in rural areas of Lesotho provide an example of such irrational preferences for modern construction (Selwyn 1971). Given this interpretation of technology adoption, recommendations are made to change the attitudes of the managers and bureaucrats and to emphasize the importance of indigenous methods and appropriate technology through education and training. The United Nations through its education programs and support of housing and building research centers has tried to respond to this interpretation.

The fourth set of arguments center around consumer preference. Consumers influenced by advertisement and close communication with advanced economies, demand modern housing, bridges and roads. The supply sector responds to consumer demand. In the context of income inequalities, the income elasticity of modern products, and lack of effective demand among the poor majority it is not surprising that the construction sector has responded with modern outputs that uses capital intensive technology. Since modern construction, using steel and glass, requires advanced technology, capital intensive technology is chosen by the supply sector. That is, choice of capital intensive technology for construction is in response to the consumer demand for modern products.

It is undoubtedly true that all of these factors -- price distortions, inadequate research, institutional biases, and consumer preferences are all involved in the choice of modern technology. However, the important issue is not that disparities between equilibrium prices and market prices exacerabates the employment/output conflict, which they undoubtedly do, but in seeking explanations for the reasons that underly factor price distortions. The answer to the paradox lies not in advocating a return to the "perfect market" and to a neo classical world where factors are priced appropriately, but in unravelling the forces which cause factor price distortions. In a similar vein, questions should be raised regarding the other arguments on technological determinism. What are the reasons for the biases of the manager, technicians and the modern firm? In the conventional analyses noted above, the social/political forces that bring about such distortion are ignored. Only the impact of these biases and distortions on technology choice are traced. Price distortions in capital, labor and foreign exchange markets are assumed to be planning errors. Why do governments of developing countries continue to increase such distortions, inspite of best analytical advice to the contrary? The point to note is that such distortions favor the elite -- owners of capital and the luxury consumers.

A long term solution to the problem is predicated on an understanding the underlying forces responsible for these distortions. In Section 3 an alternative explanation, drawn from the perspective of political economy, is provided.

3. The Construction Sector and the use of Productive/Unproductive Labor

While conventional analysts view the dualism in the construction sector as modern and traditional, or formal-informal, this analysis uses the two Marxian categories "productive" and unproductive" labor to explain technology choice and adoption. While all construction activity is involved in commodity production (and can therefore be considered productive in the general sense of the term), not all construction activity is productive in the Marxian notion of the term. In the Marxian notion, productivity of labor is not determined by the labor process, nor by the character of the commodities produced, i.e., the process or the output. Productive labor is determined by the social relations of production within which the labor is expended. To be classified as productive, the labor must be expended in a wage labor -- capital relation. For example, construction activity by skilled self employed craftsman -- bricklayers, masons, roofers -- working on their own account is not "productive" from the Marxian standpoint. Money expended by a homeowner or a local municipality for office buildings and roads, using self employed labor does not create the funds to rehire the labor in the next period. It does not create surplus value and is thus not productive labor. The laborer does not get the benefits of extra output in the case of "productive" wage earning labor, while in "unproductive" labor the benefits of output increase, through improved technology, accrues to the laborer.

In the Marxian analytic framework, surplus value, arises from the difference between the value of labor power (i.e., wages) and the value which the labor power creates through its labor. The greater the difference between the two, the greater the surplus value appropriation by the owners of capital in the construction sector. Since wages in the construction sector are determined by demand and supply of labor (modified through union negotiations in the organized labor market) and the output of that labor is a function of technology, the more efficient the technology, the greater the difference between the two magnitudes. The capitalist's interest in increasing this difference encourages the adoption of modern technology.

Most construction activity in developing countries is of the "unproductive" variety, done by jobbing laborers. Any benefit from new technology, such as through increased productivity, ability to handle more complex jobs and like innovations in the "unproductive" group accrues to the laborer. Such technology will increase surplus labor time for the labor, and increase the laborer's income. The excess product will be appropriated by and will benefit the self employed laborer and the economy at large. These innovations in the low cost sector will not permit surplus appropriation by the modern capitalist construction sector.

It is the contention of this paper that the lack of interest in low cost technology can be traceable to the absence of institutional mechanisms for encouraging surplus labor time. All attempts at slum upgrading, where such self employed artisans with improved low cost technology can be used, do not interest economic sectors - capitalist and financial. As their interest lies in surplus appropriation, price distortions, institutional biases, and value transmissions that increase surplus appropriation are favored. Adoption of technology becomes pertinent when low cost housing, can be produced by construction firms -- using wage labor. In such cases mass production methods, use of new construction materials, and like are adopted. Institutional forces -- finance, marketing and so on -- provide help to "low cost" housing rather than to low income households likely to use "unproductive" labor for construction.Any interest in technology that increases surplus labor time through -- technical, institutional, financial innovations -- thus must be encouraged by an enlightened public sector interested in efficiently augumenting social welfare.

The category of productive labor provides a basis for understanding the capital intensity bias in technology. There is likely to be interest in increasing the surplus product of labor, only when the surplus product can be appropriated as surplus value. In the context of capital -- wage labor relations any technology which affects the productivity of capital investment is useful for the accumulation process for the construction firm and in the economy. If this argument is valid, then the observed capital intensive expansion of the construction industry can be interpreted as capital in search of surplus value.

Capital intensity implies the substitution of labor power by machines. Since new technology increases output at a faster rate than old technology, firms that can adopt the new technology increase their surplus product. As wages are paid according to a social average, the capital intensive firms are able to increase their surplus value. Since construction firms are compelled to compete with each other for the limited contracts available in a developing country each firm has the incentive to modify its production process so that it is more efficient in its ability to appropriate surplus value. A firm's ability to appropriate surplus value (make profits in a neoclassical sense) and yet provide low bids, will be a function of its rate of adoption of capital intensive "efficient" technology. It is this desire which determines technology choice in the formal construction sector. Adoption of innovations through factor price distortions and the other arguments discussed in Section 2 are thus encouraged, if not promoted, by the formal/modern sector.

There will be two types of spillover effects of this capital intensive technology:

a)   within the productive sector, and
b)   for the nonproductive sector.

Within the productive sector of the construction industry in developing countries there is considerable variation in production functions (usually correlated with size, scale of operation, contact with advanced economies, etc.). The spillover effects within the productive sector will be for the more efficient firms (high K/L ratios) to increase their market share by displacing less efficient producers with older vintage technology. This will lead to concentration and centralization of resources in the long run. It will also compel the less efficient firms to move in the direction of more efficient capital intensive technology, irrespective of whether the technology is appropriate with the factor endowments of the firm or the economy at large. Since the adoption of capital intensive technology is possible only if capital costs are low, there is political pressure for subsidizing capital and thence the factor price distrotions that perpetuate and accentuate this bias. Therefore, factor price distortion are <u>necessary</u> for the increasing adoption of capital intensive technology. While factor price distortions are instrumental for the promotion of capital intensive technologies these distortions are encouraged for the purpose of surplus value appropriation by the larger construction firms.

In fact all the four arguments for Capital Intensive bias, mentioned earlier, can be accommodated in this framework of analysis. The attitudes of decision makers, the education and the training process, the ability to conduct research and development can all be viewed as compatible with the objective of the creation and appropriation of the surplus value. In as much as the less capitalized firms are unable to adopt new technology at the same rate as the more capitalized firms, they are in the short run forced to adjust by extracting more surplus value from the laborer (by driving down wages or lengthening the work day). In their need for survival such firms will change their factor inputs -- shifting along the existing production function, instead of adopting new technology (changing the production function).

Such adjustments, possible only in the short run, are made by the older, more inefficient construction firms, rather common in developing countries. Over time, some of them may be driven out of existence, whereas others will seek access to subsidized capital or search for "innovative" managers capable of extracting surplus value in order to switch to the modern construction technology.

The "unproductive sector" will have to absorb the labor "thrown off" by the progressive elimination of the smaller, less capitalized firms. Ultimately the ability of the unproductive' sector to absorb will decline, through labor surplus and competition in this sector. In the intermediate and long run there will be a shrinkage in the self employed sector. The marginal self employed will be forced to seek wage labor (i.e., join the productive sector) leading to progressive capitalization of the construction sector, increasing expansion of the modern sector, and reinforcement of the capital intensity bias. However, a "vestige" of "unproductive" labor will continue to remain because of individual preferences for self employment, the need for skilled craft labor for specific jobs, (e.g., restoration), and small jobs (such as adding components, maintenance and rehabilitation, etc.) i.e., specialized tasks in which the capital intensive firms are not interested in competing. If however, any of these tasks become sufficiently large, the productive sector can and will outbid the unproductive sector because of its higher rate of capitalization and access to "efficient" technology. Thus, the spillover effect on the "unproductive" sector will be the undermining of the base of its existence.

4. Conclusion

The ability to produce surplus value and to realize surplus value varies across space. It is not an accident that capital intensive construction firms are located in the metropolitan areas and large cities. First, they need adequate infrastructure for their functioning, access to low cost finance capital and contact with decision makers that award the limited contracts. Therefore, transportation and communication are vital. In resource poor developing countries only a few cities have the necessary public sector investment and agglomeration economies. Second, capital intensive firms, are able to pay higher wages. Higher wage managerial and technically qualified personnel are reluctant to move to non metropolitan areas.

Studies of the location of capital intensive firms (classified by size and scale) show movement over time down the urban heirarchy. Thus the integration of the construction sector is not only vertical, but has a very important spatial component (Pederson 1970, Pred 1975, Friedmann 1978). Since there will be uneven development of the construction industry, the pressure of competition and conversion to socially inappropriate technology will move outward from the metropolitan areas to nonmetropolitan areas. Thus the most "inefficient" construction technology is found in backward regions, smaller urban centers and rural areas. Their ability to survive is dependent on using the ample factor -- labor -- paying lower wages. Since the impulse for technology moves down the urban hierarchy (vertical diffusion) and down the scale of the firm, there is little or no impetus for the invention of and the adoption of technical efficiency in the "unproductive" sector. The more rapid the growth of the economy, the better the spatial integration, the faster will this displacement occur. The income inequalities that will flow from such a process cannot be traced in the paper, but are obvious.

Geographers can contribute to the policy debate by emphasizing the need for technological improvement of small scale enterprises, that have the "appropriate" factor endowments for the economy. Access to finance is particularly important, as capitalization is predicated on the availability of finance (even the largest firms depend on credit for adoption of technology). It will allow the self employed sector, either as individuals or as cooperatives, to appropriate the surplus product as surplus time. This implies the need for low income finance (not to be confused with low cost finance) for the development and adoption of technology that can benefit this sector. It is the responsibility of the public sector to assume a large role in achieving this objective. Institutional forces should be set in motion for the adoption, at the small scale and local level, of improved technology that exists in scientific establishments, research centers and institutions. In as much as these factor endowments vary locally, the role of the geographer becomes crucial, for determining the patterns of resource endowments and delineating the "appropriateness" of technology consistent with these endowments in an area.

References

Baer, Werner and Michel E. A. Herve (1966). 'Employment and industrialization in developing countries,' Quarterly Journal of Economics, Vol. 80, No. 1, pp. 88-107.

Bhalla, A.S. (1975). Technology and Employment in Industry: A Case Study Approach, I.L.O. Geneva.

Chenery, H., M.S. Ahhwalia, C.L.G. Bell, J.H. Duloy and R. Jolly (1974). Redistribution with Growth, Oxford: Oxford University Press.

Eckaus, R.S. (1958). 'The factor proportions problem in underdeveloped areas, American Economic Review, Vol. 45, No. 4, pp. 539-65.

Friedmann, John (1978). 'The role of cities in national development,' in Systems of Cities: Readings on Structure, Growth and Policy, (eds.) L.S. Bourne and J.W. Simmons, Oxford University Press.

Hawrylshyn, Oli (1978). 'Capital - intensity biases in developing country technology choice,' Journal of Development Economics, Vol. 5, No. 3, pp. 215-36

Lipton, M. (1977). Why Poor People Stay Poor: A Study of Urban Bias in World Development, London: Temple Smith.

Pederson, P. (1970). 'Innovation diffusion within and between national urban systems,' Geographical Analysis, Vol. 2, No. 3, pp. 203-54.

Pickett, James, D.J.C. Forsyth and N.S. McBain (1974). 'The choice of technology, economic efficiency and employment in developing countries,' World Development, Vol. 2, No. 3, pp. 47-54.

Pred, A. (1975). 'Diffusion, organizational spatial structure and city-system development,' Economic Geography, Vol. 51.

Selwyn, P. (1971). 'The tyranny of the technician,' International Development Review, Vol. 1, pp. 17-20.

Sen, A.K. (1975). Employment, Technology and Development, Oxford: Clarendon Press.

Singer, H.W. (1973). 'The development outlook for poor countries: technology is the key,' <u>Challenge</u>, Vol. 16, No. 2, pp. 42-47.

Stewart, Frances (1978). 'Inequality, technology and the payments systems, '<u>World Development</u>, Vol. 6, No. 3, pp. 275-93.

Streeten, P. (1979). 'Basic needs: premises and promises,' <u>Journal of Policy Modelling</u>, Vol. 1, pp. 136-46.

16 Financing urban development in developing countries

VED PRAKASH

1. Introduction

Rapid urbanization, low level of income and net savings, and high costs associated with urban development and urban services are the critical factors contributing to the deteriorating urban environment in most of the developing countries. Seriousness of the urban situation is recognized but public policy, planning, programming, and resource allocation, and financing aspects of urban development are generally unintegrated and disjointed. In many of the developing countries, especially in Asia, even if urban development is according a top priority, fiscal resources may be quite deficient. In part, this may be due to the adoption of inappropriate planning standards and technologies. With a very few exceptions, the seriousness of the resource mobilization problem has not yet been grasped. Unconventional and far reaching changes are essential in the revenue and borrowing powers of the urban local government bodies, urban land policies, and inter-governmental fiscal relations.

The primary focus of this study is local (urban) government finance in the developing countries in Asia -- revenues raised by local governments from their own resources as well as intergovernmental fiscal transfers. It is essential that any study of resource mobilization and financing policies for urban development, especially in the developing countries, must be undertaken in the broader context of:

1) the urbanization process;
2) urbanization policies and national development plans;

---

[1] With special reference to the developing countries in Asia and the Pacific (countries included are primarily those designated by the Asian development Bank as its Developing Member Countries (DMC's)).

[2] This paper draws upon an earlier report prepared by the author for the Asian Development Bank, Manila ("Fiscal Policy and Resource Mobilization for Urban Development in Asia," August 1977). Additional support was provided by the Graduate School, University of Wisconsin, Madison for field work in the Republic of China and Korea and the Philippines, during the summer of 1978 and travel support for participation in the conference.

3) national and regional income and social accounts;
4) capital and current costs associated with alternative
    standards and technologies; and
5) institutional arrangements and capacities of various levels of
    governments relative to urban development and provision of
    urban services.

Since fiscal instruments and financial policies may influence and
be impacted by other public policies and programs concerned with urban
development, such linkages deserve special attention. For example,
real estate (property) taxation in general and land taxation in particular may provide prositive incentives for certain types of development
in a particular area, it would be advantageous to coordinate tax
policies with other land use regulatory devices. Again, land acquisition and disposal policies for urban development may have far reaching
implications on the yield of property taxation.

Generally speaking, the subject matter covered by local government
finance and financial aspects of urban development including delivery
of urban public services, has not received the attention it deserves
from the academics as well as the practitioners -- economists,
planners, public administrators, and others concerned with related
public policy and development issues. This is specially so in the
developing countries due perhaps to the weak position of local
governments in general (most developing countries have unitary system
of government) and the paucity of fiscal/financial data in particular.

2. Urbanization

Magnitude and Rapid Growth

A large majority of the developing countries have been experiencing accelerated rates of population growth (because of fairly stable
birth and declining death rates) during the last three decades. Growth
of urban population has generally been much higher than the overall
rates of population growth -- largely due to increasing rural-to-urban
migration. The urban population in the less developed countries was
272 million in 1950 whereas the comparable figure was 429 million in
the developed countries, with their respective shares being 39 percent
and 61 percent of the world urban population. By 1975, urban population was 819 million in the developing countries and 731 million in the
developed countries, their respective shares changing to 53 percent and
47 percent. By the year 2000, projections indicate that less developed
countries are likely to have 2,153 million persons in urban areas and
the developed countries 1,048 million persons (67 per cent and 33 per
cent respectively) (The World Bank Staff Work Paper No. 209, 1975).
During the second half of this century the urban population in the less
developed countries is likely to increase ten-fold. It is pointed out
that "almost two-thirds of the increase in urban population of the
developing world by the year 2000 are likely to occur in Asia where two
countries, India and China, between them will account for nearly 60
percent (The World Bank Staff Work Paper No. 209, 1975).

A salient feature of the urbanization process in the developing
countries has been the invariable trend towards concentration of
population in the capital cities and large urban centers. Further,
generally countries in the middle income Asian group (Korea, Malaysia,

189

Philippines) have a higher percentage of urbanization. Again, a population concentration in the metropolitan and large cities is common in most DMC's (Developing Countries Members of the Asian Development Bank) -- feature on which the concern for the problems of urbanization is largely focussed. Finally, large cities have generally been growing as rapidly as the total urban population of the country, and there is no evidence that today's very large cities (population above five million) are encountering any natural or technological limits to this growth (Asian Development Bank, 1980, p. 6).

Policies and National Development Plans

The developing countries in Asia, like most other developing countries, are undergoing rapid socio-economic changes, and most of them are engaged in varying forms of planning for national development. A review of some of the recent national development plans indicates that most of them do not contain clearly defined objectives and targets for urbanization. These plans concentrate on the problems of economic growth and increasing financial resources, and give inadequate attention to relating economic development to spatial consequences. Some aspects of urbanization are discussed in the plans in conjunction with industrial location policy, as problems associated with housing or slums or the need to prepare "master plans" for all cities above a certain size. From public policy point of view, Dotson defines this lack of attention to urbanization and urban development in national planning as either unconscious, partial, uncoordinated, or negative (Dotson, 1972, pp. 1-2).

Balanced regional development and elimination of disparities between regions have been major objectives expressed in most national plans. But only in a few instances are concrete suggestions presented in regard to the methods for achieving these objectives. The Indian and some other national development plans, for example, include explicit location policies as a means for distributing investment in new industry more equitably among the regions. Similarly, small-scale industry is identified and considered in the context of either rural or small town development. Despite these locational attempts, many of the Indian national planners today admit that the decentralization efforts have failed, that the aggregation of industry of all scales has continued by and large in the large cities and that regional disparities have increased rather than decreased (Dandekar and Rath, 1971, pp. 25-48 and 106-146).

Another aspect of this quest for decentralization is evident in the continual interest in the development of new towns, particularly in conjunction with large scale industrial investment and administrative reforms requiring new capital cities. The model for planning most of these new towns has generally been the British "garden city" in its manifold company town varieties. The resultant cost of this kind of urbanization is enormous, both in economic and in social terms (Alonso, 1969 and Prakash, 1969).

At the metropolitan level, urban planning has by and large been modelled along the lines of European and North American examples. As a result, most of these "master planning" efforts have produced at best some interesting compilations of information about the nature of urban problems, and at worst colorful map and picture books, some of which

TABLE 1
URBANIZATION AND POPULATION GROWTH 1950-2000

	1950			1975			2000		
	Urban	Rural	Total	Urban	Rural	Total	Urban	Rural	Total
Population in Millions									
Less Developed Countries	277	1,382	1,654	661	1,912	2,573	2,153	2,939	5.092
More Developed Countries	429	402	831	670	378	1,048	1,048	267	1,315
World Total	701	1,784	2,485	1,331	2,290	3,621	3,201	3,206	6,407
Percent of Total Population									
Less Developed Countries		67			73			79	
More Developed Countries		33			27			21	
World Total		100			100			100	
Percent of Rural Population									
Less Developed Countries		77			83			92	
More Developed Countries		23			17			8	
World Total		100			100			100	

Table 1 (continued)

	1950			1975			2000		
	Urban	Rural	Total	Urban	Rural	Total	Urban	Rural	Total
Percent of Urban Population									
Less Developed Countries		39			53			67	
More Developed Countries		61			47			33	
World Total		100			100			100	

Percent Increas

	1950-1975			1975-2000		
	Urban	Rural	Total	Urban	Rural	Total
Less Developed Countries	201	50	75	163	42	76
More Developed Countries	80	(-)10	32	43	(-)26	20
World Total	121	37	60	106	32	61

Source: World Bank, op. cit.

have become sought after and hard to find collector's items[3] (Jakobson and Prakash, 1974). The conceptual poverty which has long dominated Western urban planning has been exported to the Asian metropolis despite, or perhaps because of, the considerable interest which organizations like the United Nations, the Ford Foundation, and some of the bilateral technical assistance programs have shown in problems associated with the fast growth of the primate centers of the developing countries.

In many of the developing countries in Asia (and other developing countries), the severity of the housing and urban environmental problems is recognized and concern is expressed in national development plans. However, allocation of funds in these plans and resource mobilization efforts fall far short of the public policy concerns. It appears that public policy, planning, programming, resource allocation, and financing aspects of urban developing and housing are generally unintegrated and disjointed.

The acuteness of the shortage of resources in the context of rapid urbanization has probably not yet been fully grasped.

3. Deteriorating Urban Environment

The vastness of the size of urban population, and more importantly the rapidity with which it has been growing and concentrating in the largest cities and metropolises, have many serious repercussions. The heart of the problem lies in the rapidly rising number of urban poor. Another closely related problem is provision of housing and infrastructure in the urban areas. The imbalance between the need for housing and urban services and the supply began during the World War II period, when some of the housing stock and intrastructure was destroyed and the new construction was almost at a standstill. The post-war period began with a legacy of huge backlogs of needs in both housing and urban services. The influx of refugees into cities and towns in several countries, without a commensurate increase in their economic capacity, compounded the problem. With few exceptions, the situation has been deteriorating rapidly (Grimes, 1976).

Till recently, approaches to housing policies have generally been based on estimating normative requirements -- current and future deficits in respect to housing needs. Estimates of needs are typically relative to some designated standards, e.g., number of persons per room, availability of certain environmental facilities, i.e., water supply, type of construction and so on. These standards do not generally take into account either availability of resources or economic capacities of families and/or households. Dwellings that do not meet prescribed standards and large number of slums and squatter settlements are thus included in the estimates of deficits. Such measures of deficits that rely on data for slum and squatter housing as proxies for inappropriate housing tend to overstate the seriousness of the housing problem.

---

[3] In recent years, there have been a few metropolitan planning efforts in which new conceptualizations and approaches have been developed, e.g., Calcutta and Karachi metropolitan planning efforts.

In spite of the above limitations, assessment of housing situation based on need or similar indicators suggests that housing and other urban services in the majority of developing countries have deteriorated over time. "The available data indicate that many countries are building only two to four dwelling units per one thousand population. In global terms this means that in the urban areas alone the deficit is increasing by 4 to 5 million units annually". (United Nations, 1973, p. 4-5).

The urban water supply and sanitation services have been unsatisfactory and deteriorating in a majority of the developing countries. According to a WHO survey, it was found that in 1975, 77 percent of the urban populations were supplied with reasonably adequate community water supply (57 percent had house connections and 20 percent had reasonable access to public standposts); and 75 per cent of urban population had access to reasonable sanitation facilities (25 percent were served by connections to public sewers, and the remaining 50 percent possessed household systems) in the less developed countries. In the rural areas, 78 percent of the population is without adequate water supply and 85 percent without satisfactory sanitation services.

The situation with regard to water supply and sanitation services in most of the developing countries in the Asian region is generally much worse. For example in Indonesia, only 11 percent of the urban population had access to piped water supply in 1968-69. In Western Samoa, Malaysia, Sri Lanka, and Thailand the respective percentages were 22, 27, 40 and 45 in recent years (Table 2).

TABLE 2

PERCENT OF POPULATION SERVED WITH PIPE WATER IN SELECTED RDMCs

| RDMC | Percent of Population Served by Piped Water | | |
	Year	Urban	Rural
China (Republic of)	1973	70	27
Hong Kong	1973	98	52
Indonesia	1968-69	11	--
Korea (Republic of)	1972	60	7
Malaysia	1970	27	21
Nepal	1961	48	--
Philippines	1967	63	22
Singapore	1970	94	--
Sri Lanka	1975	40	14
Thailand	1970	45	15
Western Samoa	1971	22	2

Source: Asian Development Bank, Key Indicators, October 1976, p. 5.

In the light of these conditions, HABITAT: United Nations Conference on Human Settlements, recommended that "Safe water supply and hygienic waste disposal should receive priority." While calling

194

for urgent action in most countries it was necessary to "adopt programmes with realistic standards for quality and quantity to provide water for urban and rural areas by 1990, if possible;" and to "adopt and accelerate programmes for the sanitary disposal of excreta and waste water in urban and rural areas." (Conference on Human Settlements, 1976).

A WHO/World Bank report prepared in response to the HABITAT recommendation assumed the following targets for the year 1990:

Community Water Supply - 57 percent population to be provided with house connections in urban areas and the remaining 43 percent with standposts (100 percent of rural population to be served through standposts).

Sanitation - 25 percent house connections and 75 percent household systems for urban population and 100 percent household systems for the rural population.

Based on the above targets, it has been estimated that during 1975-1990, water supply services will have to be provided for 638 million additional urban population in the developing countries. During the same period, sanitary services will have to be provided for 651 million additional persons in the urban centers. Of these projected requirements, it is likely that over 50 percent of the water supply and sanitation facilities and services are in respect of the urban centers of the developing countries in Asia if the proposed targets are also to be met by them.

In addition to housing, water supply and sanitation, massive capital outlays are also required in respect of other urban services, e.g., lands, roads and streets, electricity, education, health, transport, and so on.

4. Cost Associated with Urban Development

Comparative cost data for urban infrastructure are extremely scarce. Per capita capital outlays for urban facilities and housing as per the proposed standards in many of the countries in the region may range between $750 and $1,000. A recent publication points out that :

Available data indicate incremental costs of water supply averaging around $100 per head and sewage about the same. There are considerable variations, but these appear to depend much more on physical conditions than income level. Conventional "low income" housing costs range from a minimum rarely below $1,000 per family unit for the house construction alone to double this figure or more; $200 per head is perhaps a typical minimum. Primary school capital costs for projects with which the Bank has been associated range around $450 per student place, or $90 per head, assuming one-fifth of the population in this age bracket. Capital costs for employment vary widely from perhaps around $400 per worker in the modern sector and several times this amount in the more capital intensive advanced technology

195

occupations . . . . Large investments are also needed
for transport infrastructure and equipment, health
services, electricity, police and fire protection,
garbage collection, and other urban services (World
Bank, 1972, p. 19).

Based on 1962-64 cost data for several new towns in India, it was
found that per capita capital costs ranged from approximately $500 to
$900. Of these, development costs (e.g., land, water supply, sewerage,
drainage, street lighting, etc.) ranged between $150 and $500 per head
and the per capita outlays on housing were between $350 and $500
(Prakash, 1969).

A more recent study estimated that incremental per capita capital
costs for urban water supply may be around US $121 (1977 dollars) for
house connections and US $48 for street standposts. The sanitation
costs were estimated to be around $112 for house connections and $35
for household systems (United Nations, 1976). As per the targets
assumed in the WHO/World Bank report, average per capita capital costs
have been estimated to be around US $80 for water supply (57 percent
house connections and 43 percent standposts) and US $50 for sewerage
(25 percent house connections and 75 percent household systems).

The WHO/World Bank study points out the staggering sums of capital
investments that would be required in the developing countries during
the next fifteen years or so if the HABITAT targets (urban and rural)
were to be met: a sum of nearly US $133 billion of which US $92
billion is for community water supply and US $41 billion for sanitation
at 1977 prices. The investment requirements will be even greater after
providing for inflation and because of increasing marginal costs of
providing these services. According to the estimates, annual investment
in community water supply and sanitation during 1976-1990 would be 1.8
times and 2.3 times, respectively, the annual investments in the two
sectors during 1971-1975, or average annual investments between now and
1990, which will be 1.9 times the annual investments during the last
five years. For rural water supply and sanitation, the corresponding
annual investment rates would be 3.9 times and 4.0 times respectively.
The comparable rates for the urban areas would be 1.2 times and 2.1
times respectively.

Although cost data for urban development in the developing
countries in Asia are unavailable, it is likely that urban public
sector incremental outlays in respect to minimal standards for the very
basic facilities such as water supply, sanitation, roads, street
lighting, drainage and schools may range between US $350-500 per
capita. It may be appropriate to use these cost figures to indicate
the order of magnitude of investment requirements for urban facilities.
The population increase in urban areas in the developing countries in
Asia is currently around 10 million per year. During 1980-1990 and
1990-2000, the comparable figures are expected to be around 15 and 22
million respectively. Crude estimates of total investment requirements
during 1975-2000 may thus be between US $147 and $210 billion for
urban facilities (annual investment between US $3.50-5.0 billion during
1975-1980; between US $5.25-7.50 billion during 1980-1990; and between
US $7.70-11.00 billion during 1990-2000).

It is important to note that per capita outlays for urban infrastructure, in general, do not vary too much from one developing country to another. The ratio between the per capita infrastructure and housing costs and per capita gross domestic product may vary widely from one country to another, and this ratio is many times higher for the lowest income countries. In large part, this is due to the unavailability of intermediate technologies relative to the requirements for most elements of urban infrastructure and the economies of the different developing countries.

Because of the extreme scarcity of resources within most of the developing countries, the costs of providing urban infrastructure and other public facilities are of crucial importance in the developmental process. Economic development, industrialization, and urbanization are closely related processes. Many of the urban centers either lack or are inadequately supplied with such basic facilities as water supply, sewerage and drainage, transport and transit, and power. These urban areas are, therefore, not able to support industrialization and urbanization. In turn, this lack of industrial and other urban activities restricts their tax and revenue base, resulting in successive deterioration of municipal services, the replacement, modernization, and expansion of which is rendered imperative by rapid urban growth.

A shortage of available funds is the major constraint on capital improvements which, once built, need proper maintenance. In that capital costs influence and may largely determine maintenance and operating costs, any initial capital investment in infrastructure and other urban facilities has far-reaching implications for future allocation of resources. In the planning and programming of urban facilities, therefore, it is essential to give careful and simultaneous considerations to capital outlays as well as to the long-term impact of these projects on future budgets or maintenance and operating costs.

There are hardly any systematic studies on maintenance and operating costs for different urban services. On the basis of analysis of rather skimpy data, it is felt that annual maintenance and operating costs may exceed 10 percent of the initial capital outlays on urban services. The annual costs for land development (excluding utilities) may range between 8-10 percent, utilities between 15-20 percent, and housing between 8-12 percent of the capital costs (Prakash 1969, pp. 54-60). Thus, if per capita incremental capital costs for urban public facilities are likely to range between US $350-500 (1977 dollars), then incremental per capital maintenance costs in respect of the additional urban population may be between US $35-50.[4] As pointed out earlier, incremental capital requirements for provision of minimum basic facilities may be between US $3.50-5.00 billion per year during 1975-1980; between US $5.25-7.5 billion during 1980-1990; and between US $7.70-11.00 billion during 1990-2000. The impact of the above investments implies that municipal maintenance and operating costs in respect to new facilities alone may increase at the rate of US $350-500 million per year during 1975-1980; US $525-750 million during 1980-1990; and US $770-1,100 million during the last decade of this century.

---

[4] These services may vary in different countries and at different points in time in a given country, depending upon, among other things, interest rates and the dept retirement schedules relative to useful physical life of different facilities.

5. Planning Standards

Standards and appropriate technologies for housing and urban
development are of critical importance in the context of allocation and
mobilization of fiscal resources. Standards have generally been
adoptedon the basis of "desirable quality targets" rather than relative
to costs, economic capacity, and existing and new financial measures.
Most of the developing countries in Asia are caught in the middle in
their efforts to defend decent standards of urban development in the
face of growing needs and extremely limited means. If standards
adopted are extravagant relative to economic capacity, opportunity
costs associated with any level of investment are bound to be extremely
high, and it would be impossible to develop appropriate fiscal
instruments for financing urban services. There is some evidence to
suggest that although in humanitarian terms the standards for housing
and urban services may not be high, in terms of economic capacity in
general and ability or willingness to pay in particular, the standards
are nonetheless excessive.

6. Economic Capacity and Resource Mobilization for Urban Development

Policies and strategies for resource mobilization for financing
urban development must be reviewed within the broader framework of
national income and social accounts; national (central), state
(provincial), and local government revenues and intergovernmental
fiscal transfers; and capital and annual (maintenance and operating)
costs associated with urban service requirements. The scale and rapid
growth of urban population translates into massive capital investment
requirements and resulting long-run recurring costs in most of the
RDMCs. When these costs are juxtaposed with the extremely low level of
income and net savings, the severity of constraints and the importance
of resource mobilization come into focus.

Per capita gross national product (1979) and average annual rates
of growth during the last two decades for sixteen Asian countries are
presented in Table 3. The World Bank's 1981 Report on World Development
divides the 124 countries into five groups: (1) low-income countries
(per capita GNP of $370 or less); (2) middle-income countries (per
capita GNP between $380-4,380); (3) industrial market economies (per
capita GNP between $4,210-13,920); (4) capital surplus oil exporters
(per capita GNP between $2,410-17,100); and (5) nonmarket industrial
economies (per capita GNP between $3,690-6,430). Of the sixteen
countries included in Table 3, nine belong to Group 1 (low-income)
countries and the remaining seven to Group 2 (middle-income countries).

In a majority of the countries included in Table 3, the average
annual growth rate is under three percent. Only three countries (Hong
Kong, Republic of Korea, and Singapore) had annual growth rates above
seven percent. In real terms, per capita GNP may have declined in
several countries.

Given the low level of income and pattern of income distribution,
the level of net savings in most of the developing countries under
consideration is extremely low.[5]

---

[5] In a majority of the countries, the rate of growth for gross domestic
investment has been less than ten percent per annum during the last
two decades.

TABLE 3

PER CAPITA GROSS NATIONAL PRODUCT IN SELECTED

DEVELOPING COUNTRIES IN ASIA

Country	GNP Per Capita		Rank[1]
	1979 Dollars	Average Annual Growth (Per Cent) - 1960-79	
Afghanistan	170	0.5	11
Bangladesh	90	-0.1	4
Burma	160	1.1	10
China[2]	260	n.a.	22
Hong Kong	3,760	7.0	92
India	190	1.4	15
Indonesia	370	4.1	35
Korea, Republic of	1,480	7.1	77
Malaysia	1,370	4.0	74
Nepal	130	0.2	7
Pakistan	260	2.9	24
Papua New Guinea	660	2.8	54
Philippines	600	2.6	51
Singapore	3,830	7.4	93
Sri Lanka	230	2.2	18
Thailand	590	4.6	50

[1] Lowest to highest per capita GNP amongst the 124 countries included in the World Bank Report.

[2] Excluding the Republic of China, whose per capita GNP was $890 in 1975 and the average annual growth rate was 6.9 percent (1965-1974).

Source: World Bank, World Development Report 1981, (Washington, D.C., August 1981).

Even if urban infrastructure is accorded a high priority in the developmental context, available resources may be quite deficient in most of the countries. The World Bank, in its urban sector paper, correctly puts the problem in a proper perspective when it points out that:

> A level of net savings of 10 to 15 per cent fairly typical of the developing countries implies net savings per head below $25 a year for the majority of them and below $15 for many. Even if the totality of these savings could be mobilized for the benefit of the additional population, the amount per head of the additional population, assuming a three percent annual growth rate, would average from $500 to not much more than $800. By contrast, net national savings per head of population growth in richer countries of Latin America may exceed $4,000. Obviously, the problems for such countries, though serious enough, are of a quite different order. Such illustrative figures may appear to be unduly pessimistic in the context of urbanization problems since urban incomes and savings are well above the national average. However, though savings in the major towns are typically two or three times the national average, so also is their rate of population increase. Net savings in the towns per head of urban population increase are accordingly likely to be of the same order of magnitude as the growth between town and country tend roughly to parallel relative levels of savings (World Bank, 1972, p. 10)

Analysis of the public sector data indicates that the size of the public sector relative to the gross national product is rather small in many of the developing countries in Asia. In about half of the countries, the total public expenditures constitute less than 20 percent of the gross national product. In 1976, there were only three countries where this percentage was over 30 (Burma, Malaysia, and Pakistan). The total public expenditure relative to gross national product has changed only slightly in most of the developing countries in Asia.

Government revenue receipts (all levels) constitute less than 20 per cent of the gross national product in a majority of the developing countries in Asia. Tax revenues typically constitute between 10-20 percent of the gross national product. For a number of countries in the region, this percentage is under ten. Per capita revenue and tax receipts are presented in Table 4. It may be noted that of the 17 countries included in the table, per capita total revenues are under $50 for seven countries, between $50-100 for four, between $100-300 for another four, and in only one country is it over $300. Per capita tax revenue has been estimated for 13 countries (included in Table 4). It is less than $50 in eight and between $80 and $170 for the remaining five. In a majority of the countries, taxation provides more than 75 percent of the current revenues. Although non-tax revenues play different roles in the government revenues in different countries, they are generally not significant. It may also be pointed out that in most of the developing countries in Asia, the relative importance of

TABLE 4

PER CAPITA TOTAL CURRENT REVENUE AND TAX RECEIPTS
IN SELECTED COUNTRIES IN 1975

U.S. Dollars

Country	Current Revenues	Tax Receipts	Per Cent of of Total
Afghanistan (1974)	8	5	62
Bangladesh (1974)	8	6	77
Republic of China	213	137	64
Fiji	175	156	89
Hong Kong	275	169	65
India	31	27	85
Indonesia	26	25	96
Korea	96	81	84
Malaysia	169	154	91
Nepal	7	6	84
Pakistan	21	16	73
Papua New Guinea	81	--	--
Philippines	69	--	--
Singapore	622	--	--
Solomon Islands (1974)	52	--	--
Sri Lanka	31	26	80
Thailand	48	42	89

Source: Estimated from Asian Development Bank, Key Indicators of Developing Member Countries of ADB, Volume VIII, No. 1 (April 1977).

taxation has increased during the last decade.

Government expenditure and revenue data disaggregated by different levels are generally not available. Even if local government expenditure and revenue data were available, it would be extremely difficult to estimate urban public sector expenditures and revenue since other levels of government also finance some urban services partially or entirely. On the basis of fragmented and incomplete information that is available, it appears that the local government sector constitutes a very small proportion of the public expenditures and revenues in developing countries in general and the Asian region in particular.

For example, local public expenditures (financed from revenues raised by them, shared taxes, and grants-in-aid, etc.) constituted around five percent of the total public sector in Thailand in 1970. This percentage dropped to 4.8 in 1971 and to 4.5 in 1972 (World Bank, 1974). In the Philippines, local public expenditures accounted for 15.8 per cent of the total public sector in 1966. This percentage has been steadily declining -- 15.0 in 1968, 13.6 in 1971, 11.6 in 1973, and 7.1 in 1975. Expenditures by urban local bodies constituted 7.6 percent of the totalpublic sector in 1965, 6.4 in 1971, and 3.2 in 1975. It is interesting to note that urban (local) public expenditures as a percent of the total local public expenditures have also declined slowly -- 52 percent in 1965 to 49 percent on 1970 and 45 percent in 1975 (Sosmena and Laureta 1976,and Romualdex et al. 1970, p. 254). During 1969-1973, expenditures by local governments in Indonesia as percentage of total public expenditures declined from 17 to 15 (Smith and Smith, 1971). In Korea, local government sector plays a relatively important role compared to other countries (Republic of Korea, 1976, p. 388). Per capita expenditures in selected cities were US $10 in Manila (1970), $29 in Seoul (1971), $26 in Bombay (1971), $7 in Jakarta (1971-72), and $10 in Bangkok (1970). Relative to per capita income in these cities, it accounts for 5, 8, 9, 5, and 3 percent, respectively.[6]

Local government revenues from their own sources are quite meager even in the large cities. For example, on a per capita basis, local government revenue from own sources was US $3 in Manila (1970), $24 in Seoul (1981), $14 in Bombay (1971), $4 in Jakarta (1971-72), and $12 in Bangkok (1970). These revenues accounted for 2, 6, 5, 3, and 4 percent respectively of the per capita incomes in these cities. Local taxes generally contribute a small fraction of local government revenues. For example, per capita local tax revenue in Thailand ranged between US $0.55 in the north to $3.40 in the central regions (1972) and constituted 0.2-0.3 percent of the gross domestic product in different regions. In Seoul (1981), per capita local tax revenue was around US $8, or 30 percent, of the local revenues, and accounted for just a little over two percent of its personal income. In Bombay, per capita local tax revenue was US $7.47 in 1966-67, $7.89 in 1968-69, $9.12 in 1970-71, and $10.94 in 1972-73. Per capita local tax revenue at constant prices was $5.22, $475, $5.07, and $5.53, respectively,

------

6   Calculated from the questionnaires received from the RDMCs, World Bank's case studies of Urban Public Finances in Developing Countries; and other sources.

corresponding to the above periods. Local tax revenues constitute around three percent of income in Bombay.[7]

It should be pointed out that the local government finance data as presented in the preceding paragraphs are mainly in respect to the largest cities, where per capita incomes are several times that of the national average, and that these cities have greater access to revenue sources, and that their fiscal performances have generally been far ahead of the medium and small-sized cities. To illustrate: per capita local expenditures in Jakarta in 1969-70 were more than twice that of other cities in Indonesia. Per capita expenditures (capital and current) by the Bombay Municipal Corporation in 1962-63 was Rs.106, whereas in five cities in Bihar, the municipal expenditures averaged around Rs.16 per capita during the same year (Bhagalpur -- Rs. 13, Gaya -- Rs. 14, Patna -- Rs. 17, Ranchi -- Rs. 18, and Muzaffarpur -- Rs. 22). Revenues from local taxes constituted only a small fraction of one percent of the gross domestic product in the five cities in Bihar.

7. Public Financing of Urban Services

In many of the developing countries in Asia, urban local government expenditures and revenues (including intergovernmental transfers) constitute a much smaller proportion of their gross national product and the total public sector than is the case in most of the more developed countries. In spite of the rapid urbanization, per capita urban municipal revenues and expenditures, in the majority of the cases, have increased only slightly during the last decade or so. In all likelihood, per capita urban municipal revenues at constant prices may have remained constant or even declined in some cases. It may be pointed out that fiscal performance of different local governments varies widely even within a given country. Local governments practically everywhere are literally the creatures of the state/ provincial and/or central/national governments, and legally, the latter have the power of life and death over the former. In a sense, local bodies are their agents and undertake the services that state or other governments would have otherwise to provide. As a consequence of their political dependence, local governments are also dependent in a fiscal sense. The revenue sources of urban local bodies are limited by what is permitted by higher level(s) of government.

The revenue structure of urban local bodies varies substantially from one country to another. Locally levied taxes generally provide the single largest source of revenue for financing urban services. Non-tax revenues consisting of fees and fines and rents and prices, in terms of their relative importance, generally rank second. Intergovernmental fransfers play different but not a very significant role in financing urban services in the majority of the RDMCs. Limited information that is available suggests that the role of intergovernmental fiscal relations has been increasing gradually in many countries (Table 5).

As shown in Table 5, tax revenues play different roles in financing urban services in different countries. For example, in Thailand, tax revenues constitute 61 percent of the total local government revenues. Comparable percentages for the Philippines, Korea, and Indonesia are 55, 50, and 28, respectively. For the Municipal Corporations of

---

[7] Ibid.

TABLE 5

REVENUE STRUCTURE OF LOCAL GOVERNMENTS IN SELECTED DEVELOPING COUNTRIES

				Indonesia	India	India (Percentage)
Revenue Classification	Thailand 1971	Philippines 1974	Korea 1976	Jakarta 1972-73	Ahmedabad 1965-1971	Bombay 1971-72
Total Tax Revenues	61.4	55.0	49.8	27.9	40.1	48.8 (72.7)d
Locally Levied Taxes	21.2	22.7	29.0	21.3		
Surcharge Taxes	24.7		20.8	6.7		
Shared Taxes	15.5	32.3a				
Non-Tax Revenues	9.8	27.1	32.9	32.7	42.9	44.3 (18.3)
Fees and Fines	2.6	n.a.	–	15.5	6.5	3.4 (5.0)
Rents and Prices	6.2	n.a.	–	1.5	n.a.	2.9 (2.5)
Self-Finances Activities	1.0	n.a.	–	15.8b	36.4c	38.9 (10.8)
Grants-in-Aid & Subsidies	27.6	8.1	17.3	19.7	3.5	1.1 (1.7)
Miscellaneous Other Revenues	1.2	9.8	–	19.7	13.5	5.8 (7.2)
Total	100.0	100.0	100.0	100.0	100.0	100.0(100.0)

Totals may not add up due to rounding.
a Internally revenue allotment -- national tax sharing.
b Revenues from Casino etc.
c Includes revenues of Municipal Milk Dairy and Transport Companies.
d Percentages in parenthesis when Municipal Electric Supply and Transportation Undertaking revenues are excluded

Source: Based on information collected by the author in 1977 and 1978; World Bank Reports; and other published and unpublished materials.

Ahmedabad and Bombay in India, taxes provided around 40 and 49 percent of their respective revenues. In the case of Bombay, if the revenues of the Bombay Electricity and Transport Undertaking are excluded, tax revenues constitute about three-fourths of the total revenues.[8]

Important local taxes levied by local governments in selected Asian developing countries are listed in Table 6. The relative importance of different taxes varies widely in the local government tax structure of different countries and sometimes even in different urban municipalities in a given country.

The taxation of land and buildings plays different roles in financing urban services in different countries. It plays an important and significant role in, among others, the Republic of China, India, the Republic of Korea, Pakistan, the Philippines, and Singapore. Its role is insignificant in Indonesia and Thailand. With few exceptions, tax rates are generally low and their incidence regressive. However, in most of the countries, revenue potential of real estate taxation is not fully utilized and the present system suffers from poor assessment administration, substan-tial erosion of the tax base due to exemptions, and poor performance in terms of collection of taxes due.[9]

Tax on realty in one form or another has been utilized for financing urban services in most parts of the world. It is considered suitable for local purposes since "localization of the tax is automatic, and this is sufficient to keep the tax jurisdictions of different governing bodies from impinging on each other" (Hicks, 1961, p. 347). A carefully designed tax on real estate can be administered

---

[8] The taxes may be levied and administrered by the local governments themselves; they may be local levies collected by higher levels of governments (including surcharges taxes or tax supplements); or they may be levies of higher level(s) of government(s) who may share the proceeds of such taxes with local governments. In some cases, assessed valuation of real property may be utilized as proxies for determining beneficiary charges for specific services, e.g., for water, sewerage, and garbage collection, special rates are applied to annual rateable values in India.

[9] Poor assessment and collection may also be true of other local tax levies. To illustrate: in the five municipalities in Bihar (India), during the period 1951-52 to 1962-63, actual collection of taxes ranged between a low of ten percent (Bhagalput -- 1960-61) and 88 percent (Muzaffarpur -- 1956-57) of the taxes due. In the case of nine municipalities in the State of Haryana (India), property tax collection ranged between 28 and 58 percent of taxes due. In addition, a proportion of the taxes due are written off as bad debts each year. Generally speaking, the performance measured in terms of tax collection relative to amounts due has been deteriorating. A recent study of finances of the Bombay Municipal Corporation, however, points out that tax collection in respect to property taxes was 76 percent of assessments in 1965-66 and that this percentage has been gradually improving so that in 1971-72, it was 83 percent. In another study, it was found that during the period 1968-73, on average, only 55 percent of the property tax due was collected in Jakarta.

TABLE 6

LOCAL TAX LEVIES IN SELECTED DEVELOPING COUNTRIES IN ASIA*

Country	Important Local Tax Levies	
India	Taxation of land and build-, ings, octroi, vehicle tax, theatre tax, taxes on animals and boats, taxes on professions, trades, employment, etc., entertainment and betting tax, and tax on advertisements.	Taxation of land and buildings and octroi are most important and account for 80-90 percent of the total tax revenues in most municipalities.
Indonesia	Tax on change of motor vehicle ownership, motor vehicle tax, hotel and restaurant tax, amusement tax, fireworks tax, taxes on non-motorized vehicles, dogs and radios, taxes on land and buildings, special assessment levies, and house tax.	Motor vehicle transfer tax most important (Jakarta 46 percent in 1971-72) followed by amusement tax (19 percent), property tax (14 percent, and hotel and restaurant tax (12 percent).
Korea	Acquisition tax, registration (property tax/license tax, inhabitant tax, property tax, automobile tax, butchery tax, horse race tax, city planning tax, community facility tax, and workshop tax.	Property tax most important (31 percent) followed by acquisition tax (25 percent), entertainment tax (11 percent), inhabitant tax (10 percent), city planning (9 percent), and automobile tax (7 percent).
Philippines	Tax on real property, special education fund tax, idle land tax, special assessment levy, and national internal revenue allotments.	Property tax most important and accounted for more than two-thirds of total local tax revenues.
Singapore	No separate local taxes. The Republic of Singapore does levy a property tax.	
Thailand	House rent tax, local development tax, slaughter tax, signboard tax, surcharge on certain national taxes, (business tax, liquor tax, non-alcoholic beverage tax, and entertainment only), and shared taxes (rice export duty and the road vehicle tax).	Business, motor vehicles, land development, and house rent tax accounted for 30, 29, 16, and 16 tax, percent respectively.

* For detailed description see Pradkash, 1977.

quite efficiently and equitably and can provide large recurring revenues to urban local bodies. The reality tax, when suitably integrated with other land use regulatory devices, can be utilized as a positive tool for urban development (Dunkerley et. al., 1978; Doebele, et. al.,1979).

Besides the property taxes, non-property taxes play a significant role in financing urban public services. Local sales and income taxes are important ones. However, they are more or less nonexistent as sources of revenue for urban local bodies in the developing countries of Asia. Several local taxes presently utilized in different countries, however, do belong to the family of sales and income taxes; octroi and terminal taxes levied by a number of municipalities in India and Pakistan have certain similarities to sales taxes. Characteristics of certain taxes in Thailand (surcharge taxes on business, entertainment, and liquor and non-alcoholic beverages), Indonesia (automobile transfer tax, amusement tax, hotel and restaurant tax, and fireworks tax), and the Republic of Korea (acquisition tax, automobile tax, and entertainment and restaurant tax) are such that they belong to the family of special sales taxes. Similarly, taxes on professions, trades, callings, and employment, and various other business license taxes in India, Pakistan, and elsewhere resemble ad hoc income taxes. As pointed out earlier, several of the non-property taxes are large revenue producers in selected cities.

Municipal sales taxes have certain shortcomings as well. A general sales tax is regressive and thus is inequitable. If food items are exempt, the tax may become roughly proportional. In practice, services are generally exempt and this makes the tax somewhat capricious. Sales taxation places an administrative burden on the retailers who must collect and remit the tax to the governmental unit levying the tax and, in the absence of an effective system of audits, it may be susceptible to evasion and avoidance. On balance, however, a sales tax (general or selective) is superior to octroi as a source of revenue for urban local bodies. As a potential source of financing urban services in developing countries, sales taxation does merit careful consideration.

Municipal income taxes have not been used as extensively as the local sales taxes. In most of the Asian countries, power to tax income directly rests with the central governments, and the subnational, regional, and local governments may be constitutionally barred from levying taxes on income. No state or provincial government can grant to its local governments any tax power which it does not itself possess.

It must be recognized that use of sales and income taxes by city and municipal governments does raise some additional problems. First, in all likelihood, the national and/or the state, provincial, or regional governments may already be utilizing these taxes. Individual local government's jurisdictions, especially in metropolitan areas, may be far too small and form but a part of a much larger economic area which alone may provide a rational territorial base to administer such taxes. Imposition of such taxes by local government units, especially if the tax rates and exemptions are not uniform, would affect the location of economic and other activities, distort the land use patterns, and create unhealthy fiscal competition among them.

And last, but not least, is the question of whether local government units have the necessary administrative organization and competence to administer these taxes equitably and efficiently. Their record in this particular regard has been generally very disappointing -- experiences in the Republics of Korea and China are exceptions. Because of all these pros and cons, locally administered non-property taxes cannot be generally recommended for wide use. Nevertheless, there may be situations, especially in the case of large cities, where their utilization may be possible and even commendable.

Wherever local income and sales taxes are actually levied, their adverse features can and should be mitigated through coordination of central, state/provincial and local fiscal policies and tax measures. The two fiscal cooperation devices -- tax supplements and tax credits -- hold great promise in this regard. Under the tax supplement system, a uniform tax base may be used by more than one layer of government. The local rate is added to the state (or central) rate, both the state and local taxes are collected by the state, and the local government's share is credited to its account. The surcharge taxes in Thailand fall into this category.

The tax credit is a device similar to tax sharing, under which a taxing jurisdiction (central, state, etc.) invites a subordinate jurisdiction to share with it a prescribed portion of a tax area. The tax credit tends "to equalize the rates among jurisdictions, thereby curtailing intercommunity tax competition" (Advisory Commission on Intergovernmental Relations, 1961, p. 48). The advantages offered by intergovernmental fiscal coordination through the tax supplement and tax credit devices in respect to these and other sources of revenue must receive careful consideration, especially in view of the weak position of the local self governments in the developing countries.

Local governments all over the world have utilized a variety of other non-property taxes. Admission taxes, sometimes also known as entertainment or amusement taxes, and taxes on different types of vehicles and animals are important ones in this category. The admission tax is generally levied on the admission of persons to any place of entertainment either as spectators or audience and/or as participants in the amusements or entertainment. The amusements which are subject to tax may include movies and cinema, theatrical performances, circus shows, exhibitions, games and sports, and parimutual races. Cinemas are the major source of entertainment in the cities in the developing countries, and taxes levied at these places provide the bulk of the admission tax. The tax may be levied at a uniform flat rate, or at a proportional or graduated rate applied to the price charged for admission. In the case of parimutule races, in addition to an admission tax, a proportional tax (known as the betting tax in India) may be levied on the amounts of all bets. The administration of the tax may be entrusted either to the local bodies themselves, or the state/regional government may administer the tax and share the proceeds with municipal governments on the basis of the geographic origin of such revenues.

This tax has several advantages. The administration if fairly simple. It does not impose a great burden. It is one of the few taxes that reaches nonresidents and tourists who otherwise do not directly contribute to city revenues. The tax can provide a fair amount of revenues, especially in large cities. It has no serious disadvantages and is considered a good source of revenues for financing urban services in developing countries.

Some of the non-property taxes are good and desirable sources of revenue for the urban governments since they help diversify their revenue system. However, proliferation and indiscriminate use of non-property taxes is not desirable because a good number of them are regressive and bear hardest on those least able to pay. Careful consideration must be given to their equity, revenue productivity, cost of collection and efficient administration, and intergovernmental tax coordination aspects, and the developing countries must move cautiously in this direction.

Non-tax revenues consist of two major categories: fees and fines, and rents and prices and special service charges. Fees and fines include fees for licenses and permits and fines and forfeitures (Miller, 1953; Netzer, 1970; Stockfish, 1960). The rents and prices include rent of municipally owned property and service charges for utilities and other activities which are owned and operated by local governments.

Fees and fines are not a significant source of municipal revenue because income from this source is incidental to the process of municipal administration, especially regulation of certain activities in the broader interest of public health and welfare. The benefits of governmental activities in this regard are generally widely diffused and the value of the benefits to the community as a whole, as well as to individuals and entities, is difficult to measure. Thus, in designing rate schedules for fees and fines, the benefit principle cannot be strictly applied. However, in spite of these limitations, to the extent it is possible, an attempt should be made to make the fee charges equitable and more productive of revenue. The scope for improvements in this direction is quite considerable. For example, in municipalities where a particular trade is subject to a flat fee, it may be rational and appropriate to relate the charge to some form of ability to pay, etc. Once a revised fee schedule is adopted, it is necessary to review it periodically.

Rents and prices or user charges accrue to local governments either from their ownership or real estate (lands, markets, houses, etc.) or from their operation of public utility services and semi-commercial undertakings (water supply, sewerage, city transport, etc.). The user charges are theoretically based on the benefit principle and affect only those who really avail of the service or benefit provided. They embody a fair element of quid pro quo and are, to this extent, different from taxation.

City governments in the Asian developing countries provide a number of services on self-financing basis. Water supply, sewerage, and refuse collection are generally provided by most urban local governments. In addition, mass transit facilities (bus and/or subway) may also be owned and operated by them, e.g., Seoul Municipal Corporation owns and operates a municipal dairy. The Bombay Electric Supply and Transportation Undertaking is also responsible for the distribution of electricity to a large number of consumers within the municipal limits. In Jakarta, a number of commercial activities are carried out as local public enterprises, owned either wholly or jointly with the private sector. During the last two decades or so, it appears that the revenues from self-financed activities through service charges, etc., have been increasing in relative importance in many of the large cities.

The recent efforts towards expanding the scope of self-financing activities and greater utilization of user charges and pricing measures are important developments. They make the urban local bodies' revenue base more diversified. Generally speaking, local taxes have been found to be less income-elastic. Beneficiary charges, especially with rapid urbanization, may be relatively more elastic.

Some economic theorists consider user charges as inappropriate for financing what are defined as "pure public goods" -- services whose dominant characteristics are such that no one is denied their benefits regardless of whether he pays for it (Vieg, 1960, p. 210). It is further argued that in some cases, even when a particular public service is not a "pure public good," user charges may be feasible but not desirable. The user charges are also of limited applicability where the service produces substantial public benefits in addition to those enjoyed by the user as such, e.g., libraries (Netzer 1970, p. 186-87).

Notwithstanding the merits of these arguments, the theory of "pure public good" would need to be viewed as a relative concept. It is doubtful if it would be advisable to apply this approach to developing countries in the initial stages of their development when the accent has to be on resource mobilization and capital formation. Few developing countries can at present afford to provide as pure a public good as potable water free of charge or on a highly subsidized basis. If user charges are not related to the costs of public services, the community will have to finance them through taxation, which, in most developing countries, may well be somewhat regressive. Moreover, most user charges, where desirable, can certainly be made differential in favor of the underprivileged sections of the community. It is felt that rents and prices constitute a large and hitherto underutilized revenue resource and should therefore be exploited adequately by urban local bodies in the developing countries.

Planning and financing of urban facilities and service programs is basically an intergovernmental process. The largest proportion of fiscal resources is everywhere controlled by national and provincial governments. The capabilities of urban governments depend, therefore, not only upon their tax base and non-tax revenues, but also upon the inter-governmental transfers from national and state governments. The national or central government may transfer funds, both for capital and current programs, to local bodies directly or through the state or provincial governments, or a combination of the two methods.

Intergovernmental transfers play a significant role in local government finances in Thailand (shared taxes and grants-in-aid accounted for 43 percent of total revenues in 1971). In addition, surcharge taxes (tax supplements) provided another 25 percent of the total local government revenues. Intergovernmental fiscal transfers also play crucial roles in finances of local governments in the Philippines (in 1974, shared taxes provided 32 percent and grants-in-aid another 8 percent of the total local revenues) and the Republic of Korea (shared taxes constituted 21 percent and grants-in-aid another 17 percent of the total local revenues). Intergovernmental transfers are quite important in the case of Jakarta (26 percent of local revenues in 1972-73). However, currently, they are of marginal importance in India.

Today in most of the developing countries, intergovernmental relations are at one of the most important crossroads of their development. The urban local bodies have inadequate revenue bases and fiscal powers so that the demand for public services has been outstripping the growth of revenues. In the face of rapid urbanization, the gap between needed service expenditures and available resources is so critical that local bodies are already facing a serious fiscal crisis.

Intergovernmental finance is faced with two sets of fiscal problems: (1) a vertical one of how functions and revenues should be shared between different levels of government; and (2) a horizontal one of relations among governments within the same layer -- metropolitan cities and their surrounding suburbs. These two problems are extremely complex because local governments have been called upon to perform a number of functions which are touched with extra-local or "spillover" interests.

The higher governments' fiscal responsibilities with respect to their local subdivisions may be discharged in two general ways, neither of which is mutually exclusive. First, local government units may be granted power to tax sources which will supply sufficient revenue. Second, the state/central governments may supplement local revenues with those collected by them through their own resource powers. Since the separation of revenues device tends to favor the higher rather than the lower governments, this does not solve the problem of making available adequate revenue to the local unit. Given the deficiency of the separation device, a mixed approach is most often employed the world over, whereby supplemental revenues are transferred to the urban local bodies by the state and the national governments.

There are four major instruments of intergovernmental fiscal transfers and cooperation: (1) tax supplements, (2) tax credits, (3) tax sharing, and (4) grants-in-aid. As pointed out earlier, the tax supplement has the advantage of making the higher government's administrative capabilities available to local units and allows them discretion in setting a rate. Like the tax supplement, a tax credit is tied to a state or nationwide tax. The credit, while different in concept from the supplement, usually has the same practical effect. It allows local units access to a source of revenue used by higher governments, permits a local tax rate, and provides economy of administration. The shared tax is a third form of fiscal cooperation. The higher government sets aside a fixed proportion of the revenues collected from its tax and distributes shares to the localities on the basis of where the tax was collected. Under a shared tax system, the state or national government specifies the rate and administers the levy, but local units are generally free to use their shares as they wish. Like the supplement and credit devices, the shared tax is primarily a revenue instrument and does not contribute to the solution of fiscal problems which arise from external effects and interlocal fiscal disparities.

Grants-in-aid may be described as payments made by some higher government to a lower one with or without conditions prescribed by the former to defray either in full or in part the cost of any service or services administered by the latter. Fiscally, a grant is an appropriation of funds from the higher government's budget to local governments. It is not, therefore, a tax or shared revenue; grants have no intentional identification with any particular levy.

Although grants were conceived primarily as a measure of financial assistance, they have acquired a number of important features which add to their usefulness and put them in a distinct class of public revenues. For instance, grants are often used as measures of control and supervision over local governments. They are designed and employed to stimulate local public expenditure to promote certain nationwide goals and objectives or to underwrite the supply of certain public goods provided locally. This is done either because of national interest in a minimum level of service for all citizens or because certain services are touched with external benefits or costs, giving rise to inequities or inefficiencies, or for both of these reasons.

No less important is their role as a device for equalizing costs and opportunities among localities. By allocating more money to local bodies with the least resources or highest costs, some leveling of benefits and burdens is brought about. Grants-in-aid thus represent more than a means of intergovernmental fiscal collaboration; they provide a platform for broad policy coordination and functional cooperation.

It must be emphasized that intergovernmental fiscal relations are of crucial importance for meeting the challenge that developing countries must face in financing housing and urban development. Intergovernmental fiscal cooperation devices such as tax supplement, tax credit, and tax sharing have necessarily to play a much larger role than they do presently. Although these devices may and can provide adequate revenues to the urban local bodies to supplement locally administered tax and non-tax revenues, they fall short in many important respects, the notable ones being their inability to equalize costs and opportunities among different urban areas within the state and/or the country and to influence the local bodies to plan and provide services according to national or state priorities. A suitable system of grants-in-aid therefore must be developed and continuously reviewed to meet the goals and objectives of urban and regional development (World Bank, 1978).

The developing countries already need massive capital investments in housing, infrastructure, and several other essential urban services. The coming decades will witness a manifold increase in the demand for capital resources. Because of their life span (durability), capital projects have a long-range effect upon the lives of the urban communities and their local governments. Such projects, therefore, need to be planned with a long-term perspective and within the framework of urbanization and national development goals. In fact, urban development projects have to be integral parts of the overall national and regional development programs, although their detailed planning and implementation may very largely rest with urban local bodies or urban development authorities.

In the overall context of resource mobilization, projects for urban development must compete with other development programs for scarce capital resources. In the prevailing circumstances, their share is bound to be grossly inadequate, even in relation to their high priority needs. This implies that urban local governments or development authorities must make herculean efforts to mobilize additional resources of their own. Ursula K. Hicks correctly points out that capital investment "lies at the very heart of development from below," and that local capital formation has intrinsic importance, not only from the economic and social point of view, but also on psychological grounds (Hicks, 1961, p. 368). A bulk of capital projects for urban development are initially financed out of borrowings by public agencies at local, state, and national levels.

As pointed out earlier, urban local bodies in the developing countries have inadequate revenue powers relative to the respon- sibilities that are or should properly be placed upon them. This is so, notwithstanding the fact that in many cases they may not have even fully utilized the revenue powers already available to them. The much needed devolution of revenue resources on local governments will have, therefore, to be backed with, and even preceded by, their own earnest effort at full utilization of their revenue powers.

An equally serious and interdependent problem is the insufficient ability and access of the local governments to capital or loan funds. With the exception of a small number of them in very large cities, municipal bodies are unable to secure long-term financing against the issuance of their own bonds for various reasons. Important among these reasons, apart from legal constraints on their borrowing powers, are the weaknesses of their revenue base and unsatisfactory financial performance and housekeeping.

Data on capital investments and borrowing by urban local bodies are the most difficult to come by. At this time, such information is available for three cities -- Ahmedabad and Bombay in India and Seoul in Korea. In Ahmedabad, of the total, current expenditures accounted for 76 percent and the capital outlay 24 percent in 1965. In 1971, the comparable percentages were 88 percent and 12 percent, respectively. During this period, the overall expenditures increased at an annual rate of 6.1, the current expenditures at about 9 percent, whereas the capital outlays declined at an annual rate of around 6 percent. During 1962-63, current and capital expenditures constituted 79 and 21 percent, respectively. In 1971-72, the comparable respective figures were 84 and 16 percent. Like Ahmedabad, relative importance of the capital investments by the Bombay Municipal Corporation declined during the sixties. On the other hand, in Seoul the current expenditures in 1963 accounted for 47 percent of the total and capital outlays 53 percent. By 1970, the respective figures were 35 and 65 percent, respectively. It may also be pointed out that growth of expenditures (and revenues) in Seoul during the sixties was four to five times higher than in Ahmedabad and Bombay.

The extent of financing capital outlays from borrowing varied a great deal among the three cities. In Ahmedabad, during 1965-71, loan financing constituted between 11 percent (1971) and 16 percent (1968) of the total expenditures. During 1963-72, loan financing ranged between 11 percent (1970-71) and 26 percent (1967-68) in Bombay. In

Seoul, on the other hand, the percentage of total expenditures financed through borrowing ranged between zero (1965, 1967, 1968, 1969) and four percent (1971). Generally speaking, a very large proportion of borrowing is for utilities and self-financing projects. Foreign borrowing, in turn, may be a small fraction of total loan financing over periods of time.

The city governments have been granted extremely limited borrowing powers in the developing countries in Asia. This is an extremely serious bottleneck in light of needed infrastructure investments, especially since a strong case can be made that urban governments engage in large-scale acquisition, development, and disposal of land. The loans invariably have to be approved by provincial and national governments and sometimes by the national banks of the country. concerned. The interest rates on municipal borrowing are generally below the market rate. The durations for the repayment of loans are generally much shorter than the useful physical life of the facilities financed through borrowing.

There are two alternative approaches to facilitate loan financing for urban facilities commonly employed in different countries. First, the municipal governments are granted the statutory authority to borrow in the open market primarily through the issuance of different types of bonds. The statutes governing this authority generally place certain limitations on the borrowing powers. Second, the local government units may be granted loans by the state and the national governments for approved projects. The second alternative should by the large be preferable for the developing countries, although large cities with good financial records may also be granted the power to borrow funds directly for certain types of projects. Since the regional and national governments are engaged in large-scale borrowing for development programs, the local bodies, even if granted the borrowing power, would be in a poor competitive position.

If loan funds to urban local bodies in developing countries are largely to be provided by higher levels of government, it may be appropriate to set up special financial institutions, e.g., revolving funds, both in state and national levels. Alternatively, a special national bank with regional offices, as is the case in Mexico, may be established for facilitating loan financing for urban land and infrastructure development projects. The revolving fund boards or the special bank can then loan funds to local bodies and charge them the interest that the former have to pay plus a nominal charge for management of the funds.

For financing certain types of public improvement programs which specifically benefit certain properties and where such benefit can be measured, a special levy or tax widely known as a special assessment or similar cost-sharing scheme may be utilized for financing such capital outlays. A levy known as a valorization tax (impuesto de valorizacion) is being used very effectively in large Colombian cities for financing major portions of capital cash for construction of roads and streets (Doebele, Grimes, and Linn, 1979). "Betterment levies," which have some atributes similar to special assessments, have been tried in some of the Asian countries without much success. Many of the countries have been concerned with various aspects of land policies and taxation, and several of them have, in recent years, formulated and adopted some important selective measures.

8. Major Policy Issues, Approaches, and Conclusions

Many students of economic development, public administration, and community development specialists, and some political scientists and sociologists, have argued that dynamic local government is crucial if development is to really take root in a country. It is pointed out that "national economic development is necessarily a composite of economic activities conducted at the local level, local government is bound to be important either as a obstacle or an aid." (Bird, 1970, p. 147). Since the local governments are generally weak and have, by and large, exhibited poor performance in most of the developing countries, many economists became convinced that centralized planning and administration were essential on technical efficiency and practical grounds.

As part of a recent tax reform study in Colombia, headed by Richard A. Musgrave, the roles of local government in general and local government finance in particular were also examined, among others by Dick Netzer. He came to the conclusion that there should be no emphasis on local government in the developmental context in Colombia since "feasible development instruments are available independent of local governments and that increased revenues and expenditures at the subnational level will necessarily replace rather than supplement central government efforts and will, in any case, distort resource allocation away from the development optimum" (Ibid, p. 148).

Richard M. Bird, however, argues that in the case of large urban areas, local government efforts, in fact, supplement rather than substitute for national resource mobilization efforts:

> . . . the major problems of local finance in quantita-
> tive terms is the financing of urban development. This
> problem is concentrated in relatively few cities, and
> properly designed policies would enable and encourage
> them to do a great deal to finance their own development,
> with beneficial efforts all around. Putting more
> responsibility for financing urbanization on the urban
> areas will add to the total resources that can be
> mobilized for development and, on the whole, will do so
> in a manner consistent with the objectives of national
> tax policy. . . . This distinction between the urban
> fiscal problem -- which can and should be resolved mainly
> at the local level -- and the rural problem -- which,
> important as it is to provide basic public services to
> all citizens, may have to be handled by the national
> government or regional corporations, if it can be
> resolded at all -- is crucial (Ibid, p. 149).[11]

As pointed out earlier, the scale and rapidity of the urbanization process in the Asian developing countries is unparalleled in history. During 1950-75, of the total increase in urban population, approximately 75 percent was in cities of 100,000 or more and about 50 percent of the total was in large cities with populations of a million or more. During the remainder of this century, two-thirds of the additional population are likely to be in the million-plus cities.

The problems of resource mobilization and financing urban development in different countries in the region should be differentiated in terms of those in the large cities (say, with population of a million or more) and in other urban areas. Different sets of strategies may thus be appropriate. Investment requirements and fiscal efforts for financing long-run expenditures are so massive that the large cities must carry the major proportion of the financial responsibilities. Per capita incomes are generally positively associated with city size, thus the economic capacity in these cities may be two, three, or more times that of the national average.

The prevailing worldwide attitude among politicians and other major participants in public policy arenas is generally anti-urban, in particular anti-big city. This attitude is commonly shared by planners of all kinds. The suggestions and arguments by various commissions, committees, and others in many countries that large cities should get a very high priority in allocation of investment and other financial resources from the national government have not been heeded. Politically, they may not be feasible in the near future.

The size of the public sector is relatively small and many countries in the region rely heavily on indirect taxes. It is likely that the overall incidence of taxation is not very progressive. Since the income levels in large cities are generally several times that of national averages, it may be argued that there is room for much greater fiscal effort in the large cities; thus, the case for complete reliance on national allocation of resources is not a strong one and cannot be justified. Rapidly growing cities must, therefore, bear a large proportion of the fiscal burden of financing urban facilities and services. The task of resource mobilization for financing urban development may thus be best accomplished by giving the large cities more revenue-raising authority and more responsibility for their own expenditures.

Assignment of additional revenue and expenditure authority to local governments in large cities must be concomitant upon marked improvement of assessment and collection administration of tax and other resources that are already available to them. In respect to additional assignment of tax authority to local bodies, a system of tax supplements and tax credits may provide many advantages over local administration.

The importance of taxation of land and buildings as a financing resource for urban governments in the developing countries is considerable. Currently, property tax is a minor source and of little importance in terms of revenue in most of the developing countries in Asia. The property taxation should thus occupy an increasingly important role in efforts to finance urban services. The bases of exemptions, rates, assessment, and collection of real estate taxes must therefore be carefully examined in each country, and some radical changes may be called for. The recent experiences in the Republics of China and Korea with integrated land and property tax systems provides

---

11 Ibid., p. 149.   Recent evidence from the Asian cities such as Seoul,'   Taipei, and Bombay supports this proposition.

a basis for optimism in resource mobilization through similar fiscal devices.

The land situation is extremely critical in Asia. Urban land resources and rising land values offer major constraints and tremendous opportunities for urban growth management as well as mobilization of fiscal resources for urban development. Land taxation has a tremendous potential as a source of revenue as well as important policy instruments towards achieving other goals of urban development policies, when taxation is integrated with other land policies and programs.

Intergovernmental fiscal relations will continue to be of growing importance, although their objectives may be different for smaller urban areas and big cities. Intergovernmental fiscal cooperation devices such as tax supplements, tax credits, and tax sharing have necessarily to play much larger roles than they do presently. A suitable system of grants-in-aid must be developed to supplement the tax cooperation devices towards achieving broad policy coordination and functional cooperation; stimulating, controlling, and supervising local public agencies; and equalizing costs and opportunities among local governments to minimize the externalities and spillover effects.

Local tax revenues have generally been found to be less income-elastic than the provincial and particularly national taxes. Imbalances between expenditure requirements and resources available to urban local bodies are thus likely to continue and become cumulatively more accentuated in the future. Non-tax revenues, especially user and beneficiary charges, can potentially provide more elastic sources of revenue in the face of rapid additions to population in the large cities and rising incomes with economic development. Thus, the role of pricing policies and cost recovery methods, along with increased reliance upon other non-tax revenues may be extremely important in the resource mobilization context.

Rapid growth of large cities would require increasingly heavy investments in urban intrastructure facilities. In many of the countries, there are no capital markets from which the funds can be borrowed by the municipal governments. Only a handful of cities are able to secure even partial long-term financing against the issuance of their own bonds. Careful examination of alternative institutional arrangements (e.g., revolving funds and infrastructure development banks) to facilitate loan finance for urban capital improvement programs in a particular country would thus be crucial.

Comprehensive urban land policies may be indispensable for management of growth in the rapidly growing cities. Suitably designed land policies may also provide the most important and viable source for capital financing. In large cities, it has often been found that with rapid growth, land values increase very fast and that the volume of these increases is often greater than the investment in infrastructure. The experience of the Delhi Development Authority may provide some valuable insights. In Colombia, a large proportion of capital improvements, especially for new subdivisions, has been financed through benefit taxation known as the valorization tax. In the Republics of China, Korea, and Singapore, different approaches seem to have been instrumental in their urban development and financing strategies. It is felt that appropriate land policy measures for

financing capital improvement programs may be more important than
ensuring or facilitating municipal governments' access to loan funds.

While revenue and resource mobilization considerations are
significant, the overall system of financing urban development services
must also be continuously assessed from allocative and distributive
effects. With changing revenue structure and incresing urban public
expenditures, such effects may also change over time. A suitably
designed system of land taxation and other land policy measures can be
extremely important instruments towards achieving and harmonizing the
allocative and distributive objectives.

It should also be pointed out that the great bulk of investment
with consequences for urban and urbanizing areas originate in the
private, not the public, sector. They represent complex networks of
decisions by individuals, households, firms, and so on. Urban public
investment policies must thus be carefully designed to encourage
maximum participation by the private sector.

The findings of this study are based on information pertaining to a
limited number of countries and/or to limited numbers of cases from a
given country. These findings must thus be viewed as tentative. It
has been possible to identify the basic policy issues which appear to
be critical when dealing with questions of resource mobilization and
fiscal policy for development. Both the findings and the policy issues
need to be investigated more thoroughly and supported by further
information and analysis. In addition to cross-country studies, it is
equally important, if not more so, for further studies to concentrate
on individual countries and different urban centers therein towards the
formulation of major policies for resource mobilization and financing
urban development. These studies must be in the broader context of
urbanization processes, national development, infrastructure requirements, appropriate standards and technologies, and economic and
administrative capacities.

References

Advisory Commission on Intergovernmental Relations, (1961). <u>Local Non-Property Taxes and the Coordinating Role of the State</u>, Washington, D.C.

Alonso, W., (1970). 'What are New Towns for?.' <u>Urban Studies</u> Vol. 7

Asian Development Bank, (1980). <u>Bank's Strategy for Assistance in the Urban Development</u>, (Manila, September Draft).

Bird, R. M., (1970). <u>Taxation and Development: Lessons from Colombian Experience</u>, Cambridge, Mass.: Harvard University Press.

Dandekar, J.M. and Rath, N., (1971). 'Poverty in India,' <u>Economic and Political Weekly,</u> Vol. 6, pp. 25-48 and 106-146.

Doebele, W.A., Grimes, O.F. and Linn, J.F., (1979). 'Participation of beneficiaries in financing urban services: valorization charges in Bogota, Colombia,' <u>Land Economics,</u> Vol. 55, No. 1, February, pp. 73-92.

Doebele, W.A., 'Land readjustment as an alternative to taxation for the recovery of betterment: the case of South Korea,' <u>Proceedings of the 15th Annual TRED Conference.</u>

Dotson, Arch, (1972). 'Urbanization and national development in south and southeast Asia,' Report of the Southeast Asia Development Advisory Group. Urban Development Panel Seminars (New York: The Asia Society).

Dunkerley, H.B., Walters, A.A., Courtney, J.M., Doebele, W., Shoup, D.C., and Rivikin, M.D., (1978). <u>Urban Land Policy Issues and Opportunities,</u> World Bank Staff Working Paper No. 283, Two Volumes, Washington, D.C..

Grimes, O.F., (1976). <u>Housing for Low Income Urban Families,</u> Baltimore, Md.: The Johns Hopkins University Press.

Hicks, U.K. (1961). <u>Development From Below,</u> Oxford, The Clarendon Press.

Intergovernmental Fiscal Relations in Developing Countries, (1978).
World Bank Staff Working Paper No. 304, Washington, D.C..

Jakobson, L. and Prakash, V. (1974). 'Urban planning in the context of
new urbanization' Jakobson, L. and Prakash, (eds.)
Metropolitan Growth: Public Policy for South and Southeast
Asia, Beverly Hills, California: Sage Publication.

Miller, J.M. (1953). 'Service charge as an important revenue source,'
Municipal Finance, Vol. 25, pp. 49-53.

Netzer, D. (1970). Economics and Urban Problems, New York: Basic Books,
Inc.

Prakash, V. (1969). New Towns in India, Durham, North Carolina: Duke
University, Monograph on Southern Asia, No. 8.

Republic of Korea, Ministry of Home affairs, (1976). Financial
Abstracts of Local Government, Seoul, July.

Romualdex, E.Z., Yoingco, A.O. and Casem, A.O. (1970). Philippine Tax
System, Manila: GIC Enterprises Co., Inc.

Smith, R.S. and Smith, T.M. (1971). 'The political economy of regional
and urban revenue policy in Indonesia,' Asian Survey, Vol. XI,
No. 8, pp. 761-786.

Sosmena, G.C. and Laureta, A.G. (1976). 'Financing local governments
in the Philippines,' Tax Monthly, Vol. XVII, No. 6, pp. 1-15.

Stockfish, J.A. (1960). 'Fees and service as a source of city
revenues: A case study of Los Angeles,' National Tax Journal,
Vol. 13, No. 2, pp. 97-121.

United Nations, (1976). Report of Expert Working Group Meeting on
Community Water Supply and Sanitation, Stategies for
Development.

United Nations, World Housing Survey (1973). (Report on Item 4 of the
Provisional Agenda, Eighth Session of the Committee on
Housing, Building and Planning, Geneva 15-26 October.

Vieg, J.A. et.al., (1960). California Local Finance, Stanford, Calif.:
Stanford University Press.

World Bank, (1974). A Study of Public Finances in Thailand, Vol. IV:
Annex E--Local Government Administration and Finances in
Thailand, Washington, D.C.

World Bank, (1972). 'Urbanization: sector working paper,' Washington,
D.C., June.

World Bank Staff Work Paper No. 209, (1975). The Task Ahead for the
Cities of Developing Countries, Washington, D.C.

17 Housing and physical planning in urbanized areas

PATRIES HABERER

1. Housing and Physical Planning in Urbanized areas

1.1 Introduction

"A city can only become beautiful, convenient and clean by the united efforts of its inhabitants".

There is a lot of truth in this quotation. It is valid both in the Netherlands and India. This paper will deal with the problems of housing and physical planning, considering the possibilities of solutions by the people themselves.

It is based on Dutch experiences in planning and urban renewal. The underlying assumptions are that social action is the most important action, and that occupants are the best housing experts. In this view planning should only formalize the course of action desired by those occupants.

Seen on the map of India the Netherlands covers an area half as big as Sri Lanka. There are 13 million inhabitants on 33,250 sq. kms. The average density is 400 inhabitants per sq. km. In the western part of the country the density is much higher, up to 2,400 inhabitants per sq. km. Although there are more differences than resemblances in the physical, economic and social conditions of India and Netherlands, both countries can learn from each other, since many problems are similar, and one can learn from the other how to formulate an integrated socio-technical approach.

1.2 The Consequences of Affluence

In the urbanized regions of affluent countries, one of the big problems is to reach or restore equilibrium between the main functions. This lack of equilibrium is not a figment of a planner's imagination but it is felt daily by thousands of people commuting from home to work or in the weekends to recreation areas. Part of this problem is because of the lack of coordination between the three governmental levels we have: the Central Government, the Provincial and Local Governments. An important part however, is caused by the independant position of the private sector activities.

Regional plans are made by the provinces; they go through quite an elaborate process of approval but do not have any executive power.

Another problem -- maybe typical for an affluent society -- is the increasing pollution of water, air and soil, the scattering of activities over the relatively small space and the encroachment of natural areas.

The unlimited industrial use of water has brought our country, which is famous for its unlimited amount of water everywhere, to the position where the water is polluted to such a degree that it can be cleaned for drinking purposes only at high costs. Water flora and fauna have become extinct for quite some time in most water bodies. To keep drinking water basins free from pollution is a difficult task. Prosperity has brought auto ownership for large groups of the population. The traffic streams through the cities and landscape cause a high level of air pollution, sometimes combined with industrial airpollution to a dangerous degree; warning systems are installed to prevent calamities. Human activities are scattered all over the urbanized regions, open space is a scarce article, areas suited for outdoor recreation are difficult to find.

1.3 Some problems of urban areas in Europe

Some of the problems to be mentioned below might seem irrelevant to India. They need to be discussed nevertheless. Two or three decades ago, such problems were quite unimaginable in Europe too. Their early recognition may influence the way of thinking about the future and maybe styles of action. The commercial and industrial enterprises settle either out in the country side or in the suburbs. So the employment pattern of the city becomes less and less differentiated over time. Labour is the most costly factor in production, so automation has caused a lot of labour extensive processes and unemployment for groups with a lower and lower-middle educational level.

Telecommunication has changed the whole physical interaction pattern of business and industry. Whole units of industries and offices can be settled in remote places. A lot of urban dwellers who used to find employment close to residences now are unemployed or commuting over long distances. It must be noted that we are not speaking about the future but about developments already in evidence.

The picture emerging from the discussion might seem to be a very pessimistic view of the developments in a country that is often considered a good example of physical planning, housing and social security systems. We draw attention to these problems in this way so as to provide a framework for the description of approaches of the problems. In these approaches, the initiative for decisions and planning passes to the people directly involved. Because only with the efforts and vision of the people involved can the results of planning have a lasting value.

2. Possible Approaches Towards Physical Planning Problems

To implement plans in Dutch physical planning the public authorities are the first party to invest. The private initiative can follow but not necessarily. To obtain maximum investment in terms of money and private initiative of the people directly involved should be a main consideration for judging every action at all governmental levels. The most important part of this judgment is making explicit who is gaining and who is losing.

2.1 The new-town policy

Financial and organizational problems associated with the old overcrowded cities very often lead to a "new town" policy. Realizing new housing units in new towns seems to be cheaper and easier to manage. But once these locations get a certain size (in our country 50,000 inhabitants) the additional costs become very high. In many cases these towns stop growing leaving the inhabitants with inadequate and insufficient facilities, schools, medical centers, employment, etc. So either the inhabitants pay the price for "cheap new towns" by being dependent for a lot of their needs on the old urban areas, incurring high travel expenses, or the public authority has to do a lot of additional investments to make new towns really liveable. Further, the newly constructed dwellings are so expensive that they draw the higher and middle income groups away from the old urban areas; the population that stays behind in the old urban areas consists of low income groups, and the decay of the old urban areas starts.

2.2 Good infrastructure is vital for area development

Since little effort is made to define the kinds of and benefi-ciaries of development, the latter quite often means more roads or rail-roads that support industries and other economic development. The initial basic public investment in infrastructure leads in turn to more and more public and private investment.

Cities do not often have the governmental and organizational capaci-ties; often they do have neither land available nor money to manage this growth. So they are dependent on higher governmental levels. These levels are in most countries rural oriented, sometimes because most representatives come from the countryside or because the city is considered a less important and even negative phenomenon, but also simply because the real extent of the problems are not understood -- and more than proportional growth of costs and problems associated with the population growth is unknown.

The value of the city as an important source for culture and progress is not recognized, leading in turn to a vicious downward spiral. The living conditions become worse and worse. People who can afford leave the cities, the people that stay have hardly anything to spend. Amenities disappear, the level of education is going down; public transportation can not be maintained and the general level of maintenance goes down. The city is not a place to invest in any more. Firms tend to look for other places.

To stop this downward spiral, action has to be taken at several levels. First of all, efforts must be directed to make it possible for the local government to formulate and carry out a policy. All local governments formulate policy but very few implement policy, because they neither have the means nor the capacity. Their financial dependence on higher administrative levels makes carrying out whatever policy highly uncertain. This causes a lack of trust among residents in the local government and at the same time discourages every initiative of the population itself. People become indifferent to whatever happens and the chance that any action has success becomes smaller and smaller.

A step towards a solution for these problems is decentralization of authority and money to the local level. Then it can be the local government that sets its own priorities within constraints of the available budget. The citizen groups that want to get things done can try to convince their own -politically chosen- representatives. In setting the budgets for the big cities the amount of problems should be taken into consideration. Developing keys for dividing the available money is a matter of experimentation for years and evaluation of the expenditures afterwards.

A good public transportation system is indispensable in a highly urbanized area. For medium and long distances trains are preferable while for short distances streetcars and for large urban areas subways would be needed. Intensifying the use of existing transportation networks can be achieved by appropriate physical planning and by the use of telecommunication and automation systems.

If one views physical planning from a public transportation point of view, a very different picture emerges than the one from the usual planning schemes. Locations along the railroad get a different value. Housing should be situated in such a way that most important employment centers can be reached by public transportation. Recreational facilities must be located within the reach of the transportation network.

A strict policy for the location of employment should take care of the right balance between housing and employment. Such policies are far more powerful when accompanied by selective taxation methods. In order to make schools, shops, public services and cultural institutes accessible for large groups their location has to be close to or interwoven with the residential areas. High densities are the best guarantee for a profitable exploitation of many facilities.

For years policy makers in the Netherlands have held the view that offering a good public transportation system was sufficient to restrict the use of private cars. This view has not been sustained by experience, so an effective restriction of the use of cars should go together with the improvement of public transportation systems.

3. Possible Approaches Towards Urban Problems

The continuous housing shortage and the need of more units for smaller households has had a broad range of ramifications in the Netherlands. One of these is exemplified by (mainly) young people squatting empty buildings left behind by departing offices, industries and sometimes by dwellers. These actions are symptoms of the important underlying fact that we are not able to fulfill one of the basic needs such as adequate housing for everyone.

The high standards for housing result in the fact that less and less people can pay the rent for their own dwelling. An incredibly complicated subsidy is in place to encourage home ownership and tenancy; however, it does not prevent low income groups ending up in the worst housing with the eventual result of further decay and urban renewal. A fundamentally different approach of the housing problem is needed. This different approach should include both urban renewal and new construction.

3.1 Urban renewal

A fundamental change in the way of approaching slum clearance and urban renewal problems will be a <u>problem oriented</u> approach in such a way that the people directly involved <u>define their</u> problems. In the traditional organization, the technical and physical approach of the problems is the first step to be addressed. This approach does not work at all in situations where the inhabitants of an area are directly involved as is the case in slum and squatter improvement projects, relocation projects and in almost all the urban projects to be tackled. The problem oriented approach is the only course of action that holds out any chance to success.

First of all it should be clear whose problems are going to be solved. To quote H.V. Lanchester once more:

> "the trouble with us -- the experts, may we call
> ourselves? -- is that we are almost bound to base our
> ideals too much on the fine things we are familiar
> with, not recognizing that they may often be exotic and
> not a true interpretation of needs and character".

Consequently the individuals directly involved have to formulate their problems. Solving the problems formulated in this fashion has to be the aim of the urban improvement process. That means starting the planning process from a different perspective and place. The focus of the process will be to build up or restore the social structures of the neighborhoods to be improved.

The opinion of the inhabitants on their neighborhoods, and facilties, the amenities and their dwellings should be investigated in cooperation with them. Preferably, people trained in social action should try to initiate the process. This approach increases the duration of planning process but a careful preparation of the plans will pay back in terms of time and money saved in later stages. Once the problems are defined, the team of inhabitants directly involved and sociologists should be expanded by an economist and an architect/city planner to help find the cheapest solutions for the problems. Meanwhile, a survey of the exact situation can be made. It is useful to make the survey in cooperation with the local people in order to give them the opportunity to become accustomed with the drawings and maps. The next phase will be one of coordination. Maps of the actual situation problems and solutions with their alternatives translated into costs are to be made available.

The coordinating engineer can play a crucial role in this urban planning framework. He knows the condition of urban development in the plan area. He also has to integrate his knowledge in an open design process as a coordinating member of the team, that is in place. His technical input can identify the attractive and less attractive features of various alternatives. He is the one to advice on the phasing of the implementation of the plan and is responsible for the executive phase. At this stage, the sociologist starts the difficult task of motivating the community groups to extend their action to maintenance processes or other new fields, like employment, etc. By means of this type decentralization from higher to lower authorities a city is in the position to encourage residents to formulate their own policy, to set priorities, and to implement that policy. Improvement of slum and squatter areas in the big city will be successful, if legal instruments are available to prevent speculation with land and buildings. The specifics of these legal instruments will naturally depend on the local legal system and need not detain us here. Suffice it to say that it is an important condition in the process of urban improvement.

An important point to note while referring to the problems of coordination between local organizations is a careful delineation of the good and false ideas regarding the process of participation. Participation should be framed according to a strict set of rules. It should be kept inside reasonable time frames and entry conditions. Scope of participation and the procedural patterns should be all made clear before the process starts. One useful rule is: a person or a group has right to express itself on its own level, which implies responsibility for the costs, and a person or a group participates at the higher level, which means that their wishes are taken into account among all other considerations. The strict use of this rule will make most participation processes more clear by putting responsibilities where they belong.

3.2 New construction for housing

In our very highly concentrated cities where design of public space is an important quality, we found two different ways to approach these problems. One is in the form of rather complicated local plans that describes everything of common interest in a rather detailed fashion, letting people free to fill in the spaces. This approach is rather common, but does not guarantee at all a solution for lower income groups, since they seldom raise the money to build their own dwellings. The second and still more experimental approach is an extension of the "site and services idea":

- the government provides with a support structure for dwellings;

- those support structures can be divided in units in which facilities which are concerned necessary are provided; (in Netherlands that means water, gas, electricity, sewerage and if higher than 4 floors elevators)

- the units can be very cheap and either given or rented to the occupants;

- the occupant provides the infill; he can make that as cheap or expensive as he can pay for at that moment, making it more luxurious later on;

- Once the most serious housing need is over it will be possible to combine two units into one.

Advantages of this system are:

- control of street and urban patterns
- control of safety and construction
- control of physical standards.

The character of the support structure depends on:

- local habits
- cultural characteristics
- level of prosperity.

A lot of forms can be thought of varying from:

- the simple 'site and services' form
- basic construction with basic infrastructure
- a one or more stories construction offering the bearing
  walls of apartments, roofs and floors
- and as is experimented in our country, whole apartments
  without infill, but having bearing walls, floors, roofs
  and facades.

This is not simply a proposal to make housing cheaper. The essence of
this approach lies in the fact that the right of decisions in the basic
construction can be with the public authority -- at the level where it
belongs. The right of decisions on the infill can be with the
occupants. To distinguish responsibilities in such a way will not only
result in more and cheaper housing but also in an urban environment
that people can identify themselves with because they have a right of
decision over it.

   Maintenance will be far less a problem, because maintenance on the
infill will be the occupant's responsibility. Maintenance of the basic
construction will be the responsibility of the public authorities.
Maintenance of the dwelling environment must be organized in such a way
that the user can participate in it and is responsible for it.

   In the Netherlands, housing projects are realized by public housing
cooperations. Since labor is very expensive, maintenance costs have
been growing very much in the last decade. The housing cooperatives
try to raise the service costs (and thus indirectly the rent) in order
to keep up with these increases. The occupants, however, propose to
lower the rent, by doing the maintenance themselves. Two different
solutions in which the second one will have more lasting effects. The
only important thing to decide on is on which problems the community
has to decide and on which the individual occupant decides.

   In order to tackle the problems of organization and coordination in
between the different governmental levels and inside the urban areas,
related to the problems of big cities three solutions are evident:

- decentralization of authority to the local level;
- problem oriented approach in the big cities;
- to distinguish between decision responsibilities and
  participation between authorities and occupants.

4. Some Socio-Economic Observations

The demographic developments in Western Europe suggest an increase of the older population. The urban environment should offer amenities for this age group, which is not active anymore economically, nor as mobile as young people. They need contacts and sometimes help to do shopping, cooking and cleaning. The financially independent status of this group, thanks to the social security system, gives them freedom of choice as how to organize their own old days.

For a long time, the solution of this type of problem was sought in elderly homes -- big buildings with all possible services from normal household help to all kinds of medical treatment. These turned out to be dehumanizing. People felt themselves put aside, trying to avoid as long as possible the "old age factories".

The first step to a new response is now clear. Dwellings for old people should be just as a normal part of every complex. In these, there should be provision for decentralized help of all kinds, of shopping, meals and cleaning, and alarm systems in case of emergency. Everything should be aimed at keeping these people as long as possible part of society. One notices that a variety of handicraft skills are still present amongst these older people. To take advantage of these very scarce skills there are now even employment agencies for 65 and over where many of them are willing to do small jobs.

The other end of the demographic groups is represented by the young people between 18-27 years. They have just finished their education and quite often they do not find work and do not have many opportunities because of our stagnating economy. Their pattern of life is often very different from that of the older generation. Dwellings are expensive and difficult to obtain. In the housing sector a lot of experiments have been started to find integrated forms of living, cultural activities and employment for groups.

5. Conclusions

1. All planning efforts, instruments and methods cannot replace the will of the people directly involved to improve their situation. To motivate them to do so is one of the most important activities of planners.

2. Every effort to improve a situation will fail when the political will is lacking. In order to stimulate and keep the interest of the politicians short term successes should be placed in a framework of long term improvement strategy.

3. One of the main conclusions we can draw in the Netherlands from analyzing the effects of policies in the field of urbanization and physical planning is the fact that equal division of resources all over the country does not bring improvement for any situation or group. Concentration of attention, efforts and money in strategic positions, considering the overall cost-benefit is a much more successful strategy.

References

Haberer, Patries, (1978). <u>Urban Renewal in the Netherlands</u> (an overview), Ministry of Housing and Physical Planning, The Hague.

Haberer, Patries a.o., (1978). <u>Neighbourhood Approach</u>, The Hague.

Haberer, Patries and Frans Vonk, (1978). <u>Urban Revitalization</u>, Johns Hopkins Press, Baltimore.

Habraken, J.N., (1965). <u>Supports for Housing</u>, Eindhoven.

Lanchester, H.V., (1918). <u>Town Planning in Madras</u>, London.

18 Housing co-operatives in Ghana: problems and prospects

S. E. OWUSU

1. Introduction

One fact which cannot be disputed is that the basic necessities of life include shelter, which is just one aspect of housing. Housing is a much broader concept, which embraces the physical structure (i.e., the shelter) as well as the infrastructural and community facilities, and the ancilliary services.

Despite the fact that housing is a necessary requirement, it has constituted one of the major problems for which mankind has not found a satisfactory solution. It is not every household that can provide itself with a house. Generally, the majority of people depend on others to provide housing for hire. Where this is not adequately provided, the people tend to live in inadequate and poor housing conditions. And it is about this situation that governments of all nations have shown concern. The main concern, therefore, is how to provide and manage decent housing for the disadvantaged population.

In Ghana, as in most parts of the world, the ownership of a house for the immediate family or household is a popular desire. Ownership of the house and the land on which it stands offer the household a sense ofsecurity and pride. However, this aspiration is out of reach of most households because of the cost involved and the low incomes. As a result of these factors, most governments have instituted measures and programmes for helping the households who will not be in a position to build houses for themselves. In a number of cases the governments go in to support efforts of individuals or groups of individuals. It is the group of individuals which constitute the basic unit of the co-operative housing systems, which is the subject of this paper.

It is worthwhile placing the co-operative housing societies of Ghana into context by giving first an idea of the nature and operations of the housing sector in general.

2. Policy and Institutions of the Housing Sector

In broad terms, the ultimate aim of the government's policy for the country is to provide the population with adequate housing. This policy is being pursued in view of the important contribution of housing to the process of economic development. As a result, the objective has been to create an atmosphere within which the general public will participate effectively in the house building activities.

It is based on this broad policy that the government realized the need to encourage and develop the co-operative housing sector and earmarked an amount of ₡48.3 million for rural co-operative housing and ₡1.0 million for the urban housing cooperative development during the 1975-80 plan period (1 U.S.$ = 2.75₡).

Generally, the housing sector of Ghana is made up of the following:

(i)   the private sector:
(ii) the public sector:
(iii) the co-operative sector.

A large percentage of the housing stock in the country has been built through private initiative. It is estimated that over 80 per cent of the total output of houses in the urban areas is under the control of the private sector. This proportion is higher and in some cases it is 100 per cent in the rural areas. The fact that the private sector controls a greater proportion of the housing stock reflects, to a large extent, the method by which the houses had been financed. The private individuals build houses for their own use (i.e., owner occupier) or for rental purposes. In spite of this development, large private housing developers are not operating: this can be partially attributed to the unpredictable costs of construction materials and the consequent high cost of the basic house.

The second in importance in terms of the number of houses it controls is the public sector. Public sector housing was initiated into the country in 1939 after the earthquake which rendered many people homeless.

The third is the Co-operative sector which controls just about 763 houses.

The activities in the three sectors are conrolled both directly and indirectly by the Ministry of Works and Housing. This Ministry is the main government agency responsible for the housing sector in the country. It is the policy making body; and it has under it the following institutions which are involved in housing:

1.   Architectural and Engineering Services Corporation;
2.   Public Works Department:
3.   Town and Country Planning Department:
4.   State Housing Corporation:
5.   Tema Development Corporation:
6.   Public Servants Housing Loans Scheme Board;
7.   Ghana Water and Sewerage Corporation:
8.   Electricity Corporation of Ghana: and
9.   Rent Control Division.

Other institutions within the housing sector which do not fall under the Ministry of Works and Housing, but which have close relationship with it are:

1.   Department of Rural Development (which is now called Department of Rural Housing and Cottage Industries);
2.   Social Security and National Insurance Trust;
3.   Building and Roads Research Institute of C.S.I.R.;

4. Department of Housing and Planning Research of the University of Science and Technology, Kumasi, and
5. Local Councils.

The main organizations involved in actual house construction in the public sector are the State Housing Corporation (S.H.C), Tema Development Corporation (T.D.C.) and the Department of Rural Housing and Cottage Industries. Infrastructural services are provided by the Ghana Water and Sewerage Corporation (G.W.&S.C.), Electricity Corporation of Ghana (E.C.G.) and the Local Councils or authorities. The Department of Town and Country Planning deals with planning and the control of physical development while the local authorities play important role in the development control and the provision of sanitary facilities.

The main institutions providing finance for housing are:

1. the Bank for Housing and Construction;
2. The First Ghana Building Society, and
3. The Bank of Ghana.

In addition to these, there are the State Insurance Corporation, the Commercial Banks and the Public Servants' Housing Loan Scheme Board which have been granting mortgage loans to individual and real estate developers.

These in brief give an idea of the institutional framework for the housing sector of Ghana. In spite of the network of institutions that has been established, the supply of housing has not been able to meet the demand for it, and this is due to a number of constraints which are outlined in the next section.

3. Constraints on the Housing Sector

According to the 1960 Post Enumeration Survey and the 1971 Provisional census data on housing, the housing stock in the country increased from 701,360 houses to 959,240 houses; that is an increase of 37 percent. This increase is almost the same as the population increase. The result of this is that the supply of housing units has not been able to reach the level of the demand for it because of previous shortage. The annual output of houses for both private and public sectors between 1960 and 1971 was 26,000 units, while the projected output required to improve the housing situation is 70,000 units per annum.

The poor performance in the housing sector is due to a number of constraints. The most important constraint is the non-availability of long-term loanable funds. This is mainly due to two factors, namely, limited amount of long-term savings and the attitude of the financial institutions. Because of the limited long-term savings, these institutions are inclined to granting short-term loans. Furthermore, because the financial institutions realize that the costs of monitoring and foreclosing on rural area defaults, their limited lending facilities go to the urban dwellers. The rural dwellers are therefore denied any significant institutional financing. This financial problem is very evident among low and middle income households. It is therefore in this respect that individual resources and efforts need to be mobilized: hence the need for the co-operative approach to housing provision.

The other constraints are as follow:

(i) the difficulty in acquiring land, especially in the urban areas. Increase in the specialization of land use is making land available for housing more scarce and therefore expensive;

(ii) shortage and high cost of construction materials: and

(iii) the rapid rate of population growth (i.e., 2.7% per annum) and urbanization, which are resulting in higher rate of household formation especially in the urban areas.

As a result of these constraints, the country is currently faced with a serious housing problem. Broadly speaking, the housing problem can be stated as a shortage and sub-standard housing in the urban centers, and sub-standard (or poor) houses in the rural areas. The effect of these is overcrowding, the rate of which has been increasing as the years pass by. But it must be pointed out that overcrowding is more evident in the housing areas where most low income households find accommodation than in the high and middle incomes residential areas.

Estimates made in 1960 indicate that 82 percent of all the houses in the country were located in the rural areas. The proportion may be different in 1981, with the proportion in the urban areas increasing slightly. However, in 1960, 23.1 percent of the total national population was in the urban areas. This figure increased to 28.9 percent in 1970 and it is on the increase. It is in the light of this population concentration and the proportion of the total housing units available that the housing shortage can be seen. For the rural housing: it was found in a survey of some rural settlements that 92 percent of the houses were made of swish, most of which have developed structural defects.

4. Migration and Housing

Population growth constitutes one of the factors responsible for the current shortage and poor condition of housing in the urban areas. Migration is an important factor accounting for the growth in the urban population.

As in the case of most countries, what constitutes an urban center or town is expressed in statistical terms. In Ghana, settlements with 5,000 or more population are referred to as towns. Based on this definition, the urbanization ratio (which is defined as the percentage of population living in urban settlements) of Ghana increased from 23.1 percent in 1960 to 28.9 percent in 1970. It is estimated that this will increase to 38 percent by 1985. The growth rate for the urban centers is between 3.7 and 3.9 percent as against 2.7 percent for the whole national population. The increase in the urban population is quite high and migration is a major factor in this.

Four types of migration have been identified in the country; namely, rural-urban, rural-rural, urban-urban and urban-rural migrations. In quantitative terms, rural to rural migration is the most significant as it accounts for 59.9 percent of all migrants in the country. Rural to urban migration involves 17.7 percent of all migrants, urban to urban involves 10.9 percent and urban to rural migration accounts for 11.7 percent of all migratory movements in the country in 1960. There are no current figures on this movement, but from all indications, the pattern has not changed much. It however, appears that rural to urban migration is increasing relatively faster than the others and its implication for housing is very significant because of the limited number of settlements and therefore, space on which the population is converging.

The causes of this movement are the well known "push and pull" factors. Most of the migrants to the urban areas find employment mainly in the informal sector and in low paid jobs. A study of Anloga and Oforikrom (which are two of the predominantly migrant settlements of Kumasi) reveals that 62 percent (for Oforikrom) and 82 percent (for Anloga) of the households covered fall within the low income group with incomes of less than ₵100 per month at the time (i.e., 1977). As a result of low incomes, the majority of the migrants find housing in the slum areas and other residential areas with poor services.

There are also the rich migrants who have difficulty in obtaining accommodation, not because there are no houses for them, but because they require certain facilities. Therefore as a result of low incomes on the part of most migrants and high taste of the rich households, there tend to be "artificial shortage" of housing especially in the urban centers such as Accra and Kumasi.

5. Why Co-operative Housing Societies?

The discussion so far has been on the government policy, institutional framework and the nature of the problems of housing sector of the country. As can be realized any renewed assault on the housing problems will of necessity have to concentrate on the development of both large and small housing projects. The number of housing units that are required is great in the sense that the annual requirements for new households is not even 50 percent met by new construction.

It is not only new construction and communities that have to be planned and developed, but that the existing units and community facilities will need to be properly maintained in a way so as to effect an efficient use of the funds invested. This need is great and it is proven that good results are more likely to be achieved in circumstances where the residents participate in finding solutions. Furthermore, the results are usually better when the residents are formally organized for such participation. And housing co-operative society is one of the most widely recognized organizations for efficient community development, preservation and improvement.

One of the factors that have been frustrating the efforts of persons who would like to provide themselves with adequate and decent housing, the financial constraint appears the most important. It is with this view in mind that a number of banking institutions and schemes have been established to provide finance for housing purposes. However, as a study of the financial institutions in the country reveals, households of the low and middle income groups are the least beneficiaries of the institutional financing. These households invariably constitute a greater proportion of the nation's population. The attitudes of the financial institutions are not encouraging.

The majority of the households are not adequately suppoted by the existing financial institutions because of a number of factors including low and unstable incomes, and lack of security. The low and middle income earners can become credit worthy if they pool their resources together. This requires the formation of identifiable groups with a common objective, which in this case is the co-operative housing society.

The co-operative approach to housing is gaining root in the country as a result of the realization of the fact that it is important that we should mobilze, however small, the individual resources and group efforts into the housing task. This is even necessary because the government cannot continue its paternalistic approach to housing its population in a situation of capital shortage and high inflation.

This paper deals mainly with the housing co-operatives of Ghana. But before discussing these, there are a few terminologies which must be defined or explained in order that the case study can be understood. The following section attempts to do this.

6. Co-operative Housing - Definition, Types and Principles

Definition

A Co-operative has been defined as a legally incorporated group of people, generally of limited means, pursuing an economic purpose in which membership is voluntary and control is democratic. Co-operative housing is therefore any form of organization in which groups of people undertake co-operatively to obtain housing to be owned by those who occupy it. A co-operative society is the basic unit of the co-operative movement. The prime objective of co-operative housing societies and that which distinguishes them from other business organizations is that they aim at providing housing on non-profit basis. They are therefore both a business and a social organization.

Types: Co-operative housing societies can be classified according to the following factors:

    (i)   Life span:
   (ii)   Systems of ownership of the properties, and
  (iii)   type of activity in which particular society is engaged.

Employing these factors, they can be classified as follows:

(i)   consumer co-operatives and producer co-operatives. The consumer societies are basically management co-operatives, while the producer societies may be involved in building new housing units or buying and improving existing properties for their members. Producer societies also offer management services to their members:

(ii) Terminal and Permanent co-operative societies: Terminal or temporary co-operative is that type of society which builds single family accommodations and ceases to be a co-operative when the whole operation is completed.

The Permanent Co-operative Society is that type of society in which the members buy shares in proportion to the built-up area of the unit they occupy, and they pay monthly contributions. In such a co-operative, the members are the tenants as well as the landlords of their properties.

(iii) Primary and Secondary Co-operative Societies: This classification is based on the activities of the societies and this it stypical of the United Kingdom. A primary society is defined as the society whose members are individuals and whose objectives are to serve those members. A secondary co-operative society is one whose members are primary societies and whose objectives are to provide those primary societies with services to enable them to perform their functions adequately.

Conditions and Basic Principles of Co-opertation

Since the days of the Rochdale Equitable Pioneer Society (formed in Lancashire in England in 1844), the co-operative movement has been based on certain well-defined conditions and principles.

The co-operative housing movement is based on group action. The essential thing in the co-operative housing movement is that the group must have very strong links, and this means that the members must have a number of things that interest them and bring them together.

The second important condition is that the members must have a certain minimum regular income in order that they can make payments with regard to membership and pay for the services that the society is to provide.

There are six basic principles governing the operations of housing societies and these are formulated by the International Co-operative Alliance (I.C.A.). The current principles were approved in 1966 and they are as follows:

(i) open and voluntary membership - under this people have the freedom to join or withdraw from a co-operative society. What this principles aims to avoid is a situation where the co-operative society is imposed on the people;

(ii) Democratic Control: This deals with the equality of all members and establishes that voting rights rest in the individual members rather than the share held;

(iii) Limited Interest on share capital, and

(iv) Disposal of surplus (savings): Co-operative Societies have adopted the principle of limiting the maximum rate of interest on share capital to be paid to their members because the idea of co-operation is not to make profit on money invested. In co-operative housing profits are not distributed, but are used for the general good of the membership.

(v) Education of Members: This principle is adopted because it is
     through the process of education that the co-operatives can
     hope to raise the social standard of their members.

(vi) Politics, Religion and Race: Co-operatives adopt this
     principle of neutrality in matters of politics, religion and
     race in order to maintain the unity of the co-operative group.

It is based on these conditions and principles that the co-operative
housing movement has been able to maintain its non-profit structure
while performing its social functions. These general conditions and
principles are upheld by the co-operatives of Ghana, which are
discussed in the following sections.

Origin of the Co-operative Housing Movement in Ghana

The formal form of co-operative activities in the country started
in 1928/29 and revolved mostly around the cocoa industry. Before these
co-operative societies came into existence, there were informal
co-operative arrangements especially in the rural communities where
people teamed up for work on the farms and house construction. These
informal co-operative arrangements still exist in the rural areas and
they are termed "Nnoboa" in the Akan communities.

The first formal housing societies in Ghana were founded in about
1956 as a result of government initiative. These societies were the
results of the government's scheme for financing rural housing; that
is, the Roof Loan Scheme. These societies were purposely formed to
enable the members to have access to government sources of finance for
housing purposes. In the true sense of the word, these were not
co-operative housing societies.

It was about 15 years later that the first housing co-operative was
founded in the urban area. This is the Tema Housing Co-operative
Society Limited, which was established in 1971. The preparatory work
towards the establishment of this co-operative was however started in
1969 by the Department of Housing and Planning Research of the
University of Science and Technology, Kumasi.

Institutional Arrangements and Supporting Agencies

The housing co-operatives as well as other forms of co-operative
activities in Ghana are governed by Decree 252 of 1968. This Decree
deals with the procedure for registration, duties and privileges of
registered societies, rights and liabilities of members, methods of
handling disputes, and method for dissolving a registered society. By
regulation all established housing co-operatives are to register with
the Registrar of Co-operatives of the Department of Co-operatives, in
order to become corporate bodies. They are required to satisfy the
following conditions before they are registered:

(i) must have at least 10 members;

(ii) must have a secretary with a knowledge of accounting;

(iii) must have a management committee of seven, and

(iv) must have a piece of land on which it intends to build housing
units.

The Department of Co-operatives is responsible for the development,
supervision and extension of all co-operative activities in the
country. In the case of the development, financing and other forms of
assistance to the co-operative housing societies, other government and
quasi-government institutions are involved. These are the Ministry of
Finance and Economic Planning, Ministry of Works and Housing, Department
of Rural Housing and Cottage Industries, Department of Housing and
Planning Research, and the Ghana Co-operative and Builders Association
Limited.

7. Main Characteristics of the Co-operative Housing Societies

Co-operative housing societies in the country are organized and
administered mainly by the Department of Housing and Planning Research
(of UST, Kumasi) and the Department of Rural Housing and Cottage
Industries (of the Ministry of Youth and Rural Development). The
co-operatives organized by the Department of Housing and Planning
Research are mainly to be found in the urban areas (e.g., Tema, Kumasi
and Offinso). On the other hand the societies under the Department of
Rural Housing and Cottage Industries are to be found in both the rural
and urban settlements. According to the Department of Co-operatives,
there were 120 registered housing co-operatives in the country in July
1980, of which most fall under the Department of Rural Housing and
Cottage Industries.

The co-operatives organized by the Department of Rural Housing and
Cottage Industries are not permanent societies. They are supported by
a revolving fund and the societies cease to exist as corporate bodies
when all the loans granted to their members have been paid off and the
construction work completed. So far none of them has reached the stage
of being analyzed. The practice is that the Department of Rural
Housing and Cottage Industries has been pre-financing the buildings and
on completion a society allocates the houses to its members, and the
beneficiaries are expected to repay the loan in a period of 20 years.
The present system shows evidence of a state organization building
houses and selling them to the public on favorable low risk terms.

On the other hand the co-operatives under the Department of Housing
and Planning Research are permanent societies. Their nature however
conflicts with the main aim of most of the co-operators. The main
motive for which a good number of persons have joined the co-operative
is to own a house, but this cannot be achieved through joining
permanent societies.

In spite of this the true housing co-operatives are the ones in
Tema, Kumasi, and Offinso which come under the Department of Housing
and Planning Research. The co-operatives in the rural areas rely
solely on the initiative and funds from the Department of Rural Housing
and Cottage Industries. Without this department, these socities cease
to function and this indicates that the spirit of co-operation is not
in the members.

238

Membership status in any of the urban housing co-operatives is obtained through application and interview, and in some cases this is subject to the approval of the existing members of a society. The two main criteria for admission into a society are:

(i) place of residence, and
(ii) place of work.

Eligible persons become members only when they have paid admission fee, which currently ranges between ₵1.00 and ₵5.00. The incoming member is also required to buy one share in the society, which is at a price of ₵100.00.

There is no clear cut basis for selecting the members for the housing co-operatives organized by the Department of Rural Housing and Cottage Industries. The practice now is that the members are accepted on the ability to pay a deposit of C300.00 and a registration fee of ₵20.00. The membership of any of these societies ranges from low income workers to influential top civil servants and traders or businessmen.

In the case of the permanent societies, a member who wants to resign from a co-operative has to apply and give 30 days notice. Such a member is entitled to claim his savings plus any money he might have contributed towards the cost of a house.

The co-operatives themselves are administered by boards of elected members; that is, Chairman, Secretary and Treasurer. The officers are elected at general meetings and they serve a term of office in the first instance for a period of 3 years. The officers are not paid any remuneration as these are voluntary associations. There are other committees for various activities of the co-operatives and these assist the boards in managing the day to day affairs of the group.

The sources of funds for the housing co-operatives are:

(i) contribution of the members which come in the form of fees, dues and savings;

(ii) share capital purchased by each member:

(iii) central government funds which come in the form of mortgage loans with an element of subsidy because of the low interest rate charged; and

(iv) voluntary contributions which are made during general meetings at the end of the year.

The main source of funds is the contributions and shares of the members. The Tema Housing Co-operative Society (being a pilot project), on the other hand, has the greater part of its funds from the central government sources. Also most of the funds which were used in constructing the houses for the co-operatives which are managed by the Department of Rural Housing and Cottage Industries came from the Central Government sources.

The Central Government started funding the Tema Housing Co-operative

Society in 1971 with an initial capital of ₵68,000. It received a second loan of ₵100,000 from the government in 1974. The interest on the loan is 3 percent, with a repayment period of 30 years. Currently the government has earmarked ₵1.5 million for the co-operative sector and over half of this amount will go into the Tema Housing Co-operative Society to continue with the house construction for the 103 members.

One of the best organized housing co-operatives is the Abotare Ye Housing Co-operative Society Limited in Tema, and this Co-operative will be used to show the size of capital that can be generated. The capital of this society comes through the following sources:

(i)   Admission fee of ₵5 per each incoming member

(ii)   yearly dues of ₵5 per member:

(iii) savings of between ₵10 and ₵40 per month per member, and

(iv)   a deposit of ₵120 to qualify for a house.

The society was established in 1974 with 250 members, but by December 1980 only 116 members were left. The society has only a piece of land on which it intends to build houses, and by the end of 1979 its capital stood at ₵44,506.74.

Through a study of some of the viable housing co-operatives, it has been found that they are capable of mobilizing a substantial amount of money from their own members. This therefore implies that given the right guidance and the appropriate financial institutions, the individual financial contributions through the co-operative societies can constitute a greater part of the long term capital required for housing purposes which at the moment is in short supply in the country.

Considering the output figures, it can be concluded that the impact of the co-operatives on the housing scene has not been impressive. Between 1974/1975 and 1978/1979 the Department of Rural Housing and Cottage Industries completed 740 houses and had 694 units under construction for the co-operatives it controls.

The housing co-operatives under the Department of Housing and Planning Research completed only 23 houses and had 31 units under construction between 1971 and 1980. On the whole, only 763 houses were completed for co-operators by the end of 1980.

8. The Problems of the Co-operative Sector

The poor performance of the co-operative housing sector is due to certain factors, which relate to poor management and technical assistance, inadequate finance and supply of construction materials, and lack of adequate co-operative education. These are explained in the following paragraphs.

(i)   One of the main factors which have been hindering the proper functioning of the housing co-operatives is the lack of a promoting agency or what is popularly called Technical Service Organization (T.S.O.). Although the Department of Housing and Planning Research and the Department of Rural Housing and

Cottage Industries have been performing the functions of a promoting agency, they have not been doing it with the understanding and efficient management that are required of such an agency. The result is that a number of mistakes had been made: for example co-operatives have been established for which the members lack adequate understanding or education of what their rights and responsibilities are. This weak point in the co-operative sector has now been identified and there are plans to have a T.S.O. established to undertake this responsibility of organizing the housing co-operatives on the proper lines. As a first step the Ministry of Works and Housing established a unit under a United Nations Co-operative Adviser to see to the proper functioning of the existing housing co-operatives. This unit is now headed by a Research Fellow from the Department of Housing and Planning Research.

(ii)   As stated earlier on, the co-operatives are operating under the general co-operative societies Decree (NLCD 252) of 1968. This is supplemented by the bye-laws of each of the societies. It was found that because of lack of adequate education, almost all the existing co-operatives are operating the model bye-law drafted by the Department of Housing and Planning Research. This is not the proper method of doing this; the constitution or bye-law should deal with the obligations and responsibilities of the members, and of the relationship between the co-operative society and outside institutions. It is therefore important that the bye-laws should reflect local situations.

(iii) The housing co-operatives were founded as an alternative to state sponsored housing development, and as a means of channelling public funds into the housing sector especially the rural housing sector. Because of this there was no deliberate attempt to explore other means of attracting funds into the co-operative housing sector. This has resulted in lack of capital to undertake housing projects. The other factor which is responsible for the lack of finance is that the co-operatives have been depositing funds obtained from the shares and savings of their members in the commercial banking institutions, which are inclined to grant short-term loans as opposed to long-term lending facilities required for housing purposes.

(iv)   The fourth important problem facing the sector is the periodic shortage of materials which the whole construction industry faces. The root causes of this problem is the faulty industrialization strategy that was adopted during the first republic and that was pursued by subsequent governments. This is however, an external factor to the co-operative sector.

(v)   The fifth factor is that there is a serious lack of co-ordination in the co-operative sector. There is very little communication between the institutions involved in co-operative housing with the result that none of them knows exactly what the other is doing and the difficulties it is facing.

These then in brief outline the main problems of the co-operative housing sector. From these it is realized that the success of the sector and the socities in particular is dependent upon six interrelated factors. These facotrs are:

(i) proper guidance and technical assistance from a devoted and properly staffed promoting agency:

(ii) efficient management:

(iii) adequate finance for house construction:

(iv) commitment on the part of the members to the principles of co-operation, and this is based on adequate education on the activities of co-operative housing societies. This implies that the co-operatives must consist of people with common problems and aims:

(v) availability of resources, e.g., construction materials:

(vi) proper co-ordination of the activities of all institutions involved in the sector.

9. Potentials of the Co-operative Housing System for the Country

There are however, programmes to improve and sustain the co-operative housing sector because of its potentials. The co-operative approach to housing is being promoted because of the following reasons:

(i) to encourage and accumulate small savings of the individual persons for housing purposes:

(ii) to organize free labor in order to reduce the cost of carrying out a housing project:

(iii) to reduce the cost of housing units by cutting down on the management costs:

(iv) the use of small scale contractors and artisans for house construction:

(v) to release pressure on the central government financial sources, and through this the government can actually concentrate on the households who in all respects cannot afford to do anything about their poor or lack of housing:

(vi) to provide new houses and to maintain the houses and facilities as presently exist in the slum and rural settlements: and

(vii) to effect social integration, especially in the urban area.

These are the main potentials inherent in this sector which warrant its support and encouragement.

The co-operative approach is not by itself a cheap means of owning a house or obtaining a decent dwelling unit to rent as many are made to think. It is, however, a means of providing people without adequate financial resources and any significant security, with the shelter and related facilities at a reduced cost so that they can enjoy decent family life. The very poor people cannot be decently housed through the co-operative system except that the central government will adequately subsidize the entire project by way of providing all the relevant inputs for the people to build the houses themselves.

So far this is not the practice because a developing country like Ghana with numerous demands on the scarce governmental financial resources cannot afford to embark on such a scheme.

In spite of its shortcomings, the co-operative system has proved to have enough potentials which when adequately developed can enable a sizeable proportion of the population who will be capable of making some financial contribution to be decently housed. Housing Co-operative Societies can be developed at all income levels but in the developing countries, such as Ghana, their prospects are brighest among the middle income households. Very often these families are unable to meet the total cost of minimum, safe, sanitary and suitable housing if they acted individually. It is in this respect that co-operating with others is necessary.

10. Conclusion

As indicated, Ghana requires a large number of new housing units as well as extensive maintenance and renovation programmes for a large section of its towns and villages. In the face of this need, there is capital shortage as well as shortage of other resources. The country therefore requires the mobilization of a large segment of the population and resources in any housing programme. The co-operative housing system is a proven and a worthwhile channel through which this can be attained.

Although the co-operative housing movement in Ghana is still in its formative stages and faces a number of difficulties, it is obvious that it has potentials for solving part of the housing shortage of the urban areas, and the poor housing environment as currently can be found in the urban slum settlements and a number of rural areas. The case of Ghana is just one example of the prevailing situation in the developing countries for which a well managed and active co-operative sector can contribute significantly.

References

Afele, L.K., (1975). 'Housing financing in rural Ghana,' Current Report No. 9, B.R.R.I., Kumasi.

Digby, M., (1978). 'Co-operative housing,' Occasional Paper No. 42.

Ewusi, K. Population Growth and Housing Needs for Urban Centers in Ghana.

International Co-operative Alliance, (1971). Report of the ICA Commission and Co-operative Principles, London.

Ministry of Finance and Economic Planning, (1977). Five Year Development Plan 1975/76-1979/80, Part II, Accra.

Owusu, D.J. et al., (1973). 'A housing survey in Ghana,' Kumasi.

Owusu, S.E., (1980). Financing Housing Programmes: The Role of Co-operative Housing Societies in Urban Ghana, M. Phil Dissertation.

19 Internal migration and the Egyptian labor force

NADIA SULIMAN

1. Introduction

The exports of Egyptian labor are not a new phenomenon. Egypt's role as a supplier of labor in the Arab world has become a tradition. What is new is its magnitude, the rate of increase of migration to the Arab oil exporting countries, essentially subsequent to the oil price rises and the acceleration of investment in those countries. The Arab Oil Exporting countries are the smallest Arab countries in population. The most populous countries are the poorest in natural resources but more developed in terms of overall knowledge and skills. Over the years, these differences have contributed to pronounced patterns of migration across national boundaries and to the mobility of labor. The Egyptian labor movement (especially in some professions) is placing heavy burdens on the Egyptian economy and on the domestic labor market in Egypt.

2. Incentives Behind Egyptian Labor Migration to the Arab Countries

This large scale migration has two basic causes:

- Migration results from the desire of migrants to improve their standard of living. The most important factors which support this movement are wage differentials between origin and destination points. These differentials reach ratios of 1:25 in the case of university academic staff. In eight years of emigration to an Arab country, an Egyptian member of the academic staff can earn 3:5 times what he could earn in his entire life in Egypt, if this productive life is assumed to be 30 years (Eldin, 1979, p. 197). Educated guesses place wages in Arab oil exporting countries at 5-10 times their Egyptian equivalent.

- Migration for the whole society as the tool for alleviating the balance of payment problems through workers remittances. Egypt is undoubtedly suffering from shortages of foreign exchange earnings which act as a limiting factor on the level of economic activity in general. Foreign exchange shortage has constrained the industrial sector and was one of the major factors which led to the prevalance of excess capacity in this sector (Messiha, 1980, p. 2).

245

Egypt's position as a major labor donor to other
Arab states is due to some other factors. Because of
population explosion and limited economic resources,
Egypt's economy could not expand at a rate sufficient
to absorb labor surplus.

-    An infrastructure that produces a large number of
     university graduates every year, without adequate
     domestic opportunities for the employment of these
     graduates.

-    The cultural similarity that reduces the
     difficulties of adjustment and adaptation to an alien
     environment (Choucri, 1977).

-    The political forces underlying the movement could be
     summarized in easing internal political as well as
     social tension, resulting of the economic difficulties
     (Eldin, 1979, p. 197).

3. Migration Policies

We can distinguish three phases in the development of migration
policies in Egypt. The first phase, which extends from the mid-fifties
to around 1967, was marked by its prohibitive nature. This attitude is
revealed through the imposition of many barriers. Conscription laws
represented the most important constraint because they give the government the right to appoint by decree, a university group or any other
professional group to a given job for a period of two years, renewable.
Moreover, migration applications from non-conscripted graduates were
subject to a ministerial committee's scrutiny (Dessouki, 1978, pp.
5-6). Furthermore centralization and complication of bureaucratic
procedures were involved in obtaining passports or exit visas to
reinforce migration restrictions.

The second phase which extended from 1967 to around 1970 was marked
by its ambivalent nature. During this period, several steps were taken
to institutionalize migration by establishing an emigration department
in the Ministry of foreign affairs (Foreign Minister's decision No. 121
for 1969), and an emigration and work abroad committee (law by decree
No. 63). Their aim was to maintain contacts with Egyptian migrants
abroad, survey foreign labor market opportunities, and negotiate
bilateral agreement with recipient countries. Relaxation of restrictions during this period is witnessed by the permanent sizable number
of university graduates. Nevertheless, conscription policy continued
and quotas were still assigned to certain professions and specializa-
tions considered critical to development (Dessouki, in Messiha 1980, p.
12).

In the third phase, which extends from 1971 to the present, Egypt
has officially adopted a labor export policy, by its promulgation of
the following laws and degrees. The 1971 constitution established
emigration, permanent or temporary, as a "right" (Article 55). Law by
decree No. 73 gave migrants the right to be reappointed to their former
positions within one year of their resignation. In 1975, the
parliament ratified the treaty for man power movement between Arab
countries (Parliamentary proceedings, 1967). Law by decree No. 31 for

1976 established a higher committee to deal with the affairs of Egyptians abroad. Another presidential decree (No. 795) established the Higher Council for Manpower and training whose policy objectives were not only the satisfaction of the needs of local economic and social development, but also the fulfillment of the needs of Arab and other friendly countries (Dessouki, 1978, pp. 11-15; and in Messiha 1980, p. 12).

Emigration policy can be best understood in the light of other cognate policies such as the secondment policies and Remittances policies.

There are two types of secondment. First, organized and collective secondment which is an agreement between the government of Egypt and the Arab Countries for Egypt to send a certain number of employees per year. The duration of secondment is usually four to five years.

The second type of secondment is based on individual initiative. The employee is offered a job from an employer, applies for a non-paid leave of absence from his present job, and obtains a work permit from the Ministry of the Interior. This type of secondment may take place within Egypt itself or abroad, and is for a period of two years renewable for a maximum of four years (Messiha, 1980).

According to Remittances policies, it was compulsory for Egyptian teachers sent on secondment to Arab countries to remit 25% of their salary to the immigration countries if they were single, and 10% if they were married, at the official exchange rate.

The new import regulations, such as the "own exchange" policy was established by decree in 1974 that allows Egyptians to import consumption and capital goods with foreign exchange from earnings abroad and absolve any license requirements up to L.E. 5000 through the intermediary of the Central Bank. Also, Egyptian migrants now transfer their remittances at the incentive tourist rate, to offer them more favorable terms of exchange and to limit dealing on the black market. Moreover, new economic regulations gave migrants the right to open foreign currency accounts in Egyptian banks thus curtailing the holding of deposits in foreign exchange banks abroad. This intensive program of multiple tools and incentives was really successful in attracting remittances from abroad (Messiha, 1980, p. 14).

It is also important to refer to the brokerage agencies which have been created for mobilizing and channelling Egyptian migrant outflows. These agencies operate as facilitators for migration and as active agents for influencing individual decisions to migrate. Although these firms were largely private recently there appears to be direct government participation.

For the present Egypt has no official migration policy. In fact, the government is promotional in its orientation and even implicitly encouraging. The determination of migratory movement, however, is still one of private initiative. Lifting government restrictions has caused a marked increase in migration (Choucri, 1977, pp. 428-30).

4. Trends of the Temporary Migration of the Egyptian Labor Force

The shortage of human capital in the Arab oil producing countries is evident by the extent of projected employment of foreign manpower for the near future.

The expected need for additional human capital between 1977 and 1980 in the Arab oil producing countries is estimated to be 1.5 million workers. Egyptian migrants perform a crucial role in the development plans of the Arab countries (Messiha, 1980, p. 2).

Estimates of the total number of Egyptians working in Arab countries varies from one source to another. This phenomenon can be explained by the fact that a great number of those who emigrated left Egypt on tourist or work permit visas. In addition, non-returned students were registered in the chosen country of immigration only. Also a sizable part of the emigrated labor is this part of migrants who migrate without any dependent.

In one estimation the number is 2.5 million. In another one it is 350,000 while the Arab countries reported 369,000 Egyptians working there, and the Egyptian Government reported 430,000.

In 1978, the Ministry of Foreign Affairs in Egypt estimated their number to be 1,365,000 (Al Ahram, Sept. 18, 1978). This represents 12.8% of the labor force in Egypt.

According to the Ministry of Interior Affairs' statistics for individual and collective secondments, if we examine the trend in the flow of labor emigration from Egypt, we note that it is increasing over time. This is illustrated in Table 1.

It is clear from the table below that the outflow from Egypt has been increasing over time from 1975 till 1979 at an annual rate of 32.5%. The actual outflow in 1979 is 33.5% higher than the level in 1975.

There are marked variations in the qualifications of migrants in the total labor force which have been migrating to the various countries (Table 2). The Arab countries clearly receive the largest share of Egyptian migrants (99.2%). All other countries draw about 1% of the total number of Egyptian migrants.

In terms of the qualifications of out-migrants, 36% have the bachelor's (or higher) degree. About 32% of migrants are in the group of "with no qualification".

Table 3 displays the distribution of the emigrants according to qualification and the country of migrants in 1980.

The five large recipient countries of Egyptian migrants are Saudi Arabia, Kuwait, Yemen, Libya and Qatar. These countries alone accounted for 87.28% of all migrants to the Arab countries in 1980. Saudi Arabia alone attracted 67.15% of Egyptian migrants to the Arab countries in 1980.

Table 4 indicates the gross annual flow of highly qualified labor emigration in 1974-1979.

It is clear from Table 4 that the outflow of the highly qualified emigrants to the Arab countries has been increasing over time from 1974 till 1979 at a very steep rate.

5. Consequences of Migration

Egyptian manpower has comprised the backbone of the educated and skilled personnel in the Arab countries, to the extent that such flows, if persistent, might constitute a net drain on Egyptian manpower resources at some levels.

In 1978, the Minister of Manpower disclosed the estimated number of surplus labor in Egypt up to the year 1985 to be 975,000 workers, while as he stated, the Arab countries need nearly 1.5 million workers to fulfill the requirements of their development plans (Al Ahram, Feb. 10, 1978, 9). This was a justification for Egypt's adoption of a labor export policy. But the problem mainly centers on identifying which types of labor surplus exist, and in which sector. The Egypt's manpower plan will create significant shortage of labor from 1970-1985 in the categories of high professionals, technicians and skilled labor -- the occupational categories most crucial to the development. A surplus is predicted only in the unskilled category.

At first sight, there appear to be numerous advantages for Egyptian migration to the Arab oil countries.

(1)   The Remittances sent home by the Egyptian migrants are
      a valuable source of foreign exchange. Remittances of
      Egyptian workers abroad have increased dramatically in
      the recent years. The total remittances amounted to
      1700 million in 1980. The following table shows the
      increase since 1976.

      These remittances are very important as a source of
      foreign exchange, as a source of liquidity, a
      palliative for balance of payments problems and as a
      means of provision of hard currency (Birks and
      Sinclair, 1980, pp. 43-46).

      The widespread feeling in Egypt that remittances are
      not directed productively enough and need to be
      channelled towards investment rather than conspicuous
      consumption has led to the introduction of several
      schemes offering opportunities for Egyptians to invest
      their remittances at preferential rates. Banks have
      been established to attract expatriate Egyptian's funds

(2)   Moreover, the departure of migrants can be seen as an
      effective way of reducing unemployment.

On the other side migration has also numerous disadvantages for Egypt. Migration for employment means not only the loss of the productive capacity of the migrants during their most active years, but also the process is selective the tends to draw out many of the most

TABLE 1

GROSS ANNUAL FLOW OF LABOR EMIGRATION
1974 - 1979

Year		1975	1976	1977	1978	1979
Arab	NO	38989	57999	88383	99836	119524
Countries	%	96.5	98.14	98.25	98.38	99.21
Asian	NO	69	112	94	111	46
Countries	%	0.17	0.18	0.10	0.12	0.04
European	NO	839	644	703	641	468
Countries	%	2.05	1.08	0.78	0.63	0.40
American	NO	7	9	9	8	1
Countries	%	0.01	0.01	0.01	0.01	0.00
African	NO	498	320	753	849	405
Countries	%	1.23	0.54	0.83	0.84	0.34
Other	NO	14	9	13	17	11
Countries	%	0.03	0.01	0.01	0.02	0.01
	NO	40406	59093	89955	101462	120455
Total	%	100.00	100.00	100.00	100.00	100.00

Source: Ministry of Interior Affairs' Statistics of Individual and
Collective Secondments, 1975 - 1979.

able members within each skill level of the labor force. The loss is
therefore greater than numbers alone might suggest. The direct cost of
the "brain drain" in Egypt is the migration of skilled workers and
educated manpower who would otherwise be employed. This effectively
deprives the country of the returns from its investment in the
education of its population. The drain effect is most pronounced in
certain sectors.

The sector of university academic staff is very crucial. During
the period 1971-1975; while the number of university staff members
increased by 28% at an annual rate of 6.3%, emigration increased by 56%
at an annual rate of 12%. The most important consequences relate to
the educational system and the educational process. Thus in human
sciences, the ratio of students to each member of the staff declined
from 25.1 to 28.1 after emigration. This leads to overcrowding of the
classes and low productivity
in the educational process (Eldin, 1979, p. 40-47).

-   In the sector of construction, the effects of construction
    emigration lead to increasing labor cost internally and hence
    the cost of construction and investment should be calculated
    as part of the social cost involved in migration. Also, the

TABLE 2

THE TOTAL LABOR FORCE WHICH HAVE BEEN EMIGRATING TO THE GROUPS OF THE WORLD COUNTRIES ACCORDING TO THEIR QUALIFICATION BY THE END OF 1979

Countries Groups \ Qualification	Ph.D.	Master	Higher Diploma	Batchelor or its Equivalent	General El Azhar Secondary Certificate	Technical Secondary Certificate	Nursing	Other Intermediate Qualifications	With no Qualification	Less Intermediate Qualifications	Total	Ratio % of Total
The Arab Countries	1666	560	3912	36229	3468	17888	3011	9579	38968	4293	119524	99.21
The African Countries	13	6	32	323	1	11	1	15	-	2	405	0.34
The Asian Countries	1	1	-	43	-	-	-	1	-	-	46	0.04
The European Countries	29	10	24	199	52	58	2	32	-	23	468	0.40
The American Countries	-	-	-	1	-	-	-	-	-	-	1	0.00
Other Countries	1	1	1	6	1	-	-	-	-	1	11	0.01
Total	1700	578	3969	36801	3522	17957	3014	9627	39008	4319	120455	100.00
Ratio % Total	1.40	0.47	3.30	30.60	2.90	14.90	2.50	7.98	32.37	3.58	100.00	

Source: Ministry of Interior Affairs, Statistics of Individual and Collective Secondments, 1979.

TABLE 3

DISTRIBUTION OF EMIGRANTS FROM EGYPT BY QUALIFICATION AND COUNTRY IN 1980

The Arab Countries	Ph.D.	Master	Higher Diploma	Bachelor or its Equivalent	General El-Azhar Secondary Certificate	Technical Secondary Certificate	Nursing	Other Intermediate Qualifications	Less Intermediate Qualifications	With no Qualifications	Total	Ratio % of Total
Saudi Arabia	426	372	2221	23031	2357	12893	2210	5597	3348	35340	88290	67.15
Kuwait	236	93	360	6868	577	2366	707	1051	426	2635	15319	11.65
Libya	77	23	153	1651	64	247	162	464	27	466	3334	2.53
Iraq	174	33	45	788	40	756	10	131	136	615	2728	2.07
Algeria	62	23	92	869	21	29	-	123	4	12	1236	0.94
Tunisia	-	-	5	67	1	7	-	7	2	3	92	0.06
Moroco	15	1	-	23	2	6	-	1	2	-	50	0.03
Lebanon	95	3	3	89	12	28	-	11	19	77	337	0.25
Gaza [Palestine]	2	-	-	12	-	3	-	-	1	-	18	0.01
Syria	6	-	-	19	-	4	-	1	-	-	30	0.02
Jordan	2	1	-	83	31	662	7	117	137	449	1509	1.14
Sudan	21	3	16	562	1	66	-	35	7	35	706	0.53
Yemen	77	9	747	1332	131	302	45	272	69	261	4532	3.44
Qatar	65	16	51	785	124	570	59	144	137	1335	3276	2.49
Bahrain	2	5	18	365	15	37	1	8	12	199	662	0.50
Dobbie	5	1	33	478	72	247	11	98	52	169	1166	0.88
Aden	-	-	-	3	-	1	-	-	-	-	4	0.00
Oman Sultanate	5	17	429	1007	90	272	32	784	61	235	2942	0.23
Arabian Gulf	-	-	-	7	2	2	-	1	-	1	11	0.01
Abu-Dhabi	36	9	41	854	162	653	30	182	177	603	2747	0.08
Shariqa	-	2	5	165	24	143	6	39	22	94	499	0.37
Raas El-khima	1	-	7	65	6	30	2	13	6	11	141	0.10
United A.Emirates	30	5	76	673	85	353	19	171	57	325	1794	1.36
Total	1833	616	4313	39796	3815	19677	3312	10537	4722	42865	131476	100.00
Ratio %	1.40	0.46	3.29	30.27	2.90	14.96	2.51	8.01	3.60	32.60	60	100.00

Source: Statistics of Individual and Collective Secondments, 1980, Ministry of Interior Affairs.

252

TABLE 4

GROSS ANNUAL FLOW OF LABOR EMIGRANTION
(Highly Qualified) 1974 - 1979

Year Countries groups	1974	1975	1976	1977	1978	1979
The Arab Countries	19336	21712	29170	37170	37907	42317
The African Countries	479	438	379	663	714	374
The Asian Countries	55	54	103	82	91	45
The European Countries	614	470	403	381	340	262
The American Countries	117	6	6	6	6	1
Other Countries	1	1	2	2	2	-
Total	20602	22681	30063	39041	36850	42999

reduction in the levels of productivity due to low levels of skills of the remaining labor force should also be part of the social cost of emigration. This situation can be applied on the other sectors of skilled workers.

- In addition to the previous consequences of emigration there are also some other consequences dealing with the distribution of income in Egypt. Increased wage differentials between Egypt and other Arab states may adversely affect the distribution of income in Egypt. Thus emigration creates a class of recipients substantially above the Egyptian averages.

- A large percentage of migrants must be expected to return. This situation demands opportunities for work to absorb the returnees; otherwise massive unemployment is likely to follow when migrants return.

- Emigrants, when they go to neighboring Arab countries, acquire new patterns of consumption which are wasteful to growth, and inject the economy with these new wasteful patterns of consumption.

- Returning migrants are accustomed to certain patterns of consumption abroad which are completely different from what they used to have before their emigration. The desire to continue at the level and pattern of consumption acquired abroad, exhausts a great deal of their savings. In turn, after a certain passage of time the desire for a secondment is created.

TABLE 5

REMITTANCES OF EGYPTIAN WORKERS ABROAD
1976-1980 (millions of pounds)

Year	Total Remittances
1979	395
1977	623
1978	1232
1979	1487
1980	1700

Source: Al Ahram, 4-9-1981, 5.

Finally, it is not difficult to find evidence of a shortage of physical capital. The scarcity of foreign exchange, the continual balance of payment deficits, and the recent decision to pursue an open door policy with respect to foreign investment are all bits of evidence attesting to the scarcity of this input (Hadley, 1977).

Empirical evidence, however, suggests that whether Egypt has surpluses or shortage, human capital is underutilized and wasted. If Egypt wants to take advantage of this opportunity in the short run, it would be able to reap some of the benefits created from the huge oil surpluses in the Arab countries. This, in the view of some researchers, will improve the private welfare of Egyptian citizens and contribute to the economic development of the country. But in the long run, reliance on a labor export system to solve Egypt's problems is a high risk strategy. The way for Egypt is to start henceforth to plan for the optimum utilization of its human resources, to try to find other measures for solving its balance of payments problems.

References

Birks, J.S. and C.A. Sinclair, (1980). 'International migration and development in the Arab Region,' ILO, Geneva.

Choucri, N., (1977). 'The new migration in the Middle East: A problem for what?' International Migration Review, V. 11, No. 4, pp. 422-24.

Dessouki, A.H., (1978). Development of Egypt's Migration Policy, 1952-1978, Cairo University.

Eldin, A.M., (1979). Manpower Problems in the Arab World, Institute of Developing Economies, Tokyo, Japan.

Hadley, L.H. (1977). 'The migration of Egyptian human capital to the Arab oil producing countries: A cost benefit analysis,' International Migration Review, Vol. 11, No. 3, pp. 285-99.

Messiha, S.A., (1980). Export of Egyptian School Teachers, The A.G.C., Cairo Papers in Social Science, V. 3, Monograph 4.

20 Rural-urban migration in Papua, New Guinea

PETER MAGINDE

1. Introduction

Developing countries in Asia, Pacific today are faced with serious development problems characterized by the phenomenon of development dualism. In the large cities, the formal sector characterized by modern industry exists and is contrasted with the low income employment and poverty of the so-called urban informal sector. At the same time in the rural areas, the ever increasing population pressure on land and natural resources including food, the environmental degradation and the breakdown of rural society present an even more alarming perspective, since the greater bulk of the poor -- and the poorest of the poor -- are in rural areas. What is happening to the majority of these people caught up in the rapid rural-urban transformation (occurring in most Asia/Pacific countries) is causing considerable amount of concern among planning authorities and International agencies alarmed over the problems of uneven development and a widening in the disparity gap. The advantages of economic growth accrue to well off while the disadvantaged are deprived even of their opportunities.

2. Migration Overview

Agricultural technology aimed at increasing productivity, particularly food crops, in the densely populated parts has achieved various degrees of success. However, in many of the market and mixed economies in Asia/Pacific, rural dualism is as serious as urban dualism. Although the new agricultural technology is supposed to be neutral toward different social groups, the pattern of existing traditional land-ownership, the distribution of other assets and the social structure of these established cultures are such that the agricultural development strategy adopted, in many instances, tends to benefit primarily land-lords and large farmers (Table 1).

With very rapid growth of population in both rural and urban areas, the labor absorptive capacity of the metropolitan centers has also been found to be wanting due to the capital-intensive nature of modern industries. On theoretical grounds, it can be argued that industrial expansion, given the choice of technology and the determination of the industrial mix, in the big cities cannot cope entirely with the increasing influx of labor under conditions of premature rural-urban migration existing in these developing countries. General rural stagnation and surplus outflows in many rural areas without recompensating inflow, through government expenditure or other productive

TABLE 1

RURAL INCOME DISTRIBUTION BY PERCENT OF POPULATION,
IN SELECTED ASIAN COUNTRIES

Country	Year	Low	Rural Income as High	% Urban Income
Indonesia	1964/65	20.1	40.5	75.2
	1969/70	21.3	39.8	70.0
Malaysia	1957	19.1	42.2	55.9
	1970	13.5	51.1	46.0
Thailand	1962/63	14.9	50.9	42.5
	1970	14.3	51.1	40.7
Philippines	1961	15.9	47.4	--
	1971	13.1	51.5	48.0
Sri Lanka	1963	12.5	51.0	--
	1973	17.1	-43.0	51.0 (1969)
Pakistan	1963/64	18.0	43.0	66.0 (1970)

Source: UNCRD Working Paper, Japan, 1978.

reinvestment, has provided little alternative employment for landless laborers, except in pockets of high growth.

Under these patterns of uneven development, which are manifest in many forms, including rural-urban distortions and regional underdevelopment, the major question for regional policy is to seek alternative strategies for regional development which achieve a more equal sharing in the benefits of development. But to undertake this successfully, regional policy must not be reduced merely to its spatial dimensions but in fact must fully consider the interrelations between spatial categories and other socio-economic structures and processes. In this way can regional policy be developmental. With this as opening remarks, let me now quote from the book by Michael Todaro, in his book on Economic Development in the Third World.

> An understanding of the causes and determinants of rural-urban migration and the relationship between migration and relative economic opportunities in urban and rural areas is central to any analysis of Third World Employment problems. Since migrants comprise the majority of the urban labor force in developing nations, the magnitude of rural-urban migration has been and will continue to be the principal determinant of the supply of new job seekers. And, if migration is the key determinant of the urban labor supply, then the migration process must be understood before the nature and causes of urban unemployment can be understood in

their turn. Government policies to ameliorate the
urban unemployment problem must be based, in the first
instance, on knowledge of who comes to town and why.

The factors influencing the decision to migrate are varied and
complex. Since migration is a selective process affecting individuals
with certain economic, social, educational and demographic characteristics, the relative influence of economic and non-economic factors may
vary not only between nations and regions but also within defined
geographic areas and populations. Much of the early research on
migration tended to focus on social, cultural, and psychological
factors while recognizing, but not carefully evaluating, the importance
of economic variables.

(a) Social factors, include the desire to break away from
     traditional constraints and social organizations.

(b) Physical factors, include climatic and meteorological
     disasters such as floods, droughts.

(c) Cultural factors, include the security of the urban extended
     family relationships and the allure of the so called "bright
     city lights".

(d) Demographic factors, include the reduction in mortality rate,
     which contributes to the high rural population growth.

(e) Communication factors, relating to the improved
     transportation, urban oriented education systems and the
     modern introduction of radio, television and the cinema.

These five facts seem the most dominating facts in the Third World
Countries and Papua, New Guinea is no different. One could refer to
this factor "push and pull", forces influencing rural-urban migration
among the young, between the ages of 15 and 25. The male population is
higher than the female. Todaro, further on in his book, characterizes
the migration into three broad categories: demographic, educational,
and economic.

Urban migrants in the Third World Countries tend to be young males
between the ages of 15 and 24. However, the proportion of migrating
women seems to be on the increase as their educational and employment
opportunities expand. One consistent finding of rural-urban migration
literature seems to be a correlation between the level of completed
education and the tendency to migrate. The people with more schooling,
all other things being equal, are more likely to migrate, than those
with less schooling. The potential for ecmployment appears to be
greater in the urban areas and the field of opportunity seems wider and
brighter for the educated one while the uneducated ones have a limited
scope, minimizing migration chances.

In some countries unskilled and landless rural individuals migrate
since rural opportunities for survival are very slim. They migrate to
urban centers with a bright hope of existence of some sort. In the
1960s and 1970s we have witnessed this trend in most Third World
Countries if not in all of them. There is a massive migration of rural
populations, into urban areas, even though the unemployment figures are

258

on the increase (Table 2). The rural sector is dominated by agricultural activities, and an urban sector focusing on industrialization, the overall economic development tends to be in the urban area. There is reallocation of labor

TABLE 2

TRENDS IN URBAN-RURAL POPULATION DISTRIBUTION AND
MIGRATION IN SELECTED ASIAN COUNTRIES

	% Urban		Urban growth rate	Rural growth rate	% Urban growth from migration
	1970	1975	1970-75	1970-75	1970-75
South East Asia					
Indonesia	17.8	19.1	4.7	2.1	39.5
Malaysia	27.3	18.7	4.7	1.9	36.0
Philippines	33.1	35.8	4.8	2.0	35.0
Thailand	14.8	16.4	4.0	2.6	41.9
South Asia					
India	19.2	21.4	3.8	1.6	31.5
Nepal	4.6	5.0	5.6	2.9	34.4
Pakistan	15.9	17.0	5.3	2.7	32.9
Sri Lanka	21.9	24.2	4.3	1.6	38.0
China	23.5	25.4	3.3	1.2	50.0
East Asia					
Korea	40.0	46.1	4.9	0.5	61.8
Taiwan	60.0	63.5	5.6	0.1	41.2

Source: UNCRD, Working Paper, Nagoya, Japan, 1978.

out of the agriculture sector to the industrial sector. Urbanization and industrialization become more or less synonymous. The rational decision of the migrants, despite the existence of urban unemployment, is motivated by expected urban-rural difference in expected rather than actual earnings in the urban.

3.   Rural-Urban Migration in Papua, New Guinea

Migration in Papua, New Guinea has been in evidence prior to colonization and urbanization, though not on the massive scale as seen today:

3.1 Pre-Colonial Migration Patterns.

People lived in scattered villages and hamlets throughout the country. They moved about from one locality to the next, mostly in search or for the following reasons:

(a) Looking for food, since no established farms existed.

(b) Safety and security from enemy tribes or wild beasts or spirits.

(c) Natural or meteorological happenings such as floods or volcanoes, etc.

(d) Cross-cultural marriages and arranged feasts and exchange of gifts.

3.2 Migration Patterns in Colonial Times

(a) Employment.

- Plantation labor schemes, wherein unskilled labor is migrating to plantations such as, rubber, copra, cocoa, coffee, tea, etc. These are cheap labor -- unskilled employees on contract basis, but usually remain without returning to their homes. However, some of this type of migrants do return.
- Industrial or private employment in urban areas. Industries usually engage in employing semi-skilled labor-force for both large and small industries.
- Public employment, this is mostly skilled or semi-skilled employment with the government, or the Public Service.

(b) Educational Institutions

- employment within the institutions.
- Students within for educational purposes.

(c) Temporary migrants who come to the urban

- to visit friends and relatives.
- to seek employment.
- to be relieved from boredom in the villages/rural areas.
- to see themselves what they have been hearing so much about from others in the urban centers.

(d) The glamor and the glow of the urban areas attracts so many individuals but cannot guarantee employment opportunities.

Papua, New Guinea, like the other developing countries in Asia, is faced with rural-urban migration, which is caused by rapid developmental changes and disparities in the rural and the urban. Table 3 will reflect the migration trends and patterns in the country.

Migration rarely, if ever, means a conscious long term abandonment of rural ties and obligations; rather, all the evidence in the country

260

TABLE 3

OUTMIGRATION BY PROVINCE OF BIRTH BY SECTOR OF RESIDENCE, 1971
(absolute numbers and percentages)

	Rural Village	Rural non-Village	Urban	Total
Western	827 (18.6)	1,104 (24.8)	2,525 (56.7)	4,456 (100)
Gulf	478 (3.4)	2,636 (18.7)	10,997 (77.9)	14,111 (100)
Central	1,677 (17.8)	2,728 (29.0)	5,012 (53.2)	9,417 (100)
Milne Bay	571 (8.0)	1,937 (27.1)	4,652 (65.0)	7,160 (100)
Northern	307 (5.3)	1,832 (31.4)	3,695 (63.3)	5,834 (100)
Southern Highlands	715 (6.0)	9,268 (77.8)	1,933 (16.2)	11,916 (100)
Western Highlands	1,489 (15.2)	5,197 (53.0)	3,125 (31.9)	9,811 (100)
Chimbu	4,058 (18.0)	11,485 (51.0)	6,988 (31.0)	22,531 (100)
Eastern Highlands	955 (7.7)	5,542 (44.4)	5,974 (47.9)	12,471 (100)
Morobe	2,816 (14.9)	6,824 (36.1)	9,264 (48.0)	18,904 (100)
Madang	1,568 (13.9)	4,782 (42.4)	4,937 (43.7)	11,287 (100)
East Sepik	1,082 (6.1)	8,332 (46.8)	8,394 (47.1)	17,808 (100)
West Sepik	816 (11.5)	3,935 (55.3)	2,364 (33.2)	7,115 (100)
Manus	503 (13.3)	1,164 (30.8)	2,115 (55.9)	3,782 (100)

(Continued on next page)

Table 3 (Continued)

New Ireland	673 (15.8)	1,455 (34.3)	2,120 (49.9)	4,248 (100)
West New Britain	623 (12.8)	2,125 (43.2)	2,134 (43.7)	4,882 (100)
East New Britain	1,692 (19.0)	2,842 (43.2)	3,355 (37.8)	8,889 (100)
Bougainville	450 (17.8)	632 (25.0)	1,442 (57.1)	2,524 (100)
Total	21.300 (12.0)	74,820 (42.2)	81,026 (45.7)	177,146 (100)

Source: Papua New Guinea, Labor Department

shows that migrants as a group and as individuals maintain strong ties with their home areas.

4. Migration Frequency and Migrants to Settlers

In Papua New Guinea, at this stage, the migration frequency is quite difficult to estimate, since the majority of these movements are unwarranted and unexpected. The movement pattern of the people in the country is facilitated by the constitution of the country, which allows people freedom to move about freely in the country. Unless alterations or amendments are made to the constitution, we cannot manipulate the peoples' movements. One classic example of the unwarranted movements is that, when or during the peak coffee picking season in the Western Highlands Province, a number of close friends and relatives come to assist those who are employed all year round, because the wages vary during this period with the level of effort. These migrants are only temporary for they are not contracted workers. Often these people move to another location, where they desire to be employed, or to remain indefinitely.

Most of the internal migrations are caused by the cultural and social push and pull factors. This is particularly true in inter-provincial migration. The migration frequency increases about 2-3 months out of the year but for the rest of the period is static. This high period of migration coincides with the peak demand for labor (unskilled).

The rate of migration has been lower in the coast as compared with the interior, since the majority of the coastal labor force is made up of the mainland population (see Table 4). This also means that, the percentage of male migrants will be higher than the female migrants. However, with the current trend of education there is some increase in female migration. It is seen also that, the Provinces, which are poor or remote seem to receive no migration;instead they lose most of their scarce population. The migrants move to provinces where there is

TABLE 4

RELATIVE EFFECT OF IMMIGRATION AND OUTMIGRATION BY PROVINCE,
1966 and 1971

	Percentage of Inmigrants of total resident population		Percentage of Outmigrants of total native-born population	
	1966	1971	1966	1971
Western	1.3	2.5	3.9	6.1
Gulf	4.2	5.6	15.2	20.4
Central	18.0	21.0	5.2	6.4
Milne Bay	2.2	2.4	4.8	6.3
Northern	5.4	6.5	7.1	8.7
Southern Highlands	2.5	1.7	3.7	5.9
Western Highlands	3.2	5.5	2.6	2.9
Chimbu	1.2	1.9	8.0	12.6
Eastern Highlands	3.8	4.7	3.7	5.2
Morobe	4.9	7.6	6.3	7.8
Madang	4.8	6.2	4.3	6.7
East Sepik	3.3	3.6	5.8	9.3
West Sepik	2.1	2.6	7.2	7.3
Manus	9.9	10.1	11.6	14.8
New Ireland	15.3	15.2	6.5	7.9
West New Britain	5.5	17.4	7.6	8.9
East New Britain	16.8	20.6	5.0	9.4
Bougainville	6.0	11.8	2.5	3.1

Source: PNG Labour Department.

either an industry or some major plantation.

Urban wage is also another factor, that causes migration. The wages in our Urban Centers are higher than the rural, and act as a magnate for rural individuals. However, the unseen but important difference here is that, the standard of living in the urban is much higher than in the rural areas. A person in our urban areas spends about twice the amount in one week, as he does in the rural sector. It is true that services and conditions are more favorable in the urban but are available at a higher price. The rural migrants never see this factor, until they experience it.

5. Implication of Migration

(a) Migration drains the potential rural labor forces, sometimes failing to meet the labor requirements and the output of agricultural sector.

(b) A drop in rural agricultural sector by commodity and production, in turn, raises the commodity prices in the urban, because the production is scarce and the demand for the products is high. The agriculture sector can not obtain the labor requirements locally, so this sector has to eitheremploy outside personnel or else go into secondary production to engage skilled labor.

(c) Increasing unemployment in the urban centers or under-employment. This increase of underemployment and unemployment causes a vicious circle, wherein, we have an increase in rural-urban migration, that leads to rising unemployment and underemployment causing job rationing by educational qualification, which in turn creates increased demand for education, which puts great pressure on governments to expand school enrollments, which in turn increases in rural-urban migration. This vicious circle is not only experienced here in Papua New Guinea, but in most of the Third World.

(d) An increasing demand for housing, water and utilities. The rural migration is rarely taken into account when planning and budgeting for urban housing and utilities. Since, there is inadequate housing and other facilities, squatter settlements rise within the city boundaries. Migrants also settle on land that is not theirs in the first place, intensifying further the land shortage in the urban centers.

(e) An increase in social problems, such as urban crime, gang activities, energy crisis, prostitution, etc. These social problems are nothing uncommon to the developing countries since development brings in change, particularly within the social and cultural structure of the societies and regions. The energy crisis is particularly serious in Papua New Guinea. It has had a long dry spell, so that the hydro-power resources are running low.

(f) Over-crowding in our cities and towns causes many families to live together in one house. This is unhygenic and a health hazard for so many people to live in cramped conditions, in particular for the young children and older people. Out of such conditions diseases become widespread. In many other countries, you get slums in major cities, but it is encouraging to note that slums are not much in evidence in Papua New Guinea. However, with development they will emerge, requiring some positive steps in advance.

6. The Government's View on Rural-Urban Migration

The government of Papua New Guinea has no major policy on internal migration, because the national constitution states that the citizens are free to move about the country at their own choice and will. International migration, however, is controlled. Foreigners can enter Papua New Guinea as citizens of another country but who are coming in as tourists, or businessmen, or contract workers both with the government and the private enterprises. The government is aware of the rural-urban migration or movement, so a certain number of steps have been taken to minimize migration and reorient individuals to the rural and agricultural sectors.

(a) Decentralization

One of the major and positive steps taken by the government is the policy of Provincial Governments and decentralization. This means that, the Central Government is sharing its powers and responsibilities with the Provinces. The introduction of Provincial Governments is the main way in which the National Government is implementing its aim of decentralization. Decentralization is brought about so that the people in the rural and grassroot levels will make their own decisions and formulate policies at their level, so rural-urban migration would be minimized. They can formulate policies at the rural to improve conditions at the rural and facilitate rural sectors to be more productive.

One of the objectives of decentralization is to reorient individuals back to the rural areas to till the land and not abandon it. The decentralization is not only for political reasons but for social and economic reasons as well.

(b) Plantation acquisition scheme

This is the scheme whereby, the National Government purchases foreign owned plantations and then leases it back to the rural people with simple interest rates.

The initiative here is to motivate original landowners to go back to their own areas and live at a very minimal cost, but be productive in the agriculture sectors. The way this is directed is to divert the out-migration from the rural back to the rural areas.

(c) A third way the National Government is doing this is by providing open conditional and unconditional grants for rural improvement purposes. In the former case, grants will be repayed with interest back to the Government, whereas the unconditional grants are just like gifts for development and productive purposes.

In all of the efforts put forward by the Government an awareness is created with the belief that people will decide to return to the rural areas.

The question is, how can one realize this? I think and believe that emphasis should be placed upon agro-based rural cooperatives and industries.

7. Summary

Since migrants are assumed to respond to differentials in expected incomes, it is vitally important that imbalances between economic opportunities in rural and urban sectors be minimized. Permitting urban wage rates to grow at a greater pace than average rural incomes will stimulate further rural-urban migration in spite of rising levels of urban unemployment. This heavy influx of people into urban areas gives rise not only to socio-economic problems in the cities, but may also eventually create problems of labor shortages in rural areas, especially during the busy seasons.

Rural-urban migration is a factor which is found in every developing country, because urban areas seem attractive and employment chances are many. "The grass always looks greener on the other side." Jobs cannot be created as fast as the influx of rural population into the urban areas, so the long list of unemployed grows while employment stagnates.

Perhaps the best possibility is to expand the small-scale, labor-intensive agro-based rural industries. If this happens, then there would be a greater balance between rural and urban development than existing today. The case of Papua New Guinea is not as serious as in many major developing countries of Asia or the Third World. However, we can not deny some unemployment problems. The country mostly encounters the young male school - leavers, who after grade 10 education, enter the urban centers to seek employment. There are not many jobs for which they are qualified. They hang around the cities living off friends and relatives, causing a lot of inconvenience, and a variety of social problems in the city. To address this problem, more small-scale, labor-intensive industries have to be created in both rural and urban areas, so the employment opportunities are balanced between the two regions.

References

Conroy, John and Grania Skeldon (1975). The Rural Survey

Garmaut, Ross, Michael Wright and Richard Curtain. 'Employment, incomes and migration in Papua, New Guinea,'

Labor Statistic of Papua, New Guinea. The Department of Labour and Industry - Papua, New Guinea, The Department of Finance, Papua, New Guinea.

Lo, Fu-Chen, Kamal Salih and Mike Douglass (1978). 'Uneven development, rural-urban transformation, and regional development alternatives in Asia,' United Nations Center for Regional Development, Working Paper 78-02, Nagoya, Japan.

Skeldon, Ronald (1979). The Demography of Papua, New Guinea, Boroko, Papua, New Guinea: Institute of Applied Social and Economic Research.

Todaro, Michael P. (1977). Economic Development in the Third World, London, New York: Longman.

21 Urbanization, labor absorption and poverty in Latin America: issues and policy approaches

T. R. LAKSHMANAN

1. Introduction

Urbanization is a source of profound transformation in contemporary Latin America. While urbanization has been underway for a century, the pace has quickened in the last quarter century, when the continent has been transformed from a rural society to a predominantly urban one.

The demographic features of this transformation are well known (Fox 1974, United Nations 1974). Urbanization is occurring in Latin American countries, accompanied by national population growth rates of 2 to 3.5 per cent per annum. These high national rates translate into: a) a large natural increase in urban population and b) a high rural to urban migration. There has been, as a consequence, a very large increase in the number of cities (with more than 20,000 inhabitants), and in the population in large cities such as Sao Paulo, Mexico City, Caracas and Bogota. Further, as urbanization continues apace, existing cities are increasingly absorbing most of the population growth taking place in the countries.

While the demographic aspects of urban transformation are generally known, the economic components of urban change have received less attention. What is remarkable is that the urban areas of Latin America have been absorbing these accelerating population increases -- magnitudes and growth rates of population and labor force far higher than those experienced by the advanced countries in their corresponding periods -- in the last quarter century at rising real average incomes. Productive activities have grown enormously in these urban areas, with attendant increases in real per capita income and the increasing utilization of labor in manufacturing, commerce, and services. This is a remarkable achievement when one considers the rapid pace of growth of large cities (that seem to double in size every decade) and the conditions of low and strained financial, physical and human resources in these countries.

However, the incidence of this economic growth in the urban areas has been highly uneven. Most of the growth has often tended to be localized in certain parts of the economy, primarily the capital-intensive modern sectors, that seem to have few linkages to the 'informal' urban sector, which makes up a significant portion of the total employed urban labor force. Consequently, the benefits of growth seem to have accrued to a small segment of the urban population.

Indeed, in the urban areas of Latin America, as in other parts of the developing world, low labor utilization and low earnings characterize the lot of a significant part of the residents. Low labor utilization is manifest in terms of both open unemployment and underemployment (working too few hours or with excessively low productivity). Available evidence suggests that open unemployment in the cities of larger countries (Argentina, Brazil, Chile, Colombia, Mexico, Venezuela) averages about 6.5%. Urban underemployment, however, is far more serious, estimated as affecting between 23% to 36% of the employed workers (PRELAC 1976). The combined effect of open unemployment and underemployment (even if one accepts the lower estimate) is of a sufficient magnitude as to affect much larger proportions of the labor force than did open unemployment in advanced economies in the worst years of the Great Depression. Thus, it is not surprising that the issue of low labor utilization in urban areas has emerged as a major problem of the urban economy in Latin America.

The related problem of low earnings of many employed persons is the issue of income distribution, both in the sense of low relative shares of income some groups receive and in terms of the proportion of the urbanites on or below margins of absolute poverty. In a number of countries the share of the poorest groups in urban incomes seems to be declining. In some cases, absolute incomes in real terms appear to have been either constant or declining. As a consequence, after years of benign neglect, reduction of income inequalities and poverty have emerged as another legitimate area of policy concern.

The spate of recent analytical work stimulated by this new concern with employment and poverty have broadened the frame of analysis beyond the simple elegance and coherence of the earlier growth models to include organizational, sociopolitical, and geographical perspectives. Some of these studies explore at a disaggregated level the production structures, set in the sociopolitical contexts of different countries in a way that provides new pointers for policy relating to employment creation and poverty reduction.

This paper is addressed to a brief description of the evolution of these new analytical trends and policy interests in Latin America. It begins with a brief description of the major dimensions or urbanization in Latin America and its implications for labor utilization and poverty in the context of the development strategies that have been pursued historically. We proceed then to a review of the alternative theoretical viewpoints on income distribution and employment to assess their relevance to the observed patterns in Latin America and as guides to framing appropriate policies. While some of the theories have important perspectives to contribute, no adequate theories exist to guide policy unambiguously. Finally, we present some strategies to address the issues of urban labor utilization and income distribution.

2. Dimensions of Urbanization, Unemployment and Poverty

2.1 Urbanization Patterns

The context of contemporary urbanization in Latin America, while reminiscent in some respects of the conditions in nineteenth century Europe or North America, is notably different from that of the Victorian era in several significant ways. The rapid urbanization of

European countries in the last century occurred when those countries had a lower population base and lower growth rate, higher per capita incomes and a lower backlog of physical and medical technology than the Latin American countries today. These different initial conditions of urbanization in Latin America have important implications on the patterns of evolution of economic activities and the quality of the urban environment.

The most striking feature of the Latin American experience is the continuing rapid rate of population growth. Urbanization has been occurring in Latin America at annual rates of 1.9% (1900-1950) and 2.9% (1950-1970) as contrasted with 0.5% per annum of the corresponding period in Europe (Bairoch 1972, Fox 1974). These higher rates of population growth (reflecting declining mortality rates that result from the backlog of contemporary medical technology), combined with consistently high birth rates, translate into (a) a large natural increase in urban population and (b) a large rural urban migration.

The resulting population trends in the second half of this century are displayed in Table 1. What is noteworthy is that both rural and urban population are increasing, the latter far more significantly. Indeed, much of the population explosion appears to be the "urban explosion" as the existing cities are absorbing the lion's share of total national population increases in the larger countries (Table 2). In Argentina and Chile, however, there are absolute losses of population in the rural sector. In the other countries, in general, the proportion of total national increase absorbed by the urban sector increases with the level of urbanization in the country -- a result of both past migration flows from the rural countryside and constantly increasing proportions of urban-born residents. The present and projected trends suggest that in all these countries most of the population increase will accrue to the cities. If the composition by age and sex is taken into account, the high proportions of the young (who are still in their productive years), in the rural-urban migration flows will accentuate future urban growth through natural increase.

A second feature of the urbanization process in Latin America derives from this urban explosion. This is the large increase in the number of cities of over 20,000 residents (Fox 1974, United Nations 1974). Such cities increased from 298 in 1950 to 433 in 1960, jumped to 639 in 1970, which is to say that they more than doubled in about 20 years. By comparison, United States took 35 years (1920-1955) to double its cities (Fox 1974). Such increases in the number of cities would, no doubt, strain the economic, political and institutional capacities of these nations to plan for and adapt to the rapid urban growth increases in so short a time.

The third and perhaps the most striking feature of contemporary urbanization in Latin America is the explosive growth of large cities. Mexico City has been growing at six per cent and Bogota at two per cent per annum. Sao Paulo doubled its population in the sixties with migrants accounting for more than two thirds of the increase. If present demographic trends continue for the next two decades, these cities are expected to double every two decades, resulting in the near future in very large agglomerations (United Nations 1974). The United Nations estimates that the year 2000 agglomerations of Sao Paulo and

Mexico City will have respectively 24.6 million and 31.5 million residents.

These current and prospective increases in urban population are reflected in increases in the supply of labor that are growing at rates explosive by standards of recent world history or in comparison with the experience of developed countries (Table 3). Most countries are experiencing annual increases in their non-agricultural labor forces in excess of over 3% and often higher. Given the age structure of the present urban population in Latin America, the urban areas would well experience for the next two decades, labor force increases of over 4% annually in the larger countries. It is not surprising that these rapid expansions of labor supply have outpaced the demand for labor in urban Latin America. The expansion of manufacturing -- the hope of productive labor absorption in the traditional development theory -- will be, by itself, largely unequal to this task. It has been suggested that a manufacturing sector employing 20% per annum merely to absorb the increase in the labor force growing at 3% per annum -- this estimate does not account for increases in productivity of 3% per annum (Turnham and Jaeger 1971). By way of comparison, the fastest growing countries -- in terms of value added in manufacturing at constant prices in the sixties -- such as Panama, Mexico and Brazil managed growth rates respectively of 10.6%, 9.5% and 8.3% annually in manufacturing employment (United Nations 1974).

Consequently, except in a few countries, much of the labor force increases were, of necessity, absorbed in non-manufacturing activities -- in the handicraft manufactures, and low productivity service activities. Recent studies suggest that a significant proportion of the persons engaged in these latter activities are not fully productively employed. Further, despite recorded national increases in real GDP per capita ranging from 25 to 60% in the decade of the sixties, many urbanites engaged in these activities have experienced little or no increases in real income (Fishlow 1972, Adelman and Morris 1974, Weisskopf 1970). Thus, low labor utilization and low incomes characterize the lot of a significant number of the urban labor force.

2.2 Urban Labor Utilization and Income Distribution

It is common knowledge that the concepts of labor force, employment, and unemployment as understood in the affluent economies are difficult to apply in the context of developing countries. First a significant portion of economic activities in the latter is organized in family or extended family production units, in which the sharp distinctions between work and leisure (that help to define employment and unemployment) are not observed and which are institutions for sharing work and income. Second, real earnings in the so called urban informal sector tend to respond quickly to market pressures. The primary bread winner in a poor family cannot afford to be unemployed -- any work is preferred to none till alternatives arrive. Consequently, the rates of labor force participation vary often.

These considerations suggest that the employment problem in Latin American countries cannot be phrased as just an unemployment problem. Although rates of open unemployment are high, more important is the condition of employed groups whose earnings and consumption are low

TABLE 1

URBAN AND RURAL POPULATION TRENDS IN MAJOR AREAS OF LATIN AMERICA 1950-2000

	Population (In Millions)						Level of Urbanization (percentages)		
	1950		1975		2000				
	Urban	Rural	Urban	Rural	Urban	Rural	1950	1975	2000
A. Caribbean	5.58	11.22	13.34	15.16	29.62	18.98	33.20	46.81	60.94
B. Middle America	14.16	21.24	44.81	33.84	124.04	48.63	40.00	56.97	71.84
C. Temperate S. America	15.99	10.68	31.32	7.75	47.18	5.52	59.94	80.16	89.52
D. Tropical S. America	31.38	52.13	106.38	73.18	263.62	87.37	37.58	59.25	75.11
LATIN AMERICA	67.10	95.27	198.85	123.93	464.46	160.51	41.32	60.12	74.32

Source: United Nations Projections, 1974.

TABLE 2

NATIONAL POPULATION INCREASES ABSORBED BY THE URBAN SECTOR,

1960-70 AND PROJECTED TO 1980

(in thousands)

Country	Percent Urban in 1970	Population Increase, urban sector		Urban Population Increase/ National Population Increase	
		1960-70	1970-80	1960-70	1970-80
Argentina	66	3,368	3.627	100+	100+
Brazil	40	15,762	19,496	68	69
Chile	60	1,561	1,681	100+	94
Mexico	57	9,498	14,809	71	75
Peru	43	2,678	2,273	73	70
Venezuela	61	2,415	3,567	83	89

Source: Fox 1974, Table 5 and Table 6.

273

TABLE 3

GROWTH OF ECONOMICALLY ACTIVE POPULATION[a], 1960-70

Country	Period	Economically Active Population (thousands) 1970	Annual Growth Rate, 1960-70 (%)	
			Total	Non Agriculture
Argentina	1960-70	8,823	1.7	2.1
Brazil	1960-70	28,044	2.8	4.2
Colombia	1964-73	6,395	3.0	3.9
Costa Rica	1963-73	578	3.9	6.1
Chile	1960-70	2,721	1.5	1.9
Dominican Republic	1960-70	1,241	4.2	8.1
Ecuador	1962-74	1,817	2.5	4.1
El Salvador	1961-71	1,134	3.5	4.7
Guatamala	1964-73	1,752	2.8	4.0
Honduras	1961-70	776	3.2	3.7
Mexico	1960-70	12,473	2.3	3.9
Panama	1960-70	489	4.1	5.2
Paraguay	1962-72	739	2.3	3.1
Peru	1961-72	3,836	2.1	3.3
Venezuela	1961-71	3,015	2.9	4.0
Developed Countries	1950-70		1.0	

(a) Persons 15 years and older

Source: PRELAC 1976, Turnham and Jaeger 1971.

TABLE 4
OPEN UNEMPLOYMENT IN LATIN AMERICAN COUNTRIES AND CITIES AROUND 1970

Country and City	National Unemployment Rate	Urban Unemployment Rate	
		Age Group 15 and Over	Age Group 15-24
Argentine (1970)	1.9		
Buenos Aires		4.7	6.3
Brazil (1970)	6.9		
Sao Paulo		6.6	
Colombia (1970)	7.4		
Bogota (1968)		13.6	23.1
Cali (1968)		14.9	
Medellin (1967)		14.5	
Chile (1969)	5.0		
Santiago (1970)		6.7	12.0
Peru (1972)	5.7		
Lima (1970)		7.0	
Venezuela (1971)	6.2		
Caracas (1970)		8.0	14.8

Source: PRELAC 1976, Turnham and Jaeger 1971, Frankel 1975, Schafer
1976.

because their productivity is low.

Conventional measures of unemployment based on concepts of 'involuntary' traditions of the developed countries are often misleading measures of the nature of the labor situation in Latin America. Such measures, however, help identify important special groups in the labor force who are openly employed. Thus a high proportion of the openly unemployed are the young (age group 15-24) in the cities of Latin America (Table 4). These are well educated persons (seeking non-manual work) with little or no work experience and are dependents rather than heads of households (Turnham and Jaeger 1971). For them, immediate needs for some income generating work are less imperative than for the urban majority who cannot afford to be openly unemployed.

The latter however, are often employed in relatively unproductive work that does not yeild enough income to ensure a minimum standard of living. They are the urban underemployed. Several measures of such urban underemployment have been used. These have included the following: the proportion of persons working less than 40 hours per week; the proportion of workers who are working part time but who would like to work full time; the percentage of self employed workers in non-agricultural jobs; and the proportion of the employed workers who earn less than some 'poverty line' income such as the minimum wage (Schaefer 1976, PRELAC 1976, Turnham and Jaeger 1971). Of these measures, the income approach -- through the choice of a mimium wage or income level -- to identify the underemployment is perhaps the most appropriate to convey the notion of the urban 'working poor'. Two such estimates -- one at the national level, another for an individual urban area -- of underemployment based on data on income distribution and earnings are presented in Tables 5, 6, and 7.

In the six large countries listed in Table 5 (accounting for about 85 per cent of the labor force in Latin America) underemployment is the crux of its employment problem, since it characterizes 32 per cent of the urban workers. This is equivalent to an open unemployment rate of about 18 per cent -- yielding in all 23 per cent of total labor underutilization. Almost a fourth of the urban labor force is not used productively. This level of underutilization of labor (which is even higher in the countryside) is more serious than that experienced by the western industrialized countries during the Great Depression.

The underemployment in Sao Paulo -- one of the fastest growing cities in Latin America -- is estimated at 34.6% (open unemployment is 6.6%). What is most noteworthy about Table 6 is that underemployed workers are in no way concentrated in the urban tertiary service sectors, as is generally believed (McGee 1971). Further, young workers who experience a high level of underemployment often combine lack of skills and part time work. Underemployment is concentrated not only among the young, but also among those with little or no education (Schaefer 1976). Urban migrants have a higher incidence of underemployment. This is because the rural urban migrants are often concentrated in the low paying construction and personal service sector. However, it appears that the migrants move up the income ladder in Sao Paulo -- the 'older' migrants with between six to ten years of urban residence approach non-migrants in terms of both income and occupation (Schaefer 1976).

Thus, in urban Latin America, the crux of the employment problem lies in the proportion of the labor force earning inadequate incomes. A related problem is the unequal income distribution in urban areas.

In general, moderate and high income inequality characterizes the Latin American countries and their urban areas. In some countries, urban incomes are more unequal than rural incomes (Brazil, Colombia); in others, rural incomes are more unequal (Mexico, Ecuador). In still others, the income concentrations in urban and rural areas are comparable (Venezuela, Chile). In general, however, absolute levels of urban mean incomes are at least twice as high as rural incomes, and increase with city size, even if one allows for spatial differences in prices within a country.

Although Latin American countries are relatively high income developing countries, a sixth of the population is below the poverty level of USA $75 (1969 prices). In some countries such as Brazil, urban incomes are becoming more unequal with the poor receiving a lower share of the urban income in 1970 than they did in 1960. However, the mean incomes in urban Brazil have grown so fast that in spite of the decreasing shares of national incomes, the real incomes of the poor seem to have increased. The evidence in other countries suggest, however, a worsening condition of the poor.

We now turn to a consideration of the existing theoretical apparatus for understanding the urban income distribution and labor utilization.

3. Theory and Income Distribution

The existing theoretical apparatus for understanding the mechansims of income distribution in developing countries, especially those of Latin America can be viewed as comprising three classes of theories:

a) General theories that attempt to explain at a very high level of abstraction how income is distributed and its probable future distribution. Three broad theories of this type focusing on functional distribution of income are the Neoclassical, Post-Keynesian and Marxian. A fourth macro theory is the Dependency theory, developed in response to the dynamics of economic and social change in Latin America.

b) Theories of Personal Income Distribution. Personal distribution of income has greater significance that functional distribution, since the latter does not permit (1) self-employed workers, (a large sector in Latin America and one that includes a significant portion of the poor) to be differentiated and (2) the identification of the real earnings of the managerial sectors that receive income both from their capital and labor.

c) Theories of changes in income distribution with development. Two issues are addressed in these inquiries relevant to developing countries: How does economic growth affect income distribution? What is the effect of an income distribution on growth?

TABLE 5

LABOR FORCE UNDERUTILIZATION IN URBAN LATIN AMERICA AROUND 1970

| Country | Labor Force in Non-Agriculture (thousands) | Open Un- Employment Rate (%)[a] | Non-Agricultural Underemployment | | Total Labor Underutilization Rate (%) |
			Underemploy- ment Rate (%)	Equivalent[a] Unemployment Rate (%)	
Argentina	7,505	1.9	27.8	12.0	12.9
Brazil	16,079	6.9	43.5	21.8	28.7
Colombia	3,709	7.4	39.2	20.2	27.7
Chile	2,056	5.0	37.9	17.3	22.3
Mexico	7,180	3.8	27.9	11.8	15.6
Venezuela	2,309	6.2	42.9	20.5	26.7
All Countries Listed	38,830	5.5	37.0	17.6	23.1

a These are based on national "Economically Active Population' estimates. The last column -- showing total labor utilization -- may be underestimated to the degree that urban unemploy- ment rates are underrepresented here.

Source: PRELAC 1976, Table 8.

TABLE 6

UNDEREMPLOYMENT BY SECTOR IN GREATER SAO PAULO, 1970

Sector	Number		Underemployed as Proportion of Employed (%)
	Underemployed	Total Employed	
Primary	36,645	53,722	68.2
Secondary	483,151	1,411,990	34.2
Tertiary	495,329	1,461,553	33.9
Total	1,015,125	2,927,265	34.6

Source: Schaefer 1976, Table 23.

TABLE 7

UNEMPLOYED AND PROPORTION OF EMPLOYED POPULATION BY AGE GROUP

FOR GREATER SAO PAULO, 1970 (%)

Age Group	Non-Migrant	Migrant	Total
10-19	67.9	73.6	69.7
20-24	23.1	30.9	25.9
25-39	10.8	15.1	12.2
40 and over	8.7	14.9	9.7
All ages (10 and over)	22.5	31.4	26.1

Source: Schaefer 1976, Table 24.

3.1 General Theories of Income Distribution

3.1.1 Neoclassical theory

Neoclassical theory is essentially a microeconomic, general equilibrium theory of input and output pricing. Marginal productivity is the basis for payment of all factors and the income of an individual is merely the sum of the multiplication of his endowment of factors and their marginal products. Relative factor prices are in turn adjusted to harmonize with the factor intensity of the bill of goods demanded in relation to factor payments. The link to macroeconomics is made through the notion of an aggregate production function. For a given level of technology, the distribution of national income between labor and capital (the functional distribution) results from these factors' marginal productivity and intensity of use, the latter in turn depending upon the relative prices of labor and capital. The evolution of shares of labor and capital over time depends on changes in relative factor quantities, elasticity of substitution between factors, the bias (labor or capital saving) in technical change and the shifts in demand patterns.

The neoclassical theory, while subscribed to and refined by numerous theorists, has been under attack from two perspectives (Bronfenbrenner 1971, Ferguson and Nell 1972, Pen 1971, Cline 1975). A major criticism of the neoclassical theory is its assumption that an aggregate production function exists, with the possibility that "capital" exists as a measurable input (Harcourt 1969). This criticism which is part of the so-called "Cambridge Controversy" (between Cambridge, MA and Cambridge, U.K.) has cast doubt on the concept of capital's marginal product as the basis of factor payments to capital owners.

The relevance of this theory to the developing countries is severely limited by the nonfulfillment of many of its assumptions. The implicit assumption of homogeneity in the economic structure and integration of agents through market relations is undermined by the serious distortions in the labor and capital markets in developing countries. High, non-clearing wages in the urban modern sector and the institutionally determined wage rates resulting from 'surplus labor' conditions do not represent neoclassical wage determination. In view of the small size of modern industry in these countries, monopoly conditions may exist with consequent distrotions in the payments to capital. Further, capital markets are ill developed and fragmented with likely windfall gains to some firms (Cline 1975). The general applicability of the neoclassical theory of functional income distribution to Latin American countries is consequently very much in doubt.

3.1.2 Post-Keynesian theory

The theory developed by Kaldor views income distribution as a function of demand. Wage earners have a lower propensity to save as compared to capitalists whose investments expand productive capacity. Thus the manner in which income is distributed between wage earners and capitalists determines the level and composition of expenditures. The theory further states that there exists a given investment rate (given the assumption of a stable capital-output ratio) that the aggregate savings rate must equal this investment rate and given the different propensities to save among the capitalists and wage earners, there is only one division of income among the two classes that will equalize the average savings rate and the necessary investment rate.

Several assumptions of this theory do not obtain in the developing economies. These economies are resource rather than demand constrained and investment adjusts to available savings, not vice versa as required in the theory. Other assumptions relating to stable capital-output ratio and the different saving propensities of the two classes are highly unrealistic in the institutional and political contexts and unemployment rates of Latin America (Foxley, 1976).

3.1.3 The Marxian approach

Marxian thought views the distribution problem in the framework of a struggle between the capitalist and worker classes, a struggle determined by the relations of production. The capitalists who own the means of production appropriate the surplus value of labor by keeping wages at the subsistance level for the mass of unemployed workers (the so-called "industrial reserve army"). As the economy grows, with further capital accumulation, the surplus labor gets absorbed, with a likely rise in real wages. In this context, according to theory, capitalists introduce labor-saving technology, restore the reserve army of labor, reduce real wages and relentlessly attempt to maintain their profit rates.

Classical Marxian theory was Eurocentric, concerned with primarily the stage of capitalism that resulted in imperialism and its effects on the class struggle in Europe. It tended to see the expansion of capitalism into developing countries as simply a process ofdestruction and replacement of pre-capitalist structures. Baran (1958) extended it to countries arguing that the high inequalities of income in developing countries were due to the method of contact between developed and developing countries. For although contact hastened the disintegration of precapitalist structures and thus created some preconditions for rapid development, the role of middle classes in the developing countries was different. Unlike its role in the West, it formed an alliance with the traditional aristocracy and foreign groups to guarantee its welfare rather than generate support for the poorer classes. At the same time, Baran views the entry of capitalism into developing countries as destructive of the social support mechanisms of feudal systems, further accentuating exploitation.

Marxist analysis was developed to explain historical realities that are significantly different from contemporary development processes. As a consequence, the more traditional versions of Marxist conceptual- ization, which were developed to describe historical realities of income distribution tend to be too simplistic in the identification of social classes and their conflicts. The two-fold division of society is of little help in Latin American societies where a number of other social classes and a multipolar power structure seems to be emerging. How common are the interests of workers in the urban modern sector with those in the urban 'informal' sector or rural smallholders? The dependency theorists to be described next have shown that even Baran's assumption that capitalism in a developing country is a framework for economic stagnation, social backwardness and archaic technology is far too simplistic.

3.1.4 Dependency theory

The theory of dependency is a response by Latin Americans to the perceived failure of the dominant development strategy of capital-intensive import substitution industrialization. It represents an attempt on the part of Latin Americans to establish a new paradigm. As such it serves as a framework for organizing explanations for a variety of phenomena -- income distribution, poverty, labor absorption, the provision of housing and other amenities in urban areas, etc. -- and their interactions.

Widely used growth models that assume a closed economy (e.g., Harrod, Domar) mask the role of international relationships in the development process of the advanced countries and thus turn attention away from the effect of these relationships on the developing countries. Theories of international trade that assume perfect competition and mobility of factors and parity in international power relations do not reveal the unequal terms of trade incident on developing countries. The dependency theory, developed in response to the drawbacks of traditional theory, therefore began with an identification of the history, institutions and structures that define the parameters within which economic activities operate in Latin America. The initial expression of this theory by Prebisch was structuralist (an appreciation of different historical relations and national contexts), with his argument that the underdevelop-ment of Latin America was due to its position in the world economy and to its adoption of liberal capitalist policies. We proceed to a summary of the other varieties of dependency theory.

Within the broad theory, there are a number of different analytical traditions (O'Brien 1975):

a)   The structuralist perspective: This stems from the original Economic Commission for Latin America (ECLA) notions developed by Prebvisch. More recent work by O. Sunkel and L.C. Furtado represents a continuation and greater elaboration of this perspective (Furtado 1965, Sunkel 1969).

b)   The Neo-Marxist perspective: This branch of the theory has been actively developed, among others, by Dos Santos, A.G. Frank and Milton Santos (Dos Santos 1973, Frank 1969, M. Santos 1972).

In addition, the literature is enriched by some sociologists (e.g., A. Quijane and F. Cardoso) who appear to be straddling both the perspectives.

The central notion of the theory of dependency is that development and underdevelopment are partial, interdependent aspects of the same world system. Development is viewed as a world wide unified process of structural change and underdevelopment characterizes those countries that do not possess an autonomous ability to grow and develop and are dependent on the countries at the "Centre". Thus the theory starts with the world economic structure and attempts to develop the rules for the evolution of dependent economies. It is through the analysis of historical and present day problems that the theory tries to show that the internal dynamics of Latin American society and its underdevelopment has been primarily determined by its position in the world economy and the consequent links between its external structures (Furtado 1965).

Within this broad framework, the different analysts emphasize different aspects of how and why changes in the world lead to changes in Latin America. In Dos Santos's view, dependency is a 'conditioning' situation that makes the underdeveloped countries to be both backward and exploited (Dos Santos 1972). Cardoso provides an integrated view of economic, political, and social processes in analyzing development of different countries.

Income distribution if viewed as highly concentrated in those countries which are most dependent on the developed countries (Sunkel 1969). The emerging dependency is viewed as resulting, among other things, from the multinational corporations which restructure the internal production system in Latin American countries, and create fundamental sociological effects. The products of the multinational corporations are intended for the small bourgeois and middle class, with "internationalized" consumption patterns. Growth rates and composition of growth become dependent on those consumption goods which are supported by the unequal pattern of income distribution and resource allocation in keeping with that distribution. Capital intensive industrialization strategies continue and these inequalities continue and widen.

It must be obvious that any attempt to chart the complex cross-currents of dependency theory is bound to be selective. The theory is an electic creation, drawing on and often adding to a number of other theoretical streams -- Marxism, structuralism and nationalism. Conse-quently, the theory provides many significant perspectives for understanding development and underdevelopment. But a perspective is only a beginning. The theory does not specify any mechanisms of dependency. What are the characteristics of dependency? The criteria are sufficiently vague that Canada can qualify as a dependent country and yet by most indications is a developed country (O'Brien 1975).

The empirical evidence that has been presented in support of the theory is often casual and slim. In particular, the evidence offered about income distribution and its changes is scanty. More rigorous empirical evidence is called for. Yet the basic point of the theory that a critical part of the understanding of processes of development lies in the analysis of the relationships between internal and international structures -- is valid. But the theory, in its present form, is very much a higher level framework or hypothesis that defines a broad problem area within which other specific models can be framed. It is in this role that the dependency theory dominates Latin American literature on various aspects of development.

3.2 Theories of Personal Income Distribution

A number of theories that attempt to explain the personal income distribution exist.

The human capital theory developed by Mincer and elaborated by others as an income distribution theory of human capital postulates an optimizing behavior on the part of individuals (Mincer 1968, Becker 1962). An individual choosing an occupation that demands a longer training period forgoes income during training, but receives higher earnings later as a compensation. Individuals invest in themselves rationally on the basis of estimates of probable present discounted value of alternative life-cycle streams of income.

While the theory has been focused on formal schooling, recent work suggest the importance of including preschool and informal family investments into a more complete theory of human capital.

The human capital theory is primarily developed under assumptions of competitive labor markets and ignores the principle of "non--competing" groups. A major class of objections to this theory is directed at this assumption and the overemphasis of the role of education by human capitalists on production and income distribution. The objective is that it is not capital accumulated through education but ability and institutions that really account for what is attributed to education.

One group of such critics suggest that education merely serves as a "filter" that screens out a limited number of individuals to be placed in a few higher paying jobs, partly at the cost of others -- education thereby playing an important role in reinforcing income inequalities and class structures. In the developing countries family background (or incomes) determine schooling -- a reverse causation not admitted by human capital theory (Fishlow 1972, Sant' Anna, Merrick & Mazumdar 1976).

The second group of critics are the "segmented labor market theorists". Both developing and developed economies are characterized by labor markets that are segmented from one another, and those weaken competitive constraints and perpetuate inequalities (Sahota 1978).

The thrust of these criticisms of human capital theory in the context of developing countries is that earnings are not determined by marginal productivity considerations alone, but often by such factors as status. An improvement in education for the poor may not do them much good (Sant'Anna, Merrick & Mazunder 1971). The human capital theory must be therefore viewed with caution in developing countries. This is all the more so, since the theory is politically attractive.

3.3 Theories of Changes in Distribution with Development

The literature concerned with the evolution of income distribution with economic growth over time in developing countries suggest that incomes become more unequal in the early stages of economic growth, improving later, producing the typical inverted U-shaped curve (Kuznets, 1963). The Kuznets view argues that the rich accumulate assets proportionately more than the poor and further industrialization and urbanization tend to concentrate incomes in the middle periods of growth. However, in the latter stages welfare state policies improve the distribution of income. This hypothesis has bene widely subscribed to and 'supported' by a great number of empirical studies (Weiskoff 1970, Adelman and Morris 1973).

While the Kuznets hypothesis has been popular for some time, recent work suggests that there is no warrant for anything more than a modest suggestion that inequality is likely to rise after the early subsistence stage in a developing economy, once a surplus arrives for some group to appropriate (Cline 1975).

Some countries -- Brazil and Venezuela -- show worsening distribution, while others Colombia and Argentina -- show a reverse trend. Similar patterns are evident for urban and rural income distributions. As stated earlier, it is prudent to conclude the evolution of income distribution is related to a country's inherited social structure combined with its particular policies. Some structures and policies lead to more unequal distribution than others. There is no "natural" tendency for incomes to get more unequal before they become more equal, though public policies in housing, health, education, etc. are often anti-poor and may as a consequence increase inequalities. In other words, policy efforts to lessen income concentration at least in the relatively higher income Latin American countries are not confronted by inexorable structural factors that would lead to increase in inequalities.

Recent theoretical work questions the traditional assumption that any shift of income from the rich (who save) to the poor(who consume) would reduce savings, investment and growth (Cline 1975). Empirical simulation studies of the effects of alternative income distribution policies show no significant adverse effects of such policies (Cline 1972).

The main point of this discussion is that the widely prevalent tendency to interpret the Kuznets notion as an "iron law" describing inevitable adverse effects of early growth on income distribution in developing countries is unwarranted. First, there is no 'natural' tendency for incomes to be unequal in early development; income distribution at this stage of growth is indeed manipulable by policy. Second, more equitable income redistributions would have no significant adverse effects on economic growth.

4. Strategies for Urban Poverty Reduction

What appears to emerge from this review of theories is that for such an important subject as income distribution far too little is known and the divergence of opinion far too wide for comfort in policy guidance.

The various theories of distribution of income are either too aggregate and abstract to be of great use or postulate conditions too variant from the reality in the low income countries. Given these complexities, one theory is unlikely to encompass this complexity. What may be useful is to forego the development of broad general, theories and to design theoretical models addressed to specific policy issues. What follows in the form of policy approaches is in this spirit.

Since the income of an urban household derives partly from the incomes from work and partly from the goods and services (housing, transportation, utilities, etc.) provided in the urban environment, the strategies for urban poverty alleviation are a mixture of two types: those that augment the income from work of the poor and those that improve the quality of environment of the urban poor.

The work related strategies attempt to increase the employment opportunities and the level of earnings of the poor. Two broad analytical approaches have guided such strategies in the past. The first derives from the surplus labor models that focus on the transfer labor from the traditional rural sector to urban modern sector (Lewis 1954, Fei and Ranis 1964). This approach of developing the modern sector, combined with the capital-intensive import substitution industrialization in Latin America is now widely recognized as a failure. The second approach views underutilization of labor as stemming from factor price distortions imbedded in many development policies, in particular the capital-intensive bias in labor abundant societies.

The second broad class of strategies are those that directly improve the quality of life of the poor by increasing the flow of services from the urban built environment -- shelter, locational, environmental, educational and health services. A strategy to help the poor should attempt to increase their access to these public facilities and services.

What is required, therefore, is a combination of the work related and quality of life strategies. These two strategies are highly complementary since an increase in earnings augments the consumption standards of the poor which in turn, increases human capital and earnings capacity.

4.1 Work Related Strategies

A major component of this strategy is to increase the adoption of labor-intensive techniques in the economy. This is particularly true in a number of sectors in industry, in construction, etc. The potential for this policy of increasing the intensity of labor use is being pursued actively in the literature on 'appropriate technology'.

Since the informal sector contains a large number of the self-employed urban poor, another strategy is to remove the existing discrimination against small producers. Small scale firms use more labor and in some sectors are even more effective than large scale capital-intensive units in output or employment generation for a given stock of capital. Yet in many cases, large scale capital intensive units receive a variety of government subsidies. Elimination of such subsidies, provision of technical, managerial services and improvement of access to markets, skilled labor and scarce materials to the small firms would be warranted. Improved access to capital markets, with easier terms of credit are an important ingredient.

Further, the linkages between the small firms in the informal sector and the modern sector can be increased and built on as in subcontracting arrangements. Such input-output relations between the informal and formal sectors, which played important roles in the growth of the urban economies in a corresponding period of Japanese develop-ment, are currently handicapped in many Latin American countries. This results from the tendencies to vertical integration of various large corporations (domestic and foreign) -- partly from the desire to assure supplies and streamline management. Improved market relationships between small producers and the modern sectors must be developed.

4.2 Quality of Life Strategies

The scope of these strategies is very much determined by the overall level of resources. But many Latin American countries are relatively high income developing countries and the scope for the improvement of the urban services for the poor is not insignificant.

Equally importantly, it is necessary to redirect existing policies of urban service provision so as to help the poor. It was stated earlier, that there is an anti-poor bias in housing, health and educational services. A similar pattern is evident in the provision of water supply and sewer service.

The anti-poor bias is a combination of a variety of biases in the provision of Services (Beier, et al., 1975). Thus, public investments -- in highways, water and sewer facilities, etc. -- are often biased so as to benefit those who exercise political and economic power and exclude the poor. This bias is further reinforced by biases in pricing these services at below cost levels, so as to need government subsidies, which in turn limit expansion of roads or utilities to the urban periphery where the poor live. Further, many of the services and goods are designed at inappropriately high standards -- in housing, utility connections, etc. -- that tend to exclude the poor.

The poor who are excluded end up paying, for example, for water, much higher prices than those who are better off and consume far less of these services. The failure to provide adequate services to the poor is most adverse on their housing environment. A minimum of these environmental services would encourage the accumulation of savings among the poor and their investment in housing.

The major thrust of redistributive policy to improve the quality of life of the poor is twofold:

a)   a reorientation of priorities in the provision of housing, environmental and social services to remove the bias against the poor and to directly aid the poor.

b)   the provision of better facilities for the poor both for housing and productive enterprises. This may provide land in quantities and locations to facilitate the settlement of the poor.

References

Adelman, Irma and Cynthia Morris (1973). Economic Growth and Social Equity in Developing Countries, Stanford, California: Stanford University Press.

Bairoch, P. (1973). Urban Unemployment in Developing Countries, Geneva: I.L.O.

Baran, P. (1958). 'On the political economy of backwardness,' in A. Agarwala and S. Singh (eds.), The Economics of Underdevelopment, New York: Oxford University Press.

Bronfenbrenner, M. (1971). Income Distribution Theory, Chicago, Illinois: Aldine-Atherton.

Chenergy, H., M.S. Ahluwalia, C.L.G. Bell, J.H. Duloy and R. Joily (1974). Redistribution with Growth, New York: Oxford University Press.

Cline, William R. (1972). Potential Effects of Income Redistribution on Economic Growth: Latin American Cases, New York: Praeger.

_____ (1975). 'Distribution and development: A survey of literature', Journal of Development Economics, pp. 359-400.

(ECLA) Economic Commission for Latin America (1974). 'Income distribution in selected major cities of Latin America and in their respective countries,' Economic Bulletin for Latin America, pp. 13-44.

Fei, J. and G. Ranis (1964). Development of a Labor Surplus Economy: Theory and Policy, Homewood, Illinois: Richard D. Irwin.

Ferguson, C.E. and Nell, Edward J. (1972). 'Two boods on the theory of income distribution: A review article,' Journal of Economic Literature, Vol. 10, pp. 437-53.

Fields, Gary S. (1977). 'Who benefits from economic development? A reexamination of Brazilian growth in the 1960's,' American Economic Review, Vol. 67, No. 4, September, pp. 570-82.

Fishlow, Albert (1972). 'Brazilian size and distribution of income,' American Economic Review, Vol. 62, May, pp. 391-402.

Fox, R.W. (1974). Regional Urban Population Growth Trends: Argentina, Brazil, Chile, Mexico, Peru, Venequela, Economics and Social Development Departm,ent, General Studies Divsion, Inter American Development Bank, Urban Population Series No. 4, Washington, D.C.: July.

Foxley, Alejandro (1976). Income Distribution in Latin America, Cambridge: Cambridge University Press.

Frank, A.G. (1969). Capitalism and Underdevelopment in Latin America, Revised Edition, New York: Monthly Review Press.

Frank Jr., Charles R. and Richard Webb (1977). 'An overview of income distribution in less developed countries: Policy alternatives and design,' in C.R. Frank Jr. and R. Webb (eds.), Income Distribution and Growth in Less Developed Countries, Washington, D.C.: Brookings, pp. 7-44.

Furtado, C. (1965). 'Development and stagnation in Latin America: A structuralist approach,' Studies in Comprehensive International Development 1, pp. 159-75.

Haq, Mahbub ul (1974). 'Employment in the 1970s: A new perspective,' International Development Review, pp. 9-13.

Kravis, I.G. (1960). 'International differences in the distribution of income,' Review of Economics and Statistics, Vol. 42, No. 4, pp. 408-16.

Kuznets, S. (1963). 'Quantitative aspects of economic growth of nations: VIII distribution of income by size,' Economic Development and Cultural Change II, 2, pp. 1-80.

Lewis, W.A. (1954). 'Economic development with unlimited supplies of labor,' The Manchester School, Vol. 22, pp. 139-91.

Lipton, Michael (1977). Why People Stay Poor, Cambridge, MA: Harvard University Press.

Little, I.M.D.,Tibor Scitovsky, and Maurice Scott (1970). Industry and Trade in Some Developing Countries, London: Oxford University Press.

McGee, T.G. (1971). The Urbanization of the Third World: Explorations in Search of a Theory, London: Bell.

Merrick, T. and F.A. Binto (1974). Study of the Labor Market in a Rapidly Growing Urban Area, Washington, D.C.: World Bank.

Mincer, Jacob (1958). 'Investment in human capital and personal income distribution,' Journal of Political Economy, Vol. 66(4), August, pp. 281-302.

O'Brien, Philip J. (1975). 'A critique of Latin American theories of dependency,' in Beyond the Sociology of Development (eds.) I. Oxaal, T. Barnett, and D. Booth, London: Routledge and Kegan Paul, pp. 7-27.

Pen, Jan (1971). Income Distribution, Harmondsworth, Middlesex: Penguin Books.

Prebisch, Raul (1977). 'Peripheral capitalism and urban expansion,' A paper presented at the Symposium on Urbanization, Labor Absorption, and Environmental Quality. The Johns Hopkins University, March, apperaring as Chapter 3 of this book.

Sahota, G.S. (1978). 'Theories of personal income distribution: A survey,' Journal of Economic Literature, Vol. 16(1), March, pp. 1-55.

Sant' Anna, Anna Maria, Thomas W. Merrick and Dypak Mazumdar (1976). Income Distribution and the Economy of the Urban Household: The Case of Belo Horizante, World Bank Staff Working Paper No. 237, June.

Dos Santos, T. (1973). 'The crisis of development theory and the problem of dependence in Latin America,' in Underdevelopment and development (ed.), H. Bernstein, Harmondsworth, Middlesex: Penguin Books.

Schaefer, Kalmann, assisted by C. R. Spindel (1976). Sao Paulo, International Labor Organization, A WEP study, Geneva.

Sunkel, O. (1969). 'National development policy and external dependency in Latin America,' Journal of Development Studies, Vol. 6, No. 1, pp. 23-30.

Thomas, Vinod (1978). The Measurement of Spatial Differences in Poverty: The Case of Peru, World Bank Staff Working Paper No. 273, January.

Turnham, D. and I. Jaeger (1971). The Employment Problem in Less Developed Countries: A Review of Evidence, for O.E.C.D., Paris, K.M.S.O. London.

United Nations (1974). Urban Population Projections, Population Research Division.

Weisskoff, Richard (1970). 'Income distribution and economic growth in Puerto Rico, Argentina and Mexico,' Review of Income and Wealth, Vol. 16, December, pp. 303-32.

22 Urban transport policy, land use, and the energy crisis in India and other developing countries

S. K. MUKHERJEE

1. Introduction

The Study of Urban Transport Policy for Large and Medium Sized Cities in India (Mukherjee, 1979), the summary results of which are reported in this paper, was sponsored by the National Transport Policy Committee at the Planning Commission as a basic study for formulating national policy for urban transportation. The National Transport Policy Committee was set up by the Planning Commission to formulate a national transport policy tailored to meeting the new plan priorities and to study all aspects of transport policy including urban transport in India. The objectives of the study on Urban Transport Policy for Large and Medium Sized Cities in India were the following:

i.   to prepare a status report on Urban Transport Policy in Indian Cities based on a study of the transportation systems, existing, under construction and being planned for various large-and medium-sized Indian cities.

ii. To analyze the need for transport projects such as underround railways for meeting the transportation needs of large urban communities.

iii. To suggest the proper mix of various modes of urban transportation and to evaluate different modal choices and technical options for urban transportation in relation to:

   a) Employment;
   b) Social cost including environmental and ecological factors;
   c) Energy cost of transportation; and
   d) Accessibility of the transport mode, for recommending an appropriate mix in the various modes of transport.

iv   To study the interrelationship between land-use and transportation needs and how better land-use planning could help in improving the quality of urban transport.

v.   To suggest an appropriate tariff structure for urban transportation system including the issue of providing subsistence to socially justifiable selected groups.

During the course of the study the four large metropolitan cities -- Bombay, Calcutta, Delhi, and Madras, as well as other next level cities including Ahmedabad, Bangalore, Hyderabad, and Baroda, were visited and discussions were held with the organizations responsible for transportation planning and execution, and urban and land use policies. Relevant information on transportation planning and statistics were obtained from various Class I cities including almost all state capitals who responded to the requests sent. Documents relating to urban development and transportation planning and specific mass transportation projects for all the cities were analyzed and this was supplemented through additional information collected during visits to various cities.

It was not intended to carry out any specific surveys during the course of the study as in almost all cities such surveys have been carried out during the last decade and various working groups have also studied the transportation problems of these cities. The specific emphasis given during this study was to prepare a status report on urban transportation in India and to recommend the future direction that should be taken in the area of urban transport in India. This was specifically needed as it was observed that the traffic and transportation problems in the large metropolitan areas have increased to such a point as to make life in these cities for the citizens almost unbearable. It was also felt that many of the large and medium cities in India are facing the burden of high capital investments for providing public transportation facilities for evergrowing demands from passengers. In some of the cities, the requirements for rapid transit systems, sometime of underground construction and involving extremely high investments per passenger-kilometer, have been recommended during the last two decades. No decisions have been taken on the construction of such facilities except the underground tube railway at Calcutta. Delays in initiating such projects or viable alternatives have compounded the suffering of the commuting public in these cities.

2. Transportation Demand and Land Use Policy

There has been some re-thinking as to whether the growing transportation demands in the urban areas should always be met with large investments in public transport facilities. It has become obvious that the public transport undertakings are usually operating at a loss and have become financial burdens on the municipal corporations or the state and central governments. It is also felt that the provision of cheap and subsidized public transport corridors in the large cities have created linear city development along these corridors and increased the need for daily long trips. It appears that continuation of this trend by the provision of additional transport facilities would only create even more unmanageable situations in future, ultimately leading to a state when the whole urban transportation system would collapse under pressure of overcrowding. It would be impossible to meet the large investments needed to augment and operate the mass transportation facilities to handle the growing demand.

It is increasingly being realized that the solution to the problem of increasing demand for urban transportation lies in essentially changing the existing urban land use policy and directing the future growth of cities in a more desirable pattern to minimize the need for subsidized transportation for large numbers of people through long distances. It is felt that the policies dealing with urban development, land use, and relative locations of residential, commercial, and industrial activities within urban areas could not be isolated from studies of urban transport policy as these policies determine to a large extent the future transportation demand in urban areas.

3. Effect of Subsidized Tariff Policy in Urban Public Transport Systems

Another aspect of the urban transport policy has also been receiving increasing attention of the urban and transportation planners. The tariff policy is the other important factor besides land use pattern on which the future transportation demands will depend. Public transportation both by rail and bus has been heavily subsidized in the urban areas since their introduction. In spite of the poor financial situation in which various transport enterprises find themselves, the tariff structures often fail to generate enough revenues to cover the operating costs of the public transportation mode. The transportation market, however, is not uniform and it is seen that simultaneously with the public bus system, other more expensive private transport modes such as taxis, private cars, three-wheelers, and public modes (e.g., mini-buses, special buses, contract buses, etc.) are operating often with commercial success as they are charging higher fares. It is obvious that at least a large section of the urban community are able and willing to pay a higher price for reliable, speedy, and comfortable transportation. Somehow the public transport undertakings have not been able to take advantage of this situation. The public transport enterprises are burdened with the social responsibility of carrying the bulk of the passenger load at heavily subsidized rates. But the profitable ventures such as mini-buses are operated by private groups.

The effect of a subsidized tariff policy is usually two fold, and in the long term both effects are harmful to the urban area and to the cause of public transportation. Subsidized public transportation, especially by rail along a few limited corridors, has created sprawling suburban bedroom communities in cities like Bombay and Calcutta. People have moved further and further away from the city center and are commuting through longer distances to their workplaces still located in the central business district (CBD) in the older part of the city. The employers have not moved to the suburban areas but are increasing job opportunities in the central city as they could get people from distant suburban areas to come to the central area through subsidized public transport. This process, if continued indefinitely, will lead to large urban conglomerates which would be difficult and very costly to manage as resources would not be available for investment in urban services such as transportation, water supply, sewage, power, education, and health facilities. The subsidized tariff structure is also responsible for such poor financial situation of the transport enterprises, that they could hardly cover their operating expenses and have to depend always on the public exchequer for funding future developments and even for maintenance and operation of the existing transport facilities. It is expected that if a rational tariff structure is gradually introduced in the urban areas, still keeping in mind the need for subsidies from limited groups of poor or unemployed constituents, it would not only curb undue growth of transportation demand and attempt to stop the continuing urban sprawl, but would also create a better financial situation for the transport enterprises so that they would be in a position to provide better transport service for the urban commuters.

4.   Optimal Modal Mix for Urban Transportation

Similarity between traffic congestion and transportation problems between the major cities of the developed countries and in the developing countries, such as India, should not obscure some of the fundamental differences. The cities in the developing countries and specifically those in India are experiencing a much faster rate of population growth and this requires a higher level of investment in the transportation sector. There has been rapid increase in the number of automobiles including taxis in India during the last two decades, particularly noticeable in cities like Delhi and Bombay. These are mainly used by private businessmen, citizens, and Government/company officials. The growth of public buses and commercial vehicles has also been rapid. But still the number of automobiles in Indian cities is much smaller when compared with the cities in the developed countries. The congestion that is experienced in Indian cities is more due to the enchroachments on the inadequate road space, uncontrolled movement of slow and fast moving vehicles and pedestrians on the road space, and poor traffic planning and regulation prevalent in most cities. Private modes of transportation serve only a small proportion of the urban population and in the large metropolitan areas of Bombay and Calcutta more than 80 percent of the people depend on the public transportation system. In Delhi, Madras, Bangalore, Ahmedabad, and other medium-sized cities, the share of public transportation is still in the region of 40-60 percent, mainly due to the inadequacy of the existing public transportation system and the prevalence of cheaper private modes of transport such as scooters and bicyles. Large number of people still walk or use bicycles to go to their work places. The prevalent need for Indian cities, large, medium, or small, is the provision of an efficient mix of urban transportation modes suited to the land use pattern, transportation needs, energy use, and resource availability of these cities.

None of the medium-sized cities have gone for street cars, a highly efficient form of urban transport introduced in Calcutta and Bombay at the beginning of the century, mainly due to the rapid emergence of petrol and diesel buses in the 1940s and 1950s and the prevailing low prices of petroleum products used as fuels. Calcutta's street car (tram) system had remained stagnant for more than 30 years now, as no new investments have been made following independence. Only in recent years a project is being considered for the reactivation of the tram services in Calcutta. Electrified rail services for urban commuters in Bombay were opened in the 1930s based on available hydro power. Currently, the five corridors spanning the length of the city are unable to cope with the increasing urban commuter traffic though about half the load is shared by the efficient bus system operated by Bombay Electricity Supply and Transport Corporation (BEST). In Calcutta, train services were introduced mainly for suburban passengers commuting from adjoining rural or semi-urban communities which were later electrified during the sixties. But the rail services in Calcutta only bring passengers to the two eastern and western terminals of the city. They have to use other forms of transport, and a large number of them walk, to reach their usual destination at the Central Business District where most of the jobs are located. The city and the outlying suburbs are mainly served by the trams, private and public buses and mini-bus systems, but the total carrying capacity of this system has been highly inadequate for more than a decade. Suburban train services in Delhi and Madras are also present in a limited extent. Almost all the other Indian cities are totally dependent on public and private buses, though many smaller cities have no public transport system to speak of and auto-richshaws and cycle-rickshaws often form the only mode of transport available.

In general, the existing facilities for public transportation are inadequate in almost all cities in India, large, medium, and small. Though there are differences between the cities, buses and trains operate at near crushing loads especially during the peak office hours except where standing limits are strictly enforced. Marginal increases in capacity provided during the last decade have not imporved the situation due to growth in passenger trips and poor maintenance and replacement policy for buses, street cars, and trains. The annual growth in transit trips has been abour 4-5 percent in most of the cities and in some of the cities even higher. The 1981 traffic projections for Bombay made by Traffic Cell group in 1968 were realized in the mid seventies, and in Delhi also the growth of urban traffic has been very fast during the last decade. In almost all cities the fare in public transport systems have been very low right from the beginning and it has been always politically difficult to increase fares. Due to the poor financial conditions of the transport organizations they have to always depend on public funding not only for expansion of transport facilities, but even for replacement of older vehicles. As a result many of the urban transport undertakings are experiencing a reduction in their effective capacity of buses on the road over the years on the face of increasing passenger demand. This is true for Calcutta State Transport Corporation and also for the Calcutta Tramsways Company.

In this state of public transportation in Indian cities, there is a need to determine the optimal modal mix for urban transportation in large- and medium-sized cities. The small cities would possibly exclusively depend on some form of bus services and personal modes of travel in the near future and their problems are not discussed here. During the last 10-15 years, recommendations have been made for two new types of public transport systems or facilities for large- and medium-sized cities. Increasingly, there have been demands for the provision of rapid transit systems of surface, underground or elevated type built with financial support from the Central Government along the corridors with high intensity of transit demand. Specifically, it has been suggested that some form of rapid transit systems involving high capacity train services are essential when cities cross a population level of one million. At present only Bombay has rapid surface rail transit system along its five North-South corridors and project proposals have been under the consideration of the Central Government for two additional corridors for augmenting the capacity of the train services, one mostly of underground construction. An underground tube railway is under construction in Calcutta now and the first phase consisting of a north-south line is expected to be in operation by 1983-84. There have been proposals to construct rapid transit systems in cities such as Madras, Delhi, and Bangalore. For Madras, only certain marginal investments have been agreed upon and in Delhi, a circular surface railway has been recently sanctioned. The extremely high investments required for rapid transit systems, specifically through congested city areas which need underground construction, is already a major concern for the government and it is desirable to investigate the role such rapid transit systems will play in Indian cities in the future. Even if resources are available for such investments, construction of these facilities create major dislocations to traffic and commercial activity during the period of 5-8 years needed for construction. The augmentation of subsidized rapid transit systems along corridors of high demand also tends to reinforce the past trends of land use pattern and urban sprawl and in the process lead to even higher transit demands in the future requiring further investments.

There are also the other modes of public transportation such as mini-buses, special buses, contract buses, etc., which are essentially higher priced 'fixed-route' forms of public transport which could perhaps cater to only a small percentage of the total demand for such service, specifically belonging to the higher income group. It is also necessary to study the role of such facilities in the modal mix of future urban transportation systems in Indian cities. There are other new solutions available for introduction in our cities, some of which needs special attention due to the impending energy crisis. This consists of mainly the electric trolley buses (ETB), modern tram services like metro-rail and other light rail services which are being introduced now in various European cities. There is also a new solution to the urban transport problem available in elevated monorail or suspended transportation systems (such as U-Bahn system in West Germany) which would be less capital-intensive when compared to underground transportation system and can provide an effective solution in some Indian cities. The role of such solutions for urban transport problems needs to be examined both in the case of large metropolitan cities and the next level cities in India.

5. Urbanization and Growth of Indian Cities

To analyze the success or failure of Urban Transport Policy and its execution in the past and to recommend a policy for the future a proper study for the process of urbanization and growth of cities and towns in India must be carried out. India is often categorized as being predominantly a rural country as more than 80 percent of the total population live in the rural areas. But the process of urbanization has been quite rapid in India during the last few decades with resulting problems of urban poverty, unemployment, and inadequacy of housing and other urban infrastructure, such as roads and public transport facilities. The important characteristics of the current urban problems in the developing countries are the scale and intensity of the problems and the paucity of resources. In future, most of the large cities of the world would be located in the developing countries and already large cities in these countries such as Calcutta, Bombay, Bangkok, and Seoul are reaching population figures quite close to the 'old' large cities of the world, such as New York, London, and Tokyo. Past policies to contain urbanization in the developing countries have not really been successful and as the process of urbanization is often accompanied by rapid growth in income and employment opportunities, it might not even be in the best interests of the countries to stop the economic growth of cities like Bombay or Seoul. These cities are vibrant and dynamic as shown by their rapid rate of economic development and industrialization, while many other cities have remained stagnant over decades. It is increasingly being recognized now that it is almost impossible to stop migration of people into the big cities, contain their growth in size and inhibit the mushrooming of squatter colonies, as commonly seen in the cities of developing countries, even if these are desirable objectives. What is perhaps possible, and even this needs a strong political will, is to influence their growth in desirable directions and orient their land use policies in a way so that the city grows into an organic and vital agglomeration of multiple nodes or centers each thriving with economic, social and cultural activities and does not become a monolithic concrete jungle laced only with freeways and railways for transporting people and vehicles through long distances.

While there are individual differences among various cities due to the multitude of factors responsible for their growth, the general pattern of urbanization in India has been characterized by the high rate of growth in the large cities (or Class I cities), a state of stagnation in medium-sized cities of less than 100,000 population (Class II and III cities) and decline in the growth in smaller cities and towns. The larger cities have been attracting migrants not only from rural areas, searching for employment as unskilled workers or petty vendors, specially after agricultural calamities, but also people from small towns who come to the large cities for better fortune in employment and trade. All the large cities with more than 1 million in population, including the four metropolitan regions of Bombay, Calcutta, Delhi, and Madras, have grown quite steadily during the last few decades, some at rather a fast rate. Many of the medium-sized cities have shown even faster rates of growth mainly due to the industries that have been located, often changing the past character of these cities from quiet townships to busy industrial centers humming with industrial activity. Many of these cities have benefited by the regional trends in industrial location policy of the central government and encouragement provided by the state governments in the form of infrastructural facilities and tax relief.

In spite of various attempts in the past, industrialization in India has not touched small towns and rural areas indicating that the incentives provided by central and state governments have not been attractive enough to overcome the resistance shown by entrepreneurs to locate industries in small towns, rural, and backward areas, which are faced with multitudes of problems due to lack of adequate infrastructural facilities such as power, water supply and transportation network, lack of skilled labor as well as absence of urban facilities such as schools, and hospitals, social amenities which are preconditions for attracting professional and managerial class to these areas.

In the foreseeable future the same pattern of urbanization is expected to prevail in India, as the basic social and economic forces which encourage growth of urban areas including the 'pull' and 'push' factors remain the same in spite of recent emphasis by the government to give higher priority to the development of rural growth. In the absence of appropriate policies for directing urban growth regulating land use pattern and zoning of various urban economic activities, and the absence of statutory framework to control unplanned growth brought about by land speculation and urban market forces, large cities of India are growing into sprawling metropoli of several million people living and working in very high population densities. Subsidized public transportation by buses and railways have also distored the urban layout by separating 'jobs' from 'homes' by long distances

requiring high capacity public transportation systems to carry several
million people to their jobs in the morning and to their homes in the
evening. Such investments are often beyond the reach of the urban
governments and the consequent delays in augmenting capacities for
public transportation create overcrowding and suffering for the
people. Creating additional facilities also tend to reinforce the
existing trend of growth in demand for travel through longer distances,
thus inviting complete collapse of the urban transportation system in
future. There is a need for policies not only to contain urbanization
and growth of population in the large cities of India, and direct the
growth towards smaller towns and rural areas, but the continuing growth
in the large- and medium-sized cities need to be directed to reduce the
demand of transportation as far as possible consistent with the
necessary economic and social activities, by better land use policies
and creating almost self-sufficient small urban communities within the
large metropolitan areas. There is increasing recognition of this fact
in the recent metropolitan structural plans for Calcutta prepared by
Calcutta Metropolitan Development Authority (CMDA), Bombay Metropolitan
region by the Bombay Metropolitan Regional Development Authority
(BMRDA) and also in Delhi and Madras, but large next level cities which
are also following the same pattern are yet to show awareness in this
area. Recently, urban development authorities have been constituted in
several of these cities and it is expected that these agencies would
develop appropriate structural plans for directing future growth in
these cities.

According to the 1971 census, about 20 percent of India's
population lived in urban centers. The data in Table 1 shows that the

TABLE 1
TREND OF URBANIZATION IN INDIA 1901-1971

Census Year	Percentage of urban to rural pop.	Percentage of population in each class of towns to urban population					
		Cl. I 100,000 & over	Cl. II 50,000 99,999	Cl.III 20,000 49,999	Cl. IV 10,000 19,999	Cl. V 5,000 9,999	Cl. VI below 5,000
1901	10.05	20.93	11.84	16.50	22.06	22.38	6.29
1911	10.29	24.19	10.90	17.69	20.46	19.81	6.95
1921	11.13	25.31	12.43	16.89	18.91	19.03	7.43
1931	12.00	27.31	11.95	18.76	18.97	17.32	5.63
1941	13.86	35.40	11.77	17.71	16.27	15.38	3.45
1951	17.30	41.77	11.06	16.73	14.02	13.02	3.22
1961	17.98	48.37	11.89	18.53	13.03	7.23	0.95
1971	19.87	52.41	12.15	17.36	12.04	5.24	0.80

progress of urbanization in India remained quite slow from the
beginning of the present century until about 1941. A sudden increase
in the growth of urban population was noticed during 1941-51 and this
was mainly due to the effect of the Second World War and the migration
of a large number of refugees following the partition of India during
Independence from the British rule. In the following decade this tempo
of urbanization did not continue at the same pace in spite of
industrial growth in the country. During the last decade of 1961-71
there was again a relatively faster pace of urbanization. The share of
Class I cities increased from 35.40 percent in 1941 to 52.41 percent in
1971. The share of Class II cities and Class III cities almost
stagnated and the share of Class IV, V, and VI cities registered a
decline in these years. The decline has been very sharp in Class V and
Class VI as shown in Table 1. The uneven trend in the growth of cities
in various classes is illustrated more vividly in Figure 1.

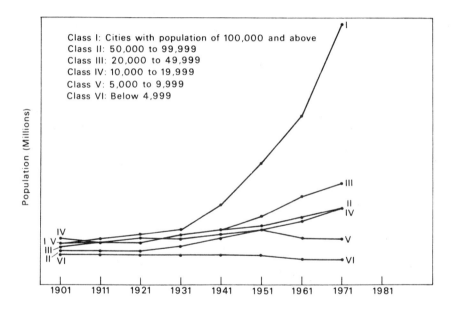

Figure 1. Distribution of Urban Population in India in Various
Classes of Cities, 1901-1971.

Source: Indian National Report on Human Environment Submitted by
the Government of India to the United Nations Conference
on the Human Environment, May 1971.

The differential rates of growth of cities and towns in India show
a definite pattern within the general trend of urbanization in the
country. It showed that larger cities grew much faster at the expense
of rural areas and even smaller urban areas. The basic reasons, as
discussed in the last section, are (i) concentration of employment and

commercial opportunities in the large cities, (ii) rapid population growth in the country and decline in per capita agricultural land and low levels of rural income, (iii) improvement in transportation and communication between large cities and the hinterland, and (iv) rapid westernization of the large urban areas providing modern facilities for living and entertainment, aspired by not only the managerial and professional classes but also by the clerical and industrial workers as well as migrants from the rural areas. The nine largest cities with 1 million and higher population, Calcutta, Bombay, Delhi, Madras, Hyderabad, Ahmedabad, Bangalore, Kanpur, and Pune, accounted for more than 25 percent of the total urban population in 1971 and during the last two decades they have been growing at about 4 percent per year, about twice the population growth rate. These cities are going to face most complex problems of urban transportation during the next 10-20 years and the study was focused to analyze the problems of this group of cities and recommend appropriate urban transport policy. However, the highest growth rate was experienced by the group of 104 cities having population between 1 million and 3 million. Average annual growth rate of these cities was 29.6 percent during 1941-51 and about 10 percent during 1951-71. Rapid growth of many of these cities have been due to the location of industrial plants and commercial activities which have started to concentrate on cities of this size, as the larger cities are becoming saturated and industrial land for large industries is becoming scarce. Table 2 shows the growth of population in selected large cities and other industrial cities, ports, and capital cities. Some of the steel cities, industrial cities, and new capital cities have grown very rapidly during the last two decades as shown in the table. Thus, an analysis of the past trends of growth in Indian cities illustrates the imbalances in the spatial distribution of industrial location and commercial activities. The industrial units have concentrated in the existing large- and medium-sized cities, thus, pulling in population from smaller cities, towns, and rural areas to the cities they are located in.

In view of the past trends in urbanization in India, the high rate of growth of large- and medium-sized cities, and the resulting complex urban problems that have been created, several important issues are raised. We have been following the urbanization patterns of the western developed countries in the past, where due to the advantages of agglomeration large industrial and commercial cities have developed. Most of these older large cities (e.g., London, New York, Chicago, etc.) have invested in surface or underground rapid transit systems in the earlier part of this century and the cities which came up later have developed highly efficient

urban road networks and are more dependent on private automobiles for urban transportation. Some of these cities are also investing large amounts to build rapid transit systems now. Being a resource-poor country, though our cities are becoming quite large, we cannot invest similar amounts either to build extensive rapid transit systems or large network of urban highways, the latter solution being also inappropriate as only a small mainority can afford to own automobiles in India. Thus, we must face the basic issues as to whether in the developing countries we should develop large cities of similar size and centralized urban structure as prevalent in the Western-developed countries. We have already seen that the urban transport problems of the large four metropolitan cities in India have already reached a

TABLE 2

GROWTH OF POPULATION IN SOME SELECTED CITIES

	POP. in 1951 (000)	POP. in 1961 (000)	POP. in 1971 (000)	Decade Growth Rate 1951-61	Decade Growth Rate 1961-71
Large Cities (Higher than 1 Million)					
Calcutta Urban	4588	5736	7005	25	22
Greater Bombay	2966	4152	5969	40	44
Delhi (incl. New Delhi)	1431	2359	3630	64	54
Hyderabad	1127	1248	1799	11	44
Madras	1416	1729	2470	22	43
Bangalore	773	1199	1648	54	43
Ahmedabad	837	1149	1588	37	38
Kanpur	705	971	1278	38	31
Pune					
Steel Cities					
Jamshedpur	218	328	465	50	42
Durg Bhilainagar	20	133	245	565	84
Durgapur	-	41	207	-	397
Rourkela	-	90	173	-	91
Bokaro Steel City	5	N.A.	108	-	new
Bhadrawati	42	65	101	55	59
Other Industrial Cities					
Surat	237	306	472	29	64
Vadodara	211	309	407	46	57
Ludhiana	153	244	401	59	64
Ranchi	106	140	256	32	83
Kota	65	120	213	85	77
Ghaziabad	43	70	128	63	82
Port Cities					
Cochin	166	277	438	67	56
Calicut	158	220	334	39	73
Visakhapatnam	108	211	362	95	72
Capital Cities					
Bhopal	102	222	392	118	96
Chandigarh	-	99	233	-	135
Bhubaneshwar	16	38	106	138	176
Patna	283	364	491	29	35

stage where they are considered unsolvable even after investing large resources. If the same trend of urban growth and centralized structure is continued in the next level cities, they would reach similar sizes and would face even larger problems as the metropolitan cities as it would be even more difficult to find resources for building rapid transit facilities and urban road network in these cities. Thus, the important questions are the following: (a) what is the optimum size of a city in a developing country like India in terms of population and (b) whether some measures should be taken to restrict the growth of population in the cities?

At least, theoretically, it would be possible to determine the optimum size of a city that would minimize the total cost of providing all urban services such as power, water supply and sewage, transportation, health, and commercial services, while the city would still be economically viable in providing enough employment opportunities for its population, past experience tells us that it would be extremely difficult to restrict the growth of population in the cities. Cities are like living organisms and they grow due to their own vitality as a result of the economic and social forces released by the society through individuals as well as institutions. The basic instruments related to the location of industrial and commercial activities, however, could be utilized to restrict growth of large cities beyond a point, and these could be partially successful.

A more important issue perhaps would be the necessity to regulate not so much the absolute size of the cities but the urban structure and land use pattern that is followed in our cities. Being a resource-poor country, highly centralized cities as found in Western countries with a single central business district (CBD), and people living in distant suburban communities are not appropriate for India and probably it is not consistent with our way of life and cultural heritage. Perhaps, our large cities should be composed of multinodal or poly-nucleated structure with a large number of partially self-sufficient communities living close together and connected by strong transportation links. If better telecommunication facilities are available and public transportation is not subsidized, then it might be possible to build such cities or orient existing city designs to such future patterns.

The ideal city perhaps would be where most of the people live not too far from their work places and can either walk or use a bicycle or take a short ride in a public transport to go to work. But as there would be some restrictions on the location of industries within an urban region, and integrated family structure being still prevalent in India, this ideal solution might not be workable. But most large cities now can work towards decentralizing some of their commercial and government activities and create new CBD's close to residential areas. Usually such alternative CBD's need certain critical mass of offices and commercial activities to be moved their before others follow the trend and usually government offices should be the first to move to provide the lead to other institutions. Similarly, central areas of many of our cities have traditionally also acted as warehousing and transportation centers for commercial vehicles as well as wholesale markets for grains, vegetables, etc. Such activities could be moved away from the city center to the urban periphery thus reducing both passenger and goods movements.

It is evident that we should not take the existing urban structure and land use pattern of our cities as well as the existing transportation demands for granted and only concentrate on finding technological solutions to the urban transportation problem by building new facilities. It is possible to change the urban structure and land use pattern of our cities gradually, so as to make them more efficient by reducing the total transportation demand, both the absolute number of trips and the average load, while not restricting the economic activities which would provide income and employment. Urban development authorities in cities like Calcutta, Bombay, Delhi, and Madras have initiated such actions, but other medium-sized cities should also follow their example before it is too late for these cities to evolve a more appropriate and optimal urban structure and land use policy. In the past, subsidized public transportation in Indian cities has usually distorted the urban structure and the harmful effects are obvious to see in our large metropolitan cities. This is one of the instruments of public policy which is often neglected and provision of subsidized public transport is lauded as a socialistic measure for income redistribution. To develop an optimum urban structure which is highly efficient while being low-cost, proper land use policy must be accompanied by an appropriate cost reflecting tariff policy for urban transportation and much more attention needs to be given to this specific area of urban policy.

6. Energy Implications of Urban Transport Policy

Developing countries have been adversely affected by the four fold increase in oil prices in 1973-74 and the periodic increases resorted to by OPEC since then. India also has been affected, mainly due to the increasing trend in the oil import requirements for the country, which has been somewhat moderated due to the discovery of various offshore fields near the West Coast. But still the import requirement for petroleum is increasing and it has not yet been possible to introduce strict methods for conservation due to the dependence of transport, agriculture and industrial sectors on this convenient fuel (Murthy and Shenoy, 1979). The Fuel Policy Committee (Government of India, 1974), which carried out a comprehensive study of the energy sector in 1971-74, recommended that coal should be considered as the principal source of energy in the country and that oil should be substituted wherever technically and economically feasible by other forms of energy to reduce the quantity of import and to maximize indigenous production. But containing the growth of oil demand is a difficult task. Due to the disruption in the supply of petroleum during the revolution in Iran, the Iraq-Iran war and the price increases announced by OPEC during 1979-80, not only the price but the continued availability of adequate amounts of petroleum has been a matter of deep concern for the developing countries.

The implications of the energy crisis should be viewed with a sense of urgency by the urban and transportation planners. Except in Bombay and in a minor way in Madras and Calcutta, where intra-urban movements by electrified rail transport is possible, all urban areas, large, medium, and small, are totally dependent on petroleum-based fuel for private and public transportation, and any disruption in the supply of petroleum products will totally paralyze our cities and also stop all economic activities. In a worldwide scramble for the limited supply made available by OPEC countries, such disruption could be a real possibility. There lies, thus, an urgent need in India that an alternative mode of public transport, and also private transport not based on petroleum fuel should be introduced as soon as possible, so that enough experience is gained for switchover to such a mode as and when the need arises. Unfortunately, none of the cities appear to have seriously considered this problem facing them, and all of them are continuing to increase their bus fleet without considering electrified modes of public transportation. Except Calcutta, all other large cities have demolished their tram or trolley bus systems. Several cities have prepared projects for the introduction of electrified rail-based rapid transit systems. But except for the Metrorail in Calcutta, no other project has been sanctioned mainly due to shortage of adequate funds. Even after the energy crisis, road-based transportation system mainly dependent on petroleum-based vehicles is still being encouraged. This is not due to absence of alternative modes or ideas. The electric tram system in Calcutta has been carrying bulk of passengers all these years, even though there have been no major investments in the system after the independence. It is well-known that most of the European cities are using either street cars (trams), ETB's or some other modern electrified system such as metro-rail and some cities in U.S. have been operating street cars and ETB's. Perhaps the time is opportune that we experiment with such alternative modes in India and based on demands from all the cities in India, a domestic industry could be based to manufacture vehicles and equipment for such a new electrified mode for public transportation. As electric trams are more expensive and track bound, it is proposed that ETB's should be seriously considered for implementation in all large and medium and even some smaller cities in India.

It was desired to determine the energy consumption in the public transport systems in Indian cities, specifically in the case of diesel fuel for which import of crude oil is needed (Murthy and Shenoy, 1979). This should give some idea regarding our dependence on imported petroleum for public transport systems. The study was carried out for the year 1982-83 for the cities of Ahmedabad, Bombay, Calcutta, and Madras based on average vehicle-kilometers driven in the past, average diesel consumption per kilometer and future fleet strength. In case of Ahmedabad, it was found that during 1971-72 to 1976-77, the kilometer/liter was improved from 3.43 to 3.59. Based on annual kilometers driven and fleet strength, the average consumption/bus/year was found to be 14102.4 liters. Based on a fleet strength of 665 in 1982-83, this led to 9.378 million liters of diesel consumption for AMTS. The crude equivalent on the basis of 25 percent of diesel oil recovery amounted to 0.208 million barrels and at $32/bbl, the foreign exchange cost of crude oil would be U.S. $6.67 million. As there has been further increase in crude prices and more to follow by 1982-83, the savings in foreign exchange if all AMTS buses could be replaced by alternative mode of transportation would be of the order of U.S. $7.0 million or more per year.

In case of Bombay, the total bus fleet in 1982-83 was assumed to be 2354 buses. Based on average annual vehicle days of 334 and route km/vehicle day of 226 and diesel consumption of 2.8 kms/liter from past data, the total consumption of fuel by BEST buses is estimated at 63.46 million liters of diesel fuel.[1] The corresponding crude requirements would be 1.41 million barrels and foreign exchange cost at U.S. $32/bbl. would be U.S. $45.12 million. For Calcutta, assuming CSTC would operate 1429 buses in 1982-83 and assuming same route km/vehicle day as Bombay, it is estimated that 38.524 million liters of diesel oil would be consumed in 1982-83. This is again equivalent to 0.856 million barrels of crude oil with foreign exchange cost of U.S. $27.39 million at $32/bbl. In case for PTC of Madras assuming a fleet of 1975 in 1982, diesel consumption is estimated at 42.595 million liters. The crude equivalent would be o.947 million barrels of crude oil costing $30.29 million. Such an analysis could not be carried out for Delhi as capacity of Delhi buses were expressed as 1000/passenger/day and data on daily kms covered were not available. In any case, even adding together the diesel consumption of these 4 cities, it is seen that the total requirement for diesel in operating public buses (in Calcutta there are 1400 private buses also) would be 15.4 crore liters requiring approximately 3.42 million barrels of crude oil costing about U.S. $110 million in foreign exchange. In case ETB is introduced in these cities to even replace 10 percent of the diesel fleet, an annual savings of U.S. $11 million would be obtained in 1982-83. This analysis could be extended to all the other cities to study the extent of our dependence on diesel buses and the national cost of such a policy, if continued indefinitely, in terms of foreign exchange costs.

---

[1]   This is equivalent to 63,400 kilolitres of HSDO consumed by BEST only. This figure could be compared to the estimated figure of 153,000 HSDO consumption by all road transport vehicles in Bombay in 1978-79 forecast by NCAER in their report on Energy Demand in Greater Bombay, January 1975.

References

Mukherjee, Shishir K., (1979). Urban Transport Policy for Large- and Medium-Sized Indian Cities, Report submitted to the NTPC, Planning Commission, Government of India, Indian Institute of Management, Ahmedabad, India.

Murthy, K.K. and Asha Shenoy, (1979). Energy Intensity of Transportation Mode, Report submitted to the NTPC, Planning Commission, Government of India, National Institute for Training in Industrial Engineers, Vihar Lake, Bombay 400 087.

Government of India, (1974). Report of the Fuel Policy Committee, New Delhi, India.

PART IV
Resources and Rural Development

23 Location difference and economic activity in the presence of a metropolitan city: an econometric study for West Bengal, 1997

R. N. DE AND C. R. PATHAK

1. Introduction

Decentralization processes of economic activities take place slowly in a developing economy. The identification of the rate of decentralization of an economic activity among a set of spatial units is the basic objective of the present study. However, there have been several attempts at estimating a functional hierarchy between spatial units in the central place theory. The present study investigates the relationships between functional hierarchy and locational gaps in relation to a highly centralized place of economic activity in a two-dimensional setting. They would enable us to assess the rates of change of functional hierarchy at different points of a locational gap. That is, the rates of change in functional hierarchy between spatial units will in turn indicate the rates of decentralization processes of economic activities between the spatial units concerned. Thus, we focus on the prevailing process of decentralization of economic activity between spatial units within a region or between regions within a national economy.

Spatial units adjacent to a central place of economic activity remain in a favorable position, whereas the other spatial units located far from the central place are not able to benefit from the locational advantage, unless they are having some special attributes like natural resource of high importance to human beings. This is because investments in a developing economy are alloted in an inverse proportion to the locational difference of spatial units in relation to the central place. Consequently, in the present situation of the Indian economy investment falls as the distance between a spatial unit and the centrality of economic activity increases. Thus, the regional inequality between spatial units is sustained. Therefore, a measure of functional hierarchy between spatial units does not simply provide us with a clear concept regarding the decentralization process, unless a relationship between functional hierarchy and physical distance is established.

2. Description of a Case Study

In view of measuring the above mentioned relationship, we have studied urban economic activity in West Bengal at a district level. The data relate to the year 1977. Two important sectors of economic activity have been chosen, viz. manufacturing and tertiary activity. We will show that the patterns of the abovementioned relationships for

the respective sectors are not at all similar. The estimation of the
relationships implies two stages. In the first stage we are required
to measure functional hierarchy among the districts for the two
sectors. The second stage is concerned with estimating an appropriate
relationship between functional hierarchy and locational difference.

Functional hierarchy is a measurable function based on different
variables obtained from each sector. The basic information available
is in terms of number of workers in each sector. Here the point to be
noted is that the variables to be derived should preserve their
comparability over different spatial units. As far as the measure for
functional hierarchy is concerned, we employ the method of unequal
weighting system (Kendall 1939). The estimation of the relationship
between functional hierarchy and locational difference is of much
importance. We will carry out a detailed investigation on the
methodology at hand.

Since Calcutta is the only metropolitan city in West Bengal and
possesses a strong gravity for attracting investments in non-agricultural activity, we will develop an index of physical distance of the
districts in relation to Calcutta. Thus, the physical distance for
Calcutta itself has been put equal to zero. The physical distances
between Calcutta and a certain spatial unit is measured by the shortest
geographical difference between the center of Calcutta and the center
of the spatial unit. The geographical centers of the districts of
Howrah, Hooghly and 24 Paraganas, Siliguri for Darjeeling district, and
the respective headquarters of the remaining districts have been chosen
as the centers for measuring physical distances. For this, we have
used a district-level map of West Bengal. It may however be noted that
the choice of these centers evidently implies a certain subjective
element. It would have been better if we could have taken the average
route distance between Calcutta and the towns of each spatial unit.
However, as the data were not available to us, we had to take the
physical distance as described above.

3. The Model Used

Let there be $(p_1, p_2, \ldots p_k)$ variables chosen to measure the
level of economic activity for every spatial unit. Here, functional
hierarchy is measured by the level of economic activity. Therefore, if
y is the prevailing level of economic activity in a spatial unit, y is
a function of the p_i's. That is, $y = F(p_1, p_2, \ldots p_k)$.

We want to estimate the function G in the system $y = G(x)$ where x
denotes the physical distance between Calcutta and the spatial unit
concerned. We now define the rate of centralization as $\dfrac{dy}{y}$

We have chosen the following functional forms for G:

(i) $y = G_1(x) = K\, a^{b^x}, \ b > 0, \ a > 0, \ y > 0, \ x \geqslant 0$

(ii) $y = G_2(x) = a + bx > 0$

For the first type of function we have:

$$\frac{dy}{y} = \frac{dG_1}{dy} = (\log a)(\log b)\, b^x dx, \ a > 0, \ b > 0$$

310

We can now get two types of centralization rates. When log a < 0 and b < 1, or log a < 0 and b > 1, we find that the rate of centralization is decreasing. It is increasing when log a > 0 and b < 1, or log a > 0 and b < 1. It is however interesting to note that the rate of centralization becomes zero, when b is unity. That would imply that a perfect decentralization is prevailing among the spatial units.

For the second type of function, we find:

$$\frac{dy}{y} = \frac{\frac{dG_2}{dy}}{y} = \frac{b}{y} \, dx = \quad dx, \, (a + bx) > 0$$

If $b > 0$, $\frac{dy}{y}$ is decreasing; if b < 0, $\frac{dy}{y}$ is also decreasing. If $b = 0$, $\frac{dy}{y}$ vanishes implying a case of perfect decentralization. Thus, we find that the rate of centralization is always decreasing for a linear relationship. However, it may be noted that the second type of function with a decreasing rate of centralization is always better than the first type of function. Now, we shall first estimate the level of economic activity, after which we shall attempt to identify the relationship between the level of economic activity (y) and physical distance (x). We have already mentioned that we have chosen two sectors of non-agricultural economic activity, viz. manufacturing and tertiary activity. The former activity is mainly made up by urban workers engaged in manufacturing and repair services, while the latter includes the following subsectors: wholesale and retail trade, restaurants and hotels, transport, storage, warehousing and communication, and finally financing, insurance, real estate and business services. The data on workers in different sectors are available in a published report (Economic Review 1979-80) from the government of West Bengal. The data relate to 1977. For constructing different variables in each sector or sub-sector, we need urban and rural population data for 1977. Using the growth rates during 1961-1971, we have obtained projected estimates for the year 1977. We have selected the following five variables (for each sector i):

Q_{1i} = Urban workers in sector i per thousand of total workers (urban + rural) in the district.

Q_{2i} = Urban workers in sector i per thousand of total urban workers in the district.

Q_{3i} = Urban workers in sector i per hundred sq. kms. of urban area in the district.

Q_{4i} = Urban workers in sector i per thousand of urban population in the district.

Q_{5i} = Urban workers in sector i per thousand of total population in the district (i = 1,..5).

In order to derive level of economic activity we have transformed the variables in order to improve mutual correlations. The transformed variables are given below.

Manufacturing activity:

Sector 1: $P_{i1} = \log (Q_{i1} + 1)$ for i = 1,4

$= \log (10Q_{i1} + 1)$ for i = 5

Tertiary activity:

Sector 2: $P_{i2} = Q_{i2}$ for $i = 1, \ldots 5$

Sector 3: $P_{i3} = \log(10Q_{i3} + 1)$ for $i = 1, 4$

$\qquad = \log(Q_{i3} + 1)$ for $i = 2, 3$

$\qquad = \log(100Q_{i3} + 1)$ for $i = 5$

Sector 4: $P_{i4} = \log(10_{I4} + 1)$ for $i = 1, 4$

$\qquad = \log(Q_{i4} + 1)$ for $i = 2, 3$

$\qquad = \log(100Q_{i4} + 1)$ for $i = 5$

Sector 5: $P_{i5} = Q_{i5}$ for $i = 1, \ldots 5$

Now we derive the levels of economic activity by aggregating five variables into a single one with the help of the unequal weighting system (Kendall 1939; see Appendix I).

Manufacturing Activity:

$y = 0.034305\ P_{11} + 0.047490\ P_{21} + 0.028076\ P_{31}$

$\quad + 0.055363\ P_{41} + 0.023974\ P_{51}$

Tertiary Activity:

$Y = -0.076800\ Z_2 + 0.332459 Z_3 + 0.402652 Z_4 + 0.341690 Z_5$

Where

$Z_2 = 0.0038128\ P_{12} + 0.0031881\ P_{22} + 0.0000049 P_{32}$

$\quad + 0.017316\ P_{42} + 0.015601 P_{52}$

$Z_3 = 0.0555110\ P_{13} + 0.059630\ P_{23} + 0.032607\ P_{33}$

$\quad + 0.054676\ P_{43} + 0.029000\ P_{53}$

$Z_4 = 0.044540\ P_{14} + 0.040272\ P_{24} + 0.033421\ P_{34}$

$\quad + 0.036042\ P_{44} + 0.034525\ P_{54}$

$Z_5 = 0.0099422\ P_{15} + 0.0097368\ P_{25} + 0.000013551\ Y_{35}$

$\quad + 0.045608\ P_{45} + 0.042644\ P_{55}$

4. Relationships Between Physical Distance and Economic Activity

The next phase of our estimation concerns the estimation of relationships between physical distance and level of economic activity for manufacturing and tertiary activity. We have plotted the scatters in Figures 1 and 2. For the manufacturing activity it is evident that either G_1 or a combination of G_1 and G_2 would yield a decreasing rate of centralization. When we try to estimate G_1 (taking all observations together), we observe that the size of manufacturing activity is falling with an increasing rate of centralization. Thus, the estimate of G_1 gives a concave curve which does not fit with the scatter. But when for the first nine observations (Calcutta, Howrah, Hooghly, 24 Paraganas, Burdwan, Nadia, Midnapore, Bankura and Burdwan; See Figure 1) we estimate G_1; we obtain a relationship that indicates that manufacturing activity is decreasing with a decreasing rate of centralization. The curve looks convex and is in agreement with the scatter shown in Figure 1. Since the observation relating to Birbhum appears in the transitional zone, we estimate G_2 taking into consideration the last 8 observations (Birbhum, Murshidabad, Purulia, Malda, W. Dinajpur, Cooch-Behar, Jalpaiguri and Darjeeling). This is also in agreement with the scatter. Therefore, we obtain the following relationship between level of manufacturing activity and physical distance form Calcutta:

$$y = 1.23380 \ (0.97879)^{1.05593^x}$$

$$R^2 = 0.85488 \text{ (based on the first 9 observations)}$$

$$= 0.98279 - 0.000851 \ x \text{ (based on the last 8 observations)}$$

$$R^2 = 0.2709$$

For the tertiary activity, we have plotted the scatter in Figure 2. If the observation related to Calcutta is excluded, we observe that the relationship is linear. The estimated relationship is given below:

$$y = 0.8434 + 0.0019 \ x$$

$$R^2 = 0.5774 \text{ (based on the last 15 observations.}$$

Conclusions

The following facts emerge from our analysis. Although the districts of Burdwan, Howrah, Hooghly, 24 Paraganas and Calcutta are having a very high level of manufacturing and repairing activity, they do not have even a medium level of tertiary activity (except Calcutta). The reason is very obvious. As far as the districts of Burdwan, Howrah, Hooghly and 24 Paraganas are concerned, they are close to Calcutta and therefore dependent on the tertiary economy of Calcutta. Consequently, tertiary activity in these districts could not grow in proportion to the level of manufacturing activity in these districts owing to the pull of tertiary activity in Calcutta. This suggests that a pivotal centralized marketing system was prevailing in West Bengal in 1977. A reverse phenomenon holds good for districts which are located very far from the district of Calcutta. Thus, the wide locational differences between Calcutta and these districts have caused tertiary activity in these districts to grow. These districts are for example Jalpaiguri, Darjeeling, Cooch Behar and Purulia, where the level of tertiary activity is high or very high compared to the level of manufacturing activity (low or very low). The analysis related to the relationships between the level of economic activity and physical distance suggests that it is difficult for tertiary activity of any area to grow, if the area is closely located to another area which already has a reasonably high potential of tertiary activity. Again

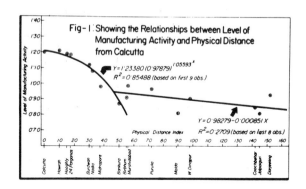

Fig-1: Showing the Relationships between Level of Manufacturing Activity and Physical Distance from Calcutta

$Y = 1.23380 (0.97879)^{1.05593^x}$

$R^2 = 0.85488$ (based on first 9 obs.)

$Y = 0.98279 - 0.000851 X$

$R^2 = 0.2709$ (based on last 8 obs.)

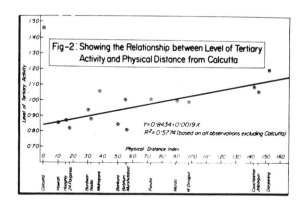

Fig-2: Showing the Relationship between Level of Tertiary Activity and Physical Distance from Calcutta

$Y = 0.8434 + 0.0019 X$

$R^2 = 0.5774$ (based on all observations excluding Calcutta)

tertiary activity of an area situated far from the highly developed area can grow, when it escapes from the grip of the highly developed area. However, this is not the case for manufacturing activity.

The relationship between level of manufacturing activity and physical distance gives a concave curve for the first set of observations, and a straight line for the last set of observations. Furthermore, we have obtained a straight line for tertiary activity. This indicates a better process of decentralization than a non-linear one. Since this study provides a rate of centralization at each level of economic activity, it sketches a guideline for reorientation required to decentralize an economic activity over spatial units.

APPENDIX I

The Weighting System

Let $I = r_i \dfrac{(x_i - \bar{x}_i)}{s_i} + r_2 \dfrac{(x_2 - \bar{x}_2)}{s_2} + \ldots \ldots + r_n \dfrac{(x_n - x_n)}{s_n}$

where x_i =   mean value of ith variable $i = 1, ..n$
     s_i =   standard deviation of x_i
     n   =   number of variables to be aggregated.

For the unequal weighting system, the r_i's represent the correlation coefficient between I and x_i, $i = 1, \ldots n$; λ in the largest latent root of the correlation matrix of the constituent variables.

For the equal weighting system, $r_i, = 1$, so that the r_i's no longer represent correlation coefficients between I and x_i, $i = 1$, ...n. The correlation coefficients between I and x_i are equal in the system. The standard deviation of I is equal to the correlation coefficient between I and x_i's.

Here for both methods, we slightly alter the form of I for the estimation procedure. I has a mean equal to zero. We adjust it to get a mean of unity. Define now z which has been used as the index for activity as follows:

$$Z = I + 1 = b_1 x_1 + b_2 x_2 + \ldots \ldots + b_n x_n$$
where $b_i = r_i / s_i k$, $i = 1, \ldots n$
and $k = \sum_{i=1}^{n} r_i \bar{x}_i / s_i$

APPENDIX II

Sectoral Subdivision

Subsectors
1.   :   Manufacturing and repair services
2.   :   Wholesale and retail trade
3.   :   Restaurant and hotels
4.   :   Transport, storage, warehousing and communication
5.   :   Financing, insurance, real estate and business services.

Subsectors 2, 3, 4 and 5 make up the tertiary activity, while subsector 1 makes up the manufacturing activity.

315

Calculation of Activity Indices

A: For computing the index of manufacturing activity, we calculated the following correlation matrix between P_{11}, P_{21}, P_{31}, P_{41} and P_{51}:

	P_{11}	P_{21}	P_{31}	P_{41}	P_{51}
P_{11}	1.0000				
P_{21}	0.9117	1.0000			
P_{31}	0.7820	0.6326	1.0000		
P_{41}	0.9137	0.8424	0.7936	1.0000	
P_{51}	0.9057	0.7857	0.8884	.9086	1.0000

Y (the index of manufacturing activity)

$$= \begin{array}{l} 0.034305\ P_{11} + 0.04790\ P_{21} + 0.028076\ P_{31} \\ (0.96892) \qquad\quad (0.89508) \qquad\qquad (0.87669) \end{array}$$

$$\begin{array}{l} + 0.055363\ P_{41} + 0.023974\ P_{51} \\ \ \ (0.95742) \qquad\quad\ (0.96319) \end{array}$$

Figures in brackets indicate the correlation coefficients between the index of manufacturing activity and the respective variables.

B: For computing the index of tertiary activity, we have to obtain four indices for the four subsectors 2, 3, 4 and 5.

B_1 : Let Z_2 denote the index of wholesale and retail trade activity which has been obtained on the basis of the following correlation matrix between P_{12}, P_{22}, P_{32}, P_{42} and P_{52}:

	P_{12}	P_{22}	P_{32}	P_{42}	P_{52}
P_{12}	1.0000				
P_{22}	0.5946	1.0000			
P_{32}	0.8660	0.5020	1.0000		
P_{42}	0.7738	0.7370	0.7949	1.0000	
P_{52}	0.9124	0.4994	0.9863	0.7860	1.0000

$$Z_2 = \begin{array}{l} 0.0038128 P_{12} + 0.0031881 P_{22} + 0.0000049 P_{32} \\ \ \ (0.93469) \quad\ \ (0.72186) \quad\ \ (0.94051) \end{array}$$

$$\begin{array}{l} + 0.017316 P_{42} + 0.015601 P_{52} \\ \ \ (0.91252) \qquad\quad (0.94885) \end{array}$$

Figures in brackets indicate the correlation coefficients between the index of wholesale and retail trade activity and the respective variables.

B_2 : Let Z_3 denote the index of restaurant and hotel activity which has been obtained on the basis of the following correlation matrix between P_{13}, P_{23}, P_{33}, P_{43} and P_{53}:

	P_{13}	P_{23}	P_{33}	P_{43}	P_{53}
P_{13}	1.0000				
P_{23}	0.6528	1.0000			
P_{33}	0.7319	0.5447	1.0000		
P_{43}	0.6765	0.8122	0.7199	1.0000	
P_{53}	0.8491	0.4428	0.7914	0.5877	1.0000

$$Z_3 = 0.055510P_{13} + 0.059630P_{23} + 0.032607P_{33}$$
$$\quad\ (0.90880)\ \ \ (0.79258)\ \ \ (0.88079)$$

$$+\ 0.054676P_{43} + 0.029000P_{53}$$
$$\quad (0.87720)\qquad\ (0.85515)$$

Figures in brackets indicate the correlation coefficients between the index of restaurant and hotel activity and the respective variables.

B_3 : Let Z_4 denote the index of transport, storage, warehousing and communication which has been obtained on the basis of the following correlation matrix between P_{14}, P_{24}, P_{34}, P_{44} and P_{54}:

	P_{14}	P_{24}	P_{34}	P_{44}	P_{54}
P_{14}	1.0000				
P_{24}	0.9103	1.0000			
P_{34}	0.8639	0.7885	1.0000		
P_{44}	0.9399	0.9688	0.8640	1.0000	
P_{54}	0.8406	0.6556	0.8619	0.7586	1.0000

$$Z_4 = 0.044540P_{14} + 0.040272P_{24} + 0.033421P_{34}$$
$$\quad\ (0.97381)\qquad\ \ (0.92617)\ (0.93436)$$

$$+\ 0.03642P_{44} + 0.034525P_{54}$$
$$\quad (0.96972)\qquad\ (0.87600)$$

Figures in brackets indicate the correlation coefficients between the index of transport, storage, warehousing and communication and the respective variables.

B_4: Let Z_5 denote the index of finance, insurance, real estate and business services activity which has been obtained on the basis of the following correlation matrix between P_{15}, P_{25}, P_{45} and P_{55}:

	P_{15}	P_{25}	P_{35}	P_{45}	P_{55}
P_{15}	1.0000				
P_{25}	0.9174	1.0000			
P_{35}	0.9961	0.9152	1.0000		
P_{45}	0.9800	0.9686	0.9765	1.0000	
P_{55}	0.9974	0.9005	0.9976	0.9700	1.0000

$$Z_5 = 0.0099422P_{15} + 0.0097368P_{25} + 0.000013551P_{35}$$
$$\quad (0.99363) \quad (0.95434) \quad (0.99254)$$

$$\quad + 0.045608 \ P_{45} + 0.042644 \ P_{55}$$
$$\quad (0.99415) \quad (0.98858)$$

Figures in brackets indicate the correlation coefficients between the index of finance, insurance, real estate and business services activity and the respective variables.

B_5 : Let Y denote the index of tertiary activity which has been obtained on the basis of the following correlation matrix between Z_2, Z_3, Z_4 and Z_5:

	Z_2	Z_3	Z_4	Z_5
Z_2	1.0000			
Z_3	0.7743	1.0000		
Z_4	0.2735	0.3219	1.0000	
Z_5	0.9196	0.5922	0.3403	1.0000

Y (= the index of tertiary activity)
$$= 0.076800Z_2 + 0.332459Z_3 + 0.402652Z_4 + 0.341690Z_5$$
$$\quad (0.77779) \qquad (0.77779) \qquad (0.77779) \qquad (0.77779)$$

Here, we have followed the system of equal weighting (instead of unequal weighting), for which each Z_2, Z_3, Z_4 and Z_5 is equally correlated with Y (being the index of tertiary activity). Figures in brackets show a correlation coefficient of 0.77779. This has been so as we do not want to discriminate between variables in their orders of representation in the index of tertiary activity. Each Z_2, Z_3, Z_4 and Z_5 is treated as equally important for constructing the index of tertiary activity (for the equal weighting system see also Pal, 1971, and De, 1980).

Indices of Activity and Distance

Districts	Index of Manu-facturing activity	Index of tertiary activity	Index of Physical Distance from Calcutta
(1)	(2)	(3)	(4)
1. Burdwan	1.1243	0.9413	30
2. Birbhum	0.9111	1.0050	55
3. Bankura	0.8747	0.8459	50
4. Midnapore	0.9670	1.0595	37
5. Howrah	1.2074	0.8563	10
6. Hooghly	1.1901	0.8697	15
7. 24 Paraganas	1.1870	0.8198	17
8. Nadia	1.0785	0.8821	32
9. Murshidabad	0.9866	0.8071	56
10. West Dinajpur	0.9068	0.9922	98
11. Malda	0.8113	0.9973	89
12. Jalpaiguri	0.8138	1.0586	145
13. Darjeeling	0.9276	1.2037	152
14. Cooch Behar	0.8508	1.0932	142
15. Purulia	0.9656	1.1080	72
16. Calcutta	1.1972	1.4601	0
Mean Value	1.0000	1.0000	--

References

Berry, B.J.L., (1960). 'An inductive approach to the regionalization of economic development', in: Essays on Geography and Economic Development, N. Ginsburg (ed.), The University of Chicago Press, Chicago.

Christaller, W., (1966). Central Places in Southern Germany, Prentice-Hall, Englewood Cliffs (N.J.).

Croxton, F.E., D.J. Gowden, and S. Klein, (1973). Applied General Statistics, Prentice Hall of India Private Ltd, New Delhi.

De, R.N., (1980). 'A note on two stages of aggregation of variables through equal weighting in every stage,' presented in the 4th World Congress of Econometric Society, held during August-September, Aix-en-Provence, France.

De, R.N., (1981). 'Economic regionalization of India 1960-61 and 1970-71: a study in quantitative methods,' Doctoral Dissertation, the Indian Statistical Institute, Calcutta.

Girshick, M.A., (1936). 'Principal components,' Journal of the American Statistical Association, Vol. 31.

Harris, C.D., (1954). 'The market as a factor in the localization of industry in the United States,' Annals of the Association of American Geographers, Vol. 44.

Holzinger, K. and H.H. Harmon, (1941). Factor Analysis: A Synthesis of Factorial Methods, The University of Chicago Press, Chicago.

Hotelling, H., (1933). 'Analysis of a complex statistical variables into principal components,' Journal of Educational Psychology, Vol. 24.

Kendall, M.G., (1939). 'The geographical distribution of crop productivity in England,' Journal of the Royal Statistical Society, Vol. 102.

Losch, A., (1954). The Economics of Location, New Haven, Yale University Press.

Pal, M.N., Prakash Rao and Tewari, (1968). 'A technique of ranking central places and determining linkages,' Paper contributed to the Symposium on Quantitative Methods in Geography, 21st International Geographical Congress, Mysore, December.

Pal, M.N., (1971). 'Quantitative techniques for regional planning,' Indian Journal of Regional Science, Vol. 3.

_____, (1974). 'Regional information, regional statistics and regional planning in India,' in: Regional Information and Regional Planning, A. Kuklinski (ed.), Mouton, The Hague.

Thurstone, L.L., (1931). 'Multiple factor ananlysis,' Psychological Review, Vol. 38.

Wilks, S.S., (1938). 'Weighting system for linear functions of correlated variables when there is no independent variables,' Psychometrika, Vol. 3.

24 Residential location decisions of multiple worker households in Bogota, Colombia

JOSE FERNANDO PINEDA

1. Introduction

The changing labor force composition of households in developing countries has stirred some interest in the impact of additional family workers on housing consumption and residential location. For Bogota in 1972 the average number of workers per family was 1.42. In 1978 this number had risen to 1.70, equivalent to an annual increment of 3%. The distribution of households by number of workers can be observed in Table 1. Households with more than one worker represented one half of the total number of households interviewed in 1978, while 20% of the interviewed families had three or more family members who declared some form of gainful occupation. From 1972 to 1978 the proportion of households with just one worker had been reduced by 10%.

One of the major obstacles to the measurement of the consequences of this phenomenon is the multiplicity of effects generated by the presence

TABLE 1

PERCENTAGE DISTRIBUTION OF HOUSEHOLDS ACCORDING TO
NUMBER OF WORKERS PER HOUSEHOLD
(Bogota 1972-1978)

Number of workers per household	Year	
	1972	1978
1	60	50
2	23	30
3	9	12
4 and more	8	8
Total	100.0 100.0	

Sources: 1972: Phase II Household Survey
1978: World Bank - DANE Household Survey (EH-21).

322

of additional workers in the household. This difficulty is further aggravated bvy the untenable nature of some traditional assumptions of residential location models (Alonso, 1964), such as the monocentricity assumption. In moving from the monocentric to the multicentric city, space looses its one-dimensional quality, making the analytical treatment of spatial processes more complex. In this brief essay (part of a larger work on residential location patterns), we present some estimates of the impact of additional workers on housing consumption and residential location in Bogota. The first part of the essay reviews briefly the residential location models and some previous findings. The second part provides a brief description of spatial processes in Bogota and the data base. The third section presents some results obtained, while the last part is a summary of conclusions.

2. Residential Location Models

In the traditional residential location models, households have two elements in their utility function: housing, Q, and other goods, Z. The price of housing is determined by a series of attributes like age of the dwelling unit, quality, amentities in the neighborhood and distance to the workzone. One of the major contributions of these models is their ability to demonstrate that a differential accessibility rent is reflected in the price of housing when the other housing attributes are controlled. As shown by Montesano (1972), the existence of an additive utility function and of transport costs that are positively associated with distance to the workplace, results in a housing price that declines with distance from the workzone. In addition, the household incurs some transport expenditures that decline with proximity to the employment center. In an equilibrium condition the marginal costs of transport with regard to distance should be equal to the absolute value of the marginal decrement in the expenditure on housing while holding its quantity and quality constant.

For each quantity of housing consumed we can then find a minimum expenditure location as shown in Figure 1. The actual amount of expenditure on housing and the remaining portion of income spent on other goods at the minimum expenditure point does not only reflect the housing expenditure, but also the optimal location for that given amount of housing and the expenditures on Z. This is graphically shown in Figure 2.

This very simple description allows us to understand the spatial impact of additional workers. Given the monocentricity assumption, an extra worker implies an incremental expenditure on transport and, ceteris paribus, a more central location. However, it also means an increase in household income which might be represented by an increase in housing consumption, forcing a more peripheral location. But in addition it also represents a decrease in the leisure time available to the household. If there is some degree of complementarity between housing and leisure time, an extra worker implies, ceteris paribus, a decrease in the quantity of housing services purchased. This effect would also indicate a more central location. White (1977) tried to derive a bid-price function for two-earner households where the husband works at the center and the wife at a peripheral location. The housing price offer curve depends on the value of the wife's leisure time (relative to her husband's) in the household's utility function. Since the slope of the bid-rent functions is known but not their intercepts,

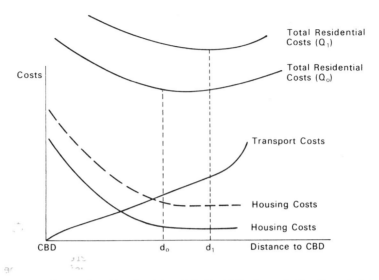

Figure 1.   The Residential Equilibrium of the Household.

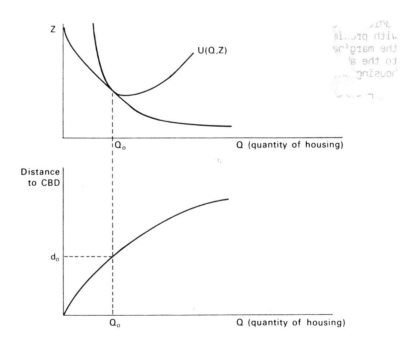

Figure 2.   Relationship Between Location, Housing
and Consumption.

White attempts to show by trial and error, that households with two workers would seek to locate closer to the wife's work place. However, this depends on the assumption that the bid rent function of two worker households is flatter between the two job centers than the one worker households. This is only true if the difference between the husband's wife's wage rates are smaller than the commuting outlays, a fact that does not necessarily hold. So, two-earner households might well stay closer to the husband's job than one-worker households.

Partially based on White's reasoning, Madden (1979) developed a model of three simultaneous equations to analyze differences in housing consumption between one- and two-earner households. The first equation explains the separation between place of work and residence for a worker in a multi-worker household as a function of each worker's wages, housing prices, number of hours worked by each household worker, and the household's unearned income. Wages are in turn a function of workplace location and worker's attributes, and housing prices depend both on the workplace-residence separation, and on a vector of market attributes. The second equation is for housing size and is in turn a function of the separation between work and residence, each worker's income, household unearned income, and household demographic characteristics. The third equation is related to quality of housing and is also a function of the variables included in the previous equation.

Madden concludes that differences in housing consumption between one-earner and two-earner households are fully explained by their differences in money income and fertility. In contrast to White's conclusions, Madden finds that men from two earner households live closer to their jobs than men with either non-employed wives or employed wives and employed children. However, none of these locational differences are statistically significant. In short, one- and two-earner households behave just the same when other relevant variables are controlled.

The methodology we use in the present study is somewhat different. First, we estimate housing prices by using the workzone stratification approach employed by Ingram (1979). The theoretical approach is based on the well known fact that workers commute down the rent gradient from their workplace and do so in the steepest direction, while workers facing the steepest gradient have the longest commuting distance. Hence different workplaces imply different residential areas and these differences in location are derived from the trade offs between housing prices and travel costs. The different workplace opportunity sets available to workers provide the basis for workplace-based price variations when using crosssection data. The hedonic price equations are obtained by regressing the rent of a unit on its constituent variables like distance to the workplace, distance from workplace to the city's CBD, type of building structure and quality of the dwelling unit. Having defined a "standard" housing unit, we estimate workzone specific housing prices by multiplying the estimated coefficients of each workzone by the respective attribute of the "standard" housing unit. If we consider rent expenditures as price times quantity, we obtain the quantity of housing by dividing monthly rent by price.

Once this quantity is assessed, we estimate the housing demand equation introducing income, household size, sex of the household head, price, and number of workers as independent variables. We also try to explain workplace-residence separation as a function of quantity of housing consumed and household characteristics. The quality of housing is taken care of in the hedonic price index. Since all workers in a household live in the same residence, their impact on location is estimated by looking at the length of the journey to work of just one of them. We have chosen the commuting distance of the household head as our dependent variable in the equation that explains workplace-residence separation.

3. The Case of Bogota

Bogota is a city of approximately 4.000.000 people located in the highlands of the Colombian Andes. During the early 1960's, its population expanded at annual geometric rates close to 7%. In the middle of the last decade its population growth rate has declined to less than 4% as a result of a decline in its birth rates (from 4.2% in 1960 to 2.6% in 1978) and a reduction in the inflow of migrants. From 1972 to 1978 its real per capita income grew at approximately 3% per year, while auto ownership expanded from 14% to 18% of all households.

The city has also become more decentralized. Estimates of the population density gradient are −0.177 and −0.112 for 1972 and 1978, respectively (cf. Pachon, 1980). The estimated density at the center for these two years went down from 356.7 inhabitants per hectare to 262.6. Employment has also become more decentralized. In 1972 the Central Business District had 22% of the total number of jobs in the city and this percentage went down to 14% six years later. Another indication of the same phenomenon is the change in employment density gradients. Using a negative exponential function, the values of the gradient are −0.240 and −0.204, while the intercepts 135 and 116 jobs per hectare for 1972 and 1978, respectively. The CBD is more or less at the center, and the wealthiest neighborhoods are located along a corridor that goes from the city center to the north. Low income households are located almost everywhere. One could say it is the upper income groups that are segregated and not the low income households. Growth of population has mainly occurred in the periphery of the city. In short, Bogota shows a marked change in its spatial structure and the signs of the emergence of a sub-urbanization process. However, given the growth of the administrative boundaries of the city, most of the population living and working in the city is covered by only one local administration. This distinguishes the city from large urban agglomerations in North America.

Our data stems from two households surveys. The first one was carried out in 1972 by a United Nations study on transportation (including roughly 4.000 households living within the administrative boundaries of the city). The survey contains information on transportation, housing, labor force, and employment location. Secondly, in 1978 the World Bank City Study project sponsored a household survey to update the 1972 information (covering 3.056 households). This survey represented a significant improvement of the quality of the information obtained, in particular with regard to income estimates. Every worker in the household was interviewed about his or her income from all sources including fringe benefits (something that was not included in the 1972 household survey). The city was divided into 38 zones, called communas by the National Statistical Agency, and expansion rates were calculated at this communa level.

4. Results

Our analysis started with some very simple measures of residential location. For each household with two or more workers we derived three distance measures: D_1 (distance between the residence and the place of work of the household head), D_2 (distance between the place of work of the secondary worker and his or her residence), and D_3 (distance between the two workzones). A closer examination of these distances on the basis of the household surveys led to the identification of five commuting patterns.

The first one may be called the short distance commuting case where both the household head and the secondary worker have their jobs close to their home. The second one is called household head commuting, where the household head travels long distances while the secondary worker stays close to home. The third pattern is the complement of the second one: the head commutes less than one kilometer and the additional worker travels longer distances. The fourth case is where both household heads and secondary workers travel long distances but to the same workzone. The last location pattern is made up by combinations of cases. Table 2 summarizes the percentage distribution of cases for Bogota in 1972 and 1978 among the five patterns illustrated. The decline in the number of short distance commuting cases from one year to the other is noteworthy.

TABLE 2
PERCENTAGE DISTRIBUTION OF RESIDENTIAL LOCATION PATTERNS
(Bogota 1972 - 1978)

Type of commuting pattern	Percentage of cases 1972	1978	Percentage change per year
Short distance commuting	14.5	6.4	-1.01
Household head commuting	11.8	7.3	-0.56
Secondary worker commuting	12.0	9.0	-0.37
Joint commuting	27.0	28.1	0.13
Other cases	34.7	49.2	1.81
TOTAL	100.0	100.0	

Next, the factors explaining the commuting pattern have been examined in greater detail. First, the age of the worker is a major determinant: very young workers and very old ones commute very short distances. Secondly education plays an important role: illiterates or workers with primary education have very short commuting distances. And thirdly, occupational status is an important factor: self-employed workers or family workers exhibit short journeys to work.

On the basis of these findings we classify additional (or secondary) workers into two categories: workers type 1, made up by

workers with high education, within 15 and 50 years old and not being
self-employed. The remaining workers are labelled workers type 2. For
each category of workers (household heads, secondary workers type 1 and
secondary workers type 2), we estimated employment density gradients
for both years. The results can be observed in Table 3. This table
indicates that the jobs of secondary workers type 2 are more
decentralized than either the jobs of household heads or secondary
workers type 1. Thus there is some correlation between the type of
skills required on the demand side of employment and its location. In
short, more qualified workers are more likely to have central job
locations, while workers type 2 certainly have more peripheral job
opportunities. If the household head's workplace is central, the
impact exerted by secondary workers on the residential location will be
different depending on the combination of worker types existing in the
household. The classification of workers by type acts as a surrogate
for job location of workers.

The next step in the analysis has been the calculation of the
hedonic price index, in order to explain in more detail the rent of
dwellings paid by various household categories in terms of distances
from home to work and to CBD, age and size of the dwelling, and other
dwelling characteristics.

In Table 4 we present the demand equation for "housing services"
corresponding to a Stone-Geary utility function of the household. The
elasticity for household head's income is statistically different from
the one obtained from secondary workers income. Secondary workers
contribute less of their earnings to housing consumption than household
heads do. The number of secondary workers in the household implies
also a decrease in housing consumption, a fact that could be attributed
to the complimentarity between household leisure time and quantity of
housing services desired: The consumption of housing decreases as the
leisure time of the household declines. In order to assess the impact
of additional workers on residential location, we take the distance
between the household head's workzone and his or her place of residence
as the dependent variable. Then Q enters as an independent variable in
combination with variables related to household composition (number of
workers by type, number of persons in the household), a series of
attributes of the household head (age, sex, occupational status,
workzone) and the income of both household heads and secondary
workers. The results are included in Table 5. The results indicate
that as housing consumption increases, travelled distance increases, a
result also predicted by residential location models (Alonso, 1964).
If income rises, the length of the journey to work also increases.
Male household heads have longer journeys to work, older males travel
shorter distances, and self-employed persons reduce their journey to
work. Secondary workers type 1 having more central locations
contribute to a reduction in the commuting distance of household heads,
while secondary workers type 2 show an increase. A separation of
workers clearly improves the understanding of their impact on
residential location. Running the same regression with no discrimination of workers by type shows no secondary workers effect. However,
the coefficient of the secondary workers income is not very clear. As
their income rises, distance travelled by the head declines. The
negative relationship might be due to the correlation between number of
workers type 1 and secondary workers income: most of the secondary
workers income comes from the earnings of type 1 additional workers.

TABLE 3

EMPLOYMENT DENSITY GRADIENTS BY TYPE OF WORKER

(Bogota 1972 - 1978)[1]

Type of worker	1972				1978			
	D_0	b	R^2	F-value	D_0	b	R^2	F-value
Household heads	166.0	0.25	.65	68.8	146.3	0.23	.66	71.9
Secondary Workers I	128.5	0.283	.55	47.7	106.1	0.45	.43	29.5
Secondary Workers II	110.0	0.22	.73	97.6	95.6	0.18	.65	72.7

[1] Equations are of the usual form: Density $= D_0 e^{-br}$, where r is distance in kilometers.

TABLE 4

CONSUMPTION OF HOUSING SERVICES (Q) FOR RENTERS WITH MONTHLY
INCOME HIGHER THAN $2,000 (Bogota 1978)
(Housing consumption standardized to Unity)

	Mean value of variables	Regression Coefficients	t Values	Mean Elasticities
Q	1.00			
Rent	2.28			
Price	3.36^1	-.2162	19.6*	-.727
Household Head Incomes	8.14^1	.0810	9.5*	.660
Secondary Worker Income	3.07^1	.0540	5.3*	.166
No. of Persons	4.37	.0327	1.8**	.143
Sex of Household Head	0.84	-.1440	1.4	
Age of Household Head	34.35	.0009	2.6*	.311
No. of Workers 1	0.25	-.2792	3.1*	-.069
No. of Workers 2	0.38	-.1381	2.3*	-.057
Constant	0.7391			
R^2	.40			
No. of Observations	908			

^{1} in thousand pesos

*   Significant at the 99% level

** Significant at the 95% level.

TABLE 5

COMMUTING DISTANCE[1] OF HOUSEHOLD HEAD (D_1) FOR RENTER WITH HOUSEHOLD MONTHLY INCOME HIGHER THAN $2,000
(Bogota 1978)

Variable	Mean Value of Variable	Regression Coefficient	t Values	Estimated Elasticity
D_1	5.264			
Q	0.74	.1100	2.50	0.64
Price	3.36^2			
Head Income	8.14^2	0.040	3.60	.16
Secondary Worker				
Income	3.07^2	-0.030	2.10	-.57
No. of Persons	4.37	0.3131	6.05	.03
Sex	0.84	0.1632	1.96	
Age	34.35	-0.2065	5.33	
No. of Workers 1	0.25	-0.3614	2.01	-.58
No. of Workers 2	0.38	0.93010	2.71	.15
Self Employed	0.24	-0.1621	2.49	
Jobs at CBD	0.17	1.1695	2.65	
Age Squared	129.89	0.0013	1.84	
Constant	9.884			
R^2	.24			
No. of cases	908			

[1] Distance measured in kilometers.

[2] In thousand pesos.

5. Conclusion

We have tried to illustrate in this short essay the impact of the number of workers in a household in terms of the selection of a place to live and the consumption of housing services. In the selection of a place to live the household takes into consideration the job locations of all members in the labor force suggesting some form of joint decision-making. The impact of the additional workers appears to have three aspects. First, the extra income earned by them increases housing consumption, leading to a more peripheral location. Second, an increase in the number of workers in the household reduces the amount of space required by the household canceling somewhat their income effect. And, thirdly, when employment is not monocentric the household head increases or reduces his travelled distance depending on whether the additional worker travels in the opposite or the same direction to the head's workzone. Since in our sample most of the household heads and secondary workers type 1 have central job locations, while secondary workers type 2 have more peripheral ones, we get opposite signs by type of workers.

References

Alonso, W.A., (1964). <u>Location and Land Use</u>, Cambridge, MA: Harvard University Press.

Ingram, G.K., (1979). 'Housing demand in the developing metropolis,' Paper presented to the Annual Meeting of the Econometric Society, Atlanta, No. 6a, CII/79.

Madden, J.F., (1979). 'Urban land use and the growth in two-earner households,' Paper presented to the American Economic Association Meeting, Atlanta, No. 6a. XII/29/79.

Montesano, A., (1972). 'A restatement of Beckmann's model on the distribution of urban rent and residential density,' <u>Journal of Economic Theory</u>, Vol. 4, pp. 329-54.

Pachon, A., (1980). 'Auto-ownership and model choice in Bogota,' <u>World Bank</u>, Washington, (Mimeographed paper).

White, M.J., (1977). 'A model of residential location choice and commuting by men and women workers,' <u>Journal of Regional Science</u>, Vol. 17, No. 1, pp. 41-52.

25 The role of intermediate cities in national development: research issues

SALAH EL-SAKHS

1. Introduction

The primary purpose of this paper is to explore some of the issues and gaps in our knowledge concerning the development and function of intermediate cities in the developing countries. The role which such cities can, or indeed do, play in national development processes has increasingly gained the attention of development specialists, planners, and policy-makers. It has recently become the specific focus of several international meetings of development experts (Fawcett, et al., 1980; UNCRD, 1982; and Mathur, 1982). Such meetings were designed to explore research issues and strategies needed for a better understanding of the nature, function, and role of such cities in socio-economic and spatial development of their regional and national systems. The planning and development of intermediate cities in developing countries has also recently become a significant objective of international assistance agencies (Randinelli, 1981; World Bank, 1980).

2. The Logic of Intermediate City Development

The development of intermediate cities is seen as a strategy to create a more balanced urban hierarchy, and thus help reduce pressure on primate cities, moderate spatial inequalities, enhance rural development, and foster embrionic or latent forces of polarization reversal. Less developed countries undergoing the process of urban concentration are faced with the challenges of: promoting national economic growth and full utilization of their resources yet, at the same time, promoting regional equity and avoiding or reducing excessive development disparities and concentration. While these two objectives may not necessarily be in conflict, particularly within a long range development perspective, (Stohr, 1975, p. 66), they require coordinated economic and spatial development policies and plans, at both regional and national levels, for the efficient distribution of population and economic activities.

Intermediate cities are expected to play a crucial role in this process. While there is no magic formula for an optimum distribution of functions, or more generally for a hierarchy of urban places, since that changes with development contexts and overtime, it does seem that a more balanced spatial and size distribution of cities would help speed up and smooth spatial transition, and ultimately enhance the efficiency of the future urban system. Although the arguments that continued concentration in large cities, beyond a reasonable minimum

size, may be necessary for overall economic efficiency, or that cities
become less efficient beyond a certain size, pose importnat research
issues, they become almost meaningless in this context. If the
capacity to organize, efficiently plan, and service very large cities
is low (which is the case in most LDCs), and if additional growth in
large cities is neither associated with nor necessary for major
additional industrial expansion, then pursuing hierarchical balance and
distributional equities become the singifincant challenges for both
short and long range urbanization and development strategies.

Cities have been described as the engines of development and their
size and spatial distribution determines their efficiency in performing
such a role. Suggestions have frequently been made for a balanced
urban hierarchy in line with the central place precepts. This means a
large spatially organized pattern of towns and cities of all sizes with
a decreasing number as sizes and functions increase. Such patterns, it
is argued, would help create a wider range of options for migrants,
vitalize rural areas through easy access to services and amentities,
counteract the attraction of primate cities through competitive
regional centers, serve the needs of urban industrial growth through
the development of sufficiently large scale economies in middle-size
cities, and help diffuse innovation and growth impulses down the urban
hierarchy.

Counter-arguments, however, have maintained that such hierarchies
failed to positively spread innovations and income effects, may
encourage greater migration from rural areas, may spread available
resources too thin to have an impact, and may reduce the overall
economic growth potential of concentrated urbanization. The optimality
of urban distributions is a function of the spatial context and the
levels of urbanization and of development. There is no magic formula
for an optimum urban distribution since it changes over time. While a
more balanced urban hierarchy would help smooth spatial transitions,
and ultimately enhance the efficiency of the future urban system, its
efficiency at any given point in time is a function of the society's
goals (with respect to inter-regional equity for example) and the
performance of its largest urban centers (Richardson, 1977, p. 12-17).

Studies of the optimum size of cities seem to point out that while
a minimum size threshold may indeed be necessary to achieve adequate
economies of scale, within a country's context, an optimum size (at
which the net benefits of additional growth become zero) is much more
questionable. The former is a function of the location and role of the
city and the development of its urban system, while the latter is a
function of internal organization and planning capacity (Richardson,
1977). Optimality thus becomes a more subjective concept related to
level of development and development goals, capacity to plan and
culturally determined tolerance levels of interaction.

Thus the notion of minimum size may indeed require high degrees of
primacy at low levels of urbanization and development (Renaud, 1981, p.
108). However, even if long term economic and spatial convergence is
an ultimate eventuality there are compelling demographic, social, and
political reasons to guide it and speed it up through public policy.
Such reasons include the imbalance between the rates of national
population and economic growth, inefficient distribution of population
in relation to resources and technological capacities, glaring spatial

and social inequities in income and development levels, and the incapacity of local institutions and resources to cope with the changing demands and complexities of urbanization and counter-urbanization processes. Thus, most of the developing countries have increasingly exhibited a policy bias for decentralization of spatial development in favor of small and intermediate-sized cities as a reaction to the failure of market spread mechanisms in enhancing the overall efficiency of the urban settlement system (Mathur 1982).

2. Identification of Intermediate Cities

The definition of intermediate cities is necessarily a relative concept. Such cities would have to be identified in terms of size and spatial distribution, economic and political interactions, and administrative and service functions within their settlement systems. While population size criteria may be convenient, they are quite inadequate within urban systems, and much more so in cross-country comparisons, for a variety of conceptual as well as statistical reasons Richardson, 1982).

However, determining intermediacy in terms of function and interaction is difficult and requires a great deal of information about individual cities as well as their national settlement systems (Randinelli, 1982). Randinelli, therefore, defined intermediate cities as those with a population between 100,000 and the largest city or cities in each system. His analysis indicated that while such cities have been growing in both number and population since 1950, their relative growth and capacity to absorb population increases has been weak in most developing nations (Randinelli, 1982, p. 360). Clearly, the evidence indicates that small cities, with less than 100,000 in population, in developing countries fared even worse in their growth relative to large cities (Table 1). Indeed the growth of intermediate and small-size cities seem to surpass that of the largest cities only in highly developed countries (Table 2).

It seems that as countries develop, and as the process of polarization reversal gains added momentum, the focus of urban growth is likely to shift in a step-wise process down the size-hierarchy of cities. That is, the process of deconcentration will first impact the secondary national urban centers then large regional centers and so on. Thus the role of intermediate cities in national development could be expected to intensify only after the polarization-reversal process begins and, even then, only in a time sequence commensurate with their size. Their latent role as a factor in helping bring about reversal trends, however, lies in their ability to prepare the stage through spatial equalization of levels of infrastructure, amenities, political awareness, and income. The United States' and, more recently, the Japanese experience tend to confirm such a sequence (Ito and Tanifuji, 1982). (See Table 2).

Maximizing the benefits and minimizing the costs of decentralization strategies in LDCs undergoing a concentration process, therefore, would largely depend on the choice of target locations and the type and mix of activities. Where the goal is to counter the primacy of the largest cities, in a step-wise process of urban deconcentration, already established cities with adequate levels of

TABLE 1

GROWTH OF URBAN POPULATION BY SETTLEMENT SIZE IN THE LESS DEVELOPED REGIONS OF THE WORLD
1960-2000 (in millions)

Region and Settlement Category	1960	1980	% Growth 1960-1980	2000	% Growth 1980-2000	% Growth 1960-2000
Africa						
less than 100,000	22.6	46.8	107	96.7	107	328
100,000 +	26.9	86.2	220	249.1	189	826
Total Urban	49.5	133.0	169	345.8	160	599
Latin America						
Less than 100,000	50.5	82.8	64	111.3	34	120
100,000 +	56.1	157.8	181	354.9	125	533
Total Urban	106.6	240.6	126	466.2	94	337
South Asia						
Less than 100,000	70.5	125.0	77	251.8	101	257
100,000 +	76.4	204.8	168	538.9	163	605
Total Urban	146.9	329.8	80	790.7	140	438
East Asia:*						
Less than 100,000	88.2	129.7	47	191.2	47	117
100,000 +	106.5	229.8	116	431.2	88	305
Total Urban	194.7	359.5	85`	622.4	73	220

* Includes Japan.

Source: P.M. Hauser and R.W. Gardner, "Urban Future: Trends and Prospects," in Population and the Urban Future, (N.Y.: UNFPA, 1980).

service and administrative infrastructure seem to provide a better chance of success for such strategies.

The size, location and function of cities plays an important role in the indentification of likely candidates. Spontaneously growing cities, where additional stimulus and administrative organization and coordination would have a major impact, provide appropriate targets "since policies can swim with the stream much more effectively than against it." (Richardson, 1977, p. 60). Such cities usually fall in the second tier in terms of function and size group, and are strategically located within the transportation and communication network, either nationally or within relatively independent large regional subsystems. They include regional and administrative centers and secondary centers of specialized economic activities (e.g., ports,

TABLE 2

POPULATION INCREASE IN THE LARGEST, INTERMEDIATE, AND
SMALL CITIES IN THE UNITED STATES AND JAPAN
1960-2000 (Population in millions)

Category	1960	1980	% Increase 1960-1980	2000	% Increase 1980-2000
United States:					
Ten largest Cities	47	65	38	76	17
Intermediate Cities	52	87	67	116	33
Cities less than 100,000	22	10	-55	17	70
Total Urban	121	162	34	209	29
Japan					
Five largest Cities	20	35	75	41	17
Intermediate Cities	9	19	111	25	32
Cities less than 100,000	29	37	27	45	22
Total Urban	58	91	57	111	22

Sources: Computed from data in Urban, Rural and City Population,
1950-2000: As Assessed in 1978, (New York: United Nations
Population Division, ESA/P/WP.66, June 1980).

mineral or hydroelectric resources, religious or cultural centers,
resort areas, etc.). Their sizes vary with city size distributional
characteristics (over 100,000 in Brazil, Mexico, Egypt, India,
Philippines and R. of Korea, less than that in Nigeria and Indonesia,
and over half a million in Japan), (Richardson, 1977, p. 60:
El-Shakhs, 1980).

3. Intermediate City Development Strategy Issues

The growth of intermediate size cities has been associated not only
with industrial decentralization (industrial estates, tax incentives,
and preferential treatment), but perhaps more importantly with the
growth in tertiary activities (services, wholesale trade, and government employment) and a greater local control over resources and the
budget. This is particularly the case when intermediate cities are not
located close to the largest city where they serve as satellite
extensions within an expanding core region.

It is therefore important to focus our attention on the effects of
redistribution of effective power, broadening the base of decision-
making, and local initiative and participation. The psychological,
social, and political factors of development need to be better understood within the context of integrated functional-area planning at
local and regional levels. The division of authority and responsibility among different levels of government, including those for
planning and budgeting, raises important issues. Frequently, municipal

authorities are delegations of national government power and depend on national decisions for the major part of their financing, organization, and operation. This often results in weak local governments who lack the power, resources, and flexibility to respond to changes within their own boundaries. It may also be non-conducive to the development of strong leadership or a clear local identity.

Efforts of national integration under conditions of concentrated fiscal and decision-making power and high degrees of regional inequalities, characteristic of most developing nations, tend to work against the growth of intermediate cities (El-Shakhs, 1982). In many countries, progress in administrative decentralization is very slow and may be out of step with local realities. Rather than fostering interdependent development, it tends to increase dependency on core regions and primate cities.

Experience indicates that economic decentralization and diffusion strategies would tend to succeed where inequalities are low, local governments are strong and locational and resource endowments are high (Stohr and Todtling, 1978). The effects of integovernmental fiscal relations (Japan, Republic of Korea), regionalization of the budget (France, Sweden) and revenue sharing with a measure of local autonomy (Nigeria, U.S.) indicate the importance of fiscal and administrative decentralization in the development of secondary and intermediate cities.

As a redistribution and equalization strategy, administrative decentralization has three distinct dimensions (or functions): economic, institutional, and political. In an economic sense, it is a redistribution of public and government employment which, in most developing countries and centrally planned economies, accounts for a substantial proportion of total formal sector employment, personal income and purchasing power. Institutionally, it provides an important component of the social infrastructure, local organizational capacity and nurtures the creation of the demand for, and supply of, local services and amenities. Politically, its effect could range from the simple creation of local bureaucratic constituency (an interest group within the national bureaucracy), to broadening the base of decision-making, participation and initiative necessary for integrated regional development.

The important role of intermediate cities in promoting integrated regional development raises a number of additional research questions regarding their own functions, growth strategies, and internal structure and planning:

a)   How and to what extent does the internal structure of population and activities impact the expansion and organization of the informal sector? How does it affect the transmission of development impulses into the hinterlands through circulatory migration?

b)   What are the symbolic and functional qualities and attributes of successful regional development centers (quality of life, nationally prominent activity, unique regional identity and specialization, communications and mass media links with their hinterlands, etc.)?

c) To what extent would the <u>metropolitanization</u> of intermediate
    cities (polycentric development, expansion along
    transportation routes, differentiation and decentralization of
    functions into neighboring satellite centers, etc.) help in
    the spatial interaction and integration and the diffusion of
    urbanization within their regions?

References

El-Shakhs, S., (1980). 'National and regional issues and policies in facing the challenges of the Urban Future,' Populations and the Urban Future, Rome: UNFPA.

_____, (1982). 'Regional development and national integration: the Third World,' Urban Affairs Annual Reviews: 22, pp. 137-58.

Fawcett. J.T. et al., (1980). Summary Report: Intermediate Cities in Asia Meeting, Honolulu: East-West Population Institute.

Ito, T. and M.Tanifuji, (1982). 'The role of small and intermediate cities in national development in Japan,' in O.P. Mathur, (ed.), Small Cities and National Development, Nagoya: UNCRD, pp. 71-100.

Mathur, Om P., (1982). 'The role of small cities in national development re-examined,' in O.P. Mathur (ed.), Small Cities and National Development, Nagoya: UNCRD pp. 6-7.

_____, (1982). Small Cities and National Development, (Nagoya: UNCRD.

Randinelli, D.A., (1981). Developing and Managing Middle-sized Cities in Developing Countries, Washington: USAID.

_____, (1982). 'Intermediate cities in developing countries: A comparative analysis of their demographic, social and economic characteristics,' Third World Planning Review: 4, pp. 357-86.

Renaud, B., (1981). National Urbanization Policy in Developing Countries, New York: Oxford University Press.

Richardson, H., (1977). City Size and National Spatial Strategies in Developing Countries, Washington: World Bank, S.W.P. #252.

_____, (1982). "Policies for strengthening small cities in developing countries,' in O.P. Mathur, (ed.), Small Cities and National Development, Nagoya: UNCRD, pp. 327-54.

Stohr, W., 1975). Regional Development Experience and Projects in Latin America, The Hague: Mouton.

Stohr, W. and F. Todtling, (1978). 'An evaluation of regional policies experiences in market and mixed economics,' in N. Hansen (ed.), Human Settlement Systems, Cambridge, MA: Ballinger.

UNCRD, (1982). Expert Group Meeting on the Role of Small- and Inter- mediate-Sized Cities in National Development, Nagoya: UNCRD.

World Bank, (1980). World Development Report.

26 Multivariate methods for soft data in development planning: a case study in natural resources

HANS BLOOMESTEIN AND PETER NIJKAMP

1. Introduction

Quantitative research in social sciences has become an important analytical tool for policy-making and planning. During the last decades, in several policy fields (such as regional and urban planning, development planning, environmental and energy planning) quantitative methods have played a crucial role in accurately describing, analyzing, predicting and planning complex systems (Nijkamp 1979, 1980).

Too little attention, however, has been paid to the limitations caused by the level of measurement of the variables used in quantitative research. In general, numerical information can be measured on a nominal, ordinal, interval and ratio scale.

The ratio scale and interval scale are usually named cardinal scales, while the nominal scale and ordinal scale are often named categorical (or qualitative) scales. Many concepts and variables used in social sciences (including regional economics, geography, planning and transportation economics) are based on measurability in a cardinal sense. Most theories and methods take for granted that phenomena to be studied can be quantified in an unambiguous manner, so that the level of measurement is mainly related to a ratio and/or interval scale. This assumption of cardinal measurability is especially a consequence of the deeply-rooted impacts of natural sciences and mathematics on social sciences.

Normally, however, reality is much more complicated, so that many concepts and variables in social sciences cannot be precisely quantified and are rather 'soft' (qualitative) in nature. In addition, very often a pseudo-metric approach is being used in order to draw seemingly realiable conclusions from quantitative data on qualitative phenomena (Adelman and Morris, 1974).

The limited validity of the traditional assumption of cardinal measurability is being increasingly realized in regional and urban economics, geography, planning and transportation economics. Examples of problems that cannot be described on an unambiguous cardinal scale include: choice of dwellings, modal choice in transportation analysis, locational choices, mental perceptions of attributes of relevant geographical items, regional and urban planning, and policy intervention in urban and regional impact analysis. All these problems are characterized by aspects which are -- in principle and/or by definition

-- non-cardinal in nature.

During the last decade, however, many attempts have been made in several disciplines (inter alia psychology, biology and demography) to deal with the paradoxical problem of 'measuring the unmeasurable'. Simultaneously, in economics and statistics increasing attention has been paid to ordinal regression analysis and so-called 'soft' multivariate techniques.

The basic aim of all these recently developed techniques is to treat soft (ordinal, nominal, qualitative or fuzzy) information by means of permissible mathematical and/or statistical operations so as to use soft data inputs in order to draw inferences that are ultimately quantitative in nature. This is certainly an intriguing and promising approach, as it opens an operational way to deal with such information in regional economics, geography, transportation and planning. In Nijkamp and Rietveld (1982) a survey and a comparison of various kinds of soft econometric and statistical tools have been presented.

The aim of this paper is fairly modest. It will deal with two different scaling algorithms which can be used to treat ordinal data so as to arrive at cardinal conclusions from the original qualitative data set. These two approaches will briefly be discussed in section 2 and 3, respectively. The use and meaning of both scaling algorithms will be illustrated by means of a case study in regional planning for Surinam (section 4). The results of this case study will also be used to compare the properties of both scaling methods.

2. Multidimensional Scaling Methods

Multidimensional scaling (MDS) methods have originally been developed in psychometrics. The rationale behind the use of MDS methods was to transform ordinal data, that describe in a N x N paired comparison table the (dis)-similarity between N objects, into cardinal units. Assuming, a symmetric paired comparison table and omitting the self-dissimilarities on the main diagonal, one has to fact $1/2\ N\ (N-1)$ ordinal dissimilarity relationships. The only way to represent these N objects as (cardinal) coordinates in a Euclidean space, is to reduce the number of dimensions. Suppose that the Euclidean space is S-dimensional $(1 < S < 1/2\ N\ (N-1)\ /\ N = 1/2\ (N-1))$. Then the co-ordinates of the N objects in a S-dimensional space can be estimated due to the fact that the transition from higher to lower dimensions implies in general the emergence of degrees of freedom which can be used to extract cardinal information from the underlying ordinal data structure. The main criterion for assessing the co-ordinates of the N objects in the new S-dimensional space is that these N points must
have a configuration such that the interpoint distances bear a maximum correspondence to the rankings in the initial dissimilarity data.

If the ordinal dissimilarities are denoted by $\delta_{nn'}$ $(n > n')$, the paired comparison table Δ for dissimilarities between items is:

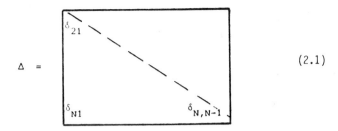

$$\Delta \quad = \qquad \qquad \qquad \qquad \qquad \qquad \qquad \qquad \qquad \qquad (2.1)$$

If this symmetric matrix is supposed to have a complete ordinal ranking without ties, the highest rank number is $1/2\ N\ (N-1)$ and the lowest 1. It should be noted that the assumption of the absence of ties is by no means necessary and that it can easily be relaxed. In such a table of ordinal dissimilarities, the transitivity conditions are not necessarily satisfied. Suppose now that the N objects are to be represented in a S-dimensional Euclidean space. Then one has to construct the following N x S configuration table which represents the co-ordinates of the N points in this space:

$$C \quad = \qquad \qquad \qquad \qquad \qquad \qquad \qquad \qquad \qquad \qquad (2.2)$$

Next one may define a distance measure (e.g., a Euclidean distance metric) between all N points at the right-hand side of (2.2):

$$d_{nn'} = \{ \sum_{s=1}^{S} (x_{ns} - x_{n's})^2 \}^{1/2} \qquad \qquad (2.3)$$

The best way to achieve an optimal fit between the ordinal data from (2.1) and the cardinal data from (2.2) is to impose the condition that the geometric configuration of (2.2) should be such that the distances represented in (2.3) do not violate the dissimilarity conditions from (2.1). This best fit can be achieved by means of some sort of least squares procedure, viz. by minimizing the (normalized) residual variance ('stress'). This stress function (or loss function) may have the following shape (although a more general Minkowski metric is also allowed):

$$\sigma = \{ \frac{\sum_{n,n'}(d_{nn'} - \hat{d}_{nn'})^2}{\sum_{n,n'}d_{nn'}^2} \}^{1/2} \ , \qquad n \neq n' \qquad (2.4)$$

where $d_{nn'}$ is already defined in (2.3) and where $\hat{d}_{nn'}$ are orderisomorph values (so-called disparities) which should be determined subject to the condition that $\hat{d}_{nn'}$ is in agreement with $\delta_{nn'}$; in other words, $\hat{d}_{nn'} \leq \hat{d}_{nn''}$, whenever $\delta_{nn'} \leq \delta_{nn''}$. Such a stress function may be regarded as a measure for the degree at which the information from C contradicts that from Δ. One possible way to determine $\hat{d}_{nn'}$ may be a monotone regression which can be formalized as:

$$\min_{\hat{d}_{nn'}} = \sum_{n,n'} | \hat{d}_{nn'} - d_{nn'} |$$

$$\text{s.t.} \hspace{9cm} (2.5)$$

$$\delta_{nn'} > \delta_{nn''} \rightarrow \hat{d}_{nn'} \quad \hat{d}_{nn''} \quad .$$

An alternative procedure is <u>inter alia</u> a rank-image method. Instead of linear distance functions, any other non-linear distance metric may be used as well.

Before (2.5) can be applied, a first 'guess' of $d_{nn'}$ has to be made. This first guess can be made after the determination of an initial configuration of (2.2); this configuration is often the result of a principal component analysis with S components applied to (2.1). Given the initial configuration, the initial distances between the points of a configuration can be calculated and substituted into (2.5); these distances are normally measured with respect to an ideal point which is specific for each individual.

Next, the monotone regression may be carried out in order to assess an initial value for $\hat{d}_{nn'}$, so that the disparities are in accordance with the (dis)-similarities. Thus, $\hat{d}_{nn'}$ is not a specific distance, but a number that is as close as possible to the original distance $d_{nn'}$, while being in accordance with the (dis)similarities.

When the initial values of $\hat{d}_{nn}$ are substituted into (2.4), a minimum stress can be calculated (in terms of x_{ns}) by means of a numerical solution procedure for minimizing (2.4) (for example, by means of a gradient method). The resulting values of the configuration can again be used to assess a new value of $\hat{d}_{nn'}$, etc., until after a number of steps $\ell = 1, 2, \ldots$ the whole procedure converges (up to a degree of accuracy ϵ). The whole procedure is represented in a simplified manner in Figure 1.

The conclusion which can be drawn from the ultimate value of the stress function are slightly subjective, so that certain rules of thumb may be helpful:

$\sigma(\%)$	20	10	5	2.5	0
Goodness-of-fit	poor	fair	good	excellent	perfect

Another subjective element concerns the choice of the dimension K. Clearly one should strive at a minimum stress with a minimum number of

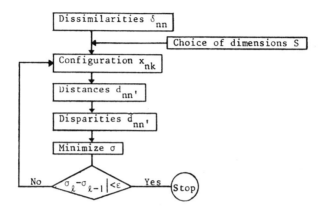

Figure 1. Simplified representation of an MDS-procedure.

dimensions involved. It is clear that the ultimate interpretation of
the configuration is also a matter of personal inventiveness of the
researcher, so that here again subjective elements may enter. Like in
factor analysis, some of the results are invariant against a
translation and rotation of the axes (provided a Euclidean distance
metric is used). A more extensive discussion of MDS can be found in
Nijkamp (1979), in which also a more detailed discussion of various MDS
algorithms (such as Torsca, Indscal, Minirsa, Minissa and Prefmap) is
included.

3. Homogeneous Scaling Methods

Homogeneous scaling (HS) methods have also been designed in the
area of psychometrics. More recently, HS methods have also been
applied in spatial economics (Blommestein and Van Deth, 1981). HS
methods may be regarded as allied and complementary to MDS methods, as
they may provide the same kind of information regarding the problem at
hand, though from a different (conceptual and technical) view point.
Furthermore, some HS algorithms provide additional information (in
terms of output) compared to standard MDS algorithms.

In general, homogeneity analysis explores the basic assumption that
different variables may reflect and measure a common "phenomenon".
This homogeneity assumption means that the basic problem to be solved
is the replacement of the various variables by a single ("stand-in")
criterion. In order to evaluate the success or reliability of this
replacement, it is necessary to define a measure for homogeneity.
Consider, for example, the following quadratic loss function (or
"badness-of-fit" function):

$$\sigma(\underline{q}) \overset{\Delta}{=} \frac{1}{J} \sum_{j=1}^{J} (\underline{q} - \underline{p}_j)^T (\underline{q} - \underline{p}_j) \qquad (3.1)$$

in which p_j $(j = 1, ..., J)$ are vectors with the successive different (possible stochastic) variables; and q is the vector which replaces all these vectors according to a certain rule to be discussed hereafter. Next, by allowing (non-)linear weighting schemes of the variables via a non-linear transformation of p_j into $\phi_j(p_j)$, the homogeneity might increase. Thus the problem is to maximize homogeneity by minimizing:

$$\sigma(\underline{q};\underline{\phi}) \stackrel{\Delta}{=} \frac{1}{J} \sum_{j=1}^{J} (\underline{q} - \underline{\phi}_j(\underline{p}_j))^T (\underline{q} - \underline{\phi}_j(\underline{p}_j)) \qquad (3.2)$$

where $\underline{\phi}_j$ is a suitably chosen non-linear transformation function.

Several techniques exist to deal with problem (3.2). A frequently used method is HOMALS (HOMogeneity analysis by Alternative Least Squares). This is an algorithm which solves a particular specification (to be discussed below) of the general optimal transformation problem (3.2). HOMALS, originated in psychometrics (de Leeuw, 1976), applies an optimal weighting algorithm to a compound matrix G of dimension (I x $\sum_j k_j$), with binary matrices G_j of order (I x k_j) as matrix components associated with criterion (or variable) j. Matrices G have (0,1) entries obtained by a binary coding of the ordinal data on criterion j. A zero element in a column of matrix G_j indicates that the corresponding ordinal number for criterion j does not occur in the initial data input of the object concerned (individual, scenario, region, etc.). Thus, G_j indicates for each object in which ordinal category k_j of the J variables (criteria) this category has scored. Now the following matrix with elements b_{is} ($i=1, ..., I$, $s=1, ..., S$) may be defined:

$$B = (X - G_j Y_j)^T (X - G_j Y_j) \qquad (3.3)$$

where X is a (IXS) matrix with object scores; Y_j is a k_jxS matrix with numerical representations of variable j with k_j categories; Y is a $(\sum_j k_j)$xS matrix defined as $[Y_1 ... Y_J]^T$; and S denotes the dimensionality chosen by the user $(1 \leq S \leq \sum_j (k_j - 1))$.

The loss function σ (X,Y) used in the HOMALS algorithm, can be written as:

$$\sigma (X,Y) = \frac{1}{J} \sum_{j=1}^{J} \text{tr} (B) \qquad (3.4)$$

Loss function (3.4) is minimized (i.e., homogeneity is maximized) by employing the principle of alternating least squares in the following basic algorithmic steps of HOMALS (de Leeuw, 1976):

Step 1:

Min! $\sigma(X; Y)$, with X fixed, $\qquad (3.5)$
Y

This yields:

$$Y_j^{\ell} = (G_j^T G_j) - 1 G_j^T X, {}^{\ell} \qquad (3.6)$$

where the superscript indicates iteration step ℓ. Clearly, the algorithm requires an initial choice for X. The initial step starts with an arbitrary choice of X subject to the normalization restriction $X^TX = I_s$, in which I_s is a (SXS) diagonal matrix with elements I on the main diagonal. Thus for step $\ell=0$ we have $Y_j^0 = (G_j^TG_j)^{-1} G_j^TX^0$, whereby X^0 is an orthogonalized configuration of arbitrarily chosen numbers (random configuration) between 0 and 1; and Y_j^0 the numerical values of variable j with k_j categories in an S-dimensional space.

<u>Step 2</u>:

$$\text{Min} \; \sigma(X; Y), \text{ with Y fixed,} \qquad (3.7)$$
$$\text{X}$$

This yields:

$$X^\ell = \frac{1}{J} G \; Y^{\ell-1}, \qquad (3.8)$$

In both steps a normalization is required to avoid degenerate solutions to be loss functions to be minimized. The HOMALS program takes the following normalization $X^TX = I_s$. Thus in both steps $\sigma(X; Y)$ is minimized subject to $X^TX = I_s$. The matrix X is normalized by a so-called Gram-Schmidt orthogonalization procedure.

The HOMALS algorithm proceeds in <u>alternating</u> steps, where in step 1 $\sigma(X;Y)$ is minimized with respect to Y for fixed X, and in step 2 $\sigma(X; Y)$ is minimized with respect to X for fixed Y. This alternating procedure terminates when $|\sigma_\ell - \sigma_{\ell-1}| < \epsilon$, where σ_ℓ is the value of the loss function in iteration step ℓ and ϵ is a criterion for accuracy or convergence selected by the user. The main structure of HOMALS programs can then be represented in the following simplified manner:

The most important output of the HOMALS algorithm consists of:

- discrimination measures for each variable (i.e., the scores or eigenvalues of each variable on each dimension of the ultimate configuration). This is comparable to the loadings of a normal factor analysis.

- the optimally-scaled values (scores) for both the I objects and the Σk_j categories of the variables (i.e., the quantification of objects and categories - after normalization - in an S-dimensional space).

4. <u>A Case Study for Surinam</u>

Since its independence in 1975, many efforts have been made to improve the development of Surinam. Integrated development strategies, however, require the fulfilment of the following conditions (Kutsch Lojenga and Nijkamp, 1981):

- a <u>simultaneous</u> consideration of all relevant economic, social, <u>physical</u> and environmental elements of a complex spatial system;

- a detailed analysis of <u>spatial</u> development potentials of the

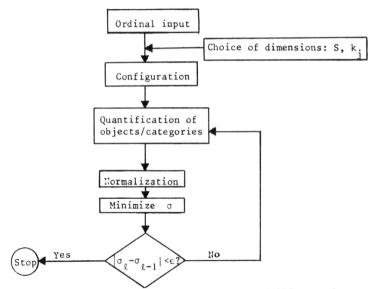

Figure 2: Simplified representation of a HOMALS-procedure.

regions studied;

—   a methodology for an integrated assessment of the <u>qualitative</u>
    (or intangible) information on the potentials of the
    successive areas;

—   a methodology for incorporating <u>policy</u> aspects and <u>conflicts</u>
    in the analysis.

These 4 elements will now briefly be discussed for the Surinam case
study. A <u>simultaneous</u> integration of relevant elements in a development
policy requires at least a detailed analysis of the following elements
for the study area at hand:

- economic   :   I.   presence of minerals (bauxite, copper,
                        nickel, e.g.)

              II.   suitability for agriculture, foresting and
                    cattle-breeding;

- environmental: III.   tourist attractiveness (water, jungle tours,
                        natural beauty);

             IV.   climate (temperature, wind);

- physical   :   V.   industrial and residential potential
                        (construction costs, hydrologic conditions,
                        etc.);

             VI.   water, (water supply, and water discharge).

- infrastructure:VII.   accessibility (road, rail, water and air transport).

These 7 elements have to be considered simultaneously in an integrated way.

A spatially disaggregated analysis of development potentials of an area requires the use of a so-called potential surface analysis which provides scores on the abovementioned 7 elements for a detailed grid system (with grids of 10 x 10 km, e.g.). A development potential is a set of regional factors that may provide a positive stimulus to the development of the region at hand. These main factors (economic, environmental, physical and infrastructural) have already been indicated above. The numerical assessment of all elements of such a development potential can be included in a regional profile containing fairly detailed information. A development potential matrix P contains all information across all regions of the system at hand:

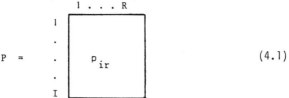

$$P = \begin{array}{c} 1 \\ \cdot \\ \cdot \\ \cdot \\ \cdot \\ I \end{array} \quad \begin{array}{c} 1 \ldots R \\ \boxed{ p_{ir} } \end{array} \qquad (4.1)$$

where p_{ir} is the estimated development potential of factor i (i=1,...,I) in region r (r=1,...,R).

Given the detailed scale of the analysis, a potential surface analysis will usually not contain cardinal information. At most, an ordinal data set can be provided. This implies that cardinal operations cannot be applied. In this respect, the use of multivariate scaling techniques may be necessary in order to draw quantitative conclusions. Such methods are able to synthesize a set of ordinal information by reducing the number of dimensions so as to allow a quantitative inference from soft data.

Finally, also policy aspects have to be included in analyses dealing with development strategies (including policy conflicts). In this respect, it may be meaningful to introduce policy scenarios which give a ranking of the importance attached to the set of development potential factors. This ranking will of course depend on political views regarding the desired development strategies. The following policy scenarios will be distinguished (Kutsch Lojenga and Nijkamp, 1981):

A neo-capitalist approach: implies inter alia: joint ventures with foreign companies, large-scale projects, capital-intensive sectors, improved infrastructure, exploitation of mineral sources, domestic investments of profils, reformation of taxes and a consumer orientation.

A socialist approach: implies inter alia: less dependence on foreign countries and multinationals, emphasis on socio-economic equity, improvement of the whole economic basis of the country, socialization of strategic sectors, and activation of population in development strategies.

A populist viewpoint: places emphasis on the following elements inter alia: more public interference with socio-economic developments, an integrated (less economic-oriented) development, self-reliance strategies, exploitation of own national opportunities, emphasis on education, and more racial integration.

These 3 policy views give rise to the following ranking of the corresponding scenario's:

(1) I → VII → V → VI → III → II → IV

(2) II → V → VII → VI → I → III → IV

(3) II → I → VII → VI → V → IV → III

The data for the abovementioned potential surface analysis have been collected for a study area of approximately 170 x 130 km in West Surinam. The total number of grids investigated was 175, so that the order of magnitude of the development potential matrix was 7 x 175. The data were collected on a scale varying from 1 to 6.

Next, of course, the ranking from the policy scenario's can be applied to these data in order to clarify the policy conflicts regarding the development of West Surinam. These results will be discussed in the next section.

5. Empirical Applications

As indicated in the previous section, the assessment of development potentials is a complicated problem (due to interdependences among profile elements, several spatial units, a wide variety of development strategies, and missing, unreliable or soft data). Consequently, a complete picture can only be achieved by the analysis of a three-fold data set: values of profile elements, spatial allocation, and development scenarios. In this respect, the two scaling methods described in sections 2 and 3 may be very helpful.

5.1 Multidimensional scaling

Two MDS algorithms (Minirsa and Kyst[1]) have been used to analyze the discrepancies between profile elements, policy scenarios and spatial units. Both algorithms led to nearly the same results. The joint metric configuration of all potential profiles, grids and scenarios is represented in Figure 3 (with a stress value of approximately 0.10).

Some brief comments will be given here:

-   The grids appear to be located mainly in three quadrants with a concentration in the right upper quandrant and partly in the left upper quadrant. The total number of regions located here is 105; their inter-cluster distance is very small, so that

---

[1] Expositions of Minirsa and Kyst can be found among others in Nijkamp (1979) and Kruskal et al. (1973), respectively.

the differ-ence in their development potentials is negligible.

- The potential profiles are distributed over three quadrants. Tourism is separately located in the right lower quadrant; availability of minerals appears to be located in the left lower quadrant while the remaining factors can be found in the right upper quadrant. The last five factors are agricultural suitability, climate, locational appropriateness, water and areal accessibility. These factors are essentially character- ized by physical features. This implies that the 105 regions depicted in this right upper quadrant derive their development potential mainly from physical factors. In a similar way, one may identify tourism-based areas (right lower cluster) which appear to be mainly mountainous areas, and resource-based areas (left lower cluster).

- Next, one may also try to interpret the axes of Figure 3. Given the point locations of the profiles and regions, one may interpret the horizontal axis in terms of given physical conditions (left-hand part) and man-perceived features (right-hand part). The vertical axis may be interpreted in terms of concentrated industrial (or rapid) growth (lower part) and integral spatial spread effects (upper part).

- The final analysis focused on the metric position of the three policy scenarios. Only a brief interpretation will be given here. It turns out that the neo-capitalist scenario is located fairly close to the mineral resources and next to the physical resources of the development areas concerned. The populist and socialist scenarios do not show great mutual differences, and show a large distance with respect to tourist aspects. Moreover, these scenarios appear to emphasize a spread of activities mainly based on the given natural conditions of the areas.

Next, the attention will be focussed on the sensitivity of the results for the size of the areas (Cliff et al., 1975) by checking the stability of the spatial configuration for a different spatial scale.

We have divided the study area into two parts, viz. a Northern part (88 grids) and a Southern part (87 grids). The joint metric configurations of regions and development potential criteria are presented in figures 4a and 4b (with stress values of approximately 0.05).

A comparison of Figure 3 with 4a and 4b provides some interesting additional information:

- Some results are clearly affected by a different spatial scale. For example, by comparing Figure 3 with Figure 4a, it is striking that variable VII (X_4) is - in contrast to Figure 3 - separately positioned in Figure 4a. Unlike Figure 3, variables III and VII are located together in Figure 4b. Similarly, variable I is jointly located with variables II, IV and VI in Figure 4b, while this is not the case in Figure 3. In all three figures, variables I (presence of minerals) and III (attractiveness for tourism) are distinctly separated from each other.

- A comparison of the joint metric representations of both
criteria and regions in the three figures enables one to draw
more detailed conclusions than those based on Figure 3 only.
By comparing Figures 3 and 4a, one can conclude that the
relative positions of regions and criteria (with the exception
of variable VII) is about the same. This implies that the
characteristics of the Northern part dominate the ultimate
configuration, obtained in Figure 3. Furthermore, Figure 3a
shows a more heterogeneous configuration of grids than Figure
4a, because of the distinctive characteristics of the Southern
part of the study area. By comparing 4a with 4b, one can see
that two homogeneous clusters of grids dominate the final
configuration in 4b. Furthermore, as mentioned above, the
configuration of development characteristics differs from 4a
(and thus from Figure 3). The clusters E_1 and E_2 perform
almost equally well with respect to criteria I, II, IV, V and
VI. However, the cluster with grids E_2 performs better with
respect to criteria III and VII.

- Finally, the tentative interpretation of the axes of Figure 3
can be refined as follows. The horizontal axis in Figure 4a
might be interpreted as a demarcation between an industrial
orientation such as mining (right-hand part), and an
agrico-environmental orientation (left-hand part); the
vertical axis as a distinction between spatial spread effects
and accessibility. In Figure 4b, the horizontal axis gives
some information about the conditions for activities related
to tourism on the one hand, and conditions for the development
of the industrial and agricultural sector on the other hand.
Figure 4b shows that the regions situated in cluster E_2 have
a comparative advantage with respect to the development of the
tourist sector. The vertical axis differentiates between the
availability of natural resources in its physical form (lower
part) and the feasibility of a development of these resources
in economic and technical terms (upper part). Figure 4b
reveals a very important piece of additional information,
viz., a large discrepancy between the availabiliby of
resources and the feasibility of the residential/industrial
potential in the Southern part of the study area.

5.2 Homogeneous Scaling

The configuration of both objects (regions) and categories
(i.e., the categorized development criteria) is presented in Figure 5.
It has been mentioned in Section 3 that HOMALS may provide additional
information. This will be illustrated for the case study considered
here.

In the first place, discrimination measures for each variable and
each dimension can be assessed. Since each variable j has k_j
categories, the discrimination measure is equal to the sum of all
between-category distances divided by the sum of all distances.
Calculation of the discrimination measures for the 7 development
potential criteria revealed that the variables I, III and VII have low
discrimination measures on both dimensions. The variables II, V and VI
score relatively well on the first dimension, while variable IV
performs well on the second dimension. The low discrimination measures

354

can be explained by the large number of tied and/or missing data for criteria I, III and VII.

A second piece of useful information is provided by the eigenvalues for each dimension. Since these eigenvalues are equal to the average discrimination measure on that dimension, it is an indication for the relative "importance" (i.e., for the final configuration of both categories and objects) of that dimension. Dimensions 1 and 2 appear to have eigenvalues of .7383 and .5168, respectively.

As HOMALS quantifies the categories of the variables (instead of the variables themselves, like in MDS models), more detailed information may be obtained. In order to facilitate the interpretation of Figure 5, only the values of the two highest category numbers are shown. Cluster E_1 performs relatively very well with respect to variable I (presence of minerals), III (tourism) and IV (climate), while E_2 scores very well on the variables V (locational conditions) and VI (water supply and discharge). Cluster E_3 scores high on II (agriculture), VI (water supply) and VII (accessibility). The spatial configuration in Figure 5 can be considered as a curved one-dimensional solution (a so-called "horse-shoe"). This suggests the following tentative interpretation of the (one-dimensional) axis. At the far left-hand side heavy industry like mining is situated; climatological factors and attractiveness for tourism is located in the middle; right from the middle, locational factors, water criteria and accessibility are situated respectively; at the far righthand side, one finds suitability for agriculture, forestry and cattlebreeding. Thus, with the help of HOMALS a relatively detailed metric interpretation of grids and development criteria is obtained.

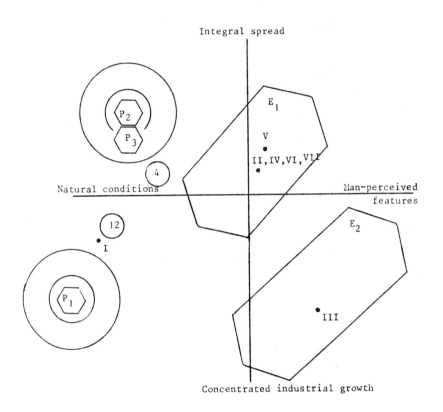

Figure 3 : Joint metric representation of grids, potential profiles and
scenarios. Black dots indicate the positions of the 7 criteria I, ..., VII.
E_1 and E_2 include the positions of 139 and 20 grids, respectively. Remaining
grids are denoted by small circles (the numerals represent the number of
regions in one point). The symbols ⬡ indicate the positions of the policy
scenarios P_1, P_2 and P_3.

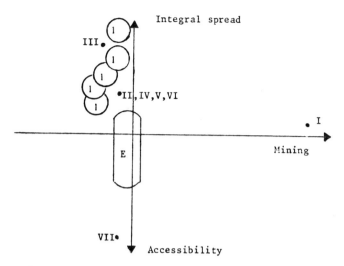

Figure 4a : Joint metric representation of regions (Northern part) and
potential profiles. Within cluster E, 83 grids are located; the
small circles represent single grids.

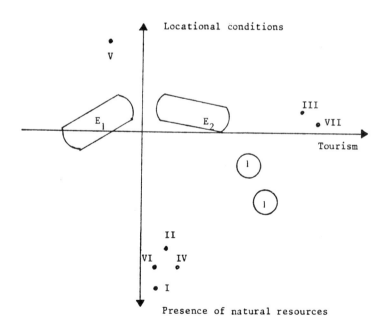

Figure 4b : Joint metric representation of regions (Southern Part) and
potential profiles. Within clusters E_1 and E_2, 56 and 29 grids are
located respectively; small circles represent single grids.

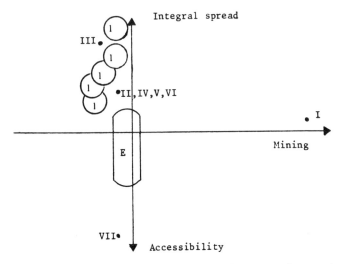

Figure 4a : Joint metric representation of regions (Northern part) and potential profiles. Within cluster E, 83 grids are located; the small circles represent single grids.

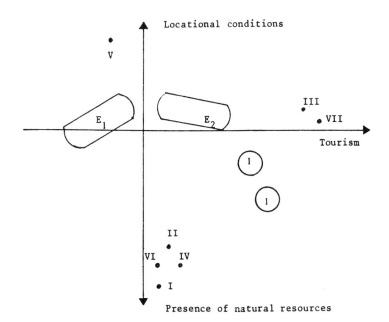

Figure 4b : Joint metric representation of regions (Southern Part) and potential profiles. Within clusters E_1 and E_2, 56 and 29 grids are located respectively; small circles represent single grids.

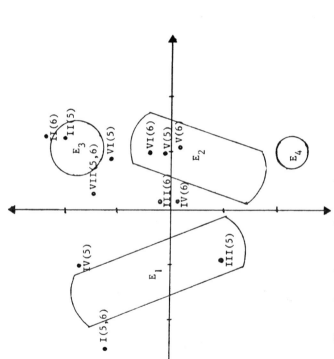

Figure 5: Joint metric configuration (HOMALS solution) of regions and categories of development criteria. Key : Within clusters E_1, E_2, E_3 and E_4, 70, 50, 25 and 15 grids are located, respectively (separate points are not shown). The criteria I, II, ..., VII have the original category numbers $n(= 1, 2, \ldots, 6)$ in brackets.

References

Adelman, I. and C.T. Morris, (1974). 'The derivation of cardinal scales from ordinal data', Economic Development and Planning, (W. Sellekaerts, (ed.)), London: MacMillan, pp. 1-39.

Blommestein, H.J. and J.W. van Deth, (1981). 'Selection of optimal urban development scenarios: A comparative study of some models for the analysis of soft information', Research Paper, Twente University of Technology, Department of Public Administration, Enschede, (mimeographed).

Cliff, A.D., P. Haggett, J.K. Ord, K. Bassett and R. Davies, (1975). Elements of Spatial Structure, Cambridge: Cambridge University Press.

Kruskal, J.B., F.W. Young and J.B. Seery, (1973). 'How to use KYST   A very flexible program to do multidimensional scaling and unfolding', Bell Laboratories, Murray Hill, N.J.

Krutsch Lojenga, F. and P. Nijkamp, (1981). 'Natural resources on spatial development potentials in development countries', Energy and Environment in the Developing Countries, (M. Chatterji, (ed.)), New York: John Wiley, pp. 245-54.

Leeuw, J. de, (1976). HOMALS, Paper presented at the Spring Meeting of Psychometric Society, Murray Hill, N.J., (mimeographed).

Nijkamp, P., (1979). Multidimensional Spatial Data and Decision Analysis, Chichester/New York: Wiley.

_____, (1980). Environmental Policy Analysis, Chichester/New York: Wiley.

Nijkamp, P. and P. Rietveld, (1982). 'Soft econometrics as a tool for regional discrepancy analysis', Papers of the Regional Science Association, (forthcoming).

27 Technological transfer in the midst of energy crises: an assessment of current practices

MANOUCHER PARVIN

1. Introduction

The available technology in the industrialized countries was developed and evolved to take advantage of abundant and low-cost fossil fuel and to save labor. The existing technology for transfer is thus capital and fossil fuel intensive. The recent catastrophic increases in relative prices of petroleum, coal, and gas, the sharp rise in costs of capital goods, and the continued availability of abundance of labor have altered the optimality of broad categories of availed technology and have shattered the expectations of the LDCs who had envisioned their future as the present of the advanced countries.

It has become now obvious that the existing standard of living achieved in advanced countries cannot be duplicated by the same means, which require high intensity use of oil in production technologies and consumption propensities. If the advanced countries had the opportunity to retrace their technological progress, a different optimum path would be chosen. The current multi-billion dollar industrial and technical efforts toward conservation of energy and pollution abatement in advanced countries attest to this developmental proposition: that increases in energy prices and environmental concerns have deformed the economic space, opening gates for the new and closing the doors for some of the existing technologies.

The theoretical study of the co-existence of various production and consumption processes using different energy-intensity technologies in an economy has already been undertaken (Parvin and Grammas, 1976, 1981). Energy requirements as intermediate inputs are also computed using input-output tables (Wright, 1975). Most recently social accounting matrices are tabulated where one of the main features is energy-based classifications of production and associated techniques, also tracing income distributional impacts (Ali Khan, 1981). The focus of attention here is not on the theoretical exploration or empirical analysis of the problem but rather the conceptual discussion of the major issues of energy scarcity, alternative technologies, and strategy of economic development today.

Thus, with non-OPEC LDCs in mind, the following questions require attention. What are the impacts of real and financial squeeze on such economies, and how has their financial status in the international money market been affected? Is the fossil fuel, capital intensive, and labor-saving technology and growth strategy, which is the only experience, also the only alternative? What is the importance and relevance of technological transfer from advanced countries to LDCs in contrast to the creation of new technologies which takes into account today's scarcities?

2. Repercussions of Oil Price Increases

Despite differences in national specificities, empirical analyses have indicated that "over the past century the change in the share of major sectors in the national product of presently advanced countries has been quite similar to the pattern derived from cross-section analysis" (Chenery 1960). Furthermore, the existence of fuel based, capital-intensive technology and imitation of a western consumption pattern have up to now necessitated a rather restricted inter-industry relationship across countries. An alternative path of development hence must embody a technology which is not fossil-fuel based and/or capital-intensive and a style of life which is not a mere imitation. Fossil fuel would still have a secondary and diminishing role in such an alternative path of development based on specificities of initial condition of a given country, economic criteria for optimization, and an envisioned or appropriate future.

For non-OPEC LDCs, the unexpected sharp rise in oil prices has caused a set of interrelated repercussions. To begin with, a distinction should be made between real and financial consequences of oil price increases. The real impact is due to the increase in the outflow of goods and services resulting from increased energy costs leading to depletion of the developmental resources and the financial strains caused by trade imbalances since OPEC has not reinvested in such LDCs or kept reserves in local currencies. Even though the more advanced LDCs have unwillingly accepted a lower growth rate, they still have had to borrow heavily to finance it. In addition, the manufacturing industries of such countries are, to various degrees, assembly line operations requiring intermediate goods from advanced countries which are, in turn, produced by the capital-energy intensive, and high-cost labor of advanced countries. The agricultural sectors also require -- to various degrees, depending on the stage of development -- imports with similar energy-capital characteristics and have become heavily dependent on foreign support, real as well as financial.

Since demand elasticities for non-primary products are in general greater than those for primary products (oil being one of the exceptions), the advanced economies are in an advantageous trade position. This advantage is further accentuated by the special role of multinational corporations in international markets. Accordingly, the balances of trade of advanced economies are more adjustable to unexpected oil price augmentations (Sagasti, 1976). This phenomenon is illustrated in Table 1 which shows that the trade balances of advanced economies with oil exporting countries have absorbed the shock of 1973-1974 OPEC oil price increases and adjusted to the pre-1974 pattern, while the LDCs trade imbalance has remained virtually unchanged.

In order to stop a sharp decrease in the growth of real output, non-OPEC LDCs have had to resort to an alarming degree of debt-financing of their programs (Aronsan, 1979). Borrowing from international financial sources and from private banking institutions has become a contemporaneous trend in international financial relations, and it has raised the fear of a widespread debt crisis with serious impacts on debtors as well as creditors (Holsen, 1977). Furthermore, it is indicated elsewhere that the increases in oil prices have increased income disparity within LDCs (Parvin, 1982). Thus with a time horizon of only one generation, only a minority of the world's population can achieve and maintain the high per capita income that is derived from fossil-fuel and capital-intensive technology. Although an energy catastrophe is not forecast, Houthakker and Kennedy predict "plenty of major problems" along the way to the year 2000 (Houthakker and Kennedy, 1978).

The relative price of oil will continue to rise and eventually at higher rates (Ramsey, 1978). The non-OPEC LDCs cannot compete over time with OECD for shrinking oil reserves.

Since the proven path implies substitution of capital and fossil fuel for labor, the following of such paths by overcrowded LDCs implies the intensification of use of scarce factors -- capital and fossil fuel -- at the expense of the abundant factor -- labor. In addition, consumer products are produced which are fossil fuel intensive consumption goods such as private automobiles.

3. Alternatives to Oil

The upsurge trend in the price of oil and natural gas has raised the likelihood of a wide range of energy substitutions in different sectors of advanced countries. The possible options in the context of depletable energy sources are coal and nuclear energy, each with hazardous environmental repercussions. It appears that a blindfolded substitution of coal for oil (in imitation of developed nations) by some non-OPEC LDCs is imminent. However, this strategy can provide a temporary relief which will have long-run adverse consequences in terms of promotion of fossil fuel-based technology.

Once the major source of energy, coal is now an option which comes to the fore immediately. Although the environmental safety hazards and high cost of liquefication and gasification of coal diminish the possibility of worldwide reliance on coal, it is worthwhile to mention that these restraints are not fixed. The continuation of research on gasification and liquefication will, most likely, reduce the costs and increase the efficiency of coal use; and regulating costs, which vary from country to country, may also decrease over time (Bergman, 1979). There is strong evidence for supporting the possibility of a coal-favored trend in advanced countries (Parvin, 1982).

Any attempt by non-OPEC LDCs to follow inter-fossil-fuel substitution will be a strategical misadventure fundamentally incapable of mitigating their internal and external economic constraints. The undesirable environmental impacts of this substitution would result in further impairment of social welfare in these countries. Also, because only six percent of the world's total coal reserves is located in Asia (excluding USSR and China), Africa, and Latin America, substitution will not reduce the dependency of these countries upon imported fossil fuel. Furthermore, the expected increase in oil and gas prices will pull along the price of coal, so that the flow of real resources of non-OPEC LDCs for energy imports would not alter significantly. Thus, such coal-for-oil substitutions lead only to a change of energy suppliers and not much more.

Nuclear fission as a pragmatic alternative for fossil fuel has turned illusive due to increasing concerns about management of hazardous radioactive wastes, threat to world peace, possibility of an accident, and the probable effects of low-level radiation over long periods. Despite the dangerous nature of processing nuclear energy and the possibility of nuclear weapon proliferation, packaged-deal nuclear technology has been imported to some of the developing countries.

Nuclear energy is not a solution, even temporarily, to capital and energy-oriented economic problems faced by non-OPEC LDCs. The reason is that the capital-intensive nature of the nuclear industry along with its need for highly technical expertise would exacerbate the current shortages of human and physical capital in these countries and increase their indebtedness and dependence on foreign techniques.

Precarious nuclear contamination and the geographical distribution of the world's uranium reserves contribute to the proposition that nuclear fission energy is not a feasible solution to the energy crisis in non-OPEC LDCs since 71 percent of the world's estimated uranium reserves are located in such countries (Source: Organization for Economic Cooperation and Energy Conservation, 1978, p. 237).

4. Paucity of Short Run Options

Apparently the policy options available to LDCs are numbered in a short time horizon. Energy conservation and the enhancement of efficient use of energy should be first on the agenda. The fact that non-commercial energy constitutes a major portion of total energy consumed in non-OPEC LDCs can support the possibility that energy/GDP ratio underestimates the actual energy consumed to produce a dollar value of output in these countries (Lambertini, 1979). Although the variation in energy/GDP ratio is partly due to geographical, economic and social specificities, the over time alteration of such ratios is feasible and implies room for conservation and improvement in efficiency without a sacrifice in output level. No strong association between gross energy input and GNP is observed (Kraft, 1980).

The energy efficiency effort must focus on the industrial and trans-portation sectors, where 80 percent of commercial energy is consumed (Lambertini, 1979). The opportunities a country has to turn its capital stock rapidly to more energy efficient directions depend on the rate of investment. Since many non-OPEC LDCs are making fresh investment in various industries, they can take advantage of this unique opportunity and engage only in energy efficient investment.

Secondly, the displacement of imported by indigenous energy sources reduces the trade deficit and ameliorates the foreign debt position. As the price of energy continues to increase, the indigenous production of oil and gas, which are currently non-economical for a number of LDCs, may become feasible. The production of primary energy in oil importing LDCs is estimated to raise to 18.5 millions of coal equivalent in 1990 from its 1976 value of 6.5 million (Lambertini, 1979). To accomplish this, non-OPEC LDCs ought to increase their knowledge of domestic energy potential and the likelihood of its utilization even at a cost higher than that of imported energy. The substitution of alcohol for gasoline in Brazil, which is expected to save $450 to $500 million in foreign exchange in the early 1980s, should be regarded as appropriate evidence of energy displacement policy (Mears, 1978). It is argued elsewhere that inter-fuel substitution provides a short run relief only (Parvin, 1982). Conse-quently, for the long run a gradual shift to renewable energy resources and creation of appropriate technology is a necessity.

5. Technological Transfer and Appropriate Future

The repercussions of oil price increase have accentuated the need for reevaluation of fossil-fuel based technologies in terms of appropriateness and for restructuring of national expectations based on new economic realities of non-OPEC LDCs. The fact that appropriate technology has received eminent attention in recent studies stems from the failure of development strategies to achieve the expected results and from the production of undesired consequences (Westphal, 1978). An interdisciplinary approach must be embraced to assess the wider impacts of technology in society and outside the realm of physical output (Long, 1979). The specificities of a particular country and avail-ability of indigenous resources should be given a prime consideration in adoption of new technology.

Failure to recognize such criteria has contributed to the creation of "dual-economies" with concentration of scarce capital in urban areas, high rate of unemployment, high cost of creating job opportunities, need for highly skilled labor and dependency on fossil fuel. Furthermore, dual economy is accompanied by impoverishment of the poor and accretion of affluence (Schumacher, 1974).

The transfer of technology has been assumed to be a less costly activity than creation of the same technology and that optimum backward-ness implies never catching up with the most advanced economies (Parvin, 1975, 1976). For a class of technological transfer this assumption is no longer valid since increasing fixed costs (capital goods input) and variable costs (energy resources input) have altered the resource condition for which the existing technology was developed in the first place. For example, would a high fossil fuel, capital intensive approach in agriculture, broadly speaking, be optimum for the Indian food production sector? (Diwan, 1981; Sarkar, 1978).

Furthermore, technological transfer, implying the sale of a package of information, rights, and services, usually is transacted between a domestic firm and a foreign firm for mutual profit-making possibilities. Generally, tariff protection and limitation of entry provided by the transferee government create a near monopolistic or drastically imperfect market for the domestic firm. Under such circumstances where Ricardian rent is abundant, would profitability be a good criterion for appropriateness of technology which is transferred? Furthermore, current literature abounds with the proposition that technologies are not value-free. The rate of income growth and its distribution depend on the type of technology adopted, the terms of its acquisition, the nature of the adaptation process itself, and finally the degree of national dependence it nurtures (Gladwin, 1978; Gaulet, 1977; Harper and Boyle, 1976; and Sunkel,

1972). Even if the transferee market were perfect and all the other negative side-effects enumerated above were minimized somewhat, would the criterion of the short-run optimum utilization of available resources in a given economy constitute an appropriate guideline with respect to appropriateness of technological choices?

Since the less the development, the greater is the number of potential avenues of development, a tenable proposal is that appropriateness of technology should be purpose specific, for example it should dovetail with a developmental strategy. The immediate goals could be translated to a multiobjective optimization function where market-worthiness of a set of activities may constitute one of the objectives. Furthermore, to avoid the costs and hazards of piecemeal technological transfers, a country must envision an appropriate future and then seek the technological progress which realizes or materializes that vision. Of course, the development strategy is neither a simple concept nor a certain process, and many mid-course adjustments will become necessary as the future unfolds intself and possibilities unimagined before appear on the horizon (Chatel, 1979 and Palmedo, 1977). For example, a strategy of decentralized agricultural life for the majority of people in India based on optimum use of a variety of low-grade renewable energy sources, coupled with industrial development to be eventually based on high-grade fusion energy, could constitute such a broad objective and strategical commitment. Low-grade energy relates to low temperature and low volume (dencentralized) nature of direct and indirect use of solar energy, while high-grade relates to high volume, high temperature availability of energy at a center. Thus, any technological transfer using large quantities of fossil fuel must be scrutinized carefully before its adoption as a transitory bridge between now and an envisioned future. The following Table gives a rough history of the use of energy resources in the past and a speculated future based on current trends and current thoughts (see Table 3).

The example of an appropriate future presented here combines the Gandhian society of decentralized sedentary life based on optimum use of renewable resources which feeds and is fed by carefully selected pockets of planned centers of industrial complexes based on fusion energy. Such a proposal, whose appropriateness -- due to limitations of space -- is not to be elaborated on here, can perhaps be a planned "dual economy" geared to different sources of energy. Income distribution in such a social arrangement will depend on political choice as well as resource market prices. The appropriate future need not be clearly stated in detail but in broad outlines. What other single criterion can be used to guide a flow of technological transfer in and out of a country such as India? It is not for scientists, even futurists, to speculate in isolation about a desired feasible future, but that must be a subject of national debate in many countries as new avenues of development are to be paved by the creation of new technologies. Certainly the trodden path should no longer be traced mechanically.

TABLE 1

(Millions of U.S. Dollars)

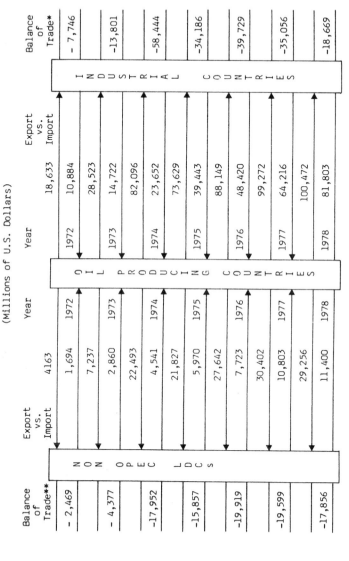

Balance of Trade**	NON OPEC LDCs — Export vs. Import		Year	OIL PRODUCING COUNTRIES	Year	Export vs. Import		INDUSTRIAL COUNTRIES — Balance of Trade*
– 2,469	4163	1,694	1972		1972	18,633	10,884	– 7,746
– 4,377	7,237	2,860	1973		1973	28,523	14,722	–13,801
–17,952	22,493	4,541	1974		1974	82,096	23,652	–58,444
–15,857	21,827	5,970	1975		1975	73,629	39,443	–34,186
–19,919	27,642	7,723	1976		1976	88,149	48,420	–39,729
–19,599	30,402	10,803	1977		1977	99,272	64,216	–35,056
–17,856	29,256	11,400	1978		1978	100,472	81,803	–18,669

Source: IMF Statistical Bureau, Direction of Trade, 1979.
* Balance of trade between oil producing and industrial countries.
** Balance of trade between oil producing and non-OPEC LDCs.
Arrows show the direction of payments.

367

TABLE 2

EXTERNAL DISBURSED DEPT OUTSTANDING AND DEPT SERVICE
OF DEVELOPING COUNTRIES, 1973-1976

(Billions of dollars)

| Item and Country Group | 1973 | 1974 | 1975 | 1976 | Debt Service | | |
					1973	1974	1975	1976
Total external debt (disbursed)								
Developing countries a/ . .	101.0	125.1	155.0	185.1	14.4	18.2	22.8	28.1
Oil-exporting countries	22.4	24.5	28.8	34.6	3.0	4.0	5.2	6.4
Non-oil exporting developing countries	78.6	100.7	126.2	150.5	11.4	14.2	17.6	21.7
Low-income developing countries (1975 per capita income $265 or less)	21.1	23.7	27.7	31.4	1.4	1.7	2.1	2.3
Other developing countries (1975 per capita income above $265)	57.5	77.0	98.5	119.1	10.0	12.5	15.5	19.4

Source: Centre for Development Planning, Projections and Policies of the United Nations
Secretariat, based on Organization for Economic Co-operation and Development,
Development Co-operation, 1976 and ibid, 1977, (Paris).

a/ The debt statistics are based on OECD/World Bank expanded reporting system, as reported by
creditors on some 130 developing countries. The figures differ from the World Bank reports
not only on account of the number of countries covered but also because of the inclusion of
additional items such as export credits reported by creditors other than suppliers' credits,
and private credits which are not guaranteed in the debtor country.

368

TABLE 3

HISTORICAL PERIODS OF ENERGY TECHNOLOGIES AND RESOURCES

RENEWABLE SOLAR ENERGY PERIODS	NON-RENEWABLE FOSSIL FUEL PERIODS	RENEWABLE ENERGY & FUSION PERIOD
ISE	**ISE**	
Wood Fuel	Wood	Nuclear Fusion Energy
Bio Mass (Including	Bio Mass	Hydroelectric
Human & Draft Animal)	Coal	Wind Energy
Wind & Water Mill	Oil	Bio Mass
Minimal Natural Gas	Water & Wind Mill	Tidal and Wave Energy
Oil	Hydro Electric (1882)	Geothermal
Coal	Geothermal	Coal and Minimal Oil Gas
		Wood
		Other ISE and DSE

0	NOW	2100 TIME
BC		

Indirect Solar Energy (ISE)

1. Forests (wood)
2. Fuel Plantation
3. Energy Crops
4. Biomass - Biogas
5. Human and Draft Animals

Direct Solar Energy (DSE)

1. Wind Mill
2. Hydroelectric Generators
3. Roof Collectors
4. Photovoltaic
5. Solar Architecture

369

References

Aronson, J.D. (ed.) (1979). <u>Debt and the Less Developed Countries</u>. Boulder,Col.: West View Press, .

Bergman, L. and M. Radetzki (1979). 'How will the third world be affected by OECD energy strategies?' <u>The Journal of Energy and Development</u>, Vol. 5, No. 1, Autumn, pp. 19-31.

Chatel, B. H. (1979). 'Technology assessment and developing countries.' <u>Technological Forecasting and Social Change</u>, Vol. 13, No. 3, April , pp. 203-211.

Chenery, H. B. (1960). 'Patterns of industrial growth'. <u>American Economic Review</u>, Vol. 50, No. 4, September (1960), pp. 624-654.

Diwan, R. (1981). 'Energy implications of Indian economic development: decade of 1960-70 and after.' <u>The Journal of Energy and Development</u>, Vol. 3, No. 2, Spring, pp. 318-337.

Gladwin, T. N. (1978). 'Technology and material culture.' In <u>The Cultural Environment of International Business</u>, edited by Vern Terstra. Southwestern, pp. 175-218.

Goulet, D. (1977). <u>The Uncertain Promise: Value Conflicts in Technology Transfer</u>. New York: IDOC, North America.

Harper, P. and Boyle, G. (eds.) (1976). <u>Radical Technology</u>. New York: Pantheon Books.

Houthakker, H. S. and M. Kennedy (1978). 'Long-range energy prospects.' <u>The Journal of Energy and Development</u>, Vol. 4, No. 1, Autumn , pp. 1-28.

Holsen, J. A. (1977). 'Notes on the 'LDC dept problem'.' <u>World Development</u>, Vol. 7, No. 2, February, pp. 145-159.

Khan, H.A. (1981). 'Basic needs and energy-intensity of technologies: a social accounting matrix for Korea with energy-based classifications of production.' Working Paper, Department of Economics, Cornell University, December.

Kraft, J. and A. Kraft (1980). 'Notes and comments on the relationship between energy and GNP.' The Journal of Energy and Development, Vol. 3, No. 2, Spring, pp. 401-404.

Lambertini, A. (1979). 'World energy prospects and the developing world.' Finance and Development, Vol. 16, No. 4, December, pp. 18-23.

Long, F. (1979). 'The Role of Social Science Inquiry in Technology Transfer.' American Journal of Economics and Sociology, Vol. 38, No. 3, July , pp. 261-274.

Mears, L. G. (1978). 'Energy from agriculture: the Brazilian experiment.' Environment, Vol. 20, No. 10, December, pp. 17-20.

Palmedo, P. F. (1977). 'Energy technology assessment: consideration of geographical scale.' The Journal of Energy and Development, Vol. 2, No. 2, Spring, pp. 207-217.

Parvin, M. (1982). 'Political economy of development with a modicum of fossil fuel and foreign exchange resources.' (forthcoming).

Parvin, M. (1975). 'Technological diffusion, optimum level of backward-ness and the rate of per capita income growth: an econometric approach.' The American Economist, Vol. 19, No. 1, Spring, pp. 23-31.

Parvin, M. (1976). 'Technology, economics and politics of oil: a global view.' Journal of International Affairs, Vol. 30, No. 1, Summer, pp. 97-110.

Parvin, M. and Grammas, G. (1981). 'Çapacity, energy and environment in developing industries.' In Energy and Environment in the Developing Countries. Edited by Manas Chatterji. New York: John Wiley and Sons, pp. 153-166.

Parvin, M. and Grammas, G. (1976). 'Optimization models for environmental pollution control: a synthesis.' Journal of Environmental Economics and Management, Vol. 3, No. 2, August, pp. 113-128.

Ramsay, C. W. (1978). 'Second thought about the energy crisis.' The Journal of Energy and Development, Vol. 4, No. 1, Autumn, pp. 49-71.

Sagasti, F. R. (1976). 'Technological self-reliance and cooperation among third world countries.' World Development, Vol. 4, No. 10/11, October-November, pp. 939-946.

Sarkar, P.L. (1978). 'Transfer of technology to less-developed countries: Indian experience with multinational corporations.' The Indian Economic Journal, Vol. 76, NO. 2, October-December, pp. 131-151.

Schumacher, E. F. (1974). Small is Beautiful. London: Sphere Books, Ltd.

Sunkel, Oswaldo (1972). 'Big business and dependencia.' <u>Foreign</u>
<u>Affairs</u>, April pp. 517-531.

Westphal, L. E. (1978). 'Research on appropriate technology.'
<u>Industry and Development</u>, No. 2, Spring, pp. 28-45.

Wright, J. D. (1975). 'The natural resource requirements of commodities.' <u>Applied Economics</u>, Vol. 7, pp. 31-39.

28 Location and agricultural risk in India

DONALD W. JONES AND CHANDRIKA KAUL

1. Introduction

Agriculture is a notoriously risky economic activity. Much has been learned about the sources of agricultural risk, and there has been a considerable amount of intellectual energy invested in the study of agriculturalists' organizational responses to risk; the role of risk in land tenure choice has been an especially heavily debated topic (Cheung, 1969; Reid, 1976; Newbery and Stiglitz, 1979; Halligan, 1980; Brown and Atkinson, 1981). The inherent riskiness of agriculture has even placed rigorous demands upon econometric investigation of agricultural activity (Nerlove, 1958).

Agriculture is a large industry in many countries, particularly in developing countries, many of which are primarily agricultural producers, and it is a very strongly space-using activity. The risk associated with agriculture derives not solely from the time lag between input application and delivery of outputs but also from the sheer spatial extent of production. Where this risk occurs within a country, has been a relatively neglected topic. Although coefficients of variation of yields for a number of crops have been examined on region and state wide basis in earlier treatises and texts such as Schultz (1953) and Heady (1952), the only explicit treatment of spatial characteristics of risk and risk-related activities in agriculture has been by Jones (1979a, 1979b, 1980) in work on location and land tenure choice. The present paper uses some of the theory developed in those papers to guide a preliminary empirical investigation of location and agricultural risk in India. In the first section, the theory is developed in an intuitive fashion. The origin of a spatial component of agricultural risk is demonstrated to be contained in transportation costs and is identifiable in a simple version of the Thunen land use model. The second section discusses the data used and the methodology of constructing several measures of risk. The measure of risk which is used in the first section is the coefficient of variation of the net farm revenue from a single crop which in the simplest case reduces to the coefficient of variation of the farm gate price of the crop. Once it is taken into account that more than one crop is usually grown in a small area, possibly by the same farmer, the covariation of the risk associated with different crops becomes of interest. Comparisons of several measures of risk, the coefficient of variation of revenue from individual crops, the coefficient of variation of total farm income, and averages of the two crop specific indexes, are made for a random sample of twenty-five percent of the districts of twelve states in

India. The locational measure used is a set of zone specific urban population potentials for each sample district. In addition, the average town and city size within each sample is used as a measure of more localized access to markets. Such measures were used satisfactorily by Jones (1979a, 1979b, 1980) in his work on agricultural location in the 19th Century United States.

In the third section, a number of new descriptive measures is presented as well as the results of some analytical work on relationships among sources of risk in specific crops, location relative to markets and implied behavioral responses.

2. Agricultural Risk, Location and Land Use

Immediate sources of risk in agriculture can be divided into output market risk, production risk, and coordination risk, in increasing order of complexity. Output market risk deals primarily with price fluctuations for the products of agriculture, whether they arise from exogenous demand shifts, supply shifts in another region (another region's production risks), or other less readily classifiable disturbances.

The Thunen land use model is useful at this point to demonstrate the locational incidence of risk. Consider the homogeneous plain populated with perfectly mobile workers and either perfectly immobile landowners or absentee landowners. Let only one homogeneous crop be produced at every location from the market, at the center of this plain, to the edge of land use, which is defined as the point of zero net (or transportation costs) marginal product of land. All farmers sell this output at the market for the same price per unit and pay transportation costs out of this gross price. Assuming for further simplicity, a zero elasticity of substitution among two inputs, land and labor, the net farm price of the output, the market price minus the transportation cost from where it was grown, is equivalent to the sum of land rent plus labor costs. Since labor is perfectly mobile and factor proportions are fixed, a constant wage bill per unit of output is subtracted at all locations. The remainder is land rent, which falls because transportation costs reduce the value of the output produced by the perfectly immobile land input. This land rent can be called farm income, or net farm income to denote that it is what remains after spatially invariant labor costs and spatially variable transportation costs have been deducted. Suppose that the price received at the market is stochastic, but is given to this small region by the outcome of a large market. Transportation costs do not vary because of variable demands placed on the transport system by agriculture; i.e., transport servicing this region is a small part of a large supply. By the assumption of a homogeneous plain, there are no local production risk differences; in fact, production is assumed to be nonstochastic. Outputs at each location do not vary, and transport costs do not vary as market prices vary. The variance of market output prices is the same for crops grown at every location and includes a nonstochastic transport cost the amount of which is larger as distance from market to farm increases. Expected net farm income is the expected rent on land, which falls as transport costs increase. So as distance from market increases, expected net farm income falls while the variance of the market price and variance of gross farm income, remains constant. Using the coefficient of variation of net farm income as a measure of risk, riskiness of farming increases with distance from the market, or from the point of disposal of output. This differential riskiness is due purely to the existence of transportation costs. Differences in the structure of the transportation market from that assumed to get this result could weaken the result; to overturn this result, a delivered output price change would have to trigger a greater percent change in the transportation rate. In terms of an elasticity of derived demand, the larger the share of transport costs in the delivered (market) price, the less likely is this a possibility, and in fact, given constant elasticities of substitution among outputs and transportation services at all locations, at some location the share of transport costs in market price would be large enough to ensure the result obtained with the strict, simplifying assumptions that the coefficient of variation of net farm income will increase with distance from the point of sale of output.

Coordination risk involves the timing of supplies of various inputs to agriculture. Water is important, but not at all if it is too late. So are seeds and fertilizer, if they can be sown and applied at the proper times. Seeds can be planted early or late and a crop can still be harvested, but it will not be the largest crop that could be obtained from the physical quantities of inputs used. This yield risk derives from simple environmental yield risk. There may be room for a systematic spatial component to this category risk. This coordination of inputs should depend on the efficiency with which markets (in the sense of supply agents and demand agents rather than in the small of a site, as the term has been used so far) operate, and it is very tempting to suppose that markets operate more efficiently closer to larger cities than far out in the countryside, particularly in developing countries (Schultz, 1953, Chapters 9 and 10, and pp. 280-82, 1964; Katzman, 1974).

Another type of risk not mentioned above is risk associated with possible changes in government policies. With more active government intervention in agriculture this is a more important source of risk. There are locational components to this type of risk but they are not directly related to distances from markets but rather to the location of the particular crop or crops affected by government policies. An example of this among the Indian crops studied here appear to be sugarcane which has the highest measure of covariance risk of revenue deriving from it, and the second highest coefficient of variation of income but has the lowest coefficient of variation of yield of any of the crops studied.

A number of options exists which farmers can employ to protect themselves against risk. One of the oldest methods is to farm separate plots. Parcelization of holdings can divide a farmer's land among locations with different local risk characteristics, e.g., use of both upland and bottom land fields can reduce the likelihood that less than catastrophic weather events will affect crops in both locations identically (McCloskey, 1975). Costs of this type of insurance effort are the additional time spent travelling among plots and the loss of land to paths between plots and possibly fences or walls between plots. Its greatest effectiveness would be to counter production risk.

Crop diversification is another device with which farmers can avoid risk, either from price or yield sources. Crops which have low correlations with the revenues from other crops, would tend to be chosen to be grown together since fluctuations in one crop would have little association with fluctuations in others. Neither boom nor bust seasons would be likely to coincide for such crops. If prices were stable, crops would be chosen according to correlation among their yields; if yields were relatively stable but prices were highly uncertain, correlations among prices would be the criteria. With both yields and prices subject to fluctuations, the returns (price times yield) correlations would be used to choose crop combinations.

Another risk reduction or insurance method is to take off farm employment. If the operator himself does not do so, some of his family members who work on the farm at peak labor demand times might take off-farm work. Commuting costs appear most clearly as a cost of this form of farm income insurance, so this diversification of employment should be engaged in closer to cities or towns where part time and seasonal work is available.

A final method of spreading risk is through choice of farm tenure. A contractual tenure arrangement assigns the rights to residual income, or the difference between the income expected at the beginning of the season and the actual income after harvest, among the suppliers of various inputs, usually the suppliers of land (the landlord) and the suppliers of labor (the tenant). A landlord who decides to operate his own farm, either by himself or with hired labor, accepts all the risk of the residual income. A cash renter will accept all the risk and his landlord will bear none since the rent is an amount stipulated beforehand. In a share arrangement, landlord and tenant each get a fixed proportion of the value of the output and thus share the risk between them in any proportion they desire. It has been pointed out that any division of risk between landlord and tenant can be achieved by the tenant farming part-time as a cash renter and hiring himself out for a fixed wage for the remainder of the time. In other words while sharecropping can spread risk around among factors suppliers, it is not necessary to achieve that risk diversification (Rao, 1971; Stiglitz, 1974; Reid, 1976). Reid (1976), however, has pointed to sharecropping as a device which can align inventiveness among different factor owners to reduce coordination risk. Newbery and Stiglitz (1979) have also shown that when some market imperfections exist, sharecropping (or tenure choice) is not a redundant risk spreading device. For instance, if crop diversification options are artificially restricted, sharecropping could be undertaken as a substitute. Thus, given Schultz's idea of a locational matrix of economic development in which factor markets work less well in remote areas where, independently of Schultz's ideas, coordination risk is probably greater, sharecropping should be a preferred form of farm tenure relative to cash rental further from cities.

Now that several risk spreading and reduction devices have been briefly presented, the substitutability or complementarity among them should be addressed. An obvious beginning point is with the commuting cost of off-farm employment. The commuting cost component of the total cost of taking off-farm employment is lower nearer to cities and towns where such jobs have heavier concentrations. However, the closer to cities farms are located and the greater are nearby wage opportunities, the more fully employed will farmers have to keep their land,

themselves, and their workers, resulting in a more even distribution
over the year of demand for labor on the farm. The availability of
farm workers will be less likely to coincide with the requirements of
urban employers who require a regular, industrially disciplined
workforce. It may in fact, be the case that higher foregone earnings
nearer cities will exceed savings in commuting costs over more
distantly located farms. Not all off-farm employment need be in cities
though. Rural non-farm employment would have a low commuting cost
component. The substitutability or complementarity of rural off-farm
work and crop diversification would depend on the seasonal characteristics of the crops and the off-farm employment. When tenure choice is
a major option, sharecropping and crop diversification should be
substitutes. To the extent that sharecropping involves more and longer
seasonal slack time than does cash renting, which would tend to be
complementary to crop diversification, there may be some measure of
complementarity between share renting and taking off-farm employment on
a seasonal basis, although travel distances would tend to be longer for
more remotely located sharecroppers.

Thus the spatial pattern of farm income diversification --
protection against risk -- would have more owner operators and cash
renters nearer cities and a higher proportion of sharecroppers, to cash
renters, in particular, at remote locations. More crop diversification
will be undertaken near cities for two reasons: it is complementary to
cash rental, and probably to owner operation, and it helps reduce slack
labor demand time near cities. More distant farmers will tend to take
off-farm employment on a seasonal basis.

3.   The Data and Construction of Risk Measures

Data from 1954-55 through 1970-71 were obtained on outputs, gross
hectares sown, yields and average prices received by farmers, for
anywhere between two and ten crops for sixty-eight districts. Absent
or largely incomplete price data reduced the number of districts
finally used in this portion of the study to forty-one. Different
districts had different combinations of crops so the full sample of 4
districts was seldom used in toto. Since most of the risk measures
used referred to the risk of a specific crop in a specific district,
risk characteristics of each of eight major crops were analyzed using
the subset of the forty-three districts in which that crop was grown.

The measure of agricultural risk which is new to this work is an
adaptation of the covariance risk measure used in portfolio analysis.
In portfolio analysis, the risk of each asset can be decomposed into
risk which is unique to it and which can be diversified away simply by
adding more assets to a portfolio, and systematic, or market, risk
which is nondiversifiable. The idea behind market risk is that one
reason all assets' returns change over time is that they are all
affected by market-wide events. From each asset's covariance with the
market return, all assets' covariances can be easily computed as well.
Thus, the return on each asset, R_i, can be divided into its unique
risk α_i, and its market risk, β_i:

$$R_i = \alpha_i + \beta_i R_m + e_i,$$

where R_m is the return on the market portfolio, and e is a random
distrubance with $E(e_i) = 0$, $E[e_i(R_m - \bar{R}_m)] = 0$, and $E(e_i$

$e_j) = 0$ for all pairs i and j, $i \neq j$. Beta is the covariance risk of the asset to which it refers.

The data available for the Indian districts did not permit computation of actual rates of return; as an alternative, the total income from each crop was regressed on the total income from all crops produced in the district. This technique biases betas toward unity for small portfolios (small numbers of crops) and for crops accounting for larger proportions of gross cropped acreage but offers the advantage of permitting variable weights per asset (crop). These regressions were performed for each crop in each of the forty-three districts over the seventeen year time span, sometimes using ordinary least squares, sometimes a Cochrane-Orcutt iterative technique, and occasionally OLS with a time trend. In less than a handful of cases were substantial differences in estimated betas produced across the three different techniques.

A second measure of the riskiness of specific crops in specific districts is the coefficient of variation of total income from a crop ($CVPQ_i$, where i = crop). Three indexes measure the risk of agricultural income in a district: the unweighted average of the estimated betas for all crops in a district (MUEB), the unweighted averate of the coefficients of variation of all crops in a district (MUCV), and the coefficient of variation of total agricultural income in a district (CVTR). Means of these risk measures are presented in Table 1. In that table, EB_i is the estimated beta for each crop, in elasticity form. The means of MUEB, MUCV, and CVTR are presented for each crop's subset of districts as well as for all districts. From Table 1, sugarcane, groundnuts and wheat are the riskiest crops in the covariance sense; they each add to the risk of agricultural income in the districts in which they are grown. Jowar and gram reduce risk more than any other crops; rice is neutral for all practical purposes; and cotton and bajra reduce risk slightly. The last column of Table 1 presents the means of coefficents of variation of prices received in each district and of yields in the different crops, as the immediate sources of the risk measured in the five indexes. It is interesting to observe that sugarcane, which has the highest average and the second highest $CVPQ_i$ has the lowest average coefficient of variation of yields. It leads all the other crops in price variability, however.

Looking at Table 2, in which the columns CVP_i and CVY_i contain the coefficient of variation across districts of the average coefficient of variation within each district over the 17 year time period, for prices and yields, the variability across districts of the yield of sugarcane was greater than the variability across districts of any other crop. The variability across sugarcane-producing districts of the price of sugarcane, while the third highest variability of any crop's price, was only about one-third the variability of its yield. This low within-district and high between-district yield variability and high within-district, low between-district price variability suggests some uniform, nonlocal price disturbance as the source of sugarcane's volatility as an income earner over the period 1954-55/1970-71. In the case of rice, there is also substantially more yield variation among districts than within; dividing rice districts into above average and below average yield groups reduces the coefficient of variation of yields to .3106 and .4757 respectively, both below the all-district figure of .5424. The all-district

TABLE 1

MEANS OF RISK VARIABLES FOR GROUPS OF DISTRICTS

Group of Districts	EB_i	$CVPQ_i$	MUEB	MUCV	CVTR	CVP_i	CVY_i
All districts	--	--	.9539	.6524	.5467	--	--
Cotton (C)	.9191	.5742	.9490	.6444	.5609	.4184	.3298
Sugarcane (SC)	1.1343	.7230	.9670	.6570	.5436	.6095	.1922
Groundnuts (GN)	1.1241	.7572	.9631	.6220	.5006	.5234	.2881
Wheat (W)	1.0461	.6861	.8889	.6798	.5902	.4006	.2416
Jowar (J)	.6761	.5496	.9382	.6379	.5409	.3787	.3854
Gram (G)	.7782	.5660	.8981	.6747	.5921	.5017	.2467
Rice (R)	.9781	.6057	.9728	.6482	.5349	.3351	.2582
Bajra (BJ)	.8865	.5545	.9235	.6237	.5132	.3694	.3660

TABLE 2

COEFFICIENTS OF VARIATION OF RISK VARIABLES ACROSS DISTRICTS,
FOR GROUPS OF DISTRICTS

Group of Districts	EB_i	$CVPQ_i$	MUEB	MUCV	CVTR	CVP_i	CVY_i
All districts	--	--	.2335	.2205	.2996	--	--
C	1.0727	.5266	.2097	.2650	.3889	.1904	.4338
SC	.4865	.2323	.2525	.2274	.3267	.2019	.5981
GN	.3975	.3048	.1922	.2329	.2936	.1137	.4442
W	.4019	.4119	.2623	.1605	.2709	.0952	.2947
J	.7947	.3948	.2402	.2331	.3384	.2125	.2489
G	.5152	.1392	.2414	.1570	.2883	.1129	.2652
R	.4234	.4306	.2517	.2231	.3406	.4308	.5424
BJ	.5208	.4599	.2189	.2624	.3035	.0960	.3470

coefficient of variation is probably picking up differences between irrigated and non-irrigated areas.

Table 1 indicates roughly similarly sized values of MUEF, MUC and CVTR in the different groups of districts, MUEB and MUCV exhibiting about a five percent variation on either side of the all-district value and CVTR about nine percent. The crop-specific risk indexes, EB and CVPQ show much more relative variability across crops. Examination of Table 2 shows that there is also much greater across-district variation in the crop-specific indexes than in the average indexes. Other important questions such as the extent to which the variance in these risk measures is accounted for by systematic location variables and non-systematic factors will not be dealt with in great detail due to lack of available space, but in the next section a summary of findings will be given.

4. Summary of Findings

The work reported above is still too preliminary to draw firm conclusions of any wide nature, but a summary of the findings will be useful.

Among the district-average risk measures (non-crop specific), MUEB, MUCV, and CVTR, it is found that average covariance risk, MUEB, increases with greater access to markets while the average coefficient of variation of revenue per crop, MUCV, and the coefficient of variation of total crop revenue, CVTR, both generally decrease closer to markets. Whether farm operators or farm laborers are taking part-time off-farm employment has not been determined yet, but larger percentages of the district workforces participating in rural household industries, rural nonhousehold industries, and especially rural construction, all lower these three measures of agricultural risk.

Crop specific risk is measured with two indexes, the covariance risk of each crop's revenue with the entire agricultural revenue in the district, EB_i, and the coefficient of variation of each crop's revenue, $CVPQ_i$. Distance from markets influences these risk measures but in crop-specific ways. Employment in rural and urban household, non-household, and construction industries reduces EB_i and $CVPQ_i$, and rural employment in these industries has larger, stabilizing elasticities.

The coefficients of variation of yields are more stable nearer markets, and again employment in the three selected industry groups is usually stabilizing, and rural employment even more so. Larger mean annual rainfall reduces CVY_i except for cotton and wheat, and possibly groundnuts.

Crop diversification in a district is measured by N, the number of major crops per ten thousand gross cropped hectares. There appears to be a wider array of crops nearer markets, and larger percentages of the workforce in the three industry groups are associated with larger N. In tests of the risk reducing effects of adding more crops, N appears to be largely endogenous and the risk indexes largely exogenous. Two motives for altering N are prominent. A higher price for each specific crop reduces the size of N; i.e., a higher price of any crop induces expansion of that crop and a reduction in the number of other crops.

Second is a risk aversion effect; higher coefficients of variation of specific prices and yields increase N. Greater price and yield risk indexes induce more diversification of crops.

Spatial patterns of crop acreage shares may be produced in the regressions of the L_i on the access measures, D_i and A. Industrial employment appears to have highly crop-specific effects on the acreage shares; these relationships are thought to be derivative of the input-output relations and seasonalities of specific crops and specific industries within the industry groups. Prices and yields do not work well as predictors of acreage shares, probably because of information loss involved in using time series averages. However, the variabilities of prices and yields perform well, suggesting that farmers shift out of crops as their prices and/or yields become riskier.

Yields of all the crops generally increase with access to markets, exceptions being sugarcane and cotton. Responses of yields to mean annual rainfall are quite crop specific. The occasional negative responsiveness of a yield to the coefficient of variation of its price suggests some risk related behavior in which farmers devote more resources to crops whose prices are more dependable. Yields are higher where more industrial employment opportunities exist, as predicted, but construction employment has less of an effect on yields than does employment in household and non-household industries.

Overall, employment in construction appears to have larger effects on risk measures and on behavior reflecting risk aversion and less influence on pure profit maximizing behavior. It is thought that the seasonality and mobility of construction activities, and possibly more common skills involved in it, make employment in construction a prime method of reducing riskiness of farm income. More locationally-fixed activities included in household and nonhousehold industries will have stronger effects on spatially less mobile profit making endeavors reflected in yields and rents per acre, but less on risk avoidance since their seasonal components are probably less pronounced and their skill demands often more specific.

A final group of regressions may present some checks on the usefulness of the indexes of access to markets and risk. Total crop revenue per gross cropped hectare is found to increase with access to markets and with average town size and to compensate for greater riskiness of total crop revenue. Thus, both the basic Thunen model feature of rents per acre declining with distance from markets and the risk-expected utility feature of increasing risk-incrasing return are found.

References

Bhalla, Surjit S. (1981). 'India's closed economy and world inflation,' in William P. Cline and Associates, World Inflation and the Developing Countries. Washington, D.C.: Brookings Institution, pp. 136-65.

Brown, D.J. and J. H. Atkinson, (1981). 'Cash and share renting: An empirical test of the link between entrepreneurial ability and contractual choice,' Bell Journal of Economics 12, No. 1, pp. 296-99.

Cheung, Stephen N.S., (1969). The Theory of Share Tenancy, Chicago: University of Chicago Press.

Conroy, Michael E. (1975). Regional Economic Growth: Diversification and Control. New York: Praeger.

Davis, Lance E. (1965). 'The investment market, 1870-1914: the evolution of a national market. Journal of Economic History 25, No. 3.

Halligan, William, (1978). 'Self-selection by contractual choice and the theory of sharecropping,' Bell Journal of Economics 9, No. 2, pp. 344-54.

Heady, Earl O., (1952). Economics of Agricultural Production and Resource Use. Englewood Cliffs, N.J.: Prentice-Hall.

Jones, Donald W., (1982). 'Land use and land tenure,' Annals of the Association of American Geographers 72, No. 3, pp. 316-31.

_____, (1983). 'Agricultural risk, farm income diversification, and land use,' Forthcoming, Geographical Analysis, 15, No. 3.

_____, (1980). 'Maps of land tenure in the United States in 1880.'

Karplus, Richard (1978). 'Capital markets in the United States: 1870-1910,' presented in the Economic History Workshop, University of Chicago.

Katzman, Martin, (1974). 'The Von Thunen paradigm, the industrial-urban hypothesis and the spatial structure of agriculture,' American Journal of Agricultural Economics 56, No. 4, pp. 683-96.

McCloskey, Donald N., (April 1975). 'English open fields as behavior towards risk,' Presented in the Agricultural Economics Workshop, Universitgy of Chicago.

Newbery, David M.G. and Joseph E. Stiglitz, (1979). "Sharecropping, risk sharing and the importance of imperfect information,' in James A. Roumasset, Jean-Marc Boussard, and Inderjit Singh (eds.), Risk, Uncertainty and Agricultural Development. New York: Agricultural Development Council, pp. 311-39.

Rao, C.H. Hanumantha, (1971). 'Uncertainty, entrepreneurship, and share-cropping in India,' Journal of Political Economy 79, No. 3, pp. 578-95.

Reid, Joseph D. Jr. (1976). 'Sharecropping and agricultural uncertainty,' Economic Development and Cultural Change 24, No. 3, pp. 549-76.

Schultz, Theodore W. (1964). Transforming Traditional Agriculture. New Haven: Yale University Press.

_____ (1953). The Economic Organization of Agriculture, New York: McGraw-Hill.

Stigler, George J. (1967). 'Imperfections in the capital market,' Journal of Political Economy 75, No. 3, pp. 287-92.

Stiglitz, Joseph E. (1974). 'Incentives and risk sharing in share-cropping,' Review of Economic Studies 41, No. 2, pp. 219-56.

29 Income contribution of the petroleum industry: a case study of the province of Alberta and implications for developing regions

SARASWATI SINGH

1. Introduction

The Alberta economy has been growing rapidly for the last two decades. It is frequently characterized as a booming province of Canada. Its unemployment rate is one of the lowest among the provinces. Its gross domestic product has been increasing rapidly. So has been the case with the government revenue and expenditure, private business investment, consumer spending and population. Other important economic indicators also show similar strength.

The rapid growth of the Alberta economy is largely attributed to the petroleum industry. However, economists are not unanimous about the extent of the contribution of the petroleum industry to the province's income. Caves and Holton (1959) concluded that although a large gross domestic[1] product was created by the petroleum industry, its income impact was greatly diminished because of the small cost of production, high profits and a high proportion of profits accruing to non-residents. On the other hand, both Hanson (1958) and Weinrich (1965) estimated that the petroleum industry created a high income and employment impact in Alberta. The conclusions of Caves and Holton are more pertinent to the present conditions in Alberta, and other developing regions than that of Hanson and Weinrich. Although the expenditures of the petroleum industry have been very high indeed, their income contributions have been relatively small. This has happened primarily because of the lack of diversification of the Alberta economy and foreign control of the petroleum industry. Therefore, this study has the following objectives:

1. To determine the magnitude of income contributions of the petroleum industry to the province of Alberta in the time

* This study was made possible by a research grant jointly awarded to Professor E.H. Shaffer and the author by the Department of Energy, Mines and Resources, government of Canada to estimate the income and employment contributions of the petroleum industry to the province of Alberta. Professor Shaffer estimated the employment impact and the author estimated the income impact. The author acknowledges with gratitude the important contributions made by Professor Shaffer to this study. Regional content of the expenditures of the petroleum industry was estimated by Mr. E. Koroluk.

period 1964 to 1970, and

2. To examine generally the policy implications for developing regions (or countries) arising out of the income contribution estimates made in this study.

This study throws light on the process of economic expansion in less developed regions (or countries), primarily caused by the export of petroleum and related products. Rapid increase in price and volume of oil and related products has created new incomes into the petroleum producing regions. Although these incomes have been substantial, they could have been larger. A considerable amount of these incomes has leaked out to other regions and countries. Therefore, from the viewpoint of economic development, it is as much important to determine the degree of leakages as it is to determine the income contributions of a resource based industry in a developing region (or a country). These likages from the newly created incomes have important policy implications. The problems of Alberta in this regard are not unique. It will be true for the provinces of Newfoundland and Nova Scotia as well, when significant production of oil takes place there. Members of OPEC countries and other oil exporting less developed countries such as Mexico face similar problems. Therefore, the analysis presented in this paper has a fair degree of generality (see also Hotelling, 1931, Devarajan and Fisher, 1981, DasGupta and Heal, 1974, Courchene and Melvin, 1980, Scarfe and Powerie, 1980, Koopmans 1973).

This paper is presented in three parts. The first part discusses the procedure used for estimating the income contributions of the petroleum industry. The second part presents the estimates of these income contributions and the third part presents the conclusions and important policy implications arising out of this study.

2. Estimation Procedure

The petroleum industry directly contributes to Alberta income through its production and capital expenditures. It indirectly contributes to Alberta income through the expenditures of the petroleum dependent industries and the government. However, indirect income contributions are limited to that portion of the expenditures of the petroleum dependent industries and the government which are atributed to the activities of the petroleum industry.

Income contributions of these expenditures can be measured with the help of a Keynesian macroeconomic model. The basic Keynesian income model can be written as:

$$Y = C + I + G + (E-M) \tag{1}$$

where

C = total consumption expenditures,
I = total private investment expenditures,
G = total government expenditures,
E = total exports, and
M = total imports.

A part of consumer, private business, non-resident and government

386

expenditures is incurred on domestically produced goods and services and the rest on imports. Suppose p is the ratio of consumer spending on goods and services produced within the province to total consumer spending. Similarly, q is the ratio of private business expenditure on goods and services produced within the province to total private business expenditures in Alberta, r is the ratio of government expenditure on goods and services produced within the province to total public expenditures in Alberta, and s is the regional content of Alberta exports. As total dollar value of imports is M, the following equation is true:

$$M = (1-p) C + (1-q) I + (1-r) G + (1-s) E. \tag{2}$$

Equation (2) divides total imports, M, into imports for consumption, for private business investment, for government and for exports. Substituting equation (2) for M into (1) gives,

$$Y = pC + qI + rG + sE. \tag{3}$$

Equation (3), ordinarily used for accounting national income, can also be used for accounting Alberta income. Through its expenditures, the petroleum industry contributes to Alberta income by increasing the magnitude of C, I, G and E.

The procedure, used in this study to estimate the income contributions of the petroleum industry, can be broken into two parts. The first part estimates the income multiplier of the expenditures of the petroleum industry in Alberta. The second part estimates the total dollar expenditures of the petroleum and petroleum dependent industries in Alberta. When the expenditure figures are multiplied by the multiplier, income contributions of the petroleum industry to Alberta are obtained. The two parts of the procedure are explained below.

If k is the marginal propensity to consume, a dollar of expenditure, $(dE = \$1)$, assuming that this expenditure is of capital nature, will generate qdE amount of income in the region in the first round, pk in the second, $(pk)^2$ in the third and so on. These income effects of one dollar of expenditure can be written as

$$dY = [1 + pk + (pk)^2 + (pk)^3 \ldots (pk)^n]qdE. \tag{4}$$

This income series can be evaluated as,

$$dY = \frac{dEq}{1-pk} \quad \text{or} \quad (dE)q \cdot \frac{1}{1-pk} \tag{5}$$

Therefore, a dollar's expenditure creates $\frac{q}{1-pk}$ amount of income. If the expenditure is G or E, the numerator in Equation (5) will change to a r or s as is the case. In order to estimate the income multiplier, the values of marginal propensity to consume and regional contents of consumer and petroleum industry expenditures (i.e., k, p, q, and s) need to be estimated.

3. Estimates of Parameters

The procedure used in this study for estimating income contributions is not beset by econometric estimation problems which are common in a single or multiple equations model. Of the parameters that need to be estimated (see Equation (5)), regional content estimates are made on population basis and the marginal propensity to consume estimate is likely to be reliable as consumption is a fairly stable function of income. Therefore, the income contribution estimates in this study are good approximations.

3.1 Estimate of Marginal Propensity to Consume

The consumption function for Alberta was estimated using a linear time-series regression equation and annual data for the period 1961-1975. The estimated values of the parameters in the function are presented below:

	Coeffi-cents	Standard error of coefficients	T-value	R^2	D-W Statistic
Personal disposal income	0.88	0.019	45.85	0.997	2.11
Constant	301.90	93.86	3.21		

The above estimated value of marginal propensity to consume, 0.88, is close to other available estimates. Gillen and Guccione (1970) estimated marginal propensity to consume for the prairie provinces, British Columbia, Ontario and Canada as 0.91, 0.90, 0.90 and 0.94, respectively. Also, these time series estimates of the marginal propensity to consume are close to the cross-section estimate of Gillen and Guccione study.

3.2 Estimate of the Regional Content of Consumer Expenditures[1]

The value of regional content of consumer expenditures, p, has been estimated for 1967 at 0.61. Statistics Canada has published sufficient data for 1967 for this purpose. However, sufficient data are not available for other years of the period for which income contribution estimates have been made. Therefore, the value of p has been assumed to be constant.

3.3 Estimates of the Regional Contents of the Petroleum Industry Expenditures

Regional contents of different expenditures of the petroleum industry in dollar were individually estimated. These estimates were multiplied by $\frac{1}{1-pk}$ to obtain the income contribution estimates of the petroleum industry. The regional content estimates of different petroleum industry expenditures will be presented later. As marginal propensity to consume, k, has been estimated at 0.88 and the regional content of consumer expenditure, p, at 0.61, the value of $\frac{1}{1-pk}$ is 2.15. Since the values of k and p are constant for the time period studied, this value is also constant over the period.

4. Estimates of the Income Contributions of the Petroleum Industry

Estimates of the income contributions of the petroleum industry will be presented in two stages. In the first stage, direct income

contributions of the petroleum industry will be presented. As
mentioned previously, direct income contributions consist of the income
arising out of the production and capital expenditures. Income
contributions of the transport phase of the petroleum industry has been
also included in the direct income contributions. In the second stage,
indirect income contributions of the petroleum industry consisting of
income contributions of oil refining and marketing, and petrochemical
industries will be presented.

Estimates of the regional contents of the expenditures of the
petroleum and its dependent industries are presented in the following
five tables. These estimates are presented both in dollars and
percentages. The procedures used for estimating regional contents can
not be described fully because of space constraints. However, as the
general reliability of these estimates is essential, basic information
concerning the use of procedures is presented in these tables.

4.1 Production Expenditures

Production expenditures consist of the expenditure incurred on
operation of wells, royalty payments to the title holders for
production, and capital and operational expenditures for natural gas
plants. Estimates of the regional contents of these expenditures are
presented in Table 1.

4.2 Capital Expenditures

Capital expenditures of the petroleum industry include
expenditure on administration and overhead, land acquisition, survey,
exploration, drilling and other developmental activity. Estimated
regional contents of these expenditures are presented in Table 2.

4.3 Transportation Expenditures

Transportation expenditures are mainly incurred on moving petroleum
products from well head to the next stage of processing such as
refining. Transportation activities consist of the operation of oil
and gas gathering lines, feeder-lines and cross-country oil and gas
pipelines. Transportation expenditures include expenditure incurred on
capital equipment, operation, regional tax, lease, rental,
construction, labor, fuel, electricity, and material and supply.

Transportation expenditures have been divided into operations and
investments for estimating regional content. Regional contents of
these expenditures are presented in Table 3.

4.4 Oil Refining and Marketing

Oil refining and marketing, and petrochemicals are the only
industries that have been considered as petroleum dependent
industries. These industries are so heavily dependent on the petroleum
industry that they would not exist otherwise.

A part of raw petroleum products is processed into final goods such
as gasoline and light oils. The rest are processed into intermediate
goods. Expenditure on refining and marketing activities is classified
into construction, investment, wage and salary, tax, supply and

TABLE 1
REGIONAL CONTENT OF PRODUCTION EXPENDITURES

Year	1964	1965	1966	1967	1968	1969	1970
	($000,000)						
Production @63%[1]	42	42	48	50	60	59	76
Gas processing @60%[2]	38	39	48	81	83	87	139
Royalties @ 90%[3]	70	71	82	96	113	122	141
Total Regional Content	150	152	178	227	256	268	356

SOURCES:
1. Canadian Petroleum Association, Statistical Year Book, 1971.
2. E.J. Hanson, Dynamic Decade, (McClelland & Stewart, Toronto, 1958), pp. 149-151 and 180-183.
3. E.J. Hanson, "Regional Employment and Income Effects of the Petroleum Industry in Alberta", a paper presented to the Council of Economics, American Institute of Mining, Metallurgical and Petroleum Engineers (AIME), Annual Conference, March 2, 1966, New York, N.Y.
4. Statistics Canada, Alberta Bureau of Statistics and petroleum industry sources.

NOTES:
1. Expenditure on production has been increasing rapidly. Its regional content, estimated at 55 percent in 1950 by Hanson, is estimated to have increased to 63 percent in 1970. This estimate is made in the following manner. Thirty-five percent of total cost of production consisted of wages and salaries. Regional content of these expenditures is very high and is estimated at 100 percent. Remaining 28 percent of regional content is contributed by the expenditure on fuel, electricity, materials and supplies.

2. These expenditures include both capital and operational expenditures. Capital expenditures have greatly varied over the years. Regional content of capital expenditures has been estimated to be 50 percent. The overall regional content of gas processing expenditures was estimated at 60 percent. Wages and salaries, which have a high regional content, constituded a significant portion of total operating cost.

3. The share of provincial government in royalty payments increased rapidly and reached four-fifths of the total in 1956. Regional content of royalty payments to the government is estimated at 100 percent. Of the remaining one-fifth of royalty payments, one-tenth was estimated to have accrued to Alberta residents and nine-tenths to corporations. On this basis, 90 percent of total royalty payments is estimated to have accrued to Alberta government and Alberta residents.equipment, land, local engineering, and operation. The estimated regional content of each of these items of expenditures is presented in Table 4.

TABLE 2

REGIONAL CONTENT OF CAPITAL EXPENDITURES

Year	($000,000)						
	1964	1965	1966	1967	1968	1969	1970
Overall @70%[1]	36	26	35	22	58	70	62
Exploration @60%[2]	19	25	41	60	52	52	49
Land acquisition @90%[3]	130	190	163	162	169	175	104
Drilling @66% and Devel. @33%[4]	100	121	109	120	130	136	122
Total Regional content	285	362	348	364	409	433	337

SOURCES:
1. Canadian Petroleum Association, Statistical Year Book, 1971.
2. E.J. Hanson, Dynamic Decade, (McClelland & Stewart, Toronto, 1958), pp. 129-132, 184-196, and 132-142.
3. E.J. Hanson, "Regional Employment and Income Effects of the Petroleum Industry in Alberta", a paper presented to the Council of Economics, American Institute of Mining, Metallurgical and Petroleum Engineers (AIME), Annual Conference, March 2, 1966, New York, N.Y.
4. Statistics Canada, Alberta Bureau of Statistics and petroleum industry sources.

NOTES:
1. Overhead expenditures include the overhead expenditures for exploration, development drilling, taxes (excluding income tax) and general expenses not included elsewhere. It is estimated that 50 percent of expenditure on administration and overhead is incurred on wages and salaries. Wage and salary payments have a very high regional content. The remaining 50 percent of the expenditure on administra tion and overhead consists of payments for office rentals, construction, materials, supplies, utility, and local taxes. Therefore, overall regional content of overhead and administrative expenses is estimated at 70 percent.
2. Exploration expenditures are primarily incurred on surveys. Survey work is mainly done by contractors, many of which are foreigners (mostly Americans) and are located in Calgary and Edmonton. These contractors employ highly skilled personnel, drilling contractors and independent geophysical and geological consultants. It is estimated that 45 percent of total expenditure on surveys are paid as salaries to geologists, geophysicists and crews, and payments to consultants. Another ten percent of total survey expenditures is estimated to have accrued to workers in Alberta manufacturing, wholesale and retail catering to survey teams. The remainder is spent on supplies and equipment. Overall regional content of exploration expenditures is estimated at 60 percent. Most of the personnel employed in survey work live in Alberta.
3. Land acquisition costs include payments for the purchase of lease, rental and fee. Presently, most of the petroleum rights in the province are held by the provincial government. Sale of leases,

and rentals for oil and natural gas acreages provided a major source of revenue to the provincial government. In the early years of the formation of the petroleum industry in Alberta, freehold and corporate holdings of subsurface rights of land were substantial. However, presently it is significantly less and 90 percent of payments for land acquisitions accrue to the provincial government and Alberta residents.

4. Expenditure on drilling and development is broadly divided into three categories. Firstly, expenditures are incurred on dry holes and capped gas wells. The average cost of drilling dry hole has been rapidly increasing over the years. Secondly, expenditures are incurred on producer wells drilled during the course of developing a field. These expenditures consist of cost for perforation, acidization, casing and tubing. Thirdly, expenditures are required for putting a well on production. These expenditures include expenditure on lifting and pumping equipment, flow lines, tanks and separators. These expenditures are known as "other developmental costs".

    Regional content of the above three types of drilling expenditures is estimated at 66 percent, 50 percent and 33 percent respectively. The figures in the fourth row of the table have been adjusted accordingly.

****

TABLE 3

REGIONAL CONTENT ESTIMATES OF TRANSPORTATION EXPENDITURES

Year	1964	1965	1966	1967	1968	($000,000) 1969	1970
Operation							
1. Canada's total transport revenue in dollars[1]	139	146	160	176	185	210	220
2. Alberta's share in percentage	45	46	46	48	49	49	49
3. Alberta's share in dollars (1x2)	63	67	74	85	91	103	108
4. Regional content in dollars @40%	25	27	30	34	36	41	43
Investment							
5. Regional content in dollars @40%[2]	20	27	63	32	36	37	37
6. Total regional content (4+5)	45	54	93	66	72	78	80

SOURCE:
1. Canadian Petroleum Association, Statistical Year Book, 1971.

2. E.J. Hanson, Dynamic Decade, (McClelland & Stewart, Toronto, 1958), pp. 165-167.
3. E.J. Hanson, "Regional Employment and Income Effects of the Petroleum Industry in Alberta", a paper presented to the Council of Economics, American Institute of Mining, Metallurgical and Petroleum Engineers (AIME), Annual Conference, March 2, 1966, New York, N.Y., p. 36.
4. Statistics Canada, Oil Pipeline Transport, Cat. No. 55-201.
5. Statistics Canada, Construction in Canada, Cat. No. 64-201.
NOTES:
1. Only a small portion of total transportation expenditures in western Canada was incurred in Alberta.
2. Wages and salaries, contractors' margin and consulting fee are estimated to constitute about 25 percent of total capital expenditure on transportation. These expenditures mainly accrued to Albertans. Another 15 percent of regional content is contributed by the payment for regional taxes, payments for right of way, purchases of regional materials and power, and receipts of owners and employees of business handling import of machinery, equipment and supplies.

****

TABLE 4

REGIONAL CONTENT ESTIMATES OF OIL REFINING AND MARKETING EXPENDITURES

Year	1964	1965	1966	1967	($000,000) 1968	1969	1970
Regional content of operating expenditures in refining and marketing @ 80%[1]	20.0	22.0	23.0	24.0	25.0	26.0	27.0
Regional content of investment expenditures in refining @ 50%[2]	3.0	3.2	2.0	5.1	2.1	1.4	3.1
Regional content of investment expenditures in marketing @ 60%[3]	2.0	2.9	3.4	3.9	5.9	4.8	5.6
Total Regional Content	25.0	28.0	28.0	33.0	33.0	32.0	36.0

SOURCE:
1. Canadian Petroleum Association, Statistical Year Book, 1971.
2. E.J. Hanson, Dynamic Decade, (McClelland & Stewart, Toronto, 1958), pp. 148-151.
3. E.J. Hanson, "Regional Employment and Income Effects of the

Petroleum Industry in Alberta", a paper presented to the Council of
Economics, American Institute of Mining, Metallurgical and
Petroleum Engineers (AIME), Annual Conference, March 2, 1966, New
York, N.Y., p. 36.
4. Statistics Canada, Construction in Canada, pp. 55-201.
5. Statistics Canada, Petroleum Refineries, pp. 45-205.

NOTES:
1. Marketing and refining expenditures consist of investments and
    operating expenditures. Bulk of expenditure on operations is
    constituted of cost of crude oil. Cost of crude oil is estimated
    to be in the range of one half to four-fifths of total sale
    proceeds. Labor costs are low and are estimated at about one-tenth
    of total operating expenditures. Profits are also low. The
    overall regional content of operating expenditures is estimated at
    80 percent.
2. The overall regional content of investments in refining is
    estimated at 50 percent.
       Cost of materials and equipment of refining construction is
    estimated to be in the range of one-third to one-half of total
    investments in refining. Such materials and equipment are largely
    imported. Wages and salaries of construction workers are estimated
    to be about one-third. Local designing and engineering costs,
    local overhead, local taxes, profits of local contractor, local
    component of material equipment and supplies and land costs are
    estimated at one-fifth.
3. Regional content of investments in marketing facilities is high.
    This is mainly because labor costs constitute a significant portion
    of total investments in marketing facilities. Also, local
    component of expenditure on materials and supplies is substantial.
    However, a significant amount of equipment and materials is also
    imported. The overall regional content of investments in marketing
    facilities is estimated at 60 percent. (continued on next page)

****

4.5 Petrochemical

   Petrochemical industry produces black carbon, polythylene,
industrial chemicals, sulphur and synthetic rubber. Crude oil and
petroleum products are refined into intermediate products which are
used by the petrochemical industry.

   Expenditures of the petrochemical industry consist of expenditure
on land, supply and material, capital, fuel, labor and power.
Estimates of the regional contents of these expenditures are presented
in Table 5.

   The direct, indirect and total income contributions of the
petroleum industry for the period 1964-1970 are presented in Table 6.
Total income contributions have been derived by applying $\frac{1}{1-\rho k}$ to the
dollar value of the regional content estimates.

5. Conclusions and Implications for Public Policy

   During the period 1964-1970, total income generated by the

394

petroleum industry in Alberta has been about one-third of the Alberta's gross domestic product. This is a substantial size of income contribution for one industrial activity. This ratio has been fairly stable up to 1968. In 1969 and 1970, it has declined.

A high degree of leakages, which reduces the size of multiplier, has taken place from the expenditures of the petroleum industry. From this viewpoint, this study has important policy implications (see also Niehans, 1975, Economic Council of Canada, 1977, Hedlin-Menzies and Associates, 1971, Gray, 1972, Safarian, 1966).

The total income contributions of the petroleum industry depended upon the volume of crude petroleum and its products, their prices and the multiplier. Ordinarily, an increase in either of the three variables could increase the income contributions of the petroleum industry to the province. During the period studied, the industry faced a buyer's market. This limited its volume of output. Oil prices were supported through the national oil policy and prorationing. Therefore, the critical factor for this study is the multiplier, particularly the regional content in the multiplier which varies across the industries.

On the basis of the regional contents estimated for different expenditures of the petroleum industry, the overall regional contents of production and capital expenditures can be estimated to be around 0.65 and 0.70 respectively.[2] When these valued are combined with the estimated value of 0.61 for the regional content of consumer expenditures and 0.88 for marginal propensity to consume, the multiplier values for production

****

TABLE 5

REGIONAL CONTENT ESTIMATES OF THE EXPENDITURES OF THE
PETROCHEMICAL INDUSTRY

Year	($000,000)						
	1964	1965	1966	1967	1968	1969	1970
Regional content of wages and electricity @ 40%	6	7	8	8	8	8	8
Regional Content of other expenditures @ 40%	34	36	43	46	45	45	44
Total regional content[1&2]	40	43	51	54	53	53	52

SOURCES:
1. Canadian Petroleum Association, Statistical Year Book, 1971.
2. E.J. Hanson, Dynamic Decade, (McClelland & Stewart, Toronto, 1958), pp. 221-222.
3. E.J. Hanson, "Regional Employment and Income Effects of the Petroleum

Industry in Alberta", a paper presented to the Council of
Economics, American Institute of Mining, Metallurgical and
Petroleum Engineers (AIME), Annual Conference, March 2, 1966, New
York, N.Y., p. 36.
4. Statistics Canada, Manufacturing Industries of Canada: Prairie
   Provinces, pp. 31-207.
5. Alberta Bureau of Statistics, Alberta Industry and Resources, 1970.
NOTES:
1. Expenditures of petrochemical industry include capital as well as
   operating expenditures. A large portion of capital expenditures is
   spent on plant and equipment which are largely imported. Specialized contractors are hired from other parts of the country to
   execute capital projects.
2. A regional content of 40 percent was estimated for the total
   expenditures of the petrochemical industry. The high regional
   content component of expenditures of the petrochemical industry
   were wages and salaries, land costs, supplies and materials, and
   local contractor's margin.

****

TABLE 6

TOTAL INCOME CONTRIBUTIONS OF THE PETROLEUM INDUSTRY

Year	1964	1965	1966	($000,000) 1967	1968	1969	1970
	Direct Income Contributions						
1. Regional content of production expenditures	150	152	178	227	256	268	356
2. Regional content of capital expenditures	285	362	348	364	409	433	337
3. Regional content of transportation expenditures	45	54	93	66	72	78	80
4. Total regional content	480	568	619	657	737	779	773
5. Multiplier	2.15	2.15	2.15	2.15	2.15	2.15	2.15
6. Total direct income contributions	1032	1221	1331	1413	1584	1675	1662
	Indirect Income Contributions						
7. Regional content of refining and marketing expenditures	25	28	28	33	33	32	36
8. Regional content of petro-chemical industry	40	43	51	54	53	53	52
Total regional content	65	71	79	87	86	85	88
9. Multiplier	2.15	2.15	2.15	2.15	2.15	2.15	2.15
10. Total indirect income contributions	140	153	170	187	185	183	189
	Total Income Contributions						
11. Total income contributions (6+10)	1172	1374	1501	1600	1769	1858	1851
12. Total income contributions as a percentage of gross domestic product of Alberta	0.30	0.32	0.31	0.31	0.31	0.30	0.27

and capital expenditures come to 1.41 and 1.52. Such low multiplier values are possible only in less developed [3] regions.

Conceptually, one needs to distinguish between two types of leakages. First type of leakages consists of remittances from wages and salaries abroad, import of capital inputs, and interest, dividend and service payments to non-residents. These leakages take place in the first round of expenditures and appear in the numerator of the multiplier equation. From the viewpoint of income generation, they reduce the size of the expenditures themselves. To the extent the above expenditures leak out, they do not create income in the province. Therefore, these leakages are very important and need to be plugged first as much as possible. Second type of leakages includes import of consumer goods and savings. They take place after the expenditures have accrued as income to the factor owners resident in Alberta. They occur in the second and following rounds of expenditures after they have accrued as income. These leakages appear in the denominator of the multiplier equation.

The concept of first and second round of leakages has significant implications for the diversification program of an economy. However, these implications are the subject matter of another paper.

FOOTNOTES

[1] Data for consumer expenditures of Canada and its breakdown into durables, non-durables and services is available. However, the corresponding breakdown for Alberta is not available.

Expenditure on durable and semi-durable goods consists of that on clothing and footwear; furniture, furnishing and household equipment; recreation and camping equipment; automobile and parts; newspapers and magazines: and jewellery and watches. As there has been little increase in the production of these goods in Alberta, the ratio of imports of durable goods to total consumer expenditures in the province may have increased.

The ratio of expenditure on non-durables to total consumer expenditures in Canada declined throughout the period 1964-70. This may also have happened in Alberta. Important non-durable goods are: food, beverages and tobacco; gas, electricity and other fuels; gasoline, oil and grease, drugs and sundries: and toiletries and cosmetics. As beverages and tobacco and certain types of food, drugs, toiletries and cosmetics are extensively imported into Alberta, the import content of expenditure on non-durables is likely to be sizeable in Alberta.

Major items of expenditure on services are: gross imputed and paid rent; medical service payments: transportation and communication service payments, recreational, educational and cultural service payments; net expenditure abroad; expenditure on restaurants and hotels: and operating expenses of non-profit organizations. Other than net expenditure abroad, none of the above items is likely to have caused a significant amount of leakage through imports. This is primarily because many of the service-providing factors moved to Alberta and the local supply of service-providing factors increased rapidly.

[2] $$x = \sum_{i=1}^{n} w_i \frac{r_i}{E_i} \quad \text{where,}$$

398

x   =   weighted average regional content of either
             production or capital expenditures,

wi =   weight of ith expenditure in total production or
             capital expenditures,

ri =   regional content of ith expenditure in dollar,

Ei =   ith expenditure in dollar

[3] P.E. Polzin estimated 2.70 as multiplier value of the
expenditure of forest industry in the state of Montana.
P.E. Polzin, "An Income Model for the State of Montana", an
unpublished paper.

R. Zuker and M. Wilson estimated that $100 of expansion in
mineral, fuel mines and wells industry of Canada induced an
income of $152. This industry included oil and gas (see R.
Zuker and M. Wilson, An Analysis of Interprovincial Income and
Employment Leakages Using an Interprovincial Input-Output
Model, Economic Development Analysis Division, Department of
Regional Economic Expansion).

References

Caves, R.E. and R.H. Holton (1959). The Canadian Economy: Prospect and Retrospect. Cambridge MA: Harvard University Press.

Courchene, T.J. and J.R. Melvin (1980). 'Energy revenues: consequences for the rest of Canada', Canadian Public Policy, Supplement, February.

DasGupta, P.S. and G.M. Heal (1974). 'The optimal depletion of exhaust ible resources', Review of Economic Studies, Symposium.

Devarajan, S. and A.C. Fisher (1981). 'Hotelling's "Economics of exhaustible resources": fifty years later', Journal of Economic Literature, March .

Economic Council of Canada (1977). Living Together: A Study of Regional Disparities, Catalogue No. Ec 22-54/1977.

Gillen, W.J. and A. Guccione (1970). 'The estimation of post-war regional consumption functions in Canada', Canacian Journal of Economics, May, pp. 276-90.

Gray, H. (1972). Foreign Direct Investment in Canada, Government of Canada, Cat. No. CP 32-15/1971, Information Canada, Ottawa,.

Hanson, E. (1958). Dynamic Decade, McClelland and Stewart Ltd., Toronto.

Hedlin Menzies & Associates, Ltd. (1971). Opportunities for Manufacturing: Prairie Region, Toronto.

Hotelling, H. (1931). 'The economics of exhaustible resources', Journal of Political Economy, April.

Koopmans, T.C. (1973). 'Some observations on optimal economic growth and exhaustible resources', Cowles Foundation Discussion Paper, March.

Niehans, Jurg (1975) 'Economic growth and decline with exhaustible resources: De Economist.

Safarian, A.E. (1966). Foreign Ownership of Canadian Industry, McGraw-Hill, Toronto,.

Scarfe, B.L. and T.L. Powerie (1980). 'The optimal savings question: an Alberta perspective', Canadian Public Policy, Supplement, February.

Weinrich, J. (1966). Economic Impact of the Gas Industry: Local, Provincial and Regional, published for the Calgary Chamber of Commerce.

30 Environmental implication of alternative economic development and energy path: framework for developing countries

NAZIR DOSSANI, ROBERT H. HONEA AND RAMA SASTRY

1. Introduction

Over the last twenty years the United States and other industrialized countries have been spending an increasing portion of their resources to correct environmental problems brought on by over 150 years of industrial development. Numerous laws and regulations dealing with air quality, water quality, land use, water use, occupational health and safety, and noise have been promulgated. This commitment is reflected in the levels of expenditures directed toward the purchase and maintenance of pollution control equipment.[1]

The share of a country's product spent on control of air, water and other pollutants tends to be directly related to its levels of economic development. The priorities and needs of a country like India differ significantly from those of developed economies. The requirements for food, housing and clothing can take precedence over the need for improved air or water quality. Despite the importance of these basic needs the attitude toward environmental concerns has been changing in developing countries. Several factors have been responsible for this change. First, there is now an improved understanding of the fact that environmental control often makes sense in simple economic terms. Second, there is a recognition of the global or multinational nature of some of the issues of concern. Problems such as the buildup of CO_2 in the atmosphere affect all countries -- developed or developing -- each of which individually, have little chance to affect it in any significant way. Third, the energy crisis has led to an increased awareness of the interrelationships among energy availability and cost, economic growth and the environment.

There is support for this emphasis in national and international institutions. The United Nations, through its environmental program, as well as its global modelling studies, is taking an active role in improving members' recognition of common environmental problems (United Nations 1979: Leontief 1977). The World Bank incorporates environmental factors into its project appraisal and financing policy (World Bank 1979). Several countries including India have organized

---

[1] In the United States over the period 1972-1979, $183 billion has been spent on pollution abatement, an amount that is roughly two percent of Gross National Product (BEA 1981).

departments of environment at the cabinet level.

This paper reports on the first phase of a study that attempts to develop methods, models and data bases to study the linkages among energy, economic growth and the environment. Since most of the authors' previous research has been in the United States, the examples used are primarily based upon the U.S. experience. The paper does attempt to draw some implications of this experience for India. The rest of the paper is organized as follows. The next section briefly reviews alternative models of economic and energy activity. The section also describes a linked energy-economic environmental system -- the Strategic Environmental Assessment System (SEAS) -- which the authors and others have been developing for the U.S. Department of Energy and which is being widely used for assessing the environmental effects of public policies. Recent applications of this paper focus on the relevance of these methods and data bases to the Indian situation. Key policy issues that link energy, environment and economic growth in India are discussed and a conceptual framework for analyzing these issues is presented. The paper concludes with the application of this framework to develop preliminary estimates of air emissions at a national level for India.

2. Linked Energy-Economic-Environmental Assessment

2.1 Introduction: The Macroeconomic Context

Analysis of environmental impacts is facilitated by the availability of a model of the U.S. economy that meets at least two principal criteria. First, that the model (or system of models) be capable of generating a consistent forecast of energy use and economic growth under a wide range of assumptions about government policy and exogenous variables (such as population growth, international oil prices, etc.). And second, that it be capable of being linked to more disaggregated sectoral and regional models whose forecasts can be used in turn to derive projection of environmental quality.

Seven widely used models of the U.S. economy are summarized below. They represent much of the conventional wisdom in the U.S. on the art of energy and economic forecasting. The discussion below focuses on the broad characteristics of the models and not on their equation-by-equation specification or their forecasting properties. A brief summary of the results is presented in Table 1. This table reveals considerable differences among the analytic frameworks of the various models. It indicates that some dimensions whose representation is central to certain models are not even included in other models. There are also significant differences among the models in their treatment of the dimensions that they do address. In many instances, such differences among the structures of the different models establish clear theoretical precedence of certain models over others relative to particular analytic dimensions. However, in any context where a model is used for purposes of forecasting or policy analysis, empirical accuracy is a more important consideration in the selection of a model than is theoretical elegance. In highly interactive analytic structures, a single deficient equation can destroy the simulation properties of the entire model. Ultimately, the selection of a specific model as a basis for forecasting or policy analysis in any particular situation should be determined by the empirical ability of

TABLE 1

STRUCTURAL CHARACTERISTICS OF THE ECONOMIC FORECASTING MODELS*

Analytic Dimension	Hudson-Jorgenson Model	Wharton Model	DRI Model	Evans Model	Turo Model	CEI Model	Fossil 2 Model
The Role of Expectations	No representation of expectations	Inflationary expectations affect monetary sector, interest rates, investment	Expectations, and errors in expectations, have extensive and pervasive effects on economic activity	Cumulative gap between actual and maximum potential GNP generates inflationary expectations and price increases	No representation of expectations	Anticipated and unanticipated government policies have differential effects on prices and output	Expected growth in energy demand determines need for investment
The Effects of Monetary Policy	No representation of monetary sector	Supply of money affects interest rates and investment in short-term, but not in long-term	Level of nonborrowed reserves affects real investment in both short- and long-term	No representation of monetary sector	Pure quantity theory of money--produces no impacts on real economic activity	In short term, anticipated monetary policy affects prices, unanticipated policy affects output. Neutral in long-term.	No representation of monetary sector
The Effects of Taxation Policy on Labor Supply	Labor supply affected by impacts of tax rates on wealth	Extremely indirect taxation effects on labor utilization, labor force participation, unemployment rate	Extremely indirect taxation effects on labor utilization, unemployment rate, labor force participation	Marginal personal income tax rates affect labor force participation, labor utilization, average wage rate	Marginal tax rate on labor income inversely affects labor force participation and hours worked	Marginal personal income tax rate inversely affects labor force participation rate	No representation of labor force
The Effects of Taxation Policy on Personal Savings	Personal saving inversely related to tax rate on labor income	Personal saving affected by any taxation policy that influences any component of consumption	Personal saving directly affected by temporary changes in tax rates through effects on variance of income	Personal saving inversely related to average personal income tax rate	Savings measured as equilibrium value of investment - no indication of effects of taxation of household saving behavior	Personal saving inversely related to personal income tax rate	No representation of personal saving
The Effects of Taxation Policy on Investment	Investment measured as savings less government and foreign deficits -- only indirectly affected by taxation policy	Taxation policies affect-non-residential fixed investment and residential investment through impact on user cost of capital	Residential and industry investment inversely related to tax rate in short-term, but positively related in long-term	Taxation policy affects investment orders through return on investment, and investment financing through interest rates and equity yields	Return on investment, and level and composition of investment, explicitly affected by a wide variety of taxation policies	Investment affected by impact of corporate profit tax rate on price of existing capital	Taxation policy affects funds available for investment and, when funds are limited, investment
The Long-Term Effects of Investment	Investment increases capital stock, productive capacity, productivity and output -- primarily through impact on wealth	Investment expands capital stock and employment, and influences subsequent real investment	Investment expands capital stock, enhancing aggregate production, productivity, unemployment rate, wage rates, and prices	Investment increases labor productivity	Investment increases capital stock, aggregate productive capacity, and productivity	Investment affects growth of capital stock, trend rate of potential output, and productivity	Investment increases capital stock after a construction delay and enhances productive capacity and prices
The Consequences of Restricted Materials Availability	The price of materials with limited availability is increased sufficiently to induce specified reduction in availability	Limitations in domestic availability induce increase in imports, or cause shortages	Model solution is restricted to feasible materials value, or consequences of shortages are simulated	The price of materials with limited availability is increased, resulting in reduced labor productivity	No representation of materials availability	The exogenous real price of oil is increased, affecting trend rate of real output, consumption, productivity	Limited materials availability causes short-term increase in imports or shortages; and long-term increase in price, profit, and investment
Representation of the International Sector	Behavioral relationships specified for import demands and export prices; export demands and import prices are exogenous	Behavioral relationships specified for numerous import and export categories	Interactive behavioral relationship specified for numerous import and export categories	Behavioral relationship specified for exports; inflation rate dependent on foreign exchange rates	Aggregate imports determined endogenously; exports and repatriated foreign-source income are exogenous	Models analogous to model of U.S. economy included for Japan, United Kingdom, France, and West Germany	Imports respond to excess domestic demand, or shortages occur
The Degree of Industry Detail	Moderate detail for energy and non-energy sectors	Extensive general detail, including moderate detail in energy sector	Extensive detail for energy and non-energy sectors	Limited industry detail	Extensive investment detail, but limited production or consumption detail	Primarily aggregate production, with side calculations for residential and non-residential construction	Extensive detail for energy sector, no other detail
Representation of Policy Initiatives	Taxation, government expenditure, energy, and (possibly) regulatory policies	Monetary, taxation, government expenditure, and energy policies	Monetary, taxation, government expenditure, regulatory, minimum wage, price control policies	Taxation, government expenditure, energy and regulatory relief policies	Primarily taxation policies; government expenditure policies also	Primarily monetary and fiscal policies, and policies affecting government debt	Wide variety of policies affecting energy: taxation, subsidization, financial incentives, foreign trade, regulation, commercialisation

Source: CONSAD 1981.

the model to develop accurate simulations of economic activity in such situations.

Comparison of the conceptual and theoretical properties of alternative models provides a valuable basis for identifying the most promising models to consider for utilization in particular situations. It can also indicate opportunities for linking two or more models to create analytic capabilities not embodied in any single model. Whenever any such conjoining of models is contemplated, care should be exercised in assuring that the fundamental assumptions embodied in the analytic structures of the models under consideration are mutually compatible.

The structure of the models described above is not directly applicable to India. In both the U.S. and India, however, the primary uses of the models are in their ability to analyze the tradeoffs among economic, energy and other impacts of alternative public decisions and in organizing the data collection and accounting framework that is necessary to study the linkages among the factors that are represented in these models.

2.2 Environmental Assessment with Linkages to Energy-Economic Models

In this section we describe a system of models called SEAS that is a set of interlinked models currently being used for environmental and energy-economic analysis in the United States (House

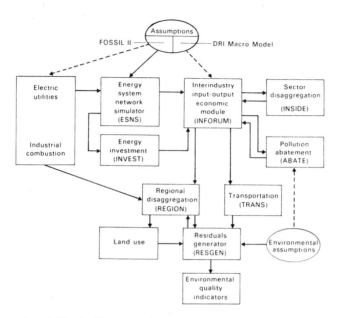

Figure 1.   A Block Diagram of SEAS.

1977, MITRE 1980).   A macro-level flow diagram of the model is given in Figure 1.   The front-end of the model is a macrodriver that generates a consistent energy and economic path for the U.S. to the year 2000. This was developed by linking the DRI and FOSSIL II models (Table 1).

To provide the detailed industry projections needed for environmental analysis, this front-end macro forecast was used to drive a detailed input-output model of the U.S. economy, the Interindustry Forecasting Model of the University of Maryland (INFORUM) (Almon 1974 and 1981).   INFORUM encompasses both a detailed input-output model as well as a comprehensive set of econometric projections for the components of Gross National Product (GNP) through the year 2000.

In addition to the detail in the input-output model there are 300 equations in SEAS dealing with product and technology mixes within these sectors.   These equations provide detail for projecting energy use, residuals, and abatement costs.   They are represented in the INSIDE module.   An important aspect of this disaggregation affects the energy sector.   SEAS disaggregates the energy projections from the Fossil II model to over 150 energy supply and demand technologies through an accounting model called the Energy System Network Simulator (ESNS).   Final demand requirements for energy investment and pollution abatement are estimated within separate modules (INVEST and ABATE) that feed back those requirements to the input-output model. National gross pollution residuals for stationary sources are calculated by applying gross pollution coefficients (units of gross pollution per unit of output)[2] to output and side equation values (RESGEN Module). Net emissions are calculated as the product of gross emissions and the percent not controlled. National residuals are assigned to regions (REGION module) using projections from regional models of the U.S. Department of Commerce and specific submodels for key energy and manufacturing studies.

The procedure for running the model involves interactions between the model and its user that are difficult to describe accurately in a brief space. The model is first targeted on the GNP and energy forecasts and energy investment requirements of the scenario generated by the DRI and FOSSIL II models. Resource requirements for specific energy technologies are estimated within an energy investment sub-model that feeds back those requirements to the input-output model's transaction matrix. Household and state and local governments purchases are determined as a function of disposable income. These and other final demands determine output levels by sector. If aggregate expenditures are greater (or less) than targeted GNP, disposable income is lowered (or raised) and the model rerun until equality with the GNP target is achieved.

3. The U.S. National Energy Plan Scenarios and their Environmental Implications

The Department of Energy is required by law to submit a national energy plan to the Congress of the United States that periodically evaluates the effects of current and projected energy trends on economic growth. The Third National Energy Plan (NEP3) presented in 1981, is a dramatic change from the earlier plans in its philosophy and approach to solving energy problems. A free market and removal of government interference from the energy sector are the guiding principles behind the Plan. The plan emphasizes the rebuilding of the nuclear energy industry (including breeder reactors) and the discontinuing of subsidies to some energy technologies such as synthetic fuels and alcohol fuels.

The energy projections of the NEP3 are not official goals of the current U.S. Administration but do reflect current policy. Table 2 displays energy forecasts for the United States at the national level. As noted earlier, these projections were generated by the DRI and FOSSIL II models. In addition to this baseline (or Mid) scenario, sensitivity analyses are conducted to assess the effects of variations in world oil prices and GNP economic growth rates. In the environmental analysis below, only the results of the Mid scenario are presented.

---

2   Output is measured either in dollars or physical units, such as Btu's, tons of steel, ect. In addition to point source residuals, SEAS also calculates residuals for nonpoint sources: transportation, urban runoff, mining, non-urban construction, and forestry. These are represented in the TRANS and LANDUSE modules.

TABLE 2

NEP3 PROJECTIONS*

	1980 Actual	1990 Range	2000 Range
Energy Production			
Oil	20.5	16-21	17-24
Natural Gas	19.8	16-21	14-21
Coal	18.9	24-30	37-45
Nuclear	2.7	6.7-8.7	7.4-14.0
Hydro-Geothermal	3.2	3.3-3.9	3.7-4.9
Renewables	1.8	2.4-3.3	3.9-7.0
U.S. Production	66.9	68-88	83-116
Net Imports			
Oil	13.3	4-15	0-11
Gas	1.0	1-3	1-3
Coal	(2.4)	(2.3-4.3)	(3.4-8.4)
Total Consumption	78.0	80-94	90-110

*All numbers are in Quadrillion Btu's. Ranges in domestic production
reflect uncertainties in assumptions about U.S. energy supply.

3.1 Broad Environmental Trends

The environmental projections related to the energy plans
include air quality, water and solid waste pollutant emissions. These
projections are generated at a wide range of detail and cannot be
adequately summarized in this paper. The national environmental
projections of NEP3 are summarized in Table 3.

The major sources of air pollution in the United States are fossil
fuel-fired power plants, industrial combustion sources and automobiles.
Significant reduction of air emissions are projected for power plants
and automobiles due to the application of stringent environmental
standards. Increased coal use by power plants is expected to generate
large amounts of sludge due to scrubbing requirements legislated by
Congress. While air pollution decreases, solid wastes increase through
1990 and 2000. Water quality problems are indicated by using measures
such as the Total Dissolved Solids (TDS) and Biochemical Oxygen Demand
(BOD). There are several other potential problems related to air
quality including CO_2, acid rain and radionuclides that are not
discussed in detail here due to the uncertainties in the pollutant
cause-effect relationship and in the contribution of the energy sector
to them.

The system also includes data bases that can be used for detailed
spatial analysis. For example, using national energy scenario data
concerning the required annual coal production to meet specific
economic or population growth levels, the SEAS framework provides for
the projection of future energy production at varying regional scales.
Figure 2 illustrates the results of such projections for surface-mined
coal. Estimates of the amounts of coal produced by county by surface
and deep mining techniques can be used to estimate the annual amounts
of land area that may be disturbed for purposes of mining and the
potential damage to streams and ground-water assessed. These
environmental damage estimates may be particularly important in the
case of endangered wildlife or surface contamination of local portable
water supplies.

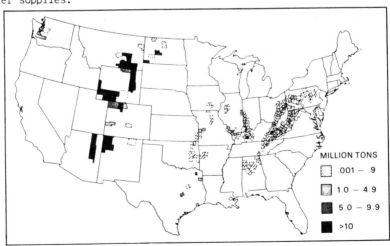

Figure 2. Projected Coal Production in U.S. Surface Mines in 2000.

TABLE 3

NATIONAL ENVIRONMENTAL PROJECTIONS - NEP3

	1975	1990	2000
TSP*	13.0	8.2	9.9
SO_x	28.3	27.8	30.2
NO_x	19.6	19.9	22.3
HC	17.2	11.8	12.9
CO	110.4	54.9	54.4
TDS	9.3	15.3	22.6
BOD	2.8	1.6	1.7
Sludge	.2	33	64

* Data in Millions of Tons. TSP=Total Suspended Particulates: So_x = Sulfur Oxides: NO_x = Nigrogen Oxides: HC = Hydrocarbons: CO = Carbon Monoxide; TDS = Total Dissolved Solids and BOD = Biochemical Oxygen Demand.

One of the most important steps in the supply of energy is the transformation process to more usable forms (i.e., electricity). This transformation process can have major impacts on the environment, with pollutants concentrated at a few points within critical distances of human population or sensitive wildlife species. The SEAS model provides for the projection of future electrical generation capacity by fuel type and by location. By maintaining an inventory of the electric utility plans for expanding or adding new capacity, this forecasting technique can be quite specific as to location, size and fuel types. To determine levels of pollutant emissions, however, these capacity levels must be transformed into estimates of electrical generation (e.g., Figure 3).

Figure 3. Power Generation from Coal Fired Power Plants in 1977 and 1990.

Through various assumptions about thermal efficiencies and knowledge about environmental regulations to be imposed, a reasonable estimate of the pollutant levels can be determined. These estimates can be used for subsequent assessment of possible environmental damage. Figure 4 shows SO_x emissions from utilities at the state level.[3] These changes in emissions can then be evaluated against an inventory of existing conditions for air quality at the county level.

This discussion has briefly touched upon the analytical potential of the SEAS framework for environmental impact assessment. In developing such a framework for a country such as India, analytical techniques and data bases would have to be modified. Because of lack

---

[3] Similar projections are available for other fuels and pollutants.

of certain kinds of data, more extensive use of surrogates will be
necessary. This issue is discussed below.

4. Environmental Analysis for Developing Economies

    4.1 Introduction

        This section attempts to bring together the concepts and
analyses described above and to apply them to the Indian context. Some
of the key policy issues and environmental concerns that have been
expressed in the literature are presented first. This is followed by a
discussion of a conceptual framework that links the energy and economic
sector with environmental impacts and provides some illustrative
applications.

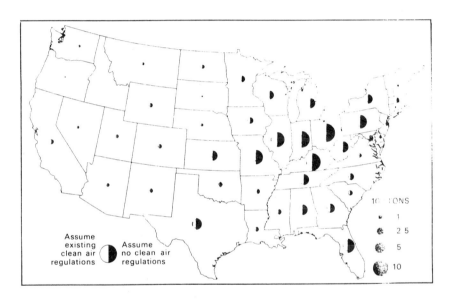

Figure 4.   Projected SO_x Emissions from Electric Utilities
             in 1995.

    4.2 Policy Issues

        The policy model described in the previous sections has been
used extensively in the U.S. While it cannot be said to be directly
relevant to developing countries, lessons derived from it and similar
model structures can yield useful insights into the types of analyses
and data bases that are needed. Moreover, despite the significant
differences in the levels of per capita income, energy use and other
factors between the United States and countries like India many of the
same tradeoffs are being made. For example, the following policy
recommendations were made by a Working Group on Energy Policy in India
after evaluation of trends in economic growth, energy supply and demand
(GOI 1979):

411

"The major thrust of the policy prescription are toward:

. The curbing of consumption of oil to the minimum
  possible level;

. Conserving the use of energy by increasing the
  efficiency of its utilization;

. Reducing the overall energy demand by lowering
  the intensity of energy consumption in the
  economy, particularly in the industries sector;

. An increased reliance on renewable energy
  sources:

. a reapraisal of our economic development
  strategies, especially those elements of the
  strategy which have a direct link to energy
  consumption like technology choice, location
  policies, urban growth, mechanization in
  agriculture, etc., with reference to the new
  awareness of the energy supply and demand in
  future."

The first four of these policy recommendations are similar to those
that underlie U.S. national energy plans and the last -- with the
exception of the issue of agricultural technology -- has also been the
subject of some study in the United States. Of course, the mechanisms
by which these objectives are expected to be achieved (e.g., reliance
on market mechanisms) are very different.

There is also a similarity in methods used for policy analysis that
is carried through in some of the scenario projections developed by the
Working Group. Two forecasts were developed by the Group:

. First, using conventional methodologies, a Reference Level
  Forecast (RLF) of energy demand was developed assuming no
  deliberate measures were initiated to manage energy supply and
  demand.

. Second, the Group estimated the level of composition of energy
  demand that could materialize if specified policy
  prescriptions were adopted. The same rates of growth of Gross
  National Product as in RLF was assumed. This is referred to
  as the Optimal Level Forecast (OLF) (GOI 1979).

This type of scenario approach has parallels in the U.S. energy and
economic forecasting experience. Also, the OLF projection showed a
strong emphasis on the greater use of coal and nuclear energy. Many of
the environmental issues surrounding the greater use of these
technologies that have emerged as important in the U.S. have relevance
to the developing countries as well.

Environmental issues for developing countries have been studied in
detail in the 'global' modelling efforts that have been undertaken in
the last ten years. For example, the Global 2000 study undertaken by

the U.S. government (CEQ 1981) has extensively described the implications of continuation of recent environmental trends on agricultural production and other economic activity. Global issues such as the effect of increasing CO_2 on the world's temperature, the effect of fossil combustion on acid rain and the hazards associated with nuclear accidents and nuclear disposal have also been addressed in this study. The implications of coal use have also been analyzed in the World Coal Study (WOCOL 1980).

Specific issues dealing with India have also emerged. Studies have found that there are dangerous concentrations of fine particulates around Bombay including carcinogenic compounds such as benzene, lead, mercury, cadmium and arsenic, primarily from coal-buring powerplants (Mojumdar 1981). The use of tall stacks, as in the West, has not solved the fundamental problem here. One study suggested that the emission of air pollutants in Bombay has increased tenfold in the last 25 years (Mayur 1979). Studies have also cited the pollution in the Ganges due to effluents from municipal and industrial waste (Mehta 1975). In the major cities particulate levels in the air, particularly in winter, are extremely high due to wood, coal and animal waste burning. Eye and lung diseases, as well as shcistosomiasis have been linked to this phenomenon (Parikh 1980).

Fortunately, there are some mitigating forces. There is a strong commitment to solar energy in the government planning framework. Also, the low level of sulfur in Indian coal has prevented SO_2 emissions from becoming a serious problem. An issue is whether appropriate policies, strongly enforced, can reverse the overall trends at a reasonable cost. As in many developing countries, there is a primary concern for meeting the needs for food, shelter and clothing. Energy plays an important role in meeting these basic necessities and the availability of an inexpensive and efficient energy supply could be a critical factor in many developing countries. Energy consumption in India is extremely small compared to the United States. In 1980, India's per capita consumption of energy was estimated to be 1.3 percent of the U.S. figure -- 13,500 Btu's per day for India vs. 995,000 Btu's per day for the United States (Mukherjee 1981b, pp. 823-851). A more detailed comparison of the basic energy data is presented in Table 4.

Approximately 50 percent of India's energy needs is met through traditional energy sources (wood, dung and vegetable wastes) and in rural areas the percentage may range as high as 95 percent. Much of this fuel use occurs with open fires; an improvement in the situation could occur by improving the efficiency of burning. Many proposals exist to improve the rural India fuel use situation, ranging from rural electrification (which is proving to be expensive), the use of windmills (again not always viable because of low wind speeds) and the use of biogas produced locally in the villages. An increasing emphasis is now being placed on finding ways to expand renewable energy supplies and use them more efficiently rather than the conventional energy sources such as coal, oil, natural gas or nuclear.

One problem is that for much of India's current (1980) consumption of about 100 million tons (metric) of coal, the pollution is essentially uncontrolled. While India's coal averages less than one percent in sulfur content (compared to a U.S. average of 2 percent), the ash

TABLE 4

PRIMARY ENERGY USE IN INDIA AND U.S.*

| | India | | U.S. | |
	Amount	Percent	Amount	Percent
Commercial				
Coal	1.970	28.0	16.5	20.9
Oil	.940	13.3	33.8	42.9
Gas	.083	1.2	20.8	26.4
Nuclear	.025	.4	2.7	3.4
Hydroelectric	.162	2.3	3.2	4.1
Other**	0	0	1.8	2.3
Noncommercial	3.880	55.0	0	0
	7.060	100.0	78.8	100.0

* Estimates in quadrillion Btus. Estimates for India are for 1978
   and for the U.S. are 1980 estimates.

**Includes wood combusion and solar. For India, wood combustion is
   included in noncommercial energy.

content of India's coal ranges from 14 to 45 percent. The particulates
and solid wastes generated from India's increased use of coal could
represent a serious pollution problem to both surface waters and
groundwaters.

It may be argued that such environmental concerns are low in priority
compared to other basic human needs, particularly in India. However,
providing for basic energy needs in an environmentally degrading manner
may lead to early deaths or diminished health. In addition, there may be
cumulative effects of pollutants such that future generations are affected
as well. One must devise ways to solve energy and other problems without
a degradation of the environment.

4.3 Conceptual Framework

The framework presented here is discussed in terms of broad
characteristics alone. It consists of five major modules:

- A national econometric-energy module that is
  capable of generating consistent scenarios of
  GNP and energy supply and demand for India;

- A detailed input-output module that disaggre-

gates and translates the final demand projections from the econometric module into a set of
industry projections;

.   A regional economic module that forecasts
        regional population, industrial activity and
        energy balances;

.   An emissions module that translated the energy,
        population and economic projections from the
        national/regional modules into a set of
        residual forecasts; and

.   A set of ambient models that use as major inputs
        the residual loading by media and, using data on
        physical characteristics of the media (e.g.,
        wind, stream flow) and source (e.g., stack
        height, gas temperature) projects ambient air,
        water and other environmental quality
        indicators.

Interaction effects will exist among modules. For example the
detailed analysis of sectoral activity implied in the input-output
module might suggest that some of the projections of the macromodel
need revision. Alternately, the input-output model can be completely
embedded in the macromodel, thereby avoiding some of the problems of
iteration and consistency. Likewise, the regional analysis might
suggest that constraints (e.g., private/public sector capital
availability) exist which require revision of national projections.

Much of the analytical basis to proceed along these lines has
already been developed. For example, Mukherjee has suggested a
framework that comprises the first two modules (Mukherjee 1981a,
1981b). Other sources of scenario projection are also available. The
Government of India planning studies provide a useful baseline against
which to analyze the impact of alternatives (GOI 1981). Another macromodel of the Indian economy available is the SIMA model developed by
IIASA (Parikh and Parikh 1979). This model unlike the Mukherjee model
is currently operational. However, it is highly aggregfate, with only
45 equations and no industry detail aside from the
agricultural/nonagricultural disaggregation.

Across them, such models offer a useful basis to develop a
consistent set of national scenarios for the Indian economy. It is in
the regional context that data problems are likely to prevent any but
the simplest of analytical schemes. The use of regional or interregional input-output models, difficult eneough in the U.S., would
appear to be precluded in India by the lack of adequate data on
production techniques, interregional flows of goods and regional final
demand. Instead, simpler regional shift-share and economic base models
are more appropriate.

Regional emissions can be linked to production activity in the
industrial, agricultural and other sectors through a scheme similar to
that described earlier. Environmental pollutants that can be estimated
could include air emmissions, water effluents, solid wastes and radioactive wastes. Ambient air and water quality models can also be

415

developed using existing methodologies. The parameters that determine air and water quality would need to be modified to be consistent with the Indian context. In particular, the open burning of agricultural, wood and animal waste would need to be incorporated explicitly since these are major sources of air pollutants. While the sulfur content of India coal is low, the interregional transport of sulfates may need to be analyzed, given the fact that these pollutants can travel extremely long distances. And some emphasis would also have to be given to the ash content of different regional coals as well as to toxic emissions.

While the framework lacks specificity, it provides a starting point. In the discussion below this framework is used to estimate air pollution emissions for India for 1978 and 2000. While these are national estimates and cannot be used to assess ambient air quality they do provide useful insights. Similar analysis can be conducted for water and other residuals.

Using residual coefficient data primarily from the U.S. (USEPA 1979) and modifying them to reflect Indian conditions (e.g., the ash and sulfur content of Indian coal) we have developed a set of coefficients measured in kilograms of pollutant per unit of product. Using these along with base year production estimates (provided primarily from the Report of the Working Group and the Sixth Five Year Plan reports) we have estimated gross national emissions for India for the base year (typically 1978-1979). These are summarized in Table 5 for the three major industrial groups: commercial energy, noncommercial energy and manufacturing sectors.

While the estimates for India presented here represent gross emis-sions, it is likely that with the possible exception of particulates, net emissions (i.e., after application of control devices) are not significantly lower. Even the application of precipitators has not been systematically implemented until recently. Emissions from noncommercial energy use are uncontrolled. Thus gross emissions are probably reasonably close to net emissions. The emissions of air pollutants are quite significant. Moreover, the sectors included in our calculations are not comprehensive. Fugitive dust (e.g., from coal mines, coal transportation, etc.) are excluded as are other emissions from nonmineral mining and small manufacturing sources.

A comparison of (gross) Indian and U.S. net emissions are given in Table 6. Particulate emissions appear to be the most serious problem with the most important source being coal burning in utilities and industry. In the European and U.S. economies also this was the first and most visible air quality problem to be attacked. In India the high ash content of coal (we have assumed an average of 25 percent compared to the U.S. average of about 13 percent) is a major source of the problem. For other pollutants estimated emissions are much lower than in the U.S. Given the smaller land area in India relative to the U.S., these emissions might result in serious problems in certain regions. The population at risk would also be significantly higher.

A preliminary assessment of the problem in a regional context could be made by using regional energy and economic activity by state and by major industry group to "share down" these national emissions estimates. Figures 5 through 8 display some of this data. Estimates of the urban/rural differences in noncommercial energy use are also

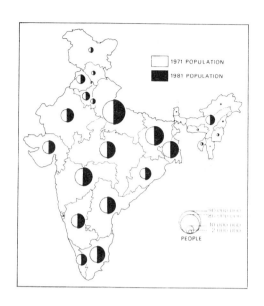

Figure 5.   Population Change by State, 1971-1981

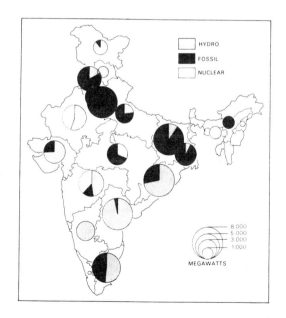

Figure 6.   Total Generating Capacity in India by Fuel
             Type, 1980

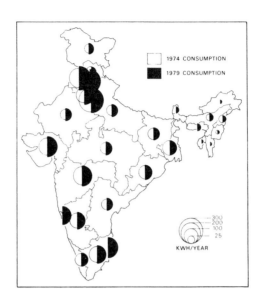

Figure 7.   Per Capita Consumption of Electricity in
            India by State, 1974-1979.

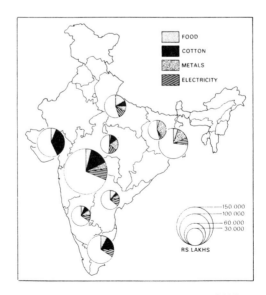

Figure 8.   Value added for Selected States, 1980.

TABLE 5

NATIONAL ESTIMATES OF ANNUAL AIR POLLUTION EMISSIONS FOR INDIA*

	TSP	SO_x	NO_x	HC	CO
Energy - Commercial	8,625	2,290	1,301	389	2,442
- Noncommercial	3,017	658	205	1,699	8,866
Manufacturing	4,391	279	31	16	6,932
	16,033	3,227	1,537	2,103	18,239

* In thousands of short tons. Pollutants refer to Total Suspended
  Particulates, Sulfur Oxides, Nitrogen Oxides, Hydrocarbons and
  Carbon Monoxide respectively.

TABLE 6

TOTAL ANNUAL EMISSIONS IN INDIA AND U.S.

	TSP	SO_x	NO_x	HC	CO
U.S.	13,020	28,275	19,606	17,240	110,423
India	16,033	3,277	1,537	2,103	18,239
India as percent of U.S.	123	11	8	12	17

available and these can also be used to allocate national emissions to a regional level.

If current trends continue (as represented in the Reference Level Forecast), coal use is projected to grow by over 400 percent, from 103 million (metric) tons in 1978 to 532 million (metric) tons in 2000. Oil use is also projected to grow significantly, from 24 million (metric) tons to 74 million (metric) tons. The implications of these growth rates for aggregate emissions should be obvious. They are reinforced by examination of short term target growth rates for key industries represented in the Sixth Five-Year Plan.

We have made crude calculations of emissions in 2000 for a reference scenario. The growth rates assumed for the energy sector were taken from the Reference Level Forecast of the Working Group; for the manufacturing sectors we assumed compound annual growth rates (over the period 1979-2000) equal to three fourths of those used in the sixth five year plan. The resulting projections of emissions are shown in Table 7. These represent gross emissions except in the case of coal burning in utilities and industries where an average removal efficiency of 30 percent was assumed. While particulate emissions continue to be the most important factor, SO_x and CO emissions emerge as being a major concern as well. Despite the low level of sulfur in coals, the use of scrubbers may prove to be advisable. Analyzing the costs associated with this and the institutional framework needed at this early stage may well be a worthwhile task.

TABLE 7

PROJECTED GROSS AIR EMISSIONS IN INDIA - 2000.*

	Total	% of Base Year
Particulates**	57,400	358.
SO_x	15,800	490.
NO_x	6,861	446
HC	2,389	113.
CO	40,800	223.

* In Thousands of Tons.

** Assumes 30 percent removal in coal fired utilities and boilers.

The solutions to the resulting problems are clearly not in restraining growth rates of the economy or the industrial sectors but in trying to achieve them through methods that have minimal adverse impacts on environmental quality. Part of this can be achieved through recognizing that pollution control can often yield net benefits in a direct monetary sense, for example, through resource recovery or

improved performance of industrial boilers (James and Siddiqi 1928).
Appropriate siting of new plants may minimize adverse impacts as well.
Care should be taken to avoid the problem of turning a local problem
into a regional one. This mistake was made in some of the early
institutional approaches in the U.S. By restricting industry from
siting in 'dirty' areas, the cleaner areas may receive the bulk of the
adverse impacts. Appropriate balancing of regional and local emissions
is needed.

The strategies for dealing with environmental problems in India
must be formulated within the context of local conditions and goals.
The mistakes of the Western experience can be avoided by analyzing the
implications of alternative national scenarios of energy use and
industrial growth. Strategies can be devised that are modest in terms
of monetary cost (especially relative to the value of industrial
output) but that can have enormous long-term benefits to an economy
that contains some of the world's most beautiful natural and cultural
resources.

References

Almon, C. et.al., (1974). 1985: Interindustry Forecasts of the AmericanEconomy, D.C. Health and Company.

Bureau of Economic Analysis (BEA), (1981). 'Pollution abatement and control expenditures,' Survey of Current Business, Vol. 61, No. 3, pp. 19-27.

CONSAD Research Corporation, (1981). The "New Economics" Implications for Economics Forecasting and Policy Analysis, Prepared for the U.S. Department of Energy, Pittsburgh, PA.

Council on Environmental Quality (CEQ), (1981). The Global 2000 Report to the President, Volumes 1-3, prepared by the Council of Environmental Quality and the Department of State, U.S. Government Printing Office, Washington, D.C.

Government of India (GOI), (1979). Report of the Working Group on Energy Policy, Government of India, Planning Commission, New Delhi.

Government of India (GOI), (1981). The Sixth Five-Year Plan. Planning Commission, New Delhi.

House, Peter, (1977). Trading off Environmental, Economics and Energy --A Case Study of EPA's Strategic Environmental Assessment System (SEAS), Lexington, MA: Lexington Books.

James, D. and T.A. Siddiqi, (1981). 'The increased use of coal in the Asia-Pacific region: achieving energy and environmental goals,' Working Paper, East-West Environment and Policy Institute, Honolulu, Hawaii.

Leontief, W. et al., (1977). The Future of the World Economy, A United Nations Study, New York: Oxford University Press.

Mayur, R., (1979). 'Fnvironmental problems of developing countries,' Annals of the American Academy, 444, pp. 89-101.

Mehta, R.S., (1975). Status of water pollution in India, In: The Hazards of Enrironmental Pollution, Proceedings of the All India Seminar on Environmental Pollution, pp. 67-71.

Mitre Corp., (1980). Introduction to the Strategic Environmental Assessment System, prepared for U.S. Department of Energy, Contract No. DE-ACO2-79 EV10092.

Mojumdar, M., (1981). 'Poverty, population and pollution,' Christian Science Monitor, November 12, 1981, p. 20.

Mukherjee, S.K., (1981a). 'Energy-economic planning in the developing countries: a conceptual model for India,' in: Chatterji, M. Energy and Environment in Developing Countries, John Wiley & Sons, Ltd.

Mukherjee, S.K., (1981b). 'Energy policy and planning in India,' Energy, Vol. 6, No. 8, pp. 823-51.

Parikh, H.K. and K.S. Parikh, (1979). 'Simulation and Macroeconomic scenarios to assess the energy demand for India (SIMA),' IIASA Research Report RR-79-15, December 1979.

Parikh, H.K., (1980). Energy Systems and Development, Delhi: Oxford University Press.

United Nations Environmental Programme (UNEP), (1979). The United Nations Environmental Programme, Nairobi, Kenya.

U.S. Environmental Protection Agency (USEPA), (1979). Compilation of Air Pollution Emission Factors, Third Edition, Research Triangle Park, N.C. 27711.

World Bank, (1979). Environment and Development, Washington, D.C.

World Coal Study (WOCOL), (1980). Future Coal Prospects: Country and Regional Assessment, Cambridge, MA: Ballinger Publishing Co.

31 Some concluding remarks on the future development of Regional Science

MANAS CHATTERJI

The greatest challenge facing manking today is the disparity in the growth rate of income between the poor countries and the advanced industrial nations. This factor has not only economic connotations, but also political, social, and humanitarian aspects. The continuance of this strain will lead to political chaos and revolution in many parts of the world. The examples are already around us. This situation is particularly true in the urban centers of the developing countries. It is in these places that economic stagnancy has been accentuated by substandard housing, poor water supply, inadequate transportation, and a low level of social services, etc. Unrealized expectations, along with modern means of education and communication, reinforce a sense of failure among the urbanites. Since industrialization goes hand in hand with urbanization, the urban areas could provide the leadership for economic development and cultural change.

The urban and regional dimension of the developmental process has been analyzed by social scientists in recent years. The articles included in this book focus on different aspects of this issue. However, there is a need for developing a comprehensive theoretical basis for action. The discipline of regional science has provided such a base. Although in the beginning it developed quite splendidly, in recent years it has failed to advance, particularly in the incorporation of current factors, such as resource availability, interregional and international conflict, international trade, and environmental pollution. So there is an urgent need to develop new theories specially designed to attack these urban-regional and resource-environmental problems in the developing countries. Some suggestions are given below.

In the field of regional population studies considerable work can be done related to population growth models, life table construction, migration, etc., for urban and regional units. We should place more emphasis on psychological behavior than on distance in migration analysis.

Although many national input-output tables have been constructed, a truly regional table is yet to be developed. It has too often been derived from the national table, since the data requirements for such tables are immense. Nevertheless, the theoretical structure for such regional models needs to be defined. The same can be said for dynamic, interregional input-output analysis and regional growth models.

Most regional science techniques and theories do not consider the change in the regional structure over time. For example, the gravity models have very little applicability, unless we interject this dynamic aspect. Interregional industrial complex analysis still needs to be developed. Although in recent years new ideas are increasingly appearing in the fields of political science and sociology, (for example, in the fields of regional conflict, regional political organization, and power structure), there have been few attempts to restructure them in the total regional system. The same is true for the management of non-profit organizations, governmental organizations, and educational and health administration.

Untapped areas in operations research, mathematics, economics, and other social sciences can give new powerful ideas to the regional scientist. One such area is typology. This field can be effectively utilized by regional scientists, since they are really concerned about the multi-dimensional nature of the distribution of points in space and their interrelationship over time. At present there are very few studies of the spatial dimension of such financial variables such as interest rates, inflation, money supply, demand deposits, and mortgage money availability.

Another area of high potential is regional econometric model building. Although many regional econometric models are currently available, they are not really "regional," for a small geographical area has been substituted for the term "nation." An econometric model relates several variables of an economy, such as gross national product, consumption, investment, exports, and imports in a system of regression equations. Some of the variables are "endogenous," that is, they affect the system, and are, in turn, affected by it. Consumption is an endogenous variable. Other variables are "exogenous," that is, they affect the system without being affected themselves. Investment is an exogenous variable. The regression relationships are formulated between the endogenous and exogenous variables, parameters are estimated by different statistical techniques, and the future values of endogenous variables are projected on the basis of the assumed value of the exogenous variables.

In addition to economic variables, a regional model should consider social and political variables, such as age structure, sex ratios, migration, and political opinion. Some models can be structured as intraregional such that they can be used for transportation, housing, and other policy areas. There are at least four situations in which an econometric model can be useful: (1) an industrial region in a developing country, (2) a highly urbanized area in a developed country, (3) a depressed area in a developed country, and (4) agricultural regions in both developed and developing countries.

It is usually difficult to obtain time series data of macro-economic variables in any developing country. However, for various reasons such data for some specific industries can be obtained. It will be worthwhile to construct an industry-wide econometric model and link it to some key macroeconomic regional variables. The same is true for input-output analysis. The data requirement for such a model is immense, particularly when we realize that we should include the small-scale industries in the input-output matrix. Some of the input-output co-efficients for a particular country can be obtained from a similar table for another country which is at the same level of economic development as the first country.

The problems of urban and regional development in the third world countries are completely different from those in the industrialized countries. No amount of re-application of the techniques developed in the rich countries will solve the problem. For example, in the case of migration analysis, it is not always a question of distance or attraction. Many other factors, such as tribal and caste systems, and marriage customs determine migration.

It is necessary to realize that whatever gain has been made in the economic development of the third world countries has been absorbed by the rich. The poor are either in the same or in a worse situation than they were in before. This structural aspect should be the paramount factor in future development of tools of analysis for the developing countries. To achieve this goal, it is imperative that we integrate the tools of regional science with those of recently developed techniques in conflict analysis and peace science.

Bibliography

Chatterji, Manas, (1976a). 'A more generalized model of regional allocation of investment,' Northeast Regional Science Review, 6.

_____, (1976b). 'Spatial Regularities: Some Empirical Evidence,' in Space, Location, and Regional Development, (ed.) Manas Chatterji, London: Pion.

_____, (1975a). 'A balanced regional input-output model for identifying responsibility for pollution created by industries which serve national markets,' International Regional Science Review, 1:(1): 87-94.

_____, (1975b). 'A dynamic balanced regional input-output model of population control,' Environment and Planning, 7: 21-34.

_____, (1972). 'The future of regional science,' Northeast Regional Science Review, 2:

_____, (1971). 'A study on the structure and growth of Indian cities,' Geographical Analysis, 3(3): 288-94.

_____, (1966). 'A regional econometric model of the World Jute industry,' Papers of the Regional Science Association, 18: 127-37.

_____, (1965). 'Local impact of disarmament, foreign aid programs, and development of poor world regions: A critique of Leontief and other growth models,' Papers of the Peace Research Society, (International), 4: 40-65.

_____, (1964). 'An input-output study of the Calcutta industrial region,' Papers of the Regional Science Association, 13: 93-102.

Fujita, Masahisa, (1978). Spatial Development Planning: A Dynamic Convex Programming Approach, Amsterdam: North Holland.

_____, (1973). 'Optimum growth in two-region two-good space systems: The final state problem,' Journal of Regional Science, 13 (2): 385-408.

Fukuchi, Takao and Nobukuni, Makoto, (1970). 'An econometric analysis of national growth and regional income inequality,' *International Econometric Review*, 11: 84-100.

Harmon, Harry J. (1960). *Modern Factor Analysis*, Chicago: University of Chicago Press.

Harris, Chauncy, (1954). 'The market as a factor in the localization of industry in the United States,' *Annals of the Association of American Geographers*, 44: 517.

Intriligator, Michael, (1969). 'Regional allocation of investment commitment,' *Quarterly Review of Economics*, 78 (4): 659-62.

Isard, Walter, (1969). *General Theory: Social, Political, Economic, Regional*, Cambridge, MA: The M.I.T. Press.

Isard, Walter and Panagis Liossatos, (1979). *Spatial Dynamics and Optimal Space-Time Development*, Amsterdam: North Holland.

Maass, Arthur A., (1958). *Area and Power: A Theory of Local Government*, Glencoe, Ill: Free Press.

Ohtsuki, Yashitaka, (1971). 'Regional allocation of public investment in a n-region economy,' *Journal of Regional Science*, 11 (2): 225-34.

Pontryagin, Lev S., et al. (1962). *The Mathematical Theory of Optimal Process*, Trans. K. N. Trirogoff, London: Wiley International.

Rahman, Anisur, (1963). 'Regional allocation of investment,' *Quarterly Journal of Economics*, 77 (1): 26-39.

Sakashita, Noboru, (1967). 'Regional allocation of investment,' *Papers of the Regional Science Association*, 19: 161-82.

Takayama, Akira, (1967). 'Regional allocation of public investment,' *Quarterly Journal of Economics*, 81 (2): 330-37.

Warntz, William, (1959). *Towards a Geography of Price*, Philadelphia: University of Pennsylvania Press.